60 HIKES *within* 60 MILES
SAN FRANCISCO
INCLUDING SAN JOSE, OAKLAND, AND SANTA ROSA

60 Hikes
within 60 MILES

SAN FRANCISCO

INCLUDING SAN JOSE, OAKLAND, AND SANTA ROSA

FIRST EDITION

Jane Huber

MENASHA RIDGE PRESS
Birmingham, Alabama

Printed in the United States of America
Published by Menasha Ridge Press
Distributed by The Globe Pequot Press
First edition, first printing

Library of Congress Cataloging-in-Publication Data

Huber, Jane
60 Hikes within 60 miles, San Francisco/Jane Huber,—1st ed.
p. cm.
ISBN 0-89732-553-2
Hiking—California—San Francisco Bay Area—Guidebooks. 2. Trails—California—San Francisco Bay Area—Guidebooks. 3. San Francisco Bay Area (Calif.)—Guidebooks I. Title: Sixty hikes within 60 miles, II. Title: Sixty hikes within sixty miles. III. Title

GV199.42.C22S269443 2003
796.52'09794'61—dc22 2003059264
CIP

Cover design by Grant M. Tatum
Text design by Karen Ocker
Cover photo David Sanger Photography/Alamy
Author photo by Hans Huber
All other photos by Jane Huber
Maps by Steve Jones and Scott McGrew

Menasha Ridge Press
P.O. Box 43673
Birmingham, AL 35243
www.menasharidge.com

For my husband Hans, who made it all possible

TABLE OF CONTENTS

ACKNOWLEDGMENTS

The faithful Bay Area Hiker community supplied many helpful suggestions that have shaped both the website and this book.

Tom Cochrane assisted in plant identification and pointed me to good wildflower displays.

Kevin Hinsta explained the difference between fairy lanterns and Mount Diablo fairy lanterns.

Bob Birkland dispensed information on Annadel State Park when cornered in the parking lot.

Robyn Ishimatsu fielded my questions about Sugarloaf Ridge State Park's geology.

Ryan Branciforte at the Sonoma Ecology Center provided a map of Jack London State Park's Sonoma Ridge Trail.

Kristi Webb answered countless queries regarding Midpeninsula Regional Open Space District preserves.

Dan Sifter educated me on trail running.

My friends and family administered equal parts support and distraction, particularly Kelly Alberta, who chased butterflies with me on Angel Island and (wisely) sat by the pool in Calistoga as I climbed Mount St. Helena.

Peabody Bradford helped me maintain my brain and has been an excellent sounding board and an understanding listener.

Russell Helms at Menasha Ridge Press gave me the opportunity to write this book and has been a thoughtful editor.

My husband Hans loved and supported me throughout the project in countless ways.

Lastly, to all who preserve and maintain Bay Area parks and preserves, a big thank you—we would be (literally) lost without you.

—*Jane Huber*

FOREWORD

Welcome to Menasha Ridge Press's *60 Hikes within 60 Miles*. Our strategy was simple: First, find a hiker who knows the area and loves to hike. Second, ask that person to spend a year researching the most popular and very best trails around. And third, have that person describe each trail in terms of difficulty, scenery, condition, elevation change, and all other categories of information that are important to hikers. "Pretend you've just completed a hike and met up with other hikers at the trailhead," we told each author. "Imagine their questions, and be clear in your answers."

An experienced hiker and writer, author Jane Huber has selected 60 of the best hikes in and around the San Francisco metropolitan area. From the greenways and urban hikes that make use of parklands to flora- and fauna-rich treks along the cliffs and hills in the hinterlands, Huber provides hikers (and walkers) with a great variety of hikes—and all within roughly 60 miles of San Francisco.

You'll get more out of this book if you take a moment to read the Introduction explaining how to read the trail listings. The "Topographic Maps" section will help you understand how useful topos will be on a hike, and will also tell you where to get them. And though this is a "where-to," rather than a "how-to" guide, those of you who have hiked extensively will find the Introduction of particular value.

As much for the opportunity to free the spirit as well as to free the body, let these hikes elevate you above the urban hurry.

All the best,
The Editors at Menasha Ridge Press

ABOUT THE AUTHOR

Jane Huber grew up roaming the rural backroads of northern New Jersey. After graduating from Boston University, she moved to New York City to pursue a publishing career. Dazzled by a visit to San Francisco, she soon pulled up stakes and moved west.

Once she got over the shock of driving a stick shift up and down the city's legendary steep streets, Huber began exploring the Bay Area's parks and open spaces. She created the Bay Area Hiker website (www.bahiker.com) in 1999 to share her love of the Bay Area's natural beauty. Huber, who currently works as a freelance writer and photographer, enjoys volunteering at open space preserves south of the city in her spare time. She lives with her husband in a San Francisco neighborhood populated with humming-birds and hawks, with views of Mount Tamalpais and Mount Diablo.

PREFACE

I remember my first Bay Area hike well. On my premier trip to San Francisco, I accompanied two friends on what they promoted as a "walk on the beach." When I showed up with sandals on, they laughed and sent me back for sneakers—this was to be a walk *to* the beach. We drove across the Golden Gate Bridge, then wound uphill through woods on a tiny, curvaceous road. We finally stopped at a parking lot (Mount Tamalpais, Pantoll), and began hiking on Steep Ravine Trail. I grew up near High Point, the tallest elevation in New Jersey (all of 1,803 feet), and I spent my youth walking along country roads and romping through rural woods. Even when I left New Jersey for six years of city living in Boston and New York City, I always walked whenever possible, usually several miles daily. None of this walking had prepared me for Steep Ravine: a descending footpath plummeting through a wooded canyon, where I had to stop and rest (going downhill) because my quads were quivering. I marveled at the foreign scenery—unknown tall trees and lush shrubs—and was suitably impressed by the throngs of happy people on the trail, but in no way did the experience pique my interest in hiking.

I eventually got the nerve to pull up stakes and move to San Francisco, and a few years later a stray impulse triggered an interest in hiking. Once I started, I found I couldn't stop: my passion raged like a fever. I sought out maps and devoured them, studying the contour lines and squiggling trails, awed at the possibilities. I acquired hiking boots, wildflower guides, and sunscreen. I ignored the worried pleas of friends and family who were sure I'd be stalked by psychopaths roaming the trails as I hiked alone. I began learning about the different vegetation and landscapes of the Bay Area: the rolling grassy ridges, steep-sided redwood canyons, and sun-baked hillsides covered with a curious mix of shrubs I would later learn was called chaparral. I'm still exploring today, chasing fragments of secondhand information about obscure trails, identifying new wildflowers, and learning to tell the difference between painted lady and American lady butterflies.

Consider yourself warned: hiking in the Bay Area can be an intense and addictive experience. Sure, other areas of California are home to more esteemed landforms and parks—Yosemite is one of many world-class parks within a day's drive, and backpackers traverse the state as they trek one of the country's longest routes, the Pacific Crest Tail. Throughout the Bay Area there are many "destination" parks, where people from all over the world flock to walk among giant redwoods or whale watch from a wildflower-dotted coastal bluff. But there are hundreds of smaller parks unknown

PREFACE

to most tourists and even lifelong residents, and short drives (or in some cases bus trips, walks, or bike rides) lead to numerous parks and preserves with stunning views, bountiful wildlife, and quiet trails. These "backyard" preserves are especially beneficial to the residents of the Bay Area's most densely packed cities, San Jose, San Francisco, and Oakland. Local parks provide close-to-home outlets for exercise and nature exploration on a daily basis—thousands of people living in the foothills of Mount Tamalpais can literally walk from their front doors for miles, all the way to the top of the mountain if they like. Locals hike parks and open space preserves bordering the towns of Berkeley, Mill Valley, and Woodside daily, and they take active roles in maintaining the trails. Getting to know your backyard means getting to love your backyard—and we fight for what we love. This dedication to open space has led many ordinary citizens in rallies to save some of our most cherished Bay Area spots. The campaign to preserve open space began in the era of John Muir, and the list of protected parklands is long and impressive. Battles continue, and development still threatens many special areas. As you make your way over trails throughout the Bay Area, think of what we could have lost and have already preserved: old growth redwoods in Muir Woods saved from logging, Point Reyes National Seashore and the Marin Headlands saved from huge housing complexes, various small parks including Edgewood and Rockville saved from development as golf courses, as well as many other "common" plots of land preserved to make life a little better for the surrounding community.

What difference does open space make to the Bay Area? It permits residents to depart from the edge of a suburban development onto a path climbing a hillside peppered with wildflowers, where butterflies and damselflies flutter. It beckons hikers off bustling city streets to a park where bobcat prints mark the trail, hawks perch in hundred year old oaks, and salmon spawn in clear, cold creeks. It draws nature lovers from all over the world to redwood canyons so majestic that some find themselves overwhelmed with emotion. These preserved lands will stand long after we're gone, and although the tallest trees will eventually fall, a new generation of saplings will find a protected home in these parks, where manzanitas will put forth sweet-smelling blossoms yearly, mountain lions will roam with stealth and grace, and carpets of wildflowers will bloom whether anyone sees them or not. Take care of these parks and preserves and treat nature with reverence—you will be handsomely rewarded with lifetime memories. I think of all I have experienced in less than 10 years of hiking Bay

PREFACE

Area trails: whales lumbering through the waters off Point Reyes' Chimney Rock; the soft sound of raindrops pattering through woods at Castle Rock; a bobcat close enough to pet, transfixed at the edge of a lake at Skyline Ridge, a coyote stepping out of the woods, then vanishing back into the trees on the high slopes of Mount Tam; fresh drifts of snow covering soaring Douglas firs after an unusual Bay Area winter storm along Skyline Boulevard; dazzling flowers everywhere, so many incredible springtime displays that I often felt giddy with all the splendor.

We never made it all the way to the beach that fateful day, but I've been back to Steep Ravine since. I now know the plants that line the trail and the creatures that roam the woods, and I sometimes utter their names under my breath in passing, like greeting old friends. My fingers lightly linger on blossoms of trillium, hound's tongue, and violet; trail over the shaggy bark on redwoods and Douglas fir; and caress the smooth trunks of aromatic bay. I watch the silent flutter of a buckeye butterfly and the slow, languid crawl of a banana slug. Unseen mammals who creep about at night have left their calling cards, and I look for coyote scat at the trail junctions and raccoon footprints in mud along the creek.

The hike through Steep Ravine to Stinson Beach, combined with a return ascent through Douglas fir woods and the high grassy ridges of Mount Tam, is one of the hikes included in this book. It's an incredible dayhike highlighting the best of Bay Area hiking, offering easy access from San Francisco, a variety of vegetation, and a sense of peacefulness laced through a wild landscape. Whether you hike for exercise, nature study, or in companionship with others, San Francisco Bay Area trails are incredibly diverse and beautiful. I hope you'll delight in discovering these parks and preserves.

HIKING RECOMMENDATIONS

▶ HIKES GOOD FOR KIDS

Angel Island State Park
Año Nuevo State Reserve
Black Diamond Mines Regional Preserve
Coyote Hills Regional Park
Crane Creek Regional Park
Edgewood Park and Preserve

Huckleberry Botanic Regional Preserve
Mount Diablo State Park: Fire Interpretative
   Trail
Rancho San Antonio Open Space Preserve
Rush Ranch
Skyline Ridge Open Space Preserve

▶ EASY HIKES WITH LITTLE ELEVATION CHANGE

Año Nuevo State Reserve
Crane Creek Regional Park
Mount Diablo State Park: Fire Interpretative
   Trail Loop

Rush Ranch
Sierra Azul Open Space Preserve

▶ HIKES WITH SUBSTANTIAL ELEVATION LOSS/GAIN

Big Basin Redwoods State Park: Waterfall Loop
Castle Rock State Park
Mission Peak Regional Preserve

Mount Diablo State Park: Mitchell Canyon
   Creek–Eagle Peak Loop
Robert Louis Stevenson State Park

▶ HIKES ACCESSIBLE BY PUBLIC TRANSPORTATION

Angel Island State Park
Bothe-Napa Valley State Park
Edgewood Park and Preserve
Marin Headlands: Gerbode Valley Loop
Mission Peak Regional Preserve
Montara Mountain
Mount Tamalpais State Park: Matt Davis and
   Steep Ravine Loop

Mount Tamalpais State Park: Mountain Home
   to Muir Woods Loop
Point Reyes National Seashore: Bear Valley to
   Arch Rock
Wilder Ranch State Park

▶ SECLUDED HIKES

Henry W. Coe State Park
Morgan Territory Regional Preserve
Point Reyes National Seashore: Estero to
   Drake's Bay

Point Reyes National Seashore: Tomales Point
Round Valley Regional Preserve

HIKING RECOMMENDATIONS

▶ HIKES GOOD FOR WILDLIFE/BIRD WATCHING

Annadel State Park
Año Nuevo State Reserve
Los Vaqueros Watershed
Montara Mountain
Monte Bello Open Space Preserve

Mount Diablo State Park: Mitchell Canyon
    Creek–Eagle Peak Loop
Point Reyes National Seashore: Tomales Point
Rancho San Antonio Open Space Preserve
Round Valley Regional Preserve

▶ HIKES GOOD FOR WILDFLOWERS

Annadel State Park
Black Diamond Mines Regional Preserve
Briones Regional Park
Edgewood Park and Preserve
Joseph D. Grant County Park
Monte Bello Open Space Preserve
Mount Burdell Open Space Preserve
Mount Diablo State Park: Mitchell Canyon
    Creek–Eagle Peak Loop

Mount Tamalpais: Phoenix Lake
Rockville Hills Community Park
Russian Ridge Open Space Preserve
San Bruno Mountain County Park
Sunol Regional Wilderness
Sweeney Ridge

▶ HIKES GOOD FOR REDWOODS

Big Basin Redwoods State Park: Waterfall Loop
Henry Cowell Redwoods State Park
Mount Tamalpais State Park: Matt Davis and
    Steep Ravine Loop
Mount Tamalpais State Park: Mountain Home
    to Muir Woods Loop

Portola Redwoods State Park
Purisima Creek Redwoods Open Space
    Preserve
Redwood Regional Park

▶ HIKES WITH SCENIC VIEWPOINTS

Angel Island State Park
Castle Rock State Park
Las Trampas Regional Wilderness
Marin Headlands: Gerbode Valley Loop
Mission Peak Regional Preserve
Mount Diablo State Park: Fire Interpretative
    Trail
Mount Diablo State Park: Mitchell Canyon
    Creek–Eagle Peak Loop

Montara Mountain
Monte Bello Open Space Preserve
San Bruno Mountain County Park
Sierra Azul Open Space Preserve
Robert Louis Stevenson State Park
Sugarloaf Ridge State Park
Samuel P. Taylor State Park

HIKING RECOMMENDATIONS

▶ HIKES GOOD FOR RUNNERS

Briones Regional Park
Edgewood Park and Preserve
Marin Headlands: Gerbode Valley Loop
Monte Bello Open Space Preserve
Mount Tamalpais: Phoenix Lake
Rancho San Antonio Open Space Preserve

Redwood Regional Park
San Bruno Mountain County Park
Sweeney Ridge
Windy Hill Open Space Preserve

▶ HIKES FEATURING WATERFALLS

Big Basin Redwoods State Park: Waterfall Loop
Castle Rock State Park
Montara Mountain
Mount Diablo State Park: Donner Canyon
  Waterfall Loop

Portola Redwoods State Park
Samuel P. Taylor State Park
Uvas Canyon County Park

▶ HIKES WHERE DOGS ARE PERMITTED

Almaden Quicksilver County Park
Black Diamond Mines Regional Preserve
Briones Regional Park
Anthony Chabot Regional Park
Crane Creek Regional Park
Las Trampas Regional Wilderness
Mission Peak Regional Preserve
Morgan Territory Regional Preserve
Mount Burdell Open Space Preserve

Mount Tamalpais: Phoenix Lake
Pinnacle Gulch
Redwood Regional Park
Ring Mountain Open Space Preserve
Rockville Hills Community Park
Sunol Regional Wilderness
Sweeney Ridge
Windy Hill Open Space Preserve

In the following categories, parentheses indicate a shorter option within a longer hike.

▶ LESS THAN 1 MILE

Mount Diablo State Park: Fire Interpretative Trail

▶ 1 TO 3 MILES

Año Nuevo State Reserve (several options)
Black Diamond Mines Regional Preserve
  (shorten via Chaparral Loop Trail)
Castle Rock State Park (Castle Rock loop, or
  out-and-back to the falls)
Henry Cowell Redwoods State Park
  (Redwood Grove loop only)

Coyote Hills Regional Park (several options)
Crane Creek Regional Park
Huckleberry Botanic Regional Preserve
Jack London State Historic Park (out-and-
  back to the lake)
Montara Mountain (Brooks Falls loop only)

HIKING RECOMMENDATIONS

▶ 1 TO 3 MILES [continued]

Morgan Territory Regional Preserve (Blue Oak-Condor loop)

Mount Burdell Open Space Preserve (Middle Burdell Fire Road instead of Cobblestone)

Mount Tamalpais: Phoenix Lake (loop around the lake only)

Mount Tamalpais State Park: Matt Davis and Steep Ravine Loop (out-and-back to the ladder only)

Mount Tamalpais State Park: Rock Spring and Potrero Meadows Loop (shorten at Laurel Dell Road; return via Benstein Trail)

Pinnacle Gulch

Rancho San Antonio Open Space Preserve (Deer Hollow Farm-Coyote Trail only)

Redwood Regional Park (return to trailhead via Stream Trail)

Ring Mountain Open Space Preserve

Rush Ranch

Sierra Azul Open Space Preserve

Skyline Ridge Open Space Preserve (loop around Horseshoe Lake only)

Skyline Wilderness Park (several options)

Robert Louis Stevenson State Park (out-and-back to Stevenson Memorial)

Tomales Bay State Park

Uvas Canyon County Park (out-and-back to Triple Falls only)

Windy Hill Open Space Preserve (loop around Sausal Pond only)

▶ 3 TO 6 MILES

Almaden Quicksilver County Park (several options)

Angel Island State Park

Annadel State Park (Steve's "S"–W. Richardson loop only)

Año Nuevo State Reserve

Black Diamond Mines Regional Preserve

Bothe-Napa Valley State Park

Briones Regional Park

Castle Rock State Park

Anthony Chabot Regional Park

Henry W. Coe State Park

Henry Cowell Redwoods State Park

Coyote Hills Regional Park

Edgewood Park and Preserve

Las Trampas Regional Wilderness

Loch Lomond Recreation Area

Jack London State Historic Park (several options)

Los Vaqueros Watershed

Marin Headlands: Gerbode Valley Loop

Monte Bello Open Space Preserve (instead of Indian Creek Trail, return via Canyon Trail)

Morgan Territory Regional Preserve

Mount Burdell Open Space Preserve

Mount Diablo State Park: Donner Canyon Waterfall Loop

Mount Tamalpais: Phoenix Lake

Mount Tamalpais State Park: Mountain Home to Muir Woods

Mount Tamalpais State Park: Rock Spring and Potrero Meadows Loop

Portola Redwoods State Park (several options)

Rancho San Antonio Open Space Preserve

Redwood Regional Park

Rockville Hills Community Park

Round Valley Regional Preserve

Russian Ridge Open Space Preserve

HIKING RECOMMENDATIONS

INTRODUCTION

Welcome to *60 Hikes within 60 Miles: San Francisco!* If you're new to hiking or even if you're a seasoned trail-smith, take a few minutes to read the following introduction. We'll explain how this book is organized and how to use it.

▶ HIKE DESCRIPTIONS

Each hike contains six key items: a locator map, an In Brief description of the trail, an At-a-Glance Information box, directions to the trail, a trail map, and a hike description. Combined, the maps and information provide a clear method to assess each trail from the comfort of your favorite chair.

LOCATOR MAP

After narrowing down the general area of the hike on the overview map (see inside back cover), the locator map, along with driving directions given in the narrative, enables you to find the trailhead. Once at the trailhead, park only in designated areas.

IN BRIEF

Here you'll get a "taste of the trail." Think of this section as a snapshot focused on the historical landmarks, beautiful vistas, and other interesting sights you may encounter on the trail.

▶ KEY AT-A-GLANCE INFORMATION

The At-a-Glance information boxes give you a quick idea of the specifics of each hike. There are 13 basic elements covered.

LENGTH The length of the trail from start to finish. There may be options to shorten or extend the hikes, but the mileage corresponds to the described hike. Consult the hike description to help decide how to customize the hike for your ability or time constraints.

CONFIGURATION A description of what the trail might look like from overhead. Trails can be loops, out-and-backs (that is, along the same route), figure eights, or balloons. Sometimes the descriptions might surprise you.

DIFFICULTY The degree of effort an "average" hiker should expect on a given hike. For simplicity, difficulty is described as "easy," "moderate," or "strenuous."

SCENERY Rates the overall environs of the hike and what to expect in terms of plant life, wildlife, streams, and historic buildings.

EXPOSURE A quick check of how much sun you can expect on your shoulders during the hike. Descriptors used are self-explanatory and include terms such as shady, exposed, and sunny.

TRAFFIC Indicates how busy the trail might be on an average day, and if you might be able to find solitude out there. Trail traffic, of course, varies from day to day and season to season.

TRAIL SURFACE Indicates whether the trail is paved, rocky, smooth dirt, or a mixture of elements.

HIKING TIME How long it took the author to hike the trail. Jane is a self-described dawdler, who often easily fritters away time watching butterflies or admiring wildflowers. On average, she covers 2 miles an hour (more mileage hiking downhill, less on steady ascents, particularly during hot weather). If you're an experienced hiker in great shape, you'll finish the hikes with time to spare, but if you're a beginner or like to stop and smell the manzanitas, allow a little extra time.

SEASON Time of year when this hike is accessible. A few parks only permit access during part of the year, but most are open year round. However, some hikes are oriented to specific seasons (usually to accommodate extremes in weather).

ACCESS Notes fees or permits needed to access the hike.

MAPS Which map is the best, or easiest (in the author's opinion) for this hike, and where to get it.

FACILITIES What to expect in terms of rest rooms, phones, water, and other niceties available at the trailhead or nearby.

SPECIAL COMMENTS Provides you with those little extra details that don't fit into any of the above categories. Here you'll find assorted nuggets of information, including whether or not your dog is allowed on the trails.

DIRECTIONS
Used with the locator map, the directions will help you locate each trailhead.

DESCRIPTIONS
The trail description is the heart of each hike. Here, the author provides a summary of the trail's essence and also highlights any special traits the hike offers. Ultimately, the hike description will help you choose which hikes are best for you.

NEARBY ACTIVITIES
Not every hike will have this listing. For those that do, look here for information on nearby sights of interest.

▶ WEATHER

Bay Area weather is mild, with a Mediterranean-like climate that generally ranges from the 40s to 70s, inviting year-round hikes. Microclimates throughout the Bay Area span a wide range of temperatures and conditions, particularly in summer and winter. On a typical summer day, the weather may be clear and warm along the Sonoma coast, scorchingly hot and dry inland around Mount Diablo, and completely fogbound in San Francisco. During the rainy season, generally from November to

INTRODUCTION

March, coastal mountains are inundated with rainfall, and the Bay Area's highest peaks are occasionally dusted with snow, City residents may go for a week without even switching on the heater. Locals learn to avoid getting caught out in weather shifts by carrying layers wherever they go, and this is a practical solution for hikers as well. Stuff a lightweight fleece jacket, one of those anoraks that compress down to nearly nothing, and a hat into your backpack and you're generally prepared for light rain and cool snaps. Beware of fog, which commonly collects on high ridges near the coast, mostly in summer; fog often blows in very quickly and can be nasty to hike in, since it completely obscures landmarks and trail junctions. A safe policy is to descend as soon as you see the fog headed your way.

Since heavy storms almost always damage trails, particularly in forested, canyon parks, check weather conditions before you head out in winter and early spring. Trails get substantially less use in winter, but I personally adore hiking through forests in light rain (Castle Rock State Park in the fog is particularly enchanting). In summer, unless you prefer hot, dry heat, avoid exposed destinations in Sonoma, Napa, Alameda, Santa Clara, and Contra Costa counties, where temperatures often soar to nearly 100 degrees. Summer is a good time to visit forested parks, particularly near the coast. Spring and autumn are the most easygoing seasons, although some parks close during high fire danger (red flag days), until the rains begin in late fall.

MEAN TEMPERATURE BY MONTH, SAN FRANCISCO AREA

JAN	FEB	MAR	APR	MAY	JUN
50°	53°	53°	54°	55°	57°

JUL	AUG	SEP	OCT	NOV	DEC
57°	59°	60°	59°	55°	50°

▶ MAPS

The maps in this book have been produced with great care and, used with the hiking directions, will help you stay on course. But as any experienced hiker knows, things can get tricky off the beaten path.

The maps in this book, when used with the route directions present in each chapter, are sufficient to direct you to the trail and guide you on it. However, you will find superior detail and valuable information in the United States Geological Survey's 7.5 minute series topographic maps. Topo maps are available online in many locations. The easiest single Web resource is located at terraserver.microsoft.com. You can view and print topos of the entire Unites States there, and view aerial photographs of the entire Unites States, as well. The downside to topos is that most of them are outdated, having been created 20 to 30 years ago. But they still provide excellent topographic detail.

If you're new to hiking you might be wondering, "What's a topographic map?" In short, a topo indicates not only distance but elevation as well, using contour lines.

INTRODUCTION

Contour lines spread across the map like dozens of intricate spiderwebs. Each line represents a particular elevation and at the base of each topo a contour's interval designation is given. If the contour interval is 200 feet, then the distance between each contour line is 200 feet. Follow 5 contour lines up on a map and the elevation has increased by 1,000 feet.

In addition to outdoor shops and bike shops, you'll find topos at major universities and some public libraries, where you might try photocopying the ones you need to avoid the cost of buying them. But if you want your own and can't find them locally, contact map retailers (see Appendix C).

▶ TRAIL ETIQUETTE

Whether you're on a city, county, state or national park trail, always remember that great care and resources (from nature as well as from your tax dollars) have gone into creating these trails. Treat the trail, wildlife, and fellow hikers with respect.

Here are a few general ideas to keep in mind while on the trail.

1. Hike on open trails only. Respect trail and road closures (ask if not sure), avoid possible trespass on private land, and obtain all permits and authorization as required. Also, leave gates as you found them or as marked.

2. Leave no trace of your visit other than footprints. Be sensitive to the ground beneath you. This also means staying on the trail and not creating any new ones. Be sure to pack out what you pack in. No one likes to see the trash someone else has left behind.

3. Never spook animals. An unannounced approach, a sudden movement, or a loud noise startles most animals. A surprised snake or skunk can be dangerous for you, for others, and to themselves. Give animals extra room and time to adjust to your presence.

4. Plan ahead. Know your equipment, your ability, and the area in which you are hiking—and prepare accordingly. Be self-sufficient at all times; carry necessary supplies for changes in weather or other conditions. A well-executed trip is a satisfaction to you and to others.

5. Be courteous to other hikers, or bikers, you meet on the trails.

▶ WATER

"How much is enough? One bottle? Two? Three?! But think of all that extra weight!" Well, one simple physiological fact should convince you to err on the side of excess when it comes to deciding how much water to pack—a hiker working hard in 90-degree heat needs approximately ten quarts of fluid every day. That's two-and-a-half

INTRODUCTION

gallons—12 large water bottles or 16 small ones. In other words, pack along one or two bottles even for short hikes.

Serious backpackers hit the trail prepared to purify water found along the route. This method, while less dangerous than drinking it untreated, comes with risks. Purifiers with ceramic filters are the safest, but also are the most expensive. Many hikers pack along the slightly distasteful tetraglycine hydroperiodide tablets (sold under the names Potable Aqua, Coughlan's, and others).

Probably the most common water-borne "bug" that hikers face is *Giardia*, which may not hit until one to four weeks after ingestion. It will have you passing noxious rotten-egg gas, vomiting, shivering with chills, and living in the bathroom. But there are other parasites to worry about, including *E. coli* and *Cryptosporidium* (that are harder to kill than *Giardia*).

For most people, the pleasures of hiking make carrying water a relatively minor price to pay to remain healthy. If you're tempted to drink "found water," do so only if you understand the risks involved. Better yet, hydrate prior to your hike, carry (and drink) six ounces of water for every mile you plan to hike, and hydrate after the hike.

▶ FIRST-AID KIT

A typical kit may contain more items than you might think necessary. But these are just the basics:

Sunscreen
Aspirin or acetaminophen
Butterfly-closure bandages
Band-Aids
Snakebite kit
Gauze (one roll)
Gauze compress pads (a half-dozen 4 in. x 4 in.)
Ace bandages or Spenco joint wraps
Benadryl or the generic equivalent— diphenhydramine (an antihistamine, in case of allergic reactions)
A prefilled syringe of epinephrine (for those known to have severe allergic reactions to such things as bee stings)
Water purification tablets or water filter (see note above)
Moleskin/Spenco "Second Skin"
Hydrogen peroxide or iodine
Antibiotic ointment (Neosporin or the generic equivalent)
Matches or pocket lighter
Whistle (more effective in signaling rescuers than your voice)

Pack the items in a self-sealing waterproof bag. You will also want to include a snack for hikes longer than a couple of miles. A bag full of GORP (Good Ol' Raisins and Peanuts) will kick up your energy level fast.

▶ HIKING WITH CHILDREN

No one is too young for a hike in the woods or through a city park. Be careful, though. Flat, short trails are probably best with an infant. Toddlers who have not quite mastered walking can still tag along, riding on an adult's back in a child carrier. Use common

INTRODUCTION

sense to judge a child's capacity to hike a particular trail, and always rely on the possibility that the child will tire quickly and need to be carried.

When packing for the hike, remember the needs of the child as well as your own. Make sure children are adequately clothed for the weather, have proper shoes, and are protected from the sun with sunscreen. Kids dehydrate quickly, so make sure you have plenty of fluid for everyone.

To assist an adult with determining which trails are suitable for children, a list of hike recommendations for children is provided on page xiii.

Finally, when hiking with children, remember the trip will be a compromise. A child's energy and enthusiasm alternates between bursts of speed and long stops to examine snails, sticks, dirt, and other attractions.

▶ THE BUSINESS HIKER

Whether you're in the San Francisco area on business as a resident or visitor, these hikes are the perfect opportunity to make a quick getaway from the demands of commerce. Many of these hikes are easily accessible from downtown San Francisco. A well-planned half-day getaway is the perfect companion to a business stay in the Bay Area.

▶ SNAKES

The most common snakes you'll encounter along Bay Area trails are nonpoisonous gopher and garter snakes. The only venomous snakes in the Bay Area are rattlesnakes, and sightings of these pit vipers are generally infrequent, occuring most commonly in dry, rocky, or exposed zones during the warmest months of the year. The standard "rules" for hiking in rattlesnake territory are:

1. Do not put your hands (or feet) where you can't see them, i.e., the top of a rock outcrop or in a log pile.

2. Be extra cautious in hot weather, as snakes are more active.

3. Scan the trail continuously as you hike.

4. Keep children from running ahead on trails. Bites to children are more severe than to adults.

5. Avoid tall grass where you can't see your feet (or a potential snake).

Should you encounter a rattler, its body language will reveal its mood. A coiled rattler is primed for a strike, while a stretched rattler is more sanguine (although snakes have been reported to "lunge"). If the snake is within striking distance, stand motionless and wait for the snake to calm down and move. Small, slow steps backward are also an option. If you're out of immediate range, you can either skirt the snake, or wait for the snake to move. Some people believe tapping the ground with a stick (from a safe distance, rather than in the snake's face) will encourage the snake to move on.

Gopher snakes resemble rattlesnakes—both snakes have a similar cream, tan, and brown pattern, but the easiest way to tell them apart (from a safe distance, of course!) is by head shape. Gopher snakes have no distinction from their "necks" to their heads, but rattlers have diamond-shaped heads. Both, by the way, make noises to warn off predators—rattlesnakes by shaking their rattles, and gopher snakes by vibrating their tails against the ground.

▶ TICKS

Ticks like to hang out in the brush that grows along trails. I've noticed that July is the peak month for ticks in our area, but you should be tick-aware during all months of the spring, summer, and fall. Ticks, actually arthropods and not insects, are ectoparasites, which need a host for the majority of their life cycle in order to reproduce. The ticks that light onto you while hiking will be very small, sometimes so tiny that you won't be able to spot them. Primarily of two varieties, deer ticks and dog ticks, both need a few hours of actual attachment before they can transmit any disease they may harbor. I've found ticks in my socks and on my legs several hours after a hike that have not yet anchored. The best strategy is to visually check every half hour or so while hiking, do a thorough check before you get in the car, and then, when you take a post-hike shower, do an even more thorough check of your entire body. Ticks that haven't latched on are easily removed, but not easily killed. If I pick off a tick in the woods, I just toss it aside. If I find one on my person at home, I make sure and dispatch it down the toilet. For ticks that have embedded, removal with tweezers is best.

▶ POISON OAK

Poison oak is a deciduous plant that grows as sparse groundcover, vine, or shrub; regardless of its form, poison oak always has three leaflets. It is easiest to spot in summer and early autumn, when the leaves flush bright red. Beware of unknown barebranched shrubs and vines in winter—the entire plant can cause a rash no matter what the season.

The rashes are caused by urushiol, the oil in the sap of poison oak. Reactions may start almost immediately, or may not appear until a week after exposure. Raised lines and/or blisters appear, accompanied by a terrible itch. Refrain from scratching because bacteria under fingernails may cause infection. Wash and dry the rash thoroughly, and apply a calamine lotion to help dry out the rash. If itching or blistering is severe, seek medical attention.

INTRODUCTION

Recognizing and avoiding poison oak is the most effective way to prevent painful, itchy rashes. Most people come into contact with the plant while bushwhacking or traveling off trail, so you can minimize your encounters with poison oak by staying on established trails. If you do knowingly contact poison oak, you must remove the oil within 15–20 minutes to avoid a reaction. Showering on the trail with cool water (hot water spreads the oil) is impractical, but some commercial products such as Tecnu clean the oil off of skin.

If you come into contact with poison oak, remember that oil-contaminated clothes, pets, or hiking gear can easily inflict an irritating rash on you or someone else, so wash not only any exposed parts of your body but also clothes, gear, and pets if applicable.

ALMADEN QUICKSILVER COUNTY PARK

▶ IN BRIEF

If you prefer your history laced with fresh air, Almaden Quicksilver is an ideal hiking destination. This nearly 4,000-acre park, a former mercury mine, hosts trails that wind past mining artifacts, shuttered shafts, and former settlements. In addition to the mining remnants, there are plenty of natural wonders here—scads of wildflowers, gorgeous oaks scattered in grassland, and a healthy animal population.

▶ DESCRIPTION

On a typical day at Almaden Quicksilver, oak leaves whisper in the breeze, rattlesnakes bask in the sun, wildflowers bloom with abandon, and coyotes scamper across grassy hillsides. It's hard to believe that the park once teemed with human activity as the most productive mine in California history. For decades, native Ohlone Indians used cinnabar, a dark reddish cinnamon-colored mineral, for pigment, trade, and religious ceremonies. When the Ohlones showed Mexican Andres Castillero the cinnabar deposits in 1845, he heated cinnabar to release its stored mercury, and soon applied for and received mineral rights to the land, although he never set up mining operations. A private firm then retained mining rights in 1846.

▶ DIRECTIONS

Drive south from San Francisco on I-280 and use the CA 1/19th Avenue merge as the mileage starting point. Drive south on I-280 about 36 miles, then exit onto CA 85 south. After about 12 miles, exit at Almaden Expressway, stay in the ramp's right lane, make the first left, and then the next right onto Almaden Expressway. Drive about 4 miles, then turn right onto Almaden Road. Drive on Almaden about 3 miles to the Hacienda Trailhead on the right side of the road.

ⓘ KEY AT-A-GLANCE INFORMATION

LENGTH: 7.8 miles

CONFIGURATION: Balloon

DIFFICULTY: Moderate

SCENERY: Grassland, oaks, and chaparral

EXPOSURE: Mostly sunny, with some shade

TRAFFIC: Quiet weekdays, steady weekends

TRAIL SURFACE: Dirt fire roads and trails

HIKING TIME: 4 hours

SEASON: Good year-round, but best in spring

ACCESS: No fee

MAPS: Park map is available at the trailhead's information signboard.

FACILITIES: Portable toilets at the trailhead

SPECIAL COMMENTS: Dogs permitted

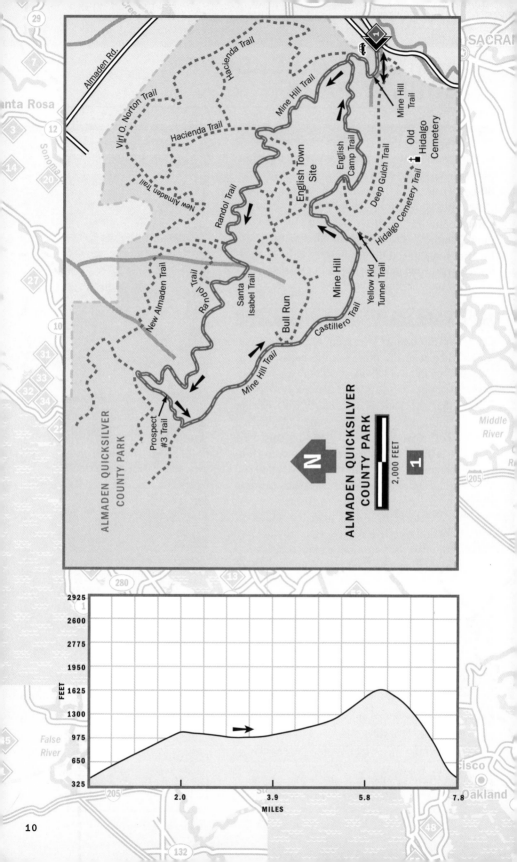

ALMADEN QUICKSILVER
COUNTY PARK

2,000 FEET

1

ALMADEN QUICKSILVER
COUNTY PARK

N

Almaden Rd.

Hacienda Trail

Hacienda Trail

Virl O. Norton Trail

New Almaden Trail

Randol Trail

Randol Trail

New Almaden Trail

Santa Isabel Trail

Bull Run

Mine Hill Trail

Prospect #3 Trail

Mine Hill Trail

English Town Site

Mine Hill Trail

English Camp Trail

Mine Hill

Castillero Trail

Yellow Kid Tunnel Trail

Deep Gulch Trail

Hidalgo Cemetery Trail

Mine Hill Trail

Old Hidalgo Cemetery

2925
2600
2775
1950
1625
1300
975
650
325

FEET

2.0   3.9   5.8   7.8

MILES

10

When full-scale operations commenced, settlements, including schools and stores, sprang up on the hillsides. Workers from all over the world mined, crushed, and heated cinnabar to produce mercury, which, although highly toxic, was essential in the processing of gold and silver, and hat production.

Mine ownership changed throughout the years, and mining ceased in 1927 when the New Almaden Corporation went bankrupt. Although piecemeal mining picked up again from 1928 to 1972, when mercury use declined and the health risks of the element became known, the mines closed for good. Santa Clara County bought the land in the early 1970s, and after a thorough cleanup, opened Almaden Quicksilver County Park in 1975. Keep in mind that although the park has been "rehabilitated," some hazards still exist. Mice in the park may harbor hanta virus, ramshackle buildings are unstable, and land surrounding old shafts and mines can still shift. Stick to the trails to stay out of trouble here.

This hike climbs on an old mining road, passes a few mine shafts, then ascends to a grassy ridge. From there it's an easy stroll around the park's tallest hill and a steady descent through manzanitas, black sage, and toyon back to the trailhead.

Begin from the trailhead on the Mine Hill Trail, a dirt fire road, once a mine road, which ascends at a moderate clip through coast live and blue oaks, California bay, and coyote brush. At 0.4 miles, the Hacienda Trail leaves right, and the English Camp Trail begins on the left. Continue straight on the Mine Hill Trail. In spring you might see a variety of wildflowers along the trail, including milkmaids and bluedicks. As the trail continues to climb, views to the surrounding mountains unfold and expand. A windy little flat called Capehorn Pass is marked by a junction and a picnic table at mile 1.1. Turn right, pass the picnic table, and then turn left onto the Randol Trail.

Angling across the hillside, the Randol Trail is nearly level. If you look past the chamise and sagebrush lining the trail, you might begin to notice remnants from the mining days. A gigantic pile of tailings on the right marks the spot of Day Tunnel, at 1.6 miles. Interpretive panels feature photos of the area during the mining boom. The Day Tunnel Trail heads uphill on the left just past the sealed tunnel site, but remain to the right on the Randol Trail.

Before long, debris piles around Buena Vista Shaft come into view on the right. At 2.2 miles the Randol Trail veers right, while Santa Isabel continues straight. Either trail is an option, but Randol is longer. Bear left onto the Santa Isabel Trail.

Spring wildflowers, including shooting stars and baby blue eyes, thrive in the shade of coast live oaks and California bays. The Santa Isabel Trail ends at the Randol Trail at 2.6 miles. Bear left and once again pick up the Randol Trail.

Without major elevation fluctuations, the trail remains an easy stroll. You'll pass through cool shaded canyons and more exposed areas as the Randol Trail travels west. Chaparral shrubs including black sage and manzanita occupy a sunny hillside on the left, delighting bees and hummingbirds with their blossoms. Finally, the trail reaches grassland and a junction at 3.8 miles. Turn left here onto the Prospect #3 Trail.

At a fairly steep grade the narrow path traverses a sloping meadow dotted with gorgeous mature blue and black oaks. A bountiful display of blossoms spreads through the grass in March—look for linanthus, johnny jump-ups, and popcorn flower. The Prospect #3 Trail veers into the woods, still climbing, but now under the shade of black and coast live oaks. The trail emerges from the woods and ends at a junction at 4.3 miles, where you'll turn left onto the Mine Hill Trail.

If you need an excuse to stop and catch your breath, a pause to admire the views is justifiable. The prominent mountain to the west is Mount Umunhum, the highest peak in the Sierra Azul range. The Mine Hill Trail ascends, slightly downslope from the ridgeline, through oaks and grassland. Just past a brief shaded stretch, a trail to Catherine Tunnel branches off to the left at 5 miles. Continue straight on the Mine Hill Trail, which tapers off to a level grade and reaches a junction at Bull Run. A picnic table on the right is a popular rest stop for mountain bikers. Stay to the right, which is now the Castillero Trail.

After a short level segment, the fire road begins a descent. On the exposed sunny hillsides along the trail you might see California coffeeberry, sagebrush, and poison oak, as well as non-native broom and pampas grass. Keep an eye out for rattlesnakes if the weather is warm. A large complex of old mining structures is visible downhill on the right. At 5.7 miles, a trail to Hidalgo Cemetery heads off on the right. Continue straight on the Castillero Trail.

Follow a steady but easy descent to the 6.1-mile mark, where you'll reach a multiple junction at the edge of English Camp. A few buildings still stand where hundreds of miners and their families lived in the late 1800s. Consult the park map and wander around if you wish—there are interpretive signs throughout the area. When you're ready, head downhill past the barns, on the English Camp Trail.

Winding downhill through grassland, continue straight at a junction at 6.3 miles—this new trail, Deep Gulch, is an alternate return route to the trailhead. As the descent sharpens a bit, the trail turns to follow a wooded canyon. Quiet hikers might surprise a bobcat loping along the trail, which is lined with toyon, black sage, manzanita, and sticky monkeyflower. Off in the distance to the right a tall brick chimney stands at the site of a mining furnace. Other than one brief uphill section, it's all downhill from here to the accompaniment of a string of power lines. The English Camp Trail ends at a junction at 7.3 miles. Turn right and descend back to the trailhead, once again on the Mine Hill Trail.

▶ NEARBY ACTIVITIES

Visit the Almaden Quicksilver Mining Museum, at 21350 Almaden Road, to learn more about the history of mercury mining at Almaden Quicksilver. Call (408) 323-1107 for more information.

ANGEL ISLAND STATE PARK

▶ IN BRIEF

Angel Island is a perfect day trip, where the journey to the trailhead rivals the hike for sheer relaxation and beauty. Since you can only reach Angel Island by boat, sit back and enjoy the ferry ride, then climb to the top of the island and back, with incredible 360-degree views nearly the entire trip. Just keep an eye on the clock to make sure you catch that last ferry.

▶ DESCRIPTION

San Francisco Bay's largest island, rising out of the water between Marin and San Francisco, has served as a cattle ranch, military base, quarantine station, immigration facility, prisoner-of-war detention center, and Nike missile site. When the federal government abandoned the island in the late 1940s, it became part of the state park system, although missile sites operated until 1962. Years of restoration, the elimination of planted non-native vegetation, and the passage of time have allowed coast live oak woods and grassy hills to make a comeback. Park staff have returned the

▶ DIRECTIONS

If you start a journey to Angel Island from a location served by BART or Muni trains, it makes perfect sense to take public transportation to the ferry landing at San Francisco's Pier 41. Take BART or Muni to the Embarcadero station, come above ground and transfer to the F line (on the Embarcadero across from the Ferry Building), and proceed west to the Fisherman's Wharf stop. Ferries to Angel Island also depart from Tiburon and Alameda. If you want to drive, the easiest and most direct route to Fisherman's Wharf from the Bay Bridge is via the Embarcadero. From the Golden Gate Bridge, take Lombard to Van Ness to North Point, then park in one of the parking garages at Fisherman's Wharf.

ⓘ KEY AT-A-GLANCE INFORMATION

LENGTH: 5 miles

CONFIGURATION: Balloon

DIFFICULTY: Easy

SCENERY: Coast live oak and California bay woods, grassland, chaparral, 360-degree views of the Bay Area from the top of Mount Livermore

EXPOSURE: Mix of sun and shade, with full sun at the top

TRAFFIC: Moderate–busy in summer, lighter in the off season

TRAIL SURFACE: Dirt trails

HIKING TIME: 3 hours

SEASON: Good all year, but ferry service is limited during the "off season," generally September–May.

ACCESS: The $12 round-trip ferry ticket includes park admission.

MAPS: The park map is available (for a fee) at the park's visitor center and at the ferry landing.

FACILITIES: Toilets and drinking water are available at the trailhead.

SPECIAL COMMENTS: Contact Blue and Gold Fleet, (415) 773-1188, for a ferry schedule. Dogs are not permitted on park trails.

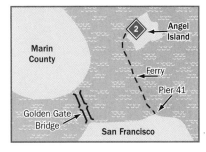

13

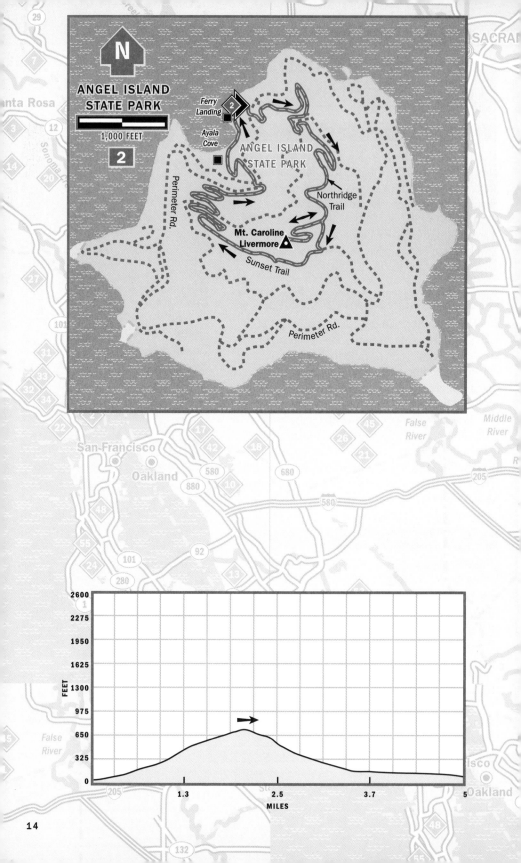

Mount Tamalpais and bay views from the Sunset Trail

island's highest peak, Mount Livermore, to its original state by restoring acres of dirt pushed off the summit by the military. With about 20 feet added back to Mount Livermore's summit, the hill is a peak again, and native vegetation has been reintroduced.

Angel Island offers two main hikes: a nearly level 5-mile circuit around the island on a fire road, and this loop, a combination of Northridge and Sunset trails, with a short out-and-back spur to the summit. The park is busy during tourist season, but when I visited with a friend in early summer, we disembarked from a nearly full ferry, then watched as the crowds made a beeline for the visitor center. On the trails, we crossed paths with only a dozen other hikers—trails are even quieter in winter, when clear days promise long views, and early spring, when the wildflower displays are legendary.

Begin from the ferry landing on the Northridge Trail, which sets off to the left (north) of the rest rooms. As it leaves the shoreline area, this footpath climbs through pine, toyon, and coast live oak, ascending some long, steep stairs past a few picnic tables, then reaches a cluster of eucalyptus and paved Perimeter Road at 0.1 mile. Continue on the far side of the pavement on the Northridge Trail, entering a more natural area where **clarkia** and Indian pink bloom in early summer, freckling patches of grass beneath coast live oak. The narrow path winds uphill through shaded woods of California bay and hazelnut. When the Northridge Trail emerges from the woods on the northernmost flank of the island, enjoy views north across Raccoon Strait to the Tiburon peninsula. Wind through a patch of manzanita charred by fire, where new shrubs are quickly reinvigorating the hillsides. At 0.9 miles, turn left onto a fire road for a few feet, then veer right, continuing on the Northridge Trail.

After one last foray through chaparral, the path, still ascending easily, takes a long tour through quiet woods of coast live oak, where you might also notice madrone, gooseberry, huge thickets of hazelnut, and poison oak. The Northridge Trail levels out as it reaches a grassy plateau dotted with coyote brush, home to iris, paintbrush, and zigadene blooming in spring; and coyote mint, venus thistle, and buckwheat flowering in summer. There are good views, west to Mount Tamalpais, and uphill to Mount Livermore's summit. Under a few pines at 1.8 miles, the Northridge Trail ends at a T junction. Turn right, following the sign to Mount Livermore.

At an easy-going rate, the trail climbs past coast live oak into grassland. You'll likely see butterflies, including California sister and a variety of swallowtails, fluttering about in summer, along with fast-moving swifts and more languid vultures and hawks riding the thermal air currents. After two bends in the trail, the path makes a final push to the summit, climbing through grassy slopes dotted with young coyote brush, reintroduced after the restoration of the peak. At 2.1 miles you'll reach the top of Mount Livermore, where views are simply incredible, and even in summer's haze include the Golden Gate Bridge stretching from San Francisco to Marin's rolling Headlands, Alcatraz Island, Mount Tamalpais, the downtown San Francisco skyline, Mount Diablo, Treasure Island, and the Bay Bridge. The picnic table and benches at the summit can be quite windy, but there are a few other sites, off the slopes of the peak, that are more sheltered. It can be tough to leave this idyllic setting, but remember that ferry schedule. Descend back to the previous junction, then continue straight on the Sunset Trail.

Dropping down onto the island's south slope, there are unobstructed views downhill to Point Blunt, an active Coast Guard station. This area is still scarred from development and restoration efforts, which have left some burned pines and a sense of disarray. The Sunset Trail crosses an old, closed road, and begins to angle across a hillside heading west. Bushes of sticky monkeyflower, coyote brush, poison oak, and sagebrush frame awesome views of the Golden Gate and the world's most famous span, with its distinctive "international orange" paint scheme so pretty against a clear blue sky. The Sunset Trail descends a ridge, offering splendid views of Sausalito, Belvedere Island, the Marin Headlands, and Mount Tam, then turns right into coast live oaks woods.

At one last little sunny viewpoint a bench invites a lingering break, and the trail then begins a campaign of switchbacks. Some shortcuts are worn into the hillside here, but please stay on the trail, which is well graded. Poison oak and Italian thistle crowd the trail in places in summer. At 3.5 miles veer right on a fire road for a few feet, then turn left back onto the Sunset Trail. Switchbacks continue, mostly through California bay and coast live oak woods. Just past a water tank and cluster of picnic tables, the trail bends left, runs along the road, then ends at 4.6 miles. Cross the road near a paved route descending to group picnic areas, then veer right, following the sign to the dock area.

This wide trail starts out paved but soon shifts to dirt. As you descend toward the visitor center, you might notice several non-native plants, including pride of madeira, a shrub with big purple flower spikes, and broom, a whispy bush that bears sweet-smelling pea-like blossoms. The trail turns sharply left, then ends at the side of the visitor center, where a grassy picnic area fronts the shoreline at Ayala Cove. Turn right and walk on a paved road the remaining distance back to the ferry landing.

▶ NEARBY ACTIVITIES

If you'd like an extended Angel Island visit, you can stay overnight in 1 of 9 primitive campsites, but you'll have to haul your gear about 2 miles from the ferry to the campsite. Visit www.angelisland.org for more information.

ANNADEL
STATE PARK

▶ IN BRIEF

If hikes were marketed like new cars, I'd say that this Annadel loop has the most meadow views per mile. This hike climbs through a forest, loops around a meadow and skirts the shore of Lake Ilsanjo, then returns through woods to the trailhead. Although Annadel is a busy park, heavily used by equestrians and cyclists as well as local walkers and runners, it's worth putting up with the crowds.

▶ DESCRIPTION

Annadel's grassy expanses are at their best in spring, when carpets of flowers bloom at the feet of mature oaks. The park is situated at the north end of the Sonoma Mountains, a long series of rolling hills that run from the outskirts of Santa Rosa to the flats of San Pablo Bay. Like Jack London State Park a few miles to the south, Annadel has pretty woods and good views, but also offers lakeside picnic spots, big sweeps of grassland, and oak savanna. Since Annadel is surrounded by residential communities, there are quite a few trailheads, many paths and trails, and lots of loop opportunities. In the last few years park staff have

▶ DIRECTIONS

Leave San Francisco on northbound US 101 and use the Golden Gate Bridge toll plaza as the mileage starting point. Drive about 50 miles north on 101, then exit on CA 12. Drive east on CA 12 toward Sonoma, for 1.5 miles, then turn left on Farmer's Lane. After about 0.7 mile, turn right onto Montgomery Drive. Drive east 3 miles, then turn right onto Channel Drive. After less than 0.1 mile, continue straight when the road makes a sharp turn right toward Spring Lake. Drive into the park, stop and pay the entrance fee at the ranger station, then continue to the parking lot at the end of the road.

ⓘ KEY AT-A-GLANCE INFORMATION

LENGTH: 6.2 miles

CONFIGURATION: Figure eight

DIFFICULTY: Easy/moderate

SCENERY: Woods, grassland, oaks, lake

EXPOSURE: First and last section shaded, the rest mostly full sun

TRAFFIC: Medium weekdays, heavy weekends

TRAIL SURFACE: Rocky dirt fire roads and trails

HIKING TIME: 3 hours

SEASON: Spring is best; it's muddy after rains, and hot in summer

ACCESS: Pay the $2 entrance fee at the ranger station.

MAPS: The park map is available at the ranger station.

FACILITIES: Pit toilets are located at the trailhead.

SPECIAL COMMENTS: Dogs are not permitted on park trails. All but one trail are multiuse.

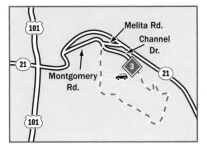

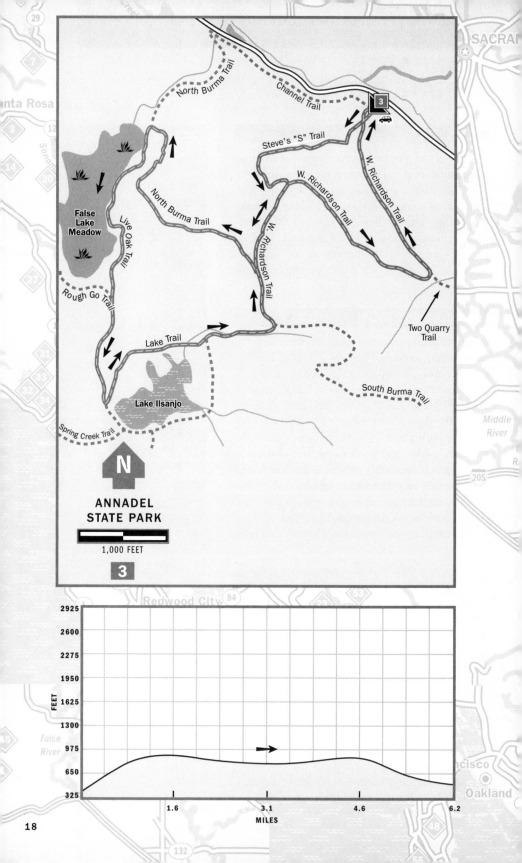

ANNADEL STATE PARK

1,000 FEET

3

cracked down on shortcuts and old, erosive routes, and the number of official trails is now much smaller—there still are faint paths and bike cuts, but all the legitimate routes are signed and appear on the map. On the trails you'll surely notice rocks and boulders all over the place, evidence of the cobblestone quarrying that took place in the area prior to the 1920s.

Begin from the middle of the parking lot, uphill on the W. Richardson Trail. After about 200 feet on a fire road, turn right onto Steve's "S" Trail. The park's sole hiking-only path begins a mostly easy climb through an open forest of California bay, Douglas fir, coast live and black oak. You might see woodland star and iris in spring. Views are obscured by the forest and noise from the surrounding neighborhoods is steady, but the hubbub fades as the trail progresses uphill. Look for shiny black shards of obsidian on the trail—native American tribes used the rock for arrowpoints and spearheads. There's so much obsidian directly on the trail that you might confuse it with broken glass. As the trail makes its way across the wooded flanks of the hillside, boulders loom in the shadows, beneath Douglas fir and California bay. Steve's "S" Trail crosses a little creek, then bends sharply left. On a spring hike I saw a deer moving through the woods out of the corner of my eye, and heard turkeys yodeling in the distance. At the 1-mile mark, the trail ends near a picnic table, at a junction with the W. Richardson Trail. Turn right.

The fire road ascends slightly, leaving the forest for a grassy savanna, where deciduous black and Oregon oaks mingle with evergreen coast live oak and manzanitas. Wildflowers you might see throughout spring include linanthus, lupines, blue-eyed grass, popcorn flower, goldenfields, bluedicks, and hound's tongue. At 1.3 miles, turn right onto the North Burma Trail.

The setting, with oaks sprinkled through grassland, is incredibly scenic and invites daydreams, but be sure to stay alert for mountain bikes on this narrow path. The North Burma Trail descends briefly along a sloping hillside, then veers left into a young forest (an old trail to the right, now closed, leads back toward Steve's "S" Trail). Douglas fir and madrone crowd the rocky level trail, but then give way to manzanita, ceanothus, and poison oak. Among the small boulders strewn about along the trail, look for shooting stars, zigadene, and blue-eyed grass in late winter, and a generous amount of golden fairy lanterns in mid- to late-April. At 1.7 miles the left side of the trail opens up to a descending meadow dotted with oaks, where lupines, popcorn flower, linanthus, and goldenfields were blooming on a mid-spring hike. As the trail proceeds slightly downhill, ceanothus, poison oak, coyote brush, manzanita, and toyon close off views, and Douglas fir, black oak, and madrone provide occasional shade. At 2.2 miles the North Burma Trail bends left to a junction. Turn left onto the Live Oak Trail.

The narrow path runs parallel to False Lake Meadow, a short distance downhill to the right, mostly screened by an assortment of young Douglas fir, and coast live, Oregon, and black oak. Since trees line the Live Oak Trail at a distance, there are plenty of grassy patches where you might see false lupine, blue-eyed grass, lupines, bluedicks, iris, shooting stars, linanthus, and zigadene, in spring. Rocks and small boulders are strewn all over the place and, in one spot along the trail, you might notice an artistic-looking pile of stones on the right. As the trail travels slightly downslope from a little knoll, you'll pass through a pocket of woods where California bay and buckeye blend into the other trees, then emerge on the western side of a meadow (although it's one of the park's largest, it's apparently unnamed). To the right there are nice, unobstructed views down to False Lake Meadow. Expect big patches of lupines along the trail in April, along with some California poppies and blue larkspur. The trail winds past an old, sprawling coast live oak, and ends at 3 miles. Bear left onto the Rough Go Trail.

Oaks and manzanita are common along the trail, which descends very gently through rocky grassland. Although Rough Go is heavily trafficked, this is a quiet part of the park, far from the trappings of suburban Santa Rosa. Two rugged Sonoma County peaks, Mount Hood and Mount St. Helena, loom off in the distance on the left. Just past a bench, the Rough Go Trail ends at 3.4 miles. Turn left onto the Lake Trail (or, if you want to take the long way around the lake, continue past this junction, then turn left at the junction with the Spring Creek Trail).

Lake Ilsanjo is the heart of the park and a regular destination for many visitors who enjoy picnicking on the shores of the little reservoir, so you'll likely cross paths with plenty of runners, equestrians, and cyclists in this part of Annadel. This level segment of the Lake Trail skirts the northern shoreline at a distance. Even when you can't see it, cries from red-winged blackbirds indicate that the water is close by, off to the right, and the trail is often muddy in all but the driest months of the year. Native bunchgrasses thrive beneath oaks, manzanita, and California bay, in an understory where California buttercups, shooting stars, and iris bloom in spring. At the south edge of the meadow you might see johnnytuck and concentrated clusters of linanthus, and goldenfields blooming in April. If you're looking for a good spot for lunch, there are many picnic tables in the area—try following one of the side paths veering off to the right and left. At 3.9 miles, the Lake Trail sweeps right, continuing its loop around the lake, and a segment of Steve's "S" Trail (signed but no longer on the park map) breaks off to the left. Make a soft left, and you're once again on the W. Richardson Trail.

The fire road starts as an easy climb along a small creek. In spring, red larkspur and yellow buttercups provide a nice contrast to the ferns and creambush beneath Douglas fir and California bay. The South Burma Trail heads off to the right at 4.2 miles, but continue to the left on the W. Richardson Trail. You may notice some mature, dead-looking Douglas firs, most conspicuous in spring and summer, when all the park's trees bear green leaves or needles. Annadel's staff has girdled some Douglas firs at the transition zones between oak savanna and evergreen forest, an attempt to stop the Douglas firs from invading the oak's territory. As these trees die and fall, they will be an important part of the healthy park ecosystem, providing habitat for many wild creatures.

The surface of the fire road may be scored with tracks made by one of most common animals at Annadel, the wild turkey. I've seen turkeys on every Annadel visit, either shuffling through oak woods, searching through the fallen leaves for insects, or tootling down the trails—these big birds make a substantial racket, gobbling back and forth to each other, and although they seem ungainly, they can move surprisingly fast. Wild turkeys can be feisty, especially the males (called toms), who keep a close watch on females (hens) during breeding season.

As the W. Richardson Trail makes its way north, look left for a last view of the meadow and Lake Ilsanjo. At 4.4 miles, you'll once again reach the junction with the North Burma Trail. Stay to the right on the fire road, and retrace your steps back to the junction with Steve's "S" Trail at 4.7 miles. Continue to the right, downhill on the W. Richardson Trail.

The fire road begins a moderate descent, through a forest of redwood, Douglas fir, California bay, and coast live oak. At a hairpin turn, about 5.4 miles into the hike, the Two Quarry Trail departs on the right, heading into the eastern part of the park. Continue on the W. Richardson Trail, which runs at the edge of the woods, presenting nice views of a little egg-shaped hill on the right. A few big-leaf maple trees call attention to themselves in autumn, when they show off their foliage. As the trail descends, traffic and household noise filters through the trees. At 6 miles, you'll return to the junction with Steve's "S" Trail. You can walk the short distance back to the trailhead on the fire road, but I prefer the path on the right, which descends a flight of steps, then ends at the south end of the parking lot.

AÑO NUEVO
STATE RESERVE

LENGTH: 4 miles

CONFIGURATION: Balloon

DIFFICULTY: Easy

SCENERY: Coastal, elephant seals

EXPOSURE: Full sun

TRAFFIC: Moderate

TRAIL SURFACE: Dirt fire roads and trails; some loose sand

HIKING TIME: 2 hours

SEASON: April–November obtain a permit (available the same day at the reserve) to walk through the wilderness area. Mid-December–late March the protection area is accessible only via guided docent walks, and you must preregister (advance reservations strongly advised).

ACCESS: Pay the $4 fee at the entrance kiosk.

MAPS: The park map is available at the entrance kiosk.

FACILITIES: Rest rooms and water are available at the trailhead.

SPECIAL COMMENTS: During the seal breeding season, access to Año Nuevo's wildlife protection area is via advance reservation only. April–November, obtain a wilderness permit at the reserve entrance. Seals are usually present throughout the year, especially during the breeding season. No food or dogs permitted.

▶ IN BRIEF

Although this park was created to protect elephant seals and other marine mammals, Año Nuevo is an incredibly restorative destination for humans as well. On this hike you can enjoy fresh sea air, views of the shoreline and mountains, and bird calls. If you're lucky and the season is right, you might glimpse seals and sea lions basking on the sandy beaches.

▶ DESCRIPTION

Año Nuevo Point was named by Spanish explorer Sebastian Viscaino to commemorate the day he first sailed past the point in 1603, on New Years Day. At that time a tribe of Ohlone Indians lived in the area, grizzly bears roamed along the coast and through the forested slopes of the Santa Cruz Mountains, and hundreds of thousands of elephant seals swam through the waters off the point. By the late 1800s, the grizzlies were gone, and the elephant seals had been hunted nearly to extinction, primarily for their oil-rich blubber. Although their population numbered less than 100 when U.S. and Mexican governments gave northern elephant seals protected status in the 1920s, they slowly began a comeback. Seals were first sighted on Año Nuevo Island in 1955, and in 1961 the first pup was born there. Seals moved onto the mainland to breed. In 1971 the point and island were purchased by the state of California and a reserve

▶ DIRECTIONS

Drive south from San Francisco on I-280 and use the CA 1/19th Avenue merge as the mileage starting point. Drive 14 miles south on I-280, then exit onto CA 92 West. Drive west 8 miles to the junction with CA 1. Turn south and drive about 28 miles to the park entrance on the right side of the road, just north of the Santa Cruz County border.

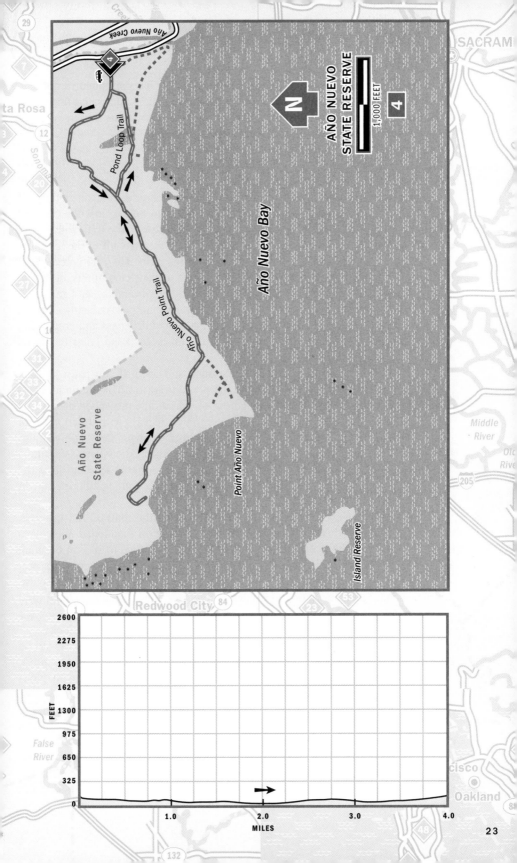

ANO NUEVO
STATE RESERVE

N

1,000 FEET

4

Año Nuevo Creek

Pond Loop Trail

Año Nuevo Point Trail

Año Nuevo Bay

Año Nuevo
State Reserve

Point Año Nuevo

Island Reserve

FEET				
2600				
2275				
1950				
1625				
1300				
975				
650				
325				
	1.0	2.0	3.0	4.0

MILES

was established. Since then the elephant seal population has continued to flourish, and sea lions and harbor seals have found both the mainland and island hospitable for breeding and migratory rest stops. Año Nuevo Reserve now hosts the largest mainland breeding colony of northern elephant seals in the world.

Begin from the parking lot on the Año Nuevo Point Trail. After about 90 feet, you'll reach a **T** junction. Turn right toward the wildlife area (if you prefer to tour the visitor center first, turn left, then return to this spot).

The first of an occasional series of interpretive signs appears, this one telling the tale of the schooner Point Arena, which was bashed into bits against the rocks at Pigeon Point in 1913. A piece of the ship stands off the side of the trail, with an old porthole nicely framing an ocean view. The Pond Loop Trail sets off to the left here; this is the path for the hike's return leg, so stay to the right. The Año Nuevo Point Trail keeps a nearly level grade as it travels through a plant community of coyote brush, poison oak, California coffeeberry, toyon, blackberry brambles, and grasses. A few shrubby Douglas fir seem totally out of place. In late summer and early autumn, yellow goldenrod is conspicuous in a sea of tawny-colored dry grass and army-green shrubs. The ocean is audible but not visible. At 0.7 miles, the Pond Loop Trail feeds in from the left. Continue straight.

The trail resembles a city boulevard, straight and wide. If you pause to look back to the east, patches of stark white soil sharply contrast to Chalk Mountain's surrounding dense forest. You'll reach the border of the wildlife protection area at 0.9 miles. In a little exhibit building there are interpretive displays with descriptions of stellar sea lions, harbor seals, California sea lions, and elephant seals. You can also view an artist's depiction of how wind and water transformed Año Nuevo's coastline, creating Año Nuevo Island. If you're visiting during the restricted season, this is the trailhead for docent-led walks. The rest of the year (with your wildlife permit in hand), proceed on the Año Nuevo Point Trail.

Gorgeous ocean views unfold as the trail runs along the coast. Off to the west, the remains of a lighthouse constructed in 1890 are visible on abandoned Año Nuevo Island, now home to birds and seals. Guidewires remind visitors to stay on the trail. As if to emphasize the point, coyote brush, bush lupine, and blackberry form protective thickets along the trail—then the shrubs thin and a boardwalk channels visitors over a damp area. Just past an exhibit about whales, the trail shifts to loose sand and dunes appear, dominating the landscape. At 1.4 miles, a path heads to the left toward the South Point. Stay to the right toward the North Point seal overlook.

Past this area the trail network is fluid, and may be changed (or closed) with no advance notice to protect the seals. The current path may vary from this account, so simply follow the guidewires and signs to stay on course. There's a tremendous amount of loose sand to climb through, and if you've ever wanted your own "Lawrence of Arabia" moment, you've come to the right place. From the top of the dunes the surroundings are scenic and peaceful, with the sound of the ocean and barking seals, birds swooping overhead, and stunning mountains just to the east. You'll pass a few sides paths, heading off to the left, optional out-and-back add-ons, assuming they're open. After the trail crosses a boardwalk, coastal plants including bush lupine, ragwort, coyote brush, beach primrose, sand verbena, sea rocket, and shrubby willow stabilize the dunes somewhat. At 2 miles the trail curves sharply left and then ends at a viewpoint above the beach. Docents can answer questions and help you identify whatever mammals are present on the day of your visit. When I last visited in autumn, a few elephant seals were romping in the water, building calluses on their chest for the fierce competition of mating season, which generally begins in December. The rest of the seals were placidly lounging on the beach. When you're ready, return to the junction of the Año Nuevo Point Trail and the Pond Loop Trail at 3.3 miles, then turn right.

The Pond Loop Trail makes its way through grasses dotted with coyote brush. The visitor center, an old barn, is visible in the distance. A few steps bring the trail down to the shores of a pond and a junction at 3.6 miles. The trail on the right descends to Cove Beach—continue straight on the Pond Loop Trail, skirting the shores of the little pond, where you might see pelicans either in the water or overhead. At 3.8 miles a trail heads south to the reserve boundary and New Years Creek. Continue to the left, climbing slightly. The trail levels out and returns to the junction with the Año Nuevo Point Trail. Bear right, and when you reach the next junction, either turn left to return to the parking lot, or continue straight to the visitor center.

▶ NEARBY ACTIVITIES

Año Nuevo's inland section hosts a trail connection to Big Basin Redwoods State Park. The *Trail Map to Santa Cruz Mountains* (map 2), published by the Sempervirens Fund, is a good guide to this area, known as Cascade Ranch.

Costanoa, a few miles north of Año Nuevo, has accommodations ranging from campsites to tent cabins and lodge rooms, in a natural, coastal setting. Visit www.costanoa.com or call (650) 879-1100 for more information.

BIG BASIN REDWOODS STATE PARK: WATERFALL LOOP

KEY AT-A-GLANCE INFORMATION

LENGTH: 11 miles

CONFIGURATION: Loop

DIFFICULTY: Strenuous

SCENERY: Redwoods, waterfalls, creeks

EXPOSURE: Mostly shaded

TRAFFIC: Heavy around park headquarters, otherwise moderate

TRAIL SURFACE: Dirt trails, with one short, steep scramble downhill over rocks at Silver Falls

HIKING TIME: 6 hours

SEASON: Good all year—waterfalls at peak in late winter and spring

ACCESS: Pay the $5 fee at the entrance station or park headquarters.

MAPS: The park map is available (for $2) at park headquarters.

FACILITIES: Toilets and drinking water are available at the trailhead.

SPECIAL COMMENTS: Dogs are not permitted on park trails.

IN BRIEF

Redwoods, creeks, and waterfalls—that's what this loop is all about. Nestled in California's oldest state park, this popular hike begins at the Big Basin park headquarters, and follows the undulating Sunset Trail downhill through forested canyons to a series of three dramatic waterfalls. The return leg, a segment of the Skyline to the Sea Trail, rises along murmuring creeks back to the trailhead.

DESCRIPTION

There is one main parking lot, in front of the massive Redwood Trail sign, and secondary lots across from the park store—begin on a path to the left of the Campfire Center, following the signs to the Skyline to the Sea Trail. After crossing Opal Creek on a little bridge, you'll reach a T junction with the Skyline to the Sea Trail. Turn right toward the Dool and Sunset trails.

At a level grade, the broad trail runs along Opal Creek, through the outskirts of the park headquarters area. Noise from vehicles and park visitors grows fainter with each step through redwood,

DIRECTIONS

Drive south from San Francisco on I-280 and use the CA 1/19th Avenue merge as the mileage starting point. Drive south on I-280 about 36 miles, then exit CA 85 south. After about 4.5 miles, exit onto Saratoga Avenue. Drive west about 2 miles into Saratoga and the junction with Saratoga-Sunnyvale, then continue straight on Big Basin Way/CA 9. Drive uphill on 9 for about 7 miles to Saratoga Gap (junction 9 and CA 35), then continue straight on Highway 9. Drive downhill on 9 for 6 miles. Where 9 sweeps left, continue straight onto CA 236. Proceed on this narrow winding road for 8.5 miles to the park headquarters (left) and parking lots (right).

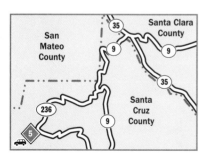

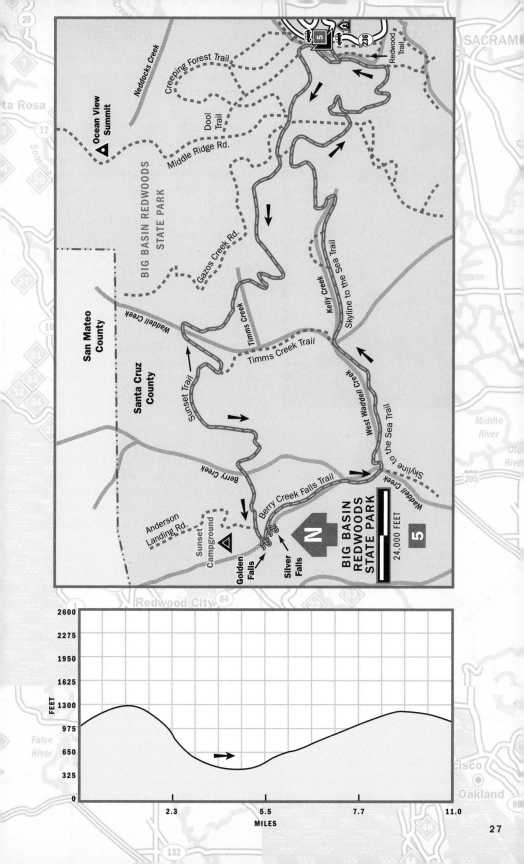

BIG BASIN
REDWOODS
STATE PARK

24,000 FEET

Five finger ferns and moss thrive in the spray of Berry Creek Falls.

huckleberry, and tanoak woods. After about 0.3 miles, Skyline to the Sea continues to the north, on its way to Castle Rock, but turn left, onto the Dool Trail. The trail rises easily through forest, then reaches a junction with the Sunset Trail, at about 0.4 miles. Turn left.

The Sunset Trail begins to climb through woods where madrone are prominent. Many of the trees along the trail are charred by fire, and some of the huge redwoods have burned-out trunks. Early settlers confined poultry in these hollowed-out trees, which became known as "goose pens." At 0.9 miles, the Sunset Trail crests at the junction with Middle Ridge Road. Continue across the fire road on the Sunset Trail, which begins an easy descent. Winding down into a redwood canyon, you might see milkwort and California harebell in summer, and in a short grassy stretch, lingering blossoms of Ithuriel's spear and vetch.

At 1.1 miles a connector to Skyline to the Sea departs on the left, but continue straight on the Sunset Trail. A few coast live oaks give way to a forest dominated by redwood and tanoak. The trail ascends gently, crosses over a knoll, and drops through woods where trilliums, redwood violets, western hearts ease, and fairy lanterns bloom in spring. At West Waddell Creek, a pretty stream graced with a few big-leaf maple, the trail rises again. The Timms Creek Trail begins at 3.9 miles off to the left as the Sunset Trail makes a sharp turn right. The Timms Creek Trail, which leads to the Skyline to the Sea Trail, is the bail-out route for hikers who are ready to return to the trailhead.

Continue on the Sunset Trail, climbing steadily straight uphill. The Sunset Trail crests near a huge fallen redwood, then begins to descend through very quiet woods. After crossing Berry Creek, the path ascends again, but soon steps out of the woods to bisect a swale of chaparral. Manzanita covers the chalky white hillsides to the left and right, and these low-slung shrubs, mixed through occasional knobcone pines, permit views south to the forested canyon surrounding the waterfalls. Bush poppy's cheerful yellow flowers stand out in a sea of green in early summer, preceding chamise's bloom and fruit on huckleberry shrubs.

As the Sunset Trail leaves the chaparral, live oaks, nutmeg, and Douglas fir bridge the transition back into redwood and tanoak. At 5.5 miles the trail to Sunset Camp breaks off to the right—continue straight, now on the Berry Creek Falls Trail. The sound of water rushing, then falling, increases as the trail descends. Then, on the right, Golden Falls comes into view. A short switchback drops the trail to the side of the fall, where water slides down a sloping wall of tawny-colored sandstone. The water rushes to a second, short drop, then pools at the top of Silver Falls. As the water shoots straight down 50 feet in a single gasp, the trail clings to the side of the cliff, descending rock stairs. The guidewire on the right is essential, and take special care when the water flow is heavy, for the steps will be slippery.

The Berry Creek Falls Trail reaches the base of Silver Falls and then levels out and follows the creek. When the creek is low, you can jump across to the right and walk a few feet to get a close look at the fall. This interlude between waterfalls is my favorite spot on the hike—West Berry Creek burbles along the trail and sunlight filters through the redwoods to an understory of ferns, where starflower, trilliums, and redwood sorrel brighten the forest floor in spring, and butterflies float through the air in summer. Just past the confluence of West Berry and Berry creeks, the trail crosses the stream and rises to overlook the top of Berry Creek Falls, a 60-foot drop distinguished by gorgeous ferns and moss covering the rocks around the water flow. There are wonderful views to the falls as the trail descends to a viewing platform near the base of the falls—if it's not crowded, this is an ideal location for lunch. Past the platform, the trail descends to a junction at 6.7 miles. Turn left onto the Skyline to the Sea Trail.

A bridge crosses the confluence of Berry and West Waddell creeks, then the Skyline to the Sea Trail climbs somewhat sharply to a bench where there is one last view to Berry Creek Falls. I lunched here on my last hike and enjoyed the waterfall view and entertainment provided by a band of marauding steller jays, who perched on a fence hoping for breadcrumbs. Past the bench, the Skyline to the Sea Trail begins a rollicking course of short ups and downs, along West Waddell Creek. Azaleas and big-leaf maples line the stream as the trail crosses the water for the south bank, where you may notice salal and wild rose in the understory of tanoak and redwood. Past some big boulders sitting in the creekbed at 7.9 miles, the Timms Creek Trail crosses the creek on the left, at the confluence of West Waddell and Kelly Creek. Continue straight on the Skyline to the Sea Trail, still climbing, here at a more straightforward uphill pace. The trail wanders through a beautiful redwood forest where in late spring, look for clintonia in bloom, a lily with magenta flowers. Later, in summer, orchids unfurl, including the native stripped and spotted corralroots, and helleborine, with purple-green flowers, an import from Eurasia. The Skyline to the Sea Trail forks, with the left leg crossing the creek—either path is an option, as they both reconnect shortly.

Past the rejoining, the Skyline to the Sea Trail crosses Kelly Creek, then begins to climb out of the canyon, away from the creek. The forest remains quiet and shaded, and you might see banana slugs along the trail, particularly in cool, damp weather. At 9 miles the connector to the Sunset Trail heads uphill to the left—continue straight on the Skyline to the Sea Trail. The ascent mellows as you reach the hike's highest elevation, over 1,300 feet. The Skyline to the Sea Trail crosses Middle Ridge Fire Road at 9.5 miles, then descends through redwoods scarred by fire. At the 10.6-mile mark, bear left at a fork toward park headquarters. At 10.9 miles, you'll return to the hike' first junction. Turn right, cross Opal Creek, and return to the trailhead.

▶ NEARBY ACTIVITIES

This is the most popular Big Basin hike (the short Redwood Trail loop is really just a walk), although there are scores of other possibilities. The website www.bigbasin.org has some brief descriptions of hiking options, and an on-line trail map. One of my favorite hikes is the out-and-back trek to Buzzard's Roost, a sandstone outcrop with incredible views of the park.

BLACK DIAMOND MINES
REGIONAL PRESERVE

KEY AT-A-GLANCE INFORMATION

LENGTH: 3.5 miles

CONFIGURATION: Loop

DIFFICULTY: Moderate

SCENERY: Grassland and chaparral

EXPOSURE: Mostly full sun

TRAFFIC: Mostly moderate, but heavy near the visitor center

TRAIL SURFACE: Dirt fire road and trails

HIKING TIME: 2 hours

SEASON: Summer is often very hot—late winter and spring are best.

ACCESS: Pay the $4 fee at the entrance kiosk.

MAPS: The park map is available at the trailhead.

FACILITIES: Vault toilets and drinking water are available at the trailhead.

SPECIAL COMMENTS: Dogs permitted

▶ IN BRIEF

Want to ramble through grassland and chaparral on one hike? This loop is a perfect tour through grassy rolling hills as well as chamise, black sage, and manzanita-covered slopes. You'll begin in the heart of the park, climb through grassland dotted with blue oaks, follow an undulating course through chaparral, climb some more back into grassland, and then descend steadily back to the trailhead.

▶ DESCRIPTION

Have you heard the one about the coal mine in Contra Costa County? It's no joke—from 1860 to 1906 the property we now know as Black Diamond Mines was the largest coal mining district in California. Nearly 4 million tons of coal (black diamonds) were mined, with as many as 900 miners populating five towns in the area. When coal mining operations ceased, underground sand mining continued until the late 1940s. The East Bay Regional Park District has preserved Black Diamond Mines as a recreation and historical park, with miles of trail laced through more than 5,700 acres of land, and remnants from the mining era accessible in several locations. Although almost all the mine shafts, portals, and tunnels are shuttered, 200 feet of Prospect Tunnel are

▶ DIRECTIONS

Depart San Francisco on the Bay Bridge and use the toll plaza as the mileage starting point. Stay to the left, northbound on I-80. Drive north on I-80 about 15 miles, then exit on CA 4. Drive east on CA 4 (toward Martinez) 25 miles, then exit onto Somersville Road. Drive south on Somersville Road 2 miles into the park, continue another mile to the entrance kiosk, and then drive a little less than 1 more mile to the parking lot at the end of the road.

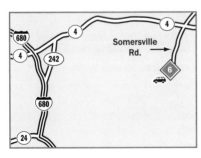

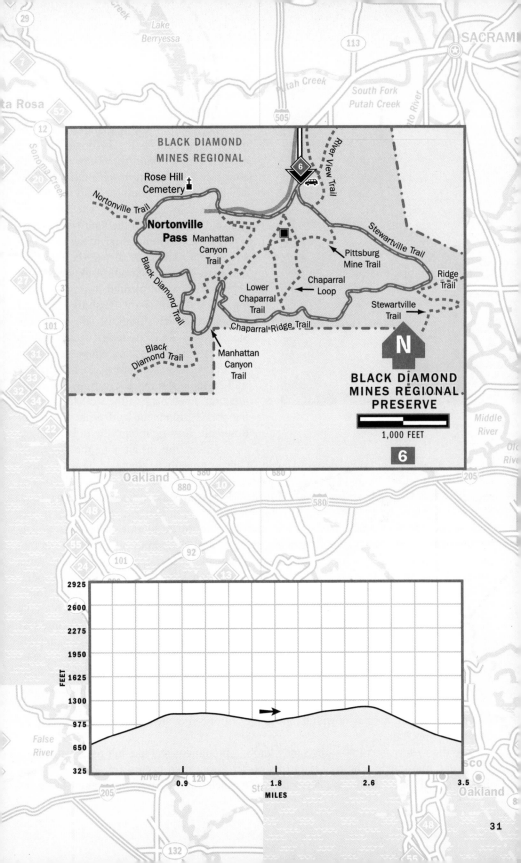

BLACK DIAMOND
MINES REGIONAL

Rose Hill
Cemetery

Nortonville Trail

Nortonville Pass

Manhattan
Canyon
Trail

Black Diamond Trail

River View Trail

Stewartville Trail

Pittsburg
Mine Trail

Chaparral
Loop

Lower
Chaparral
Trail

Ridge
Trail

Stewartville
Trail

Black
Diamond Trail

Manhattan
Canyon
Trail

Chaparral Ridge Trail

N

**BLACK DIAMOND
MINES REGIONAL
PRESERVE**

1,000 FEET

6

The Nortonville Trail toward Rose Hill Cemetery at Black Diamond Mines

open for exploration, and the park's visitor center occupies the original opening to the sand mine.

Begin from the parking lot on the paved Nortonville Trail. The broad fire road ascends gently toward the visitor center, but after just 220 feet, turn left onto the Stewartville Trail. Still gaining elevation, the fire road cuts through grassland, then reaches a gate and junction with the Railroad Bed Trail at 0.1 mile. Continue straight on the Stewartville Trail. The trees that tower above the trail here—tree of heaven, black locust, and pepper tree—were planted during the mining era. At 0.2 miles, the Pittsburg Mine Trail begins on the left. Continue straight on the Stewartville Trail. A long, steady climb begins, through grassland where you might see fiddlenecks and lupines in March. The trail crests at 0.6 miles, reaching a multiple junction. Look back to the west for views of the park's prominent bald peak, 1,506-foot Rose Hill. Turn right onto the Ridge Trail.

Off in the distance to the southwest you'll get a peek at the top of Mount Diablo. While at a nearly level grade, the trail skirts a knoll on the left. Buckeye and blue oak sprawl through grassland along the trail—this is a good spot for wildflowers all spring long. Early in the season smatterings of shooting stars, bluedicks, lupines, and buttercups are common, but an even better display occurs in late April, when Ithuriel's spear, owl's clover, and big cheerful California dandelions heavily freckle the grassland like rainbow sprinkles. Sticking downslope from the ridgeline, the trail rises a bit steeply into a dramatically different landscape of manzanita, coulter pine, yerba santa, and sagebrush. At 1.1 miles the trail crests at a little bare spot on the left—a wonderful spot for a break, offering good views of Mount Diablo and Black Diamond's valley, downhill to the left. On a mid-May hike here, I admired a bountiful display of gorgeous butterfly mariposa lilies, mixed through paintbrush. The Ridge Trail begins to descend, enclosed by thick stands of chaparral. When the trail bends left, views open up to the north, encompassing rock formations in the foreground and Antioch in the distance. Quite a few bush poppy shrubs are mixed through chamise and manzanita—look for bush poppy's bold yellow flowers in spring. The Ridge Trail descends somewhat steeply over slippery bare sandstone, then ends at a junction at 1.4 miles. The Lower Chaparral Loop Trail sets off to the right, skirting a rock formation on the way downhill toward the visitor center area. Continue straight on the Chaparral Loop Trail.

To the west, past a low-slung sandy knoll, a prominent reef-like hill rises, with rocks jutting out at an angle. The trail rises to a power tower, then begins a descent. One long straight stretch is an aromatic alley, with sweet smells wafting from manzanita blossoms (winter), black sage and pitcher sage flowers (spring), and a froth of chamise blooms (summer). A few live oaks mingle with pine and yerba santa as the Chaparral Loop Trail drops on steps and some steep grades into Manhattan Canyon. In mid-May, I have seen dozens of fairy lanterns blooming along the trail. Just after a bridge crosses the canyon at 1.7 miles, you'll reach a junction, with the trail to the right closing the Chaparral Loop. Turn left, following the sign toward the Manhattan Canyon Trail.

After a brief, winding climb through chamise and six-foot-tall manzanitas, there's a second junction. The Manhattan Canyon Trail, to the right, leads downhill back toward the trailhead. The trail straight ahead is a connector to the Black Diamond Trail. Turn left, onto the Manhattan Canyon Trail.

On a slope just uphill from the canyon floor, the narrow trail ascends through live oaks, pine, sticky monkeyflower, toyon, and manzanita. Somewhat abruptly, the canyon widens into a grassy bowl near the park boundary. Blue oaks dot the hillsides as the Manhattan Canyon Trail veers right and climbs steeply, ending at a junction with the Black Diamond Trail at 2 miles. A bench to the right just before the junction is a good place to catch your breath. Turn right onto the Black Diamond Trail.

Trailside vegetation is a mixture of grassland, pine, manzanita, and blue and live oaks. Look off to the right for views back to Chaparral Loop and Ridge trails. After a brief level interlude, the fire road begins to descend easily into chaparral, where you might see ceanothus, black sage, yerba santa, chamise, and pitcher sage. At 2.2 miles the connector to the Manhattan Canyon Trail departs on the right. Continue straight on the Black Diamond Trail, ascending at a moderate grade back into grassland. On the far side of a cattle gate beneath a power tower, there are sweeping views to the Stewartville Trail. By mid-May, the tips of high hills rising up to the northeast begin to fade from green to dull brown, drained of color. In early spring, shooting stars bloom in staggering amounts along the trail, in the grassy breaks between clusters of blue and live oaks. The Black Diamond Trail begins to descend easily, offering views northwest to Suisun Bay on clear days. At 2.8 miles the Black Diamond Trail ends at a junction with the Nortonville Trail. Turn right.

The Nortonville Trail loses elevation at a moderate grade, dropping along the side of a sloping valley to the right of Rose Hill. Owl's clover is common in the short grass of early spring, but by mid-May billowing mustard plants and thistles take over. You may see and hear red-winged blackbirds in this part of the park. At 2.9 miles a path departs on the left, leading to Rose Hill Cemetery, the final resting place for some of the residents of the mining era. This is an optional detour—a path returns to the Nortonville Trail less than 0.1 mile downhill. The Nortonville Trail sweeps right and begins a return to the main park area, with tree of heaven lining the route. At 3.2 and 3.4 miles, two forks of the Manhattan Canyon Trail depart on the right. Continue straight on the Nortonville Trail to a junction at 3.5 miles. Turn right here if you'd like to tour the visitor center (open weekends). Otherwise, turn left, and follow the Nortonville Trail another 0.1 mile back to the parking lot.

BOTHE-NAPA VALLEY STATE PARK

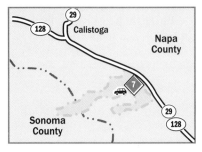

IN BRIEF

Just a stone's throw from Napa Valley vineyards, this hike starts along shaded Ritchey Creek and then climbs through redwoods into chaparral and the top of Coyote Peak. After enjoying views of Napa Valley and Mount St. Helena, you'll descend to the creek and follow it back to the trailhead.

DESCRIPTION

Tucked in a canyon in the heart of wine country, this park is easy to miss amongst the tasting rooms and vineyards of surrounding Napa Valley. Although the trailhead is close to Highway 29, it only takes a few minutes of walking to reach the banks of Ritchey Creek, where the loudest sounds are the murmur of water and bird calls. Since the park's highest trail elevation is less than 2,000 feet, Bothe-Napa offers some of the easiest all-season (shaded) hiking in Napa County.

Begin from the trailhead on the Ritchey Canyon Trail. This path, shaded by oaks and big-leaf maple, crosses a service road, meets a spur feeding in from the right, skirts an employee residence, then widens at the banks of Ritchey

DIRECTIONS

Leave San Francisco northbound on US 101 and use the Golden Gate Bridge toll plaza as the mileage starting point. Drive 20.5 miles north on US 101, then exit onto CA 37. Drive east about 7 miles, and turn left onto CA 121. Drive north about 6.5 miles, and stay right on CA 121/CA 12 East at a junction with CA 116. Drive east about 9 miles, then turn left onto CA 29. Drive north about 25 miles to the park entrance on the left side of the road (between the towns of St. Helena and Calistoga). After passing the entrance kiosk, drive past the visitor center and park at the Ritchey Canyon Trailhead (about 0.25 miles from the entry kiosk) on the right side of the road.

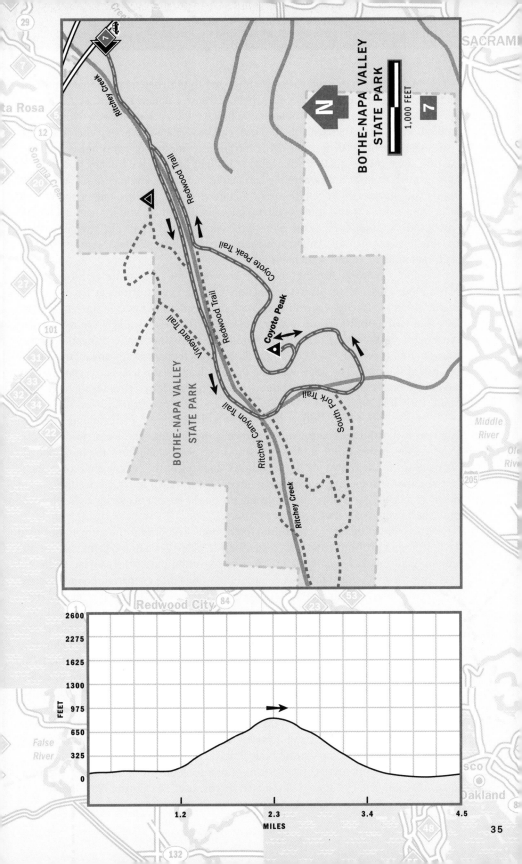

BOTHE-NAPA VALLEY
STATE PARK

N

1,000 FEET

7

Ritchey Creek

Redwood Trail

Coyote Peak Trail

Coyote Peak

Redwood Trail

Vineyard Trail

BOTHE-NAPA VALLEY
STATE PARK

Ritchey Canyon Trail

South Fork Trail

Ritchey Creek

FEET

2600
2275
1625
1300
975
650
325
0

1.2   2.3   3.4   4.5
MILES

35

Creek. Maidenhair fern, wild rose, hazelnut, and thimbleberry form a lush landscape beneath redwoods and Douglas fir, where starflower and woodland star bloom in spring. After about a half mile of level strolling, you'll reach a junction with the Redwood Trail. Stay to the right on the Ritchey Canyon Trail, crossing the creek. The park's campground, off to the right, contributes some background noise, but once past the area, things quiet down again. At a slight incline, the Ritchey Canyon Trail cuts through a grassy area where big-leaf maple, madrone, and oaks are common. In spring you may notice huge blossoms on cultivated rose bushes, one of several artifacts from this canyon's more civilized past. At 0.9 miles, you'll reach a junction with a trail doubling back to the right to the campground. Continue straight, still on the Ritchey Canyon Trail. An old stone fountain, building, and barn stand beside the trail, remnants of an old settlement.

Ignore a spur trail leading left to the Redwood Trail, and continue through a mix of redwood, oaks, and maple to the junction with the Vineyard Trail, at 1.6 miles. Stay to the left on the Ritchey Canyon Trail. With the creek burbling off to the left, the trail keeps an easy uphill pace. In winter and early spring, you'll likely see a variety of mushrooms in the shade of dense redwood stands. At the 2-mile mark, the Ritchey Canyon Trail continues off to the right deeper into its namesake canyon and the far reaches of the park. The Redwood Trail doubles back to the left. Cross the creek on a concrete bridge to a second junction, with the Spring Trail. Here, turn left onto the South Fork Trail.

Once across a little bridge, the narrow path hops over a stream and begins to climb at a mostly moderate grade, following the stream. The forest is dense and there are few plants in the understory, with huge giant chain ferns the most notable companions to the redwoods. In the quietest months of the year, when foot traffic is low, the trail is sometimes completely carpeted with fallen redwood needles. At 2.4 miles, in a small grove of young madrone, the South Fork Trail swings right. Bear left onto the Coyote Peak Trail.

The path continues to rise through redwoods deeper into the canyon, but then curves left and drops to cross the creek. As the Coyote Peak Trail regains the lost elevation, California bays along the trail mark a transition out of the canyon. Oaks and grass line the trail, which then leads out of the woods into chaparral. Looming to the north, over an undulating sea of redwood, is the top of Mount St. Helena. Here, chamise, sticky monkeyflower, yerba santa, manzanita, toyon, and poison oak crowd the trail as the grade slackens to an easy uphill. Volcanic rock is conspicuous in this area, and the going gets quite rocky. There's a short downhill, then the trail climbs to a junction at 2.8 miles, with the trail to the top of Coyote Peak departing to the right. Follow this path, which is initially very rocky and eroded, uphill, and pause at a clear spot to note the view south into Napa Valley—this is the best view from the peak, since the actual summit is surrounded with tall trees, which block the views. It's worth continuing, though, since this tiny, somewhat steep path is quite scenic, ascending through chaparral and a pocket of redwood before ending, at the top, at 2.9 miles. Backtrack to the Coyote Peak Trail, then turn right.

Golden fairy lanterns, paintbrush, and iris bloom in spring along the trail, mixed through dense chaparral dominated by chamise. The Coyote Peak Trail follows a contour around the hillside, descending back into oak, California bay, madrone, and hazelnut woods. A short stretch of chaparral permits views of redwoods farther downhill, then the trail reaches those trees, preceding a junction with the Redwood Trail at 3.6 miles. Turn right.

In April, look for both red and blue larkspur, hiding out in the shade beneath redwoods. The Redwood Trail descends easily, following the course of Ritchey Creek. At 4 miles you'll return to the junction with the Ritchey Creek Trail. Stay to the right here, and retrace your steps back to the trailhead.

▶ NEARBY ACTIVITIES

Bale Grist Mill State Historic Park, just south of Bothe-Napa Valley Park, features a water-powered grist mill built in 1846. The park occasionally has open-to-the-public milling days, where visitors can watch as grain is milled, and purchase fresh corn meal and flour. Phone (707) 942-4575 for more information.

BRIONES REGIONAL PARK

IN BRIEF

This hike reminds me of the *Goldilocks and the Three Bears* fairy tale: It's not too long and not too hard, but just about right for most people. Briones is a happy combination of soft rolling hills, grassy valleys dotted with oaks, seasonal lagoons, and tree-lined creeks. Visiting the heart of the park, this loop climbs along an old ranch road to a viewpoint, then descends past black oaks on the way back to the trailhead.

DESCRIPTION

How can a park with so many cows have so many flowers? The meeting of lush flora and hungry bovids seems a contradiction, but it somehow works at Briones, home to one of the best spring wildflower displays in the Bay Area. I also love the park in autumn, when the tall and tawny-colored grass is complimented by a riot of orange black oak leaves. Is there a bad time to visit? Not really, although the trails do get muddy after a typical winter storm's deluge.

Start from the parking area on Old Briones Road, initially a paved route. Along the flat wide trail, the vegetation is an ordinary mix of young coast live oak, blue elderberry, and coyote brush.

DIRECTIONS

Depart San Francisco on the Bay Bridge and use the toll plaza as the mileage starting point. About half a mile past the toll plaza, bear right onto I-580 East. Drive 1.5 miles, then exit CA 24. Drive 7 miles east on CA 24, then exit at Moraga/Orinda. Turn left and drive north on Camino Pablo Road for about 2 miles, then turn right onto Bear Creek Road. Drive on Bear Creek about 4.4 miles to the park entrance on the right side of the road. After passing the entrance kiosk, continue straight to the parking lot.

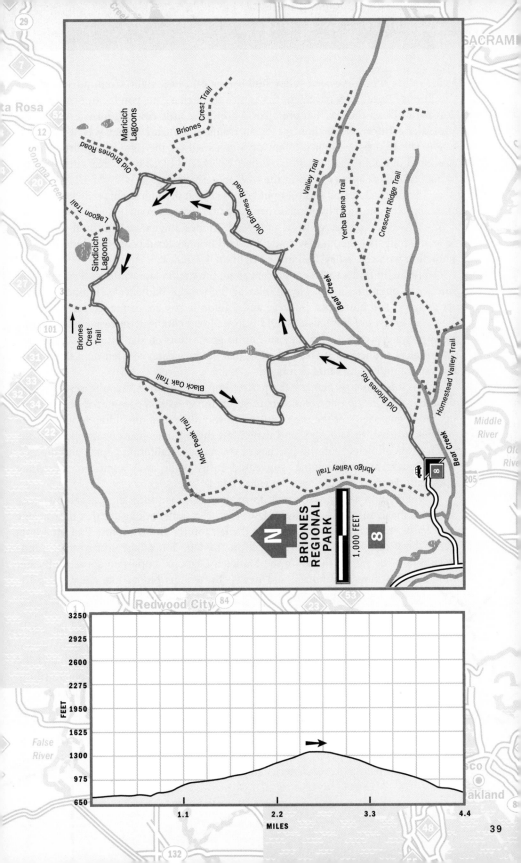

BRIONES REGIONAL PARK

N

1,000 FEET

8

Maricich Lagoons

Briones Crest Trail

Old Briones Road

Lagoon Trail

Sindicich Lagoons

Briones Crest Trail

Old Briones Road

Valley Trail

Yerba Buena Trail

Crescent Ridge Trail

Bear Creek

Black Oak Trail

Mott Peak Trail

Homestead Valley Trail

Old Briones Rd.

Abrigo Valley Trail

Bear Creek

8

FEET

3250
2925
2600
2275
1950
1625
1300
975
650

1.1   2.2   3.3   4.4

MILES

At 0.2 miles, the Homestead Valley Trail breaks off to the right. Continue straight on Old Briones Road, now pavement free. Once through a gate, you'll enter cattle range, skirting a hill on the left. On one hike, I noticed a little cow figurine nestled in the grass along the trail—an homage or an ironic statement? Either way it made me laugh. The trail rises slightly, following a creekbed on the right into a little shaded woodland of California bay and coast live, valley, and black oak. Great drifts of California buttercups sprawl beneath the trees in early spring.

The Black Oak Trail sets off uphill on the left at 0.7 miles. This trail is the return route, much more steeply pitched than easy Old Briones Road, so continue straight. A grassy valley on the left gently rises toward Briones' highest peaks. You'll pass a corral as the trail sticks to an easy grade, but Old Briones Road begins to climb just past a junction with the Valley Trail on the right, at 1.1 miles.

You might find a variety of flowers along the trail in late winter and spring, with buttercups often the first to bloom, blazing the way for fiddlenecks, lupines, California poppies, and bluedicks. Buckeye and California bay are common, particularly in the damp creases of the hillsides. Old Briones Road climbs at an easy grade, offering pretty views down into the valley and up to grassy hills on the left. At 1.7 miles the trail reaches a junction, fence, and crest. Just before a gate, veer left on a slight path, and walk uphill a few yards to a bench.

Yes, this bench is perhaps the perfect lunch destination if you're alone or with one other person (no one volunteers to sit on the grass in a cow-grazed park). There are 360-degree views of the park and the surrounding area, including Mount Diablo to the southeast. In late April and early May, the hillsides just downslope from the bench show off dense colorful patches of creamcups, California poppy, and lupines. If the flowers aren't blooming, you could easily while away some time watching hawks and kestrels soaring over the valley below.

When you're ready, walk back down the path, then turn left, pass through the gate, and make another left. After a few steps, the trails fork again, this time at one end of a big triangular junction. Stay to the left, on the Briones Crest Trail. At a level grade, the wide fire road skirts a knoll on the left. You might notice small ponds downhill on the right—those are the Maricich Lagoons, important sources of water for the park's birds, mammals, and newts. Buttercups bloom like crazy along the Briones Crest Trail in April, tinting entire hillsides lemon yellow. A row of coast live oaks lines the right side of the trail, interrupting the sea of grass.

The Lagoon Trail begins on the right at 2.1 miles, across from one of the Sindicich Lagoons. Continue straight on the Briones Crest Trail. As the trail ascends easily, there are good views downhill to the right of another lagoon. When it's full and the sun is shining, the water makes a nice mirror, reflecting puffy white clouds drifting across the bluest skies. At 2.4 miles, the Briones Crest Trail continues off to the right. Turn left onto the Mott Peak Trail. After a short ascent, the fire road crests and begins to descend, skirting its namesake peak through grassland with a few lonely oaks sprinkled here and there. On spring hikes in this part of the park, I've seen orange patches of California poppy that were so vivid and colorful I wondered if Mother Nature played paintball. Fiddlenecks are a late winter fixture along the trail.

Where the Mott Peak Trail reaches a junction at 2.7 miles, veer left onto the Black Oak Trail. The Black Oak Trail roller coasters along the ridgeline past displays of blue and white lupine. Up close in late winter's short green grass, the blooms really pop, but from a distance they make the hillsides look bruised. Black Oak bends left as the descent sharpens. In the driest months of the year, loose stones on the trail can make the descent a bit scary. I've taken the steepest section in a zigzag pattern more than once to keep from sliding. The trail runs between a beautiful oak forest on the right and a sloping grassy hillside on the left, where a few buckeyes line a creekbed. Although they blend into the woods in spring and summer, the trail's namesake trees are easy to pick out in autumn when their leaves turn orange. Black Oak levels out on the valley floor, then ends at 3.7 miles at Old Briones Road. Turn right and retrace your steps back to the trailhead.

CASTLE ROCK
STATE PARK

IN BRIEF

Castle Rock is an appropriate, majestic name for a park with so much natural beauty. Starting at the crest of the Santa Cruz Mountains, this hike descends through an evergreen forest, winds through chaparral and oaks past massive boulders and smaller sandstone formations, offers fabulous, sweeping views west, and stops at a waterfall before returning uphill toward the trailhead. On the return leg, a brief detour visits the park's namesake rock formation.

DESCRIPTION

Hikers love Castle Rock, and for good reason. It's beautiful all year-round, and has a few little extras that elevate it to the top tier of Bay Area parks and preserves. One bonus is a variety of vegetation, with woods, chaparral, and oak savanna. A second feature is Castle Rock Falls, less than 1 mile from the parking lot. This 70-foot waterfall nearly disappears in the driest months of the year, but winter storms send plenty of water rushing down in a single fall. The third and perhaps most unusual Castle Rock attribute is the tafoni sandstone formations. Although there are a few other locations in this part of the Bay Area with tafoni, Castle

DIRECTIONS

Drive south from San Francisco on I-280 and use the CA 1/19th Avenue merge as the mileage starting point. Drive south on I-280 about 36 miles, then exit onto CA 85 south. After about 4.5 miles, exit Saratoga Avenue. Drive west about 2 miles into Saratoga and the junction with Saratoga-Sunnyvale, then continue straight, now on Big Basin Way/CA 9. Drive uphill on CA 9 for about 7 miles to Saratoga Gap (junction CA 9 and CA 35), turn left onto CA 35 and drive south about 2.5 miles to the park entrance on the right side of the road.

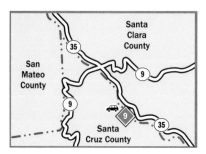

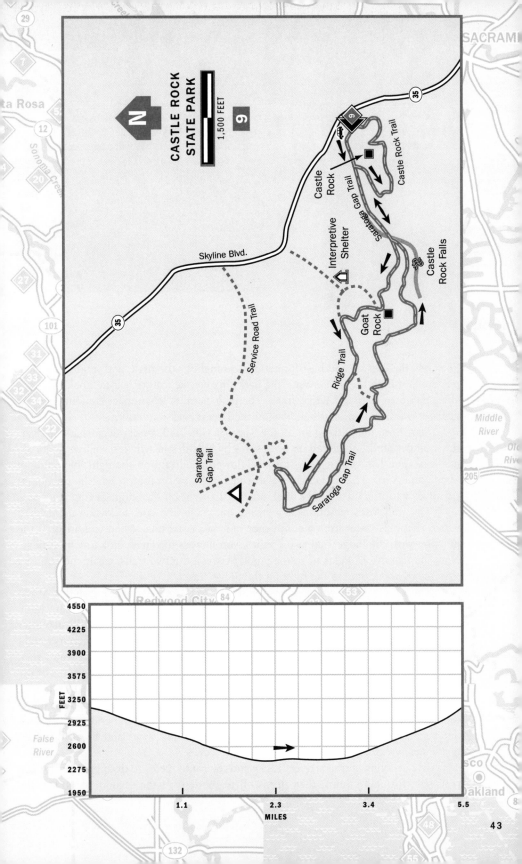

CASTLE ROCK
STATE PARK

1,500 FEET

9

Castle Rock

Castle Rock Trail

Saratoga Gap Trail

Interpretive Shelter

Castle Rock Falls

Skyline Blvd.

Goat Rock

Ridge Trail

Service Road Trail

Saratoga Gap Trail

Saratoga Gap Trail

FEET
4550
4225
3900
3575
3250
2925
2600
2275
1950

MILES
1.1   2.3   3.4   5.5

A gorgeous pocket of moss-covered tanoaks on Castle Rock's Ridge Trail

Rock has the biggest and best formations throughout the park, and interesting clusters are found on the trail around the park's namesake feature, Castle Rock, and also along Saratoga Gap and Ridge Trails. The park permits low-impact climbing, so you may see climbers working their way up the largest rock formations.

Start from the parking lot on the Saratoga Gap Trail. Under deep shade the narrow trail descends, squeezed on both sides by hillsides heavily forested with tanoak, madrone, and Douglas fir. Look for pink-flowering currant on the right, blooming in March and April. The trail crosses a seasonal creek twice, then reaches a junction at 0.2 miles with the Castle Rock Trail. Stay to the right on the Saratoga Gap Trail.

The trail loses elevation at a steady but moderate rate, following a creekbed which channels water from a confluence of smaller streams. When you arrive at the junction with the Ridge Trail at 0.7 miles, you'll cross the creek on a tiny footbridge. Note the massive Douglas fir in the crook between the two trails, easily the size of a mature redwood. Stay to the right on the Ridge Trail.

The narrow path winds a bit uphill, passing a massive white boulder. Moss-covered live oaks give way to sunny chaparral comprised of ceanothus, manzanita, yerba santa, chamise, pitcher sage, toyon, and sticky monkeyflower. You'll encounter the first of the hike's rock scrambles here. Deciding where to cast your gaze is tough, with sweeping views west, rocks and roots strewn about the trail, and weird rock outcrops visible uphill on the right. These odd pockmarked boulders are some of the park's most visible tafoni, sandstone rocks slowly shaped by exposure to rain and temperature change. Winter rains seep into the rocks, dissolving calcium carbonate, then summer's low humidity draws moisture containing the mineral to the rock's outer shell. Over time, the rocks develop interior weak spots and break from the inside out, creating dimples, holes, and small caves.

Two sections of trail are very rocky and the route seems to disappear. At the first rock pile, the trail climbs, then drops off to the left. At the second, ascend to the right, picking your way uphill until the rocks give way to more regular terrain. The trail bends right under a buckeye at the base of Goat Rock, and a set of steps brings the trail to the upper reaches of the rock formation and a junction at 1.2 miles. The path heading right leads to an interpretive shelter. Bear left, and after a few feet, follow the trail off to the left to Goat Rock overlook. A mellow path passes through oak grassland, then ends at a viewpoint surrounded by live and black oaks, manzanita, ceanothus, and chamise. Two interpretive signs help you identify landforms visible off to the distance, including Monterey Bay, the Butano Range, and Big Basin's Eagle Rock. Return to the previous junction and bear left, following the sign toward the Ridge Trail and campground.

I've seen the sides of the trail torn up—beneath madrone, California bays, and black oaks, a tell-tale sign that wild pigs had passed through. Feral pigs are troublesome residents of the Bay Area, and in this part of the Santa Cruz Mountains you don't have to look far to see the evidence of their bad behavior. The pigs, descended from escaped domestic swine and boars imported for hunting, dig through the topsoil searching for roots and acorns. Mountain lions and coyotes do kill some baby pigs, but adult pigs can tip the scales at over 300 pounds and have no predators (except the automobile). Some parks have begun a trapping and euthanasia campaign, but nonetheless the pig problem is spreading throughout the Bay Area. The path winds slightly uphill through grassland and trees, where baby blue-eyes bloom in April. At 1.4 miles you'll reach a T junction. Turn left onto the Ridge Trail.

Madrones, black and live oaks, and Douglas fir form a sparse forest along the trail as it descends easily. You may hear the sound of gunfire drifting into the park from a nearby shooting range. A little path veers off to the left, leading to a bird observatory lookout, a short out-and-back option (however, there are better views to come). At 1.7 miles, a shortcut to the Saratoga Gap Trail breaks off to the left. Continue straight on the Ridge Trail.

As the trail descends downslope from Varian Peak, thick stands of madrone, tanoak, and live oak woods close off views. Just past a spot with a rock formation and some manzanita, the Ridge Trail passes beneath some towering knobcone pines. The ridgeline thins, and the trail makes a transition from a course downslope of the ridge to the top of the ridge. There's not much understory, and some trees are completely covered with moss. Woods prevail until there's a sudden break in the tree cover, and you'll step out to the edge of a cliff. Eye-popping views unfold to the west, across miles of forested ridges. The trail heads back into a forest now dominated by madrone, and descends to a junction at 2.5 miles. The Castle Rock Trail Camp is a short distance down the trail to the right. Turn left onto the Saratoga Gap Trail.

At a mostly level grade, the trail winds through a familiar forest. After heavy rains, you may hear water tumbling down Craig Springs Creek on the right. The Saratoga Gap Trail bends left and changes its character completely. Under the dappled shade of live oaks, the trail passes beneath a rock outcrop, then descends a short segment of very steep steps cut into a boulder. A metal guidewire bolted into the rock is helpful—there's a steep drop-off on the right. Trees are left behind as the Saratoga Gap Trail ascends slightly through chaparral. Weaving through (and sometimes over) sandstone outcrops, the views west are outstanding. Along the trail, manzanita and two varieties of ceanothus (wartleaf and buckbrush) bloom in late winter and early spring, while yellow bush lupine, paintbrush, and lizardtail flower later, in early summer. Other common plants include chamise, yerba santa, and toyon. A few California bay and live oak shade the trail every once in a while. Watch out for poison oak, which is very common on the fringe of the trail. As the trail skirts Varian Peak, vegetation shifts to grassland and black oaks. The connector leading back uphill to the Ridge Trail starts at 3.5 miles. Continue straight on the Saratoga Gap Trail.

Once past a little bunch of buckeyes in a gully on the right, you'll climb back into chaparral, and get a good look ahead to steep rock-studded hillsides near Goat Rock. But there's a little surprise in a damp crease along the trail—a grove of California bay and a pocket of redwood. The tour through this cool oasis is short-lived, and the Saratoga Gap Trail rises back into chaparral. Keep your eyes open for tafoni with visible caves on the left side of the trail. There seems to be a "wow" with every step—hawks soaring overhead, flowers blooming at your feet, and always, the view. The trail squeezes between two boulders, marking a transition to a woodland of California bay, tanoak, live oaks, and Douglas fir. A pile of little boulders similar to the rock piles on the way to Goat Rock must be picked through. You might notice a huge live oak on the left, which seems to have grown out of the boulders. Waterfall lovers may quicken their steps when they begin to hear the sound of rushing water. Hop onto an observation platform on the right for a look down to Castle Rock Falls. This 70-foot sheer drop is at its best after days of heavy rain, but it trickles even in summer. The route continues uphill, following the creek. At 4.5 miles you'll return to the junction of Saratoga Gap and Ridge Trails. Turn right, and head back uphill.

When your reach the junction with the Castle Rock Trail, turn right. The trail ascends gently through a forest of tanoak, madrone, and Douglas fir, to Castle Rock. Unlike the largest tafoni formations toured so far on this hike, Castle Rock is not perched out in the open, but is nestled amongst the trees. Does is resemble a castle? It's surely big enough to house a family of Lilliputian elves, and it doesn't take too much imagination to see jutting pieces of rock, eroded into waves and cascades, as gargoyles. The trail opens up to fire-road width and passes another large rock formation on the right. Soon after, bear left, following the sign toward the parking lot. An easy descent finishes the hike, returning you to the trailhead.

▶ NEARBY ACTIVITIES

There are sandstone formations in two other parks in the Santa Cruz Mountains, Sanborn-Skyline County Park and El Corte de Madera Creek Open Space Preserve. Sanborn-Skyline sits on the east side of CA 35, across from Castle Rock, and El Corte de Madera Creek is on the west side of CA 35, about 18 miles north of this Castle Rock Trailhead. Visit the Santa Clara County Parks website (www.parkhere.org) for information about Sanborn-Skyline, and the Midpeninsula Regional Open Space District website for details about El Corte de Madera Creek (www.openspace.org).

ANTHONY CHABOT REGIONAL PARK

▶ **IN BRIEF**

This loop is a circuit through the heart of Chabot, bisecting Grass Valley, climbing to a ridge, then descending into Bort Meadow through quiet woods. I've enjoyed Chabot hikes in every season, but the park really shines in spring, during wild-flower season. If you're a beginning flower enthu-siast, this is a good, accessible place to start, with plenty of common blossoms best seen in April and early May.

▶ **DESCRIPTION**

Anthony Chabot Regional Park is shaped like a foot, with long thin toes pressing against Redwood Park and Lake Chabot settled at the heel. East Bay Municipal Water District defines the entire eastern border of Chabot, and the western boundary is mostly residential, but a ridge blocks most of the noise. If you're unfamiliar with the area, it would be easy to consider Chabot and neighbor park Redwood as one, but it's remarkable how different two adjoining parks can be—Redwood is heavily forested while Chabot hosts extensive grassland. The area around Lake Chabot is a warren of paths, leading to and from a marksmanship range, golf course, picnic areas, and campsites, but the rest of the park has an undeveloped feel.

▶ **DIRECTIONS**

Depart San Francisco on the Bay Bridge and use the toll plaza as the mileage starting point. About one-half mile past the toll plaza, bear right onto I-580 East. Drive 1.5 miles, then exit on CA 24. Drive 3.5 miles east on CA 24, then exit onto CA 13 south. Drive about 4 miles, exit at Redwood. Turn left onto Redwood and drive uphill about one-half mile, to the junction with Skyline Boule-vard. Stay in the left lane, and continue straight on Redwood about 4.3 miles to the trailhead on the right side of the road.

ⓘ **KEY AT-A-GLANCE INFORMATION**

LENGTH: 5.4 miles

CONFIGURATION: Loop

DIFFICULTY: Easy

SCENERY: Grassland, woods

EXPOSURE: Mostly full sun

TRAFFIC: Moderate

TRAIL SURFACE: Dirt fire roads and trails

HIKING TIME: 3 hours

SEASON: Summer is often hot; late winter and spring are best.

ACCESS: No fee

MAPS: Park map is available at the trail-head's information signboard.

FACILITIES: Pit toilets available at Bort Meadow, none at trailhead

SPECIAL COMMENTS: Dogs are permit-ted. Trails are usually muddy through winter and early spring.

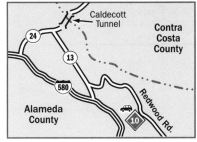

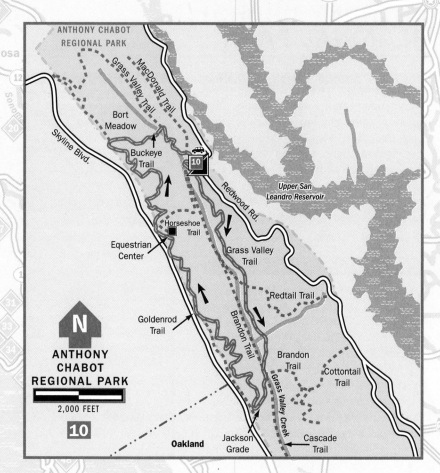

ANTHONY CHABOT
REGIONAL PARK

Grass Valley Trail

MacDonald Trail

Skyline Blvd.

Bort
Meadow

Buckeye
Trail

10

Redwood Rd.

*Upper San
Leandro Reservoir*

Horseshoe
Trail

Equestrian
Center

Grass Valley
Trail

Redtail Trail

N

ANTHONY
CHABOT
REGIONAL PARK

2,000 FEET

10

Goldenrod
Trail

Brandon Trail

Brandon
Trail

Cottontail
Trail

Grass Valley Creek

*Middle
River*

205

Oakland

Jackson
Grade

Cascade
Trail

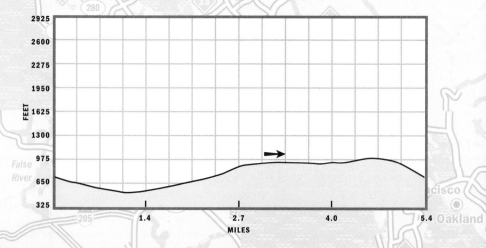

FEET				
2925				
2600				
2275				
1950				
1625				
1300				
975				
650				
325				
	1.4	2.7	4.0	5.4

MILES

Begin from the trailhead on a paved, gated road near the information signboard. As the service road sweeps downhill, there are views past the coyote brush and poison oak along the trail to Grass Valley on the left. At 0.1 mile, you'll reach a three-way junction. The road to the right continues to Bort Meadow, and the middle path leads to the Brandon Trail, which runs parallel to the Grass Valley Trail on the far side of Grass Valley Creek. Turn left onto the Grass Valley Trail.

Once through a cattle gate, you'll begin a nearly level stroll along the length of Grass Valley, a narrow meadow where wildflowers are common in spring. Some oaks, coyote brush, and poison oak shrubs dot the valley, but grassland dominates the landscape, where suncups, blue-eyed grass, and buttercups bloom in clusters in early April, and tiny-blossomed filaree makes a huge impact, overtaking hillsides with a purple hue. At mile 1 the Redtail Trail sets off uphill on the left. Continue on the Grass Valley Trail, winding slightly downhill into a grove of eucalyptus companionably mixed through some redwoods. At 1.5 miles, the Grass Valley Trail swings left toward Lake Chabot. Turn right and pass over Grass Valley Creek on Stone Bridge to a second junction, with the Cascade Trail on the left and the Brandon Trail on the right. Continue straight, now on Jackson Grade.

At a moderate pace, the fire road climbs through a mélange of vegetation, including eucalyptus, big-leaf maple, creambush, hazelnut, blackberry, wild rose, toyon, coast live oak, and coffeeberry. In spring, you are likely to see purple bush lupine and sticky monkeyflower blooming. The ascent ends at a junction with Goldenrod Trail at 1.9 miles. Turn right.

A short distance from the park boundary, the fire road runs downslope of a hillside, within audible range of Skyline Boulevard, and you'll likely hear some vehicle and residential noise. Chaparral favors this sunny area, although there are eucalyptus trees, which have extended their range out of the canyon on the right. In spring you might see bluewitch nightshade, checkerbloom, California poppy, blue-eyed grass, and bluedicks blooming beneath poison oak, toyon, broom, blue elderberry, and sticky monkeyflower. As the Goldenrod Trail veers left, a spur trail heads back to the left—continue to the right. Now, following close to Skyline Boulevard, eucalyptus trees are mostly replaced with some pine. There are good views across Grass Valley to the Upper San Leandro Reservoir watershed, managed by the East Bay Municipal Water District. At 3.6 miles you'll approach the grounds of Chabot Equestrian Center. Follow the trail signs as a skimpy path leads left, crosses an access road, and heads back into chaparral. The Horseshoe Trail sets off downhill on the right. Continue on the Goldenrod Trail.

This is a good section for wildflowers, ranging from delicate, wispy woodland star to giant, sturdy cow parsnip. In May you may see owl's clover. The trail alternates between chaparral and shade, with little substantial elevation change. California poppies occupy some grassy knolls just off the trail on the right. When you reach a T-junction with a paved service road at 4.4 miles, turn right. The road skirts a water tank, then returns to dirt. Creambush, a deciduous shrub, puts forth froths of white flowers in late spring and early summer, brightening the sides of the trail. You might also notice some big-leaf maple and hazelnut. If it's clear you should be able to make out Las Trampas Ridge to the east. At 4.7 miles, you'll reach a junction with the Buckeye Trail. Turn right.

In a park full of fire roads, this narrow hiking-only path is a gift. Steep sloping stairs drop the trail into a deeply shaded canyon, where coast live oak and California bay create a lush canopy. A little creek murmurs on the left, creating a moist, hospitable environment for hound's tongue and fringecups in spring. After a bridge crosses the creek, you'll pass a shaded rest bench that is welcome on a hot day. Watch your step as the trail runs along the stream, since the ground can be unstable. Forget-me-not one of our most charming "alien" wildflowers, covers the forest floor with a wash of light blue in late March. One last bridge transports you from woods to the edge of Bort Meadow, a wide, grassy expanse that makes a good stop for lunch or a sunny snooze. Cross the meadow to a junction on the left of the vault toilets at about 5 miles. The paved road (the same road on which this hike began) winds back to the parking lot, but a path to the right of a gated trail makes a nicer finish. This slight trail climbs through eucalyptus into coyote brush and poison oak. Loads of blue-eyed grass and buttercups bloom in April along the trail. There are also a few plum trees, favored by birds and the omnivorous coyote. When the trail forks at 5.3 miles, stay to the left. Coming to a crest, you'll reach a junction with the MacDonald Trail. Turn right and walk a few feet to the parking lot.

▶ **NEARBY ACTIVITIES**

The park's main trailheads are around Lake Chabot, where you can hike or bike around the lake on a 12.4-mile loop, then spend the night at one of several camp-sites. Call the campground office at (510) 639-4751 or the East Bay Regional Park District headquarters at (510) 635-0135 (www.epbarks.org) for more information.

HENRY W. COE STATE PARK

▶ IN BRIEF

If you yearn for a real getaway from city life, head to Henry Coe State Park. Although Coe is a substantial drive from some parts of the Bay Area, it offers superior day hikes as well as long multiday backpacking treks. This loop is one of Coe's shortest, but provides an excellent introduction to the park—touring canyons, oak savanna, and a high meadow crowned with towering ponderosa pines. Not to be missed!

▶ DESCRIPTION

Henry Coe is California's second largest state park, and with over 86,000 acres, there's plenty of room to roam. Part of the Coast Range, the park is mostly comprised of steep-sided ridges and creek-lined canyons, and sustains a variety of vegetation and terrific spring wildflower displays. With so many trails, the choices are a bit mind-boggling, and overzealous visitors often get in over their heads, hiking too far in hot weather while carrying insufficient water. I recommend the loop described below for first-timers. Hiking veterans can expand this trip to a 6.5-mile trek with significantly more elevation change by substituting the Fish Trail for Flat Frog, then looping to Hobbs Road via the Middle Ridge Trail.

ⓘ KEY AT-A-GLANCE INFORMATION

LENGTH: 4.7 miles

CONFIGURATION: Loop

DIFFICULTY: Easy/moderate

SCENERY: Oaks, grassland, ponderosa pines, views of the park and beyond

EXPOSURE: First half mostly shaded, second section mostly exposed

TRAFFIC: Light/heavy, depending on the season and day of the week

TRAIL SURFACE: Dirt trails and fire roads

HIKING TIME: 2.5 hours

SEASON: Late winter and spring are pleasant; avoid the park during heat waves.

ACCESS: Pay a $4 entrance fee at the visitor center.

MAPS: An excellent park map is available at the visitor center.

FACILITIES: Drinking water and rest rooms are available at the trailhead; the visitor center, when open, sells a small stock of cold drinks.

SPECIAL COMMENTS: Dogs are permitted in the park only on one short trail, near the park headquarters. For an easier hike, make this loop in the opposite direction—a particularly good option in hot weather.

▶ DIRECTIONS

Drive south from San Francisco on I-280 and use the CA 1/19th Avenue merge as the mileage starting point. Drive south on I-280 about 36 miles and exit onto CA 85 south. Drive south 19 miles, then merge onto southbound US 101. Drive south on US 101 about 10 miles to Morgan Hill, then exit onto East Dunne Avenue. Drive east 13 miles to the park headquarters and visitor center.

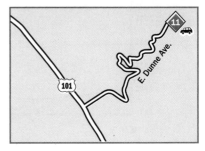

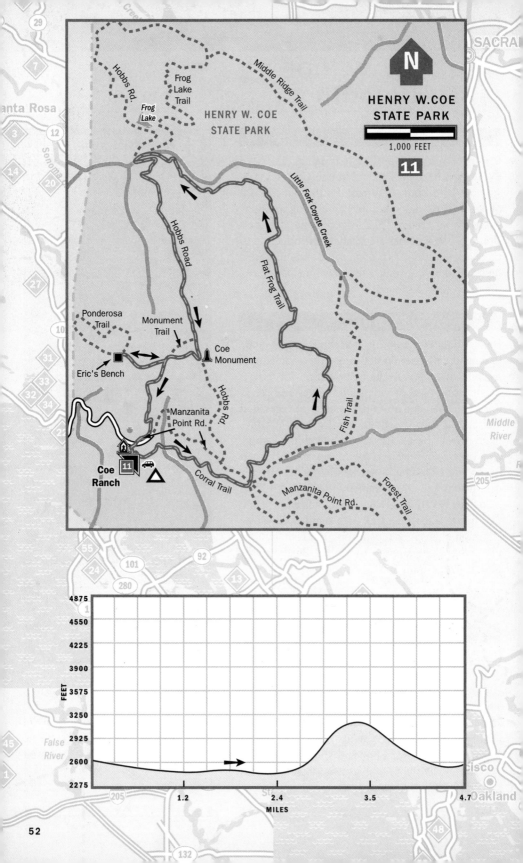

Map Labels

HENRY W. COE STATE PARK

N

1,000 FEET

11

Hobbs Rd.

Frog Lake Trail

Frog Lake

Middle Ridge Trail

HENRY W. COE STATE PARK

Little Fork Coyote Creek

Hobbs Road

Flat Frog Trail

Ponderosa Trail

Monument Trail

Coe Monument

Eric's Bench

Hobbs Rd.

Manzanita Point Rd.

Fish Trail

Coe Ranch

11

Corral Trail

Manzanita Point Rd.

Forest Trail

Elevation Profile

FEET

4875
4550
4225
3900
3575
3250
2925
2600
2275

1.2   2.4   3.5   4.7

MILES

52

Oaks loom in summer fog on the Corral Trail.

Begin from the park headquarters on the well-signed Corral Trail, which sets off at the edge of the parking lot, across from the visitor center. The narrow trail descends to cross a damp area on a wooden bridge, then begins a level journey on a ledge above a wooded gulch. On the morning of our hike, cobwebs strung through trailside vegetation glistened with dew like strands of sparking jewels. Buckeye, California bay, and live oaks shade the trail most of the way, but in a few pockets chaparral shrubs chamise, manzanita, and toyon bask on exposed hillsides. Like many of Coe's shaded paths, the Corral Trail hosts good displays of fairy lanterns in spring. The trail finally leaves the woods for good and enters oak savanna, where on a June hike thick fog obscured the landscape, and massive valley oaks standing in grassland were reduced to ghostly figures looming in the distance. Up close, disturbed vegetation under the oaks is an obvious sign of the big wild pig population inside the park—pigs dig up the ground beneath oaks while rooting for acorns. At half a mile, you'll reach a signed three-prong junction. The trail to the right leads to Manzanita Point via the Spring Trail, and the path straight ahead, to Manzanita Point Road. Veer left toward Flat Frog and Fish Trails. After a few feet, the path crosses Manzanita Point Road and reaches a junction with Flat Frog and Fish Trails. Bear left onto Flat Frog.

After hiking less than 30 minutes, there is virtually no noise from the outside world—except for occasional airplanes traveling overhead, bird songs, quails chirping unseen in the brush, squirrels scampering from tree to tree, and leaves whispering in the breeze make up the soundscape. Keeping an easy grade, this slight path follows a contour on the side of the hill, with a ravine to the right, winding through a sparse woodland of pines, California bay, manzanita, and a variety of deciduous and evergreen oaks. By mid-June, flowers on fairy lanterns are gone, leaving dangling seed pods, while great washes of elegant clarkia stain the drying grass pink. Occasionally, the trail bisects little huddles of chaparral, as well as increasing amounts of poison oak and creambush, but overall the vegetation is dominated by trees, including some big-leaf maple and madrone. With displays of pink flowers, coyote mint is common in late spring. As the ravine begins to open out, there are views across the canyon to another ridge, and ceanothus, scrub oak, cercocarpus, and toyon make appearances. Thickets of snowberry crowd the Flat Frog Trail, which bends left to follow a creek just before the trail ends at a multiple junction at 2.9 miles. Hobbs Road heads uphill both to the left and right, and the Frog Lake Trail sets off for its namesake, sharply to the right. Turn left onto Hobbs Road.

Ascending narrow Pine Ridge, a climb begins, moderate at first but then increasingly sharp. Along the fire road there's some California coffeeberry, pine, madrone, and oak above a grassy understory where you might see milkweed and pink-tinted clay mariposa lilies in early June. If you pause to look back downhill, Mount Hamilton's Lick Observatory dome is prominent in the distance to the north. In a little dip, the Monument Trail departs to the right at 3.6 miles. Continue straight on Hobbs Road, which soon crests at the flat ridge top. Just as the fire road begins to descend, turn left across from a junction with the Ponderosa Trail at 3.7 miles. A short path leads to the Henry Coe monument, a small headstone-like memorial with Coe's birth and death dates, as well as the following inscription: "May these quiet hills bring peace to the souls of those who are seeking." Coe and his family ranched this land until his death in 1943. Shortly thereafter the land was sold, but Coe's daughter Sada repurchased the property, then donated the 12,230-acre parcel to Santa Clara County in 1953. Turn back to the fire road, then cross it onto the Ponderosa Trail. This slight path can be hard to follow when the grass is tall, but the obscure section is short. Ponderosa winds slightly uphill through blue oaks and pine, then descends to a junction with the Monument Trail at 3.9 miles. Continue straight, following the sign to the vista point.

The path rises gently, then levels out in a broad, grassy plateau, topped with a few big, mature ponderosa pine, blue oak, and young madrone. In June, elegant brodaeia and yellow mariposa lily bloom through the pure stands of thigh-high grass. Off in the distance to the left (west), lower Santa Clara Valley is visible. At 4.1 miles the paths split around Eric's Bench (the paths eventually rejoin at the park boundary). This is a fantastic resting place for lunch or a water break. If you proceed a bit farther down the left fork, you'll come to an astonishingly graceful blue oak, standing alone in the grass. When you're ready, return to the junction with the Monument Trail, and turn right.

Descending steadily, the small footpath sweeps through grassland, then switchbacks through a pocket of California bay and ends at 4.5 miles. Turn right onto Manzanita Point Road, where a gate stretches across the fire road and dirt turns to pavement near a house. Manzanita Point Road descends gently toward park headquarters, then ends at 4.6 miles. Veer left onto the park road, and walk the remaining 100 feet back to the parking area.

▶ NEARBY ACTIVITIES

Coe has a very good website, which describes the most popular day hikes, offers photos of wildflowers and birds, and details camping options (www.coepark.org).

HENRY COWELL REDWOODS STATE PARK

▶ IN BRIEF

Visitors pour into Henry Cowell, drawn to the park's magnificent redwood grove, but beyond a short popular loop through the giant *Sequoia sempervirens,* there's a vast and varied park lightly traveled, except by locals. This hike is a soup-to-nuts tour through redwoods, sun-baked chaparral, and even ponderosa pines. You can also get a glimpse of a narrow-gauge train that passes through Henry Cowell on the way to Santa Cruz.

▶ DESCRIPTION

Henry Cowell Redwoods State Park, along with Pogonip Park, University of California Santa Cruz lands, and Wilder Ranch State Park, forms a greenbelt just north of the city of Santa Cruz. Cowell was a successful gold rush era entrepreneur who once owned 6,500 acres of prime Santa Cruz County real estate. His heirs donated over 1,600 acres of land abutting a county park founded to preserve one of the area's loveliest redwood groves, and the two properties became a state park in 1954.

▶ DIRECTIONS

Drive south from San Francisco on I-280 and use the CA 1/19th Avenue merge as the mileage starting point. Drive south on I-280 about 36 miles, then exit onto CA 85 South. After 7.5 miles, exit onto CA 17 South. Drive south on CA 17 about 17 miles, then exit onto Mt. Hermon Road. Turn right and follow Mount Hermon Road about 3.5 miles into Felton. Turn right onto Graham Hill Road, get into the left lane, and turn left onto CA 9. Drive about one-half mile south on CA 9, then turn left onto the signed park entrance road. Drive about one-half mile to the entrance kiosk, then continue straight 0.1 mile to the main parking lot at the end of the road.

ⓘ KEY AT-A-GLANCE INFORMATION

LENGTH: 4.8 miles

CONFIGURATION: Figure eight

DIFFICULTY: Easy

SCENERY: Woods, chaparral, redwoods, river

EXPOSURE: Mixed

TRAFFIC: Heavy near trailhead, lighter farther afield

TRAIL SURFACE: Dirt fire roads and trails, some with loose sand

HIKING TIME: 2.5 hours

SEASON: Summer is often very hot—late winter and spring are best.

ACCESS: Pay a $5 fee at the entrance kiosk.

MAPS: A park map is available at the entrance kiosk.

FACILITIES: Rest rooms and water at trailhead

SPECIAL COMMENTS: Dogs permitted on a few trails. Expect horses on most trails.

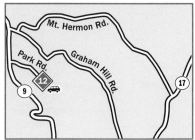

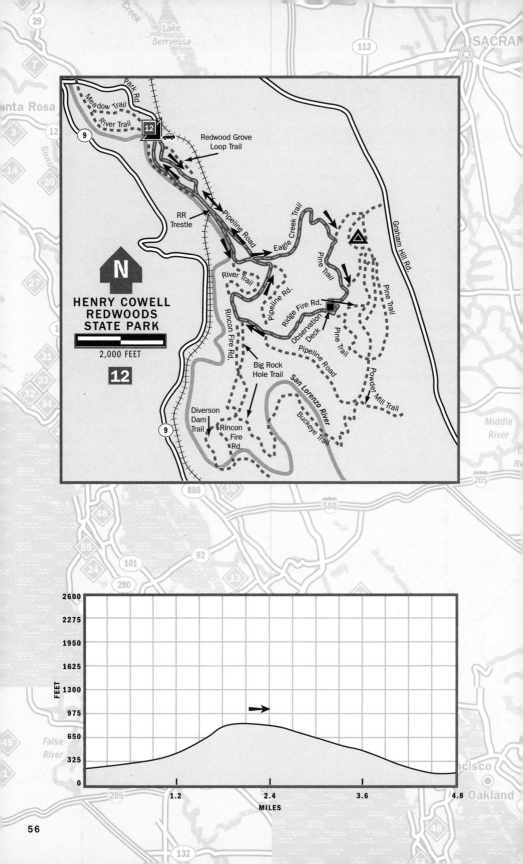

HENRY COWELL REDWOODS STATE PARK

2,000 FEET

12

Starting from the parking lot, follow the big sign toward the redwood grove. This paved, level boulevard, suitable for wheelchairs, crosses a fire road near the Nature Center, then proceeds into the grove, where towering redwoods dwarf a surrounding forest of big-leaf maple, tanoak, and California bay. At the far end of the loop, about 0.4 miles from the parking lot, slip through a gated gap in the trees, then bear right. Running parallel to the railroad tracks, the broad trail ends at a T-junction with Pipeline Road. Turn left.

The trail descends slightly to the shores of the San Lorenzo River, where big-leaf maples grace the riverbanks. If you happen through this area when a train is either coming or going, you're in for a treat—a trestle crosses directly overhead, and the sight of a chugging locomotive is particularly appealing to kids and train enthusiasts. After a brief descent, the Pipeline Trail meets the River Trail at 0.6 miles. Bear right. The slight trail winds through redwoods, joining a path feeding in from the left, then the River Trail reaches a junction. The path to the right leads to Cable Car Beach. The River Trail continues straight. Turn left onto the Eagle Creek Trail.

The trail ascends along the wall of a canyon above Eagle Creek. Although the surrounding redwood forest is young, these are some mighty tall trees—you can get a good sense of their size by perusing the fallen redwoods which litter the canyon. At 0.9 miles cross Pipeline Road, remaining on the Eagle Creek Trail. With the stream still downslope to the right, the Eagle Creek Trail ascends through a forest of redwood, tanoak, madrone, and California bay, with plenty of poison oak, hazelnut, and azalea in the understory. Once across a bridge, the Eagle Creek Trail climbs away from the creek through mixed woods of coast live oak and California bay. As the trail surface shifts to white chalky powder, chaparral plants take over—look for pines, manzanita, bush poppy, lizardtail, California coffeeberry, sticky monkeyflower, and chamise. At 1.7 miles, under a pocket of woods, you'll reach a junction, with the paths left and straight leading to the campground. Turn right onto the Pine Trail.

At a gradual ascent, the thin trail winds through chaparral. The sandy soil seems well suited to native plants, and the sides of the trail are crammed with manzanita, huckleberry, sticky monkeyflower, chinquapin, and ceanothus. Some tanoak accompany knobcone and Ponderosa pine. These two pines are easy to tell apart—knobcone feature closed cones, while the towering ponderosas, distinguished by a "jigsaw puzzle" bark pattern, bear open cones. With the ponderosas rising from the stark white soil, you might feel far from the Bay Area—although they are widely distributed through most of the state, ponderosas are very uncommon here. A path heads north to the campground from a junction at 2.1 miles—stay to the right on the Pine Trail.

The white ribbon of a trail continues ascending gently through chaparral to a multiple junction at 2.3 miles. An observation deck stands here at the park's highest elevation, offering impressive views north to the ridge surrounding Loma Prieta. This is a good spot for lunch (there's also a picnic table just off the side of the trail), but on a hot day the shade seems miserly. An interpretive sign explains that this part of the park, with its conspicuous white chalky soil, was formerly the ocean floor. When ready to continue, head west on Ridge Fire Road.

The trail does descend off a ridge, but it is no fire road—just a slight path here. Chaparral pea is mixed through manzanita, chamise, sticky monkeyflower, and pines, with some scrubby oaks and young Douglas fir. A flight of steps drops the trail back into the woods and a junction with Pipeline Road at 2.8 miles. Continue straight on Ridge Fire Road as the trail widens and heads uphill through redwoods. You may hear traffic on CA 9, a short distance to the west but out of sight. Coming to a crest, Ridge Fire Road ends at 3 miles. Turn right onto Rincon Fire Road.

Redwoods rule as the fire road drifts downhill. Ignore two paths breaking off to the left at 3.2 and 3.3 miles. Redwood sorrel, starflower, wild ginger, and iris bloom along the trail in late spring. Rincon Fire Road ends at about 3.6 miles. Turn left on Pipeline Road.

The fire road crosses Eagle Creek, then the Eagle Creek Trail. Pipeline Road descends, mostly in the shade of redwoods. You'll pass the junction with the River Trail, then enjoy a dead-on view of the railroad trestle as you retrace your route back to the junction with the Redwood Grove Loop Trail on the right at 4.4 miles. From the junction just past the trestle you can walk back through the redwoods to the right, continue straight on Pipeline Road, or veer off to the left on the River Trail. Whichever option you choose, it's about 0.4 miles back to the parking lot.

▶ NEARBY ACTIVITIES

The park has a separate area called Fall Creek Unit on Felton Empire Road northwest of the main park area. Phone the park headquarters for more information at (831) 335-4598. Roaring Camp and Big Trees Railroad runs trains through an adjacent redwood forest, and seasonally, from Felton to Santa Cruz. Call (831) 335-4484 or visit www.roaringcamprr.com.

COYOTE HILLS REGIONAL PARK

▶ IN BRIEF

There are a number of parks perched on the shores of San Francisco Bay, but Coyote Hills has the whole enchilada: excellent wildlife viewing, extensive facilities, and trails that explore not only marsh and coastline, but grassland as well. You can choose a very easy hike through Coyote Hill's marsh, or stretch your legs a bit on a few short but steep paths that roller coaster up and down grassy hills fronting the bay. This 5-mile loop does both, starting in the marsh and then traversing the hills.

▶ DESCRIPTION

A unique landform, the Coyote Hills are a small collection of grassy rolling knolls rising above the bay just north of the Dumbarton Bridge. The native Ohlone, original inhabitants of the Bay Area who settled here more than 10,000 years ago, found this area particularly bountiful, leaving a shell mound and other historical artifacts in the marsh. The park is very popular with kids, who tour Coyote Hills on school trips guided by park staff, or visit on weekends for bird-watching with mom and dad. Since Coyote Hills offers many flat trails and is a short drive from communities around Fremont, locals use the park for daily exercise. The steady

▶ DIRECTIONS

Depart San Francisco southbound on US 101 and use the US 101/I-280 split as the mileage starting point. Drive south 25 miles on US 101, then exit at CA 84 East/Dumbarton Bridge. At the eastern end of the Dumbarton Bridge, exit onto Paseo Padre Parkway/Thornton Avenue (this is the first exit after the toll plaza). Turn left and drive north on Paseo Padre about 1 mile, then turn left onto Patterson Ranch Road. Drive about 1.5 miles, past the entrance kiosk and Quarry Staging Area, to the trailhead at the end of the road (near the visitor center).

ⓘ KEY AT-A-GLANCE INFORMATION

LENGTH: 5 miles

CONFIGURATION: Loop

DIFFICULTY: Easy

SCENERY: Grassland, marsh

EXPOSURE: Full sun

TRAFFIC: Moderate

TRAIL SURFACE: Dirt fire roads and trails

HIKING TIME: 2.5 hours

SEASON: Good year-round, but marsh trails can flood in winter

ACCESS: Pay $4 fee at entrance kiosk.

MAPS: The park map is available at the visitor center.

FACILITIES: Rest rooms and drinking water at visitor center

SPECIAL COMMENTS: Dogs are permitted on most trails but are not allowed in the marsh.

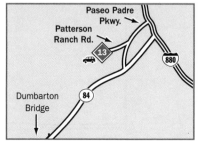

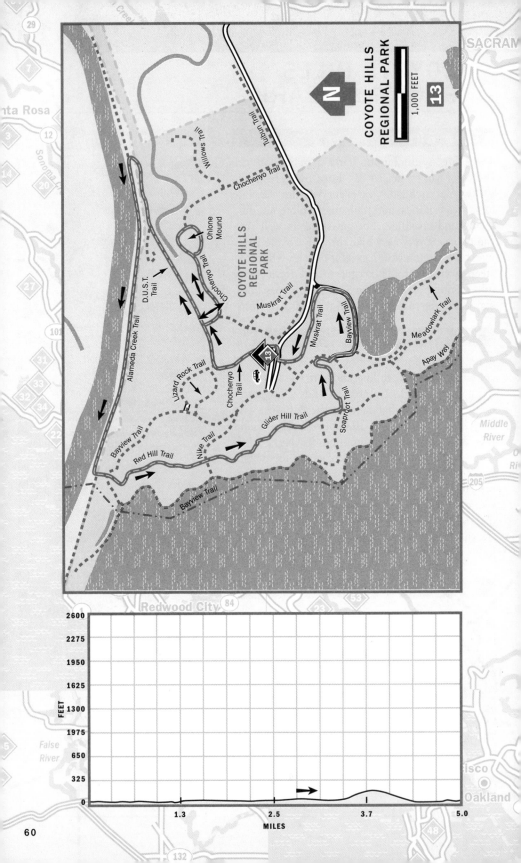

foot traffic seems not to bother the park's wildlife; I've seen a fox, jackrabbits, and many birds here.

If the visitor center is open, take a quick pre-hike tour through exhibits highlighting Ohlone settlements and native flora and fauna. Then walk back to the parking area and cross the street to a multiple trail junction. The Bayview Trail on the right runs along the road back toward the park entrance. A boardwalk and the Chochenyo Trail split off straight ahead into the marsh. If the marsh is relatively dry, the boardwalk can be substituted for the Chochenyo's dirt path, but I've seen the boardwalk completely flooded. These two trails form a triangle, so either route is suitable to begin the hike.

Initially, the wide and flat Chochenyo Trail bisects two pools lined with cattails and reeds. After just 0.2 miles, two paths head off to the left toward Lizard Rock, and the Chochenyo bends right. Continue following the Chochenyo to a junction with the Demonstration Urban Stormwater Treatment Trail at 0.4 miles then turn right for a short side trip to a shell mound, still on the Chochenyo.

Dock, pickleweed, and New Zealand spinach thrive along the trail, along with thick stands of marsh plants that mostly block views of the water. Even if you can't see them, ducks and waterfowl may be heard splashing through the marsh. There's another fork at one-half mile—bear left here or you'll end up back at the trailhead. The Chochenyo Trail proceeds at a level grade to a junction at 0.7 miles. At this fork, bear left.

Fences guard the shell mound on the right. This former Ohlone village site is being restored and is usually closed to the public, although naturalist-led tours can be arranged, and the park often hosts shell mound "open houses." Unless you're visiting on one of those days, you'll have to peer through the fence for a look at the historic area. The Chochenyo Trail continues to the left at 0.8 miles, departing from the shell mound area to the Tuibin Trail. Since there is no direct route that connects back to the D.U.S.T. Trail, follow the other end of the loop to the right, back around the shell mound site, then retrace your steps to the junction with the Chochenyo and the D.U.S.T. at 1.3 miles. Turn right onto the D.U.S.T. Trail.

The marsh surrounding the D.U.S.T. Trail was engineered to filter polluted storm runoff before it reaches the bay. A bonus benefit is that the marsh provides wildlife habitat for ducks, geese, and more "wild" birds like herons and egrets. Plants on the side of the D.U.S.T. Trail range from wispy mustard, poison hemlock, and wild radish to sturdy bushes of poison oak. In summer after the plant blossoms have dried out, you might see scores of tiny birds feeding on seeds of all these plants. After a long straight stretch, the D.U.S.T. Trail gently curves right (a very short unnamed spur goes off to the left) as the flatlands of Fremont stretch east to a series of low rolling hills. Where the D.U.S.T. Trail ends at 2 miles, turn left onto the Alameda Creek Trail.

This flat, wide, paved levee trail runs along the shore of the East Bay's longest creek as it makes its way to the bay. Although the creek is really a less-than-natural managed flood channel here, geese are common in and around the creek and in the skies above the channel, you might see birds of prey including harriers, hawks, and kestrels. A cluster of eucalyptus trees on the left punctuates the landscape and provides a little oasis of shade. Pickleweed, a groundcover often found in marshes, draws attention to itself in autumn, when it flushes a rusty red. From this elevated route, there are good views of the rest of the park, including the marshes and hills. At the hike's 3.1-mile mark, just past an Alameda Creek interpretive display, you'll reach a junction. Bear left, cross the paved Bayview Trail, and start uphill on the Red Hill Trail.

Climbing moderately through grassland, the trail quickly crests. Dry stalks on fennel plants rustle in the wind in early winter. In March, orange California poppies contrast nicely to vivid green grass and blue sky—an eye-popping late-winter color palette. A steep descent commences, and at 3.6 miles the Nike Trail crosses the Red Hill Trail. Continue straight on the Red Trail.

After another sharp climb you'll reach the park's highest elevation, a mere 291 feet. Red Hill is an apt name for this knoll, where big boulders of crimson chert jut up from the grassland. Beware of poison oak nestled among the outcrops. From here you can get a good overview of the marsh's twists and turns. The Red Hill Trail descends slightly to a level saddle, where a barely noticeable path, the Gilder Hill Trail, heads downhill to the left. Proceed uphill on the Red Hill Trail to yet another beautiful view, this one located on top of Gilder Hill. True to its name, the hill is a good place to fly a kite or model airplane; for those without such accessories, the wind can detract from a hilltop rest break. On clear days you can enjoy views of the Bay, Dumbarton Bridge, Mission Peak, the Santa Cruz Mountains, and Mount Diablo. As the Red Hill Trail steeply descends one last time, look for jackrabbits bounding through the grass and hawks hunting overhead. At 4.1 miles, you'll reach a T junction where you'll turn left onto the Soaproot Trail.

As the trail descends easily, look for the trail's namesake plant along the trail. Soaproot has long wavy leaves and narrow stalks that resemble asparagus (both soaproot and asparagus are members of the lily family). Ohlones dug soaproot bulbs and used them to make soap as well as to stupefy fish for easy gathering. The plant blooms in May through June, but blossoms don't open until late in the afternoon. After a sharp curve right, the Soaproot Trail ends at 4.4 miles. Turn right onto the Bayview Trail.

The paved Bayview Trail sweeps past Dairy Glen, a group campsite to the right. Just before South Marsh, another path continues straight while the Bayview Trail bends left and runs parallel to the marsh. Stay on Bayview, skirting a rocky hill on the left, then reach the fringes of Quarry Staging Area. There are a few well-worn shortcuts, but continue on Bayview almost all the way to the park road at 4.8 miles, then turn left, cross the parking lot, and head uphill on the signed Muskrat Trail.

Poison oak, sagebrush, coyote brush, sticky monkeyflower, and toyon mix with grass along the narrow trail. Bush lupine is a pretty accompaniment in spring, when sweet-smelling, purple-blue flowers emerge. Near a rock outcrop, a path (not on the map) doubles back to the left, but Muskrat continues straight. Veer right in front of a massive boulder, then begin a descent, with one last opportunity to gaze at the marsh, as the trail drops down a set of steps. In March, you might see shooting stars in bloom on the sides of the trail. At 5 miles, the path ends within steps of the parking lot.

CRANE CREEK REGIONAL PARK

▶ IN BRIEF

Sonoma County is best known for agriculture, wine production, and a spectacular coastline. This little county park is off the tourist beat and showcases a different side to Sonoma—a gorgeous blend of grassland, oaks, and creeks. This 1-mile loop is perfect for families with little kids, older folks, or anyone looking for an easy yet refreshing hike.

▶ DESCRIPTION

Crane Creek is a great place for a relaxing saunter. The park isn't big enough to support hikes of more than an hour, but it's a fun place to ramble, particularly in spring when wildflowers hide in the grass and the oaks leaf out. Since it is so close to Rohnert Park on weekdays local workers visit the park on their lunch breaks, and folks with dogs favor the trails for morning walks. Benches and picnic tables are sprinkled throughout the park, inviting visitors to linger.

Depart from the parking lot on the Creek Trail, to the right of the pit toilets. The trail

▶ DIRECTIONS

Leave San Francisco northbound on US 101 and use the Golden Gate Bridge toll plaza as the mileage starting point. Drive about 44 miles north on US 101, then exit at Rohnert Park Expressway. Turn right and drive southeast on Rohnert Park Expressway about 2.5 miles to a T-junction with Petaluma Hill Road. Turn right on Petaluma Hill Road, and drive south about 1.2 miles, then turn left onto Roberts Road (there's a brown "parks" sign at this intersection). Drive about 1.2 miles on Roberts Road, and where Roberts Road ends (Lichau Road makes a sharp turn right), continue straight, now on Pressley Road. Continue on Pressley about one-half mile, then turn left into the parking lot.

ⓘ KEY AT-A-GLANCE INFORMATION

LENGTH: 1 mile

CONFIGURATION: Loop

DIFFICULTY: Very easy

SCENERY: Grassland, oaks, and creek

EXPOSURE: Full sun

TRAFFIC: Moderate, with lots of daily walkers

TRAIL SURFACE: Dirt trails

HIKING TIME: 30 minutes

SEASON: Anytime of year is good, but the park is hot in summer.

ACCESS: Pay $3 entrance fee (self-register) in parking lot.

MAPS: There is a park map posted at trailhead.

FACILITIES: Pit toilets at trailhead

SPECIAL COMMENTS: Dogs permitted

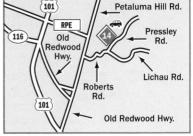

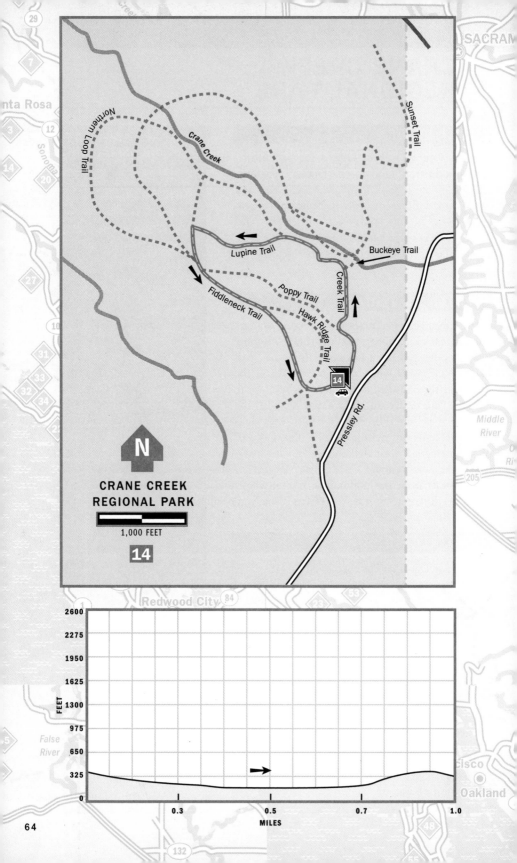

N

CRANE CREEK
REGIONAL PARK

1,000 FEET

14

descends very gently, past a picnic table, and then through grassland along a damp drainage. Pressley Road and cattle-grazed hillsides are visible on the right. The Poppy Trail sets off to the left just before a bridge at 0.2 miles. Stay to the right on the Creek Trail. Big buckeyes stand off to the sides of the trail, just slightly smaller than neighboring valley oaks. By mid-March the buckeyes are covered with lush green foliage and look as if winter never happened, while the park's valley and black oaks begin to show their new leaves as well. At 0.3 miles, the Buckeye Trail begins on the right. Buckeye crosses the creek and then ascends to join the Sunset Trail, which climbs to a hilltop viewpoint, an optional out-and-back on this hike. Bear left on the Creek Trail.

Running parallel to Crane Creek, the path weaves through a sparse collection of buckeye, coast live oak, and California bay. The creekbed on the right is crowded with willow, alder, snowberry, poison oak, and blackberry, but there is a small clearing where you can duck in for a look at the rock-lined stream. Along the trail you might see shooting stars, milkmaids, saxifrage, California poppies, popcorn flowers, buttercups, and bluedicks, all typically blooming weeks before the start of spring. At 0.4 miles, turn left onto the Lupine Trail.

The trail bisects a grassy meadow encircled by giant lichen-draped valley and black oak. This bucolic setting can be admired at length from a trailside bench, one of Crane Creek's many beautiful spots for lunch or contemplation. When the Lupine Trail reaches a junction at 0.6 miles, bear left, then after a few feet, stay to the left again, now on the Fiddleneck Trail. The Poppy Trail begins a few feet past the junction on the left, but continue straight.

Popcorn flowers, fiddlenecks, and milkmaids bloom in late winter on the right near a creekbed. The Fiddleneck Trail steps through the stream, then begins an easy climb back into grassland. Buttercups and bluedicks are common in late March. As the trail crests at 0.8 miles, the Hawk Ridge Trail splits off to the left, offering an optional route back to the trailhead. From a bench at this hilltop, you can admire the park, as well as surrounding privately held land, mostly multi-acre estates and rolling grassland still ranched. This is a good spot to spy on hawks perching in oaks or soaring overhead. Continue on the Fiddleneck's nearly level grade as the trail heads south. When the Fiddleneck Trail makes a sharp turn left, the Hawk Ridge Trail joins along, and the dead-end Overlook Loop Trail heads off to the right. With the trailhead in sight, the Fiddleneck Trail returns through grassland to the parking lot.

EDGEWOOD
PARK AND PRESERVE

KEY AT-A-GLANCE INFORMATION

LENGTH: 3.1 miles

CONFIGURATION: Balloon

DIFFICULTY: Easy

SCENERY: Mixed woodland, serpentine grassland, wildflowers

EXPOSURE: Mixture of shaded woods and exposed grassland

TRAFFIC: Some daily all year-round; heavy during spring peak

TRAIL SURFACE: Well-maintained dirt paths

HIKING TIME: 1.5 hours, plus more time searching for wildflowers

SEASON: Good year-round, exceptional March–May

ACCESS: No fee

MAPS: A park map is available at the trailhead's information signboard.

FACILITIES: Rest rooms, drinking water, and picnic area at trailhead

SPECIAL COMMENTS: Dogs are not permitted.

▶ IN BRIEF

This hike ascends gently through coast live oak and California bay woodlands, then traverses grassland where hikers visiting in Spring may see drifts of flowers. On the return leg of the loop, a tiny waterfall in a wooded canyon charms visitors after heavy rainstorms.

▶ DESCRIPTION

Edgewood Park is a little jewel of a park surrounded by a bustling highway, busy county road, and residential neighborhoods. Thousands of commuters zip past this park every day on I-280, and between the traffic noise and hum of suburban living there's no confusing Edgewood with the wilderness. However, the small park hosts an incredible wildflower display in spring and shelters a community of animals, including hawks, coyotes, deer, and jackrabbits.

Edgewood's chaparral-coated hillsides, serpentine grassland, and oak-forested canyon were nearly lost in a series of threatening developments from the 1960s to 1993, when the parcel became a San Mateo County nature preserve and park. An Edgewood advocacy group works tirelessly to preserve habitats for endangered plants and butterflies, and docent-led hikes offered by volunteers during the park's "high season" are a great way to learn about the creatures that thrive throughout

▶ DIRECTIONS

Drive south from San Francisco on I-280 and use the CA 1/19th Avenue merge as the mileage starting point. Drive south on I-280 about 20 miles, and exit onto Edgewood Road. Turn left and drive east on Edgewood Road about 1 mile and turn right into the park. There's overflow parking in a dirt lot right off Edgewood Road, and a 13-car parking lot inside the park gates.

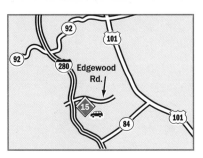

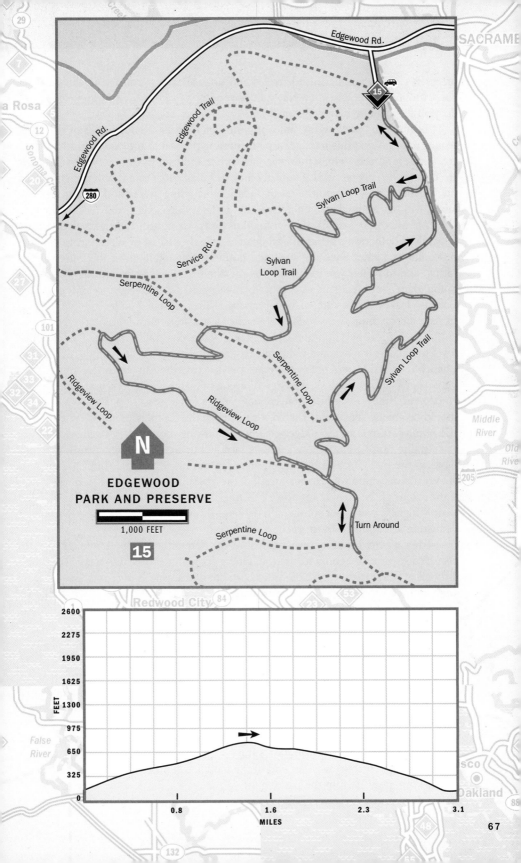

Edgewood Rd.

SACRAME

a Rosa

Edgewood Rd.

Edgewood Trail

280

Service Rd.

Serpentine Loop

Sylvan Loop Trail

Sylvan
Loop Trail

Sylvan Loop Trail

Serpentine Loop

Ridgeview Loop

Ridgeview Loop

N

EDGEWOOD
PARK AND PRESERVE

1,000 FEET

15

Turn Around

Serpentine Loop

Middle
River

Old
Rive

205

Redwood City   84

False
River

sco

Oakland

88

FEET

2600
2275
1950
1625
1300
975
650
325
0

0.8   1.6   2.3   3.1

MILES

132

the park's 467 acres. Because bicycles and dogs are not permitted in the park and horse traffic is limited to a few trails, Edgewood is very hiker friendly and a good destination for a family hike with small kids.

Begin at the parking lot, following the signs for the Sylvan Trail (not the paved service road). Along this nearly flat path running parallel to the park boundary, there are a few plum trees, which flower in late winter and fruit in early summer. The fruits are favored by coyotes, and if you're quiet you may catch one nibbling right off the side of the trail. A few other "exotic" plants, including acacia and a palm tree, are mixed with native buckeye, California bay, and coast live oak.

After about 0.2 miles, the Sylvan Trail forks. Here, bear right and climb up the canyon's shoulder on a series of switchbacks, mostly shaded by mature coast live oak and California bays. Shooting stars and hound's tongue bloom in the understory in spring, and in winter you may see birds picking berries off toyon shrubs. Poison oak is abundant, but blends in with other benign plants from autumn to spring when it loses its leaves, so beware of bare-branched shrubs. At 0.7 miles the Sylvan Trail crests, emerges from the woods, and reaches a junction. Turn left.

The Serpentine Loop and Sylvan Loop share this trail segment. Under partial cover from coast live oak and California bay, the trail skirts a hilltop on the right. From a bench crowded by sagebrush there are views across the canyon to the south. A few steps later you'll cut across the edge of a grassy plateau, then reach a multiple trail junction at 1 mile. Continue straight, now on the Ridgeview Loop. On clear days you should be able to see Mount Diablo, rising above the East Bay foothills. At a junction at 1.3 miles, turn left onto Ridgeview Loop, following the sign for "scenic overlook."

Traffic noise from nearby I-280 is steady, but tree cover blocks any vehicular views as the trail climbs a bit. When you step out into chaparral, there's a break in the vegetation where you can get a peak of the Santa Cruz Mountains to the west (this is the extent of the "scenic overlook"). A thicket of chamise lines the trail near Edgewood's highest point, but soon you'll descend through some pretty coast live oaks to a junction at 1.6 miles. Turn left.

After a brief descent, turn right onto the Serpentine Loop, 1.7 miles into the hike. Fences protect habitat as the trail enters serpentine grassland, where incredible displays of wildflowers carpet the sides of the trail in spring. Serpentine Loop reaches a junction at 1.9 miles. This is the turnaround point for the hike, but in wildflower season you might explore more in the area. Whatever you choose, when you're ready, retrace your steps back to the junction with the Ridgeview Loop.

Instead of returning uphill on Ridgeview, continue straight on the Serpentine Loop. A few zigzags drop the trail down a hillside to a junction at 2.2 miles. Keep going straight, now back on the Sylvan Trail.

Initially this part of the Sylvan Trail winds downhill through an open forest of oaks, madrone, and patches of grass, but after a pass through some chaparral, the path again settles into coast live oak and California bay woods. At 2.7 miles a wee waterfall appears after rainstorms, trickling down the hillside on the left before emptying into a creek. There's one last sunny section before the Sylvan Trail reenters woods and then meets the other end of the loop at 2.9 miles. Continue straight, and retrace your steps back to the parking lot.

JOSEPH D. GRANT COUNTY PARK

▶ IN BRIEF

On the high slopes of Mount Hamilton, Joseph D. Grant County Park sprawls over 9,000 acres of oak-dotted grassland, less than 15 miles from downtown San Jose. Even though the park is bisected by Mount Hamilton Road, it has an isolated feel to it—I've hiked for hours here and seen only cows and wild pigs. This hike begins near an old ranch compound, skirts Grant Lake, then climbs through an oak savanna to the ridgeline. After a sustained jaunt along the grassy ridge, you'll drop through grassland peppered with oaks, then retrace your steps back to the parking lot.

▶ DESCRIPTION

Begin on the signed Hotel Trail at the edge of the parking lot. The first steps are paved, but when the pavement swings right, continue straight, passing the pretty old ranch buildings on the left. After 500 feet, you'll reach a T-junction. Turn left, following the sign toward Mount Hamilton Road.

A few steps down the trail, a hard-to-spot path, the Loop Trail, departs on the right. Continue on the Hotel Trail, here a wide dirt path. Ascending easily, the trail is lined with young

ⓘ KEY AT-A-GLANCE INFORMATION

LENGTH: 7.4 miles

CONFIGURATION: Balloon

DIFFICULTY: Moderate

SCENERY: Grassland, views

EXPOSURE: Almost entirely unshaded

TRAFFIC: Light

TRAIL SURFACE: Dirt fire roads and trails

HIKING TIME: 4 hours

SEASON: Not a summer park unless you favor dehydration—best in spring. Trails are often muddy, but this is an awesome winter hike.

ACCESS: Pay the $4 fee at the park entrance (self-register if kiosk is unattended).

MAPS: A park map is available at the park entrance, and there's an information signboard at the trailhead.

FACILITIES: Rest rooms and drinking water are at the trailhead.

SPECIAL COMMENTS: Dogs are only permitted on the Edwards Trail, in the northwest corner of the park. Watch out for wild pigs throughout the park.

▶ DIRECTIONS

Depart San Francisco southbound on US 101 and use the I-280/US 101 split as the mileage starting point. Drive south on US 101 about 44 miles, then exit at Santa Clara Street/Alum Rock Avenue (just north of the I-280/I-680 junction). Drive east on Alum Rock Avenue about 4 miles, then turn right onto Mount Hamilton Road. Drive about 8 miles southeast on this narrow, winding road to the park entrance on the right side of the road. Once past the entry kiosk, go straight past the first parking area on the left, then turn left where the road splits and park near the gated entrance to the Hotel Trail.

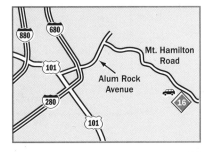

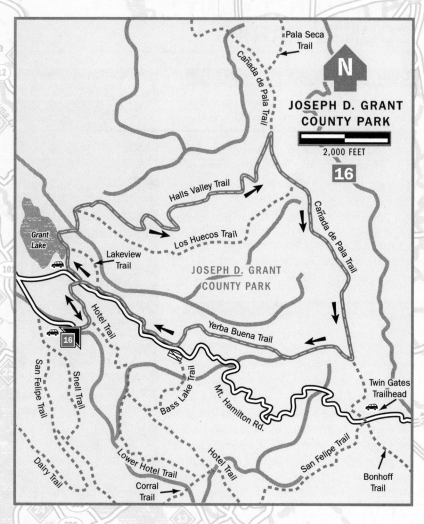

JOSEPH D. GRANT COUNTY PARK

N

2,000 FEET

16

Pala Seca Trail

Cañada de Pala Trail

Halls Valley Trail

Los Huecos Trail

Grant Lake

Lakeview Trail

JOSEPH D. GRANT COUNTY PARK

Cañada de Pala Trail

Hotel Trail

16

Yerba Buena Trail

San Felipe Trail

Snell Trail

Bass Lake Trail

Mt. Hamilton Rd.

Twin Gates Trailhead

Middle River

Dairy Trail

Lower Hotel Trail

Hotel Trail

San Felipe Trail

Bonhoff Trail

Corral Trail

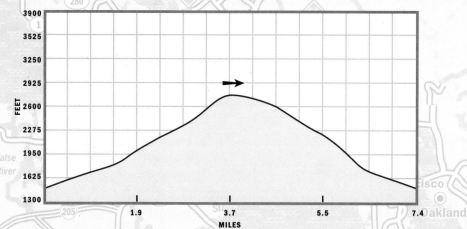

FEET

3900
3525
3250
2925
2600
2275
1950
1625
1300

1.9   3.7   5.5   7.4

MILES

coast live oak and coyote brush, and in spring, the sloping grassy hillside on the right hosts big patches of rose clover, along with smatterings of blue-eyed grass, vetch, fiddlenecks, and California poppy. A few cottonwood and alder thrive on the left on the edge of a damp creek basin where I've seen some of the park's marauding wild pig population. At 0.4 miles, the trail approaches Mount Hamilton Road. Carefully cross the street, then turn left onto the Yerba Buena Trail.

The trail approaches, then swings to the right of a small staging area and reaches a junction at 0.6 miles. Turn right toward the Halls Valley Trail. The Lakeview Trail breaks off to the right, looping back to the Yerba Buena Trail. Continue straight. Coyote brush forms thickets on the right, and just off the left side of the trail, herons and ducks swim and hunt on the shore of Grant Lake. From a junction at 0.8 miles, turn right onto the Halls Valley Trail.

The fire road dips to cross a creek, then rises again through coast live oak, valley oak, eucalyptus, and coyote brush. On my last hike, I heard the distinctive "whoof" grunts of wild pigs, concealed from view in a dense clump of coyote brush just off the trail to the right. I did not linger, since these wild pigs (descendants of game animals and escaped domesticated pigs) can run faster than I can, and some of them wield tusks. Should you come across pigs, be sure to give them a wide berth. Their eyesight and hearing are poor, so they might not see you—give them a good holler and raise up your arms to look big, and the porcines should be on their way.

The Canal Trail begins on the right at 1 mile, another "blink and you'll miss it" trail. Continue another tenth of the mile, then stay to the left/straight at a junction with the Los Huecos Trail. At an easy grade, the Halls Valley Trail begins to ascend, through coyote brush, California coffeeberry, poison oak, and black, valley, and coast live oaks. Look for yarrow, Ithuriel's spear, and checkerbloom along the trail in late April, when I saw a long dense swath of orange scarlet pimpernel at the edge of the trail. As the grade picks up slightly, you may notice California bay and a few big-leaf maples—their shade fosters a good display of shooting stars, blue larkspur, buttercups, and woodland star in spring. The Halls Valley Trail passes through a gate, crosses a creek, and then begins to climb at a steady, moderate grade. On the right in early May, California gilia blooms in a cluster of sagebrush and monkeyflower. The landscape shifts to oak savanna, with lovely blue and valley oaks standing in grassland along the trail, many of them dangling massive clumps of mistletoe, a poisonous, parasitic plant.

Weaving through a landscape of oaks and grassland, the trail permits views north to the highest hills of the park, near Antler Point. In autumn, when the grass is sun-baked blonde, your gaze may be drawn to bright red patches of poison oak on distant hillsides. On a hot day, every little bit of shade along the trail provides a brief but welcome respite from the sun. With the ridgeline in sight, the Halls Valley Trail begins a drop to another creek. Buckeyes blend through California bay on the left— look for fairy lanterns on the right slope in April. The trail makes one last push uphill to the ridge, reaching a junction with the Cañada de Pala Trail at 3.1 miles. If you'd like to add 4.5 miles to this hike, you can turn left here and loop to Antler Point— at just under 3,000 feet, the highest point in the park. Turn right on the Cañada de Pala Trail.

At the peak of wildflower season, the slopes are filled with a variety of common flowers—look for blue-eyed grass, popcorn flower, johnny-jump-ups, fiddlenecks, California poppy, checkerbloom, blue and white lupine, and bluedicks. On an early May hike I enjoyed one of the best wildflower displays I've ever witnessed in the Bay Area, with heavily concentrated blooms all around. It's a far different scene in summer and autumn, when only oaks interrupt the one-dimensional expanse of golden grassland. Cañada de Pala, the name of this rancho's original grant, rises gently, then reaches a junction with the Los Huecos Trail at 3.5 miles. Continue straight. Across a valley to the east the domes of Lick Observatory are visible, near the highest elevation on Mount Hamilton, 4,373-foot Copernicus Peak. The Cañada de Pala Trail crosses through a gate into cattle range, where cows are present in spring and summer. In April and May the transition is abrupt—say goodbye to wildflowers and hello to trim, bare grassland, and big sections of muddy trail.

As you follow an easy rolling course, look for a bench on trail right, a good spot to gaze at the long views extending downhill to Grant Lake and beyond to downtown San Jose on clear days. The fire road drops away from this hike's highest elevation, about 2,700 feet, and you should be able to see past the rolling hills along the trail to the ridge forming Grant's southwestern boundary. At 4.8 miles the Yerba Buena Trail begins on the right. If you'd like to stretch this hike to 9.5 miles, you can continue straight here, cross Mount Hamilton Road, pick up the San Felipe Trail, then turn right onto the Hotel Trail, which returns to the trailhead through the southern part of Halls Valley. To stick to this 7.4-mile hike, turn right onto the Yerba Buena Trail.

The trail begins a moderate descent through cattle range. Even when the cows are in the area, some wildflowers escape them, including owl's clover, woodland star, and blue and white lupine. Poison oak is common, growing here in shrub form. Valley oaks keep a distance from the trail, so there is little shade. Bass Lake is briefly visible downhill to the left. One short uphill precedes a steady descent past a few black oaks on the right, through grassland where mule ear sunflowers, goldenfields, johnnytuck, blue-eyed grass, Ithuriel's spear, California poppy, and buttercups bloom in spring. At 6.2 miles, the Yerba Buena Trail nears the side of Mount Hamilton Road—the gate to the road is locked, but there's a step-over bench. A path to Bass Lake sets off directly across the street, but a locked gate has blocked access every time I've visited. If you can find a way over the fence, a trip to Bass Lake would make an excellent return loop to the trailhead, via the Bass Lake and Hotel trails. Continue on the Yerba Buena Trail, which runs along Mount Hamilton Road, finally leaving the cattle range at a gate at 6.7 miles. The trail here shrinks to a narrower path, and keeps to an easy, mostly downhill grade. Look for a big gooseberry bush growing around a rock formation on the left. A trail to McCreery Lake departs on the right at 6.9 miles. Continue on Yerba Buena Tail to the next junction at 7 miles. Turn left, cross the road, and retrace your steps back to the trailhead.

▶ NEARBY ACTIVITIES

There are many hiking possibilities at this large park. For mellow, easy loops, pick trails through Halls Valley, like Lower Hotel and San Felipe. View a map at www.parkhere.org/scc/assets/docs/159660grant_park.pdf.

HUCKLEBERRY BOTANIC REGIONAL PRESERVE

▶ IN BRIEF

The most visible of the East Bay's open spaces are dominated by rolling grassland, but Huckleberry Botanic Preserve in the hills above Oakland offers a variety of vegetation. Along this short and easy 1.7-mile loop, numbered posts and a free brochure guide hikers through a wide assortment of plants, some of which are uncommon in the area.

▶ DESCRIPTION

This small preserve sits on an unusual deposit of shale and chert, "poor" soil well suited to native plants. Although surrounding neighborhoods feature some grassland, forests of eucalyptus, and redwood-crammed canyons, Huckleberry is a little oasis of chaparral and woodland plants. The mix is comprised of manzanita barrens, scads of huckleberry bushes, and a gorgeous woodland of madrone, California bay, fern, coast live oak, hazelnut, and currant. This is an arboretum-quality collection with an ever-changing palette of colors, textures, and tastes. Huckleberry Preserve hosts two segments of long trails: the Skyline National Trail and the Bay Area Ridge Trail. Skyline National Trail is a 31-mile multiuse path that passes through a string of six big East Bay parks.

▶ DIRECTIONS

Depart San Francisco on the Bay Bridge and use the toll plaza as the mileage starting point. About one-half mile past the toll plaza, bear right onto I-580 East. Drive 1.5 miles, then exit onto CA 24. Drive east on CA 24 about 5 miles, and at the far side of the Caldecott Tunnel, exit onto Fish Ranch Road (this is the first post-tunnel exit—stay in the right lane). Drive north on Fish Ranch Road about 1 mile, then turn left onto Grizzly Peak Boulevard. Drive 2.4 miles, then turn left onto Skyline Boulevard. Drive 0.6 miles on Skyline Boulevard, then turn left into the preserve parking lot.

ⓘ KEY AT-A-GLANCE INFORMATION

LENGTH: 1.7 miles

CONFIGURATION: Loop

DIFFICULTY: Easy

SCENERY: Mixed woodland and chaparral

EXPOSURE: Mostly shaded

TRAFFIC: Light

TRAIL SURFACE: Narrow dirt trails

HIKING TIME: 1 hour

SEASON: Winter for blooming manzanitas, but any time of year is good

ACCESS: No fee

MAPS: Pick up the park map at the trailhead's information signboard

FACILITIES: Pit toilets at trailhead

SPECIAL COMMENTS: Dogs are not permitted.

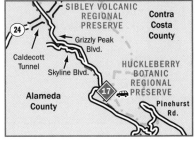

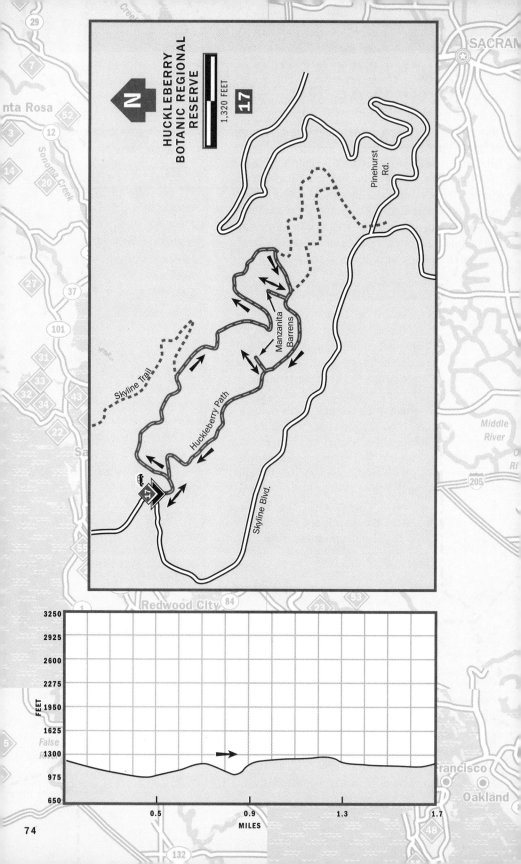

HUCKLEBERRY BOTANIC REGIONAL RESERVE

1,320 FEET

17

Pinehurst Rd.

Manzanita Barrens

Skyline Trail

Huckleberry Path

Skyline Blvd.

The Bay Area Ridge Trail extends over 230 miles through nine Bay Area counties. However, the Skyline Trail Ridge Trail segment is the only path in Huckleberry Preserve that is multi-use, so the loop on Huckleberry Path is significantly quieter than the surrounding parks. From the small staging area, walk a few feet to the information signboard, where you can pick up a brochure and map, then continue on the Huckleberry Path. Tangles of blackberry and creambush crowd a hillside on the right, but the trail quickly enters an area well shaded by coast live oaks and California bays. After 200 feet, where the two legs of the loop split, bear left. A few short zigzags drop the trail into a cool, shaded canyon, followed by a slow and steady descent. Look for the first numbered post of the tour on the right, identifying a madrone. At 0.3 miles, the Skyline Trail on the left heads out of the preserve toward Sibley Volcanic Preserve. Veer uphill to the right. California bays arch over the trail as it begins an easy ascent. The tour identifies hazelnut and sword and wood fern. A tiny-leaved sweet-smelling plant called yerba buena hugs the ground in several places. The vegetation shifts subtly to include more coast live oak. In a few exposed areas, sticky monkeyflower and California coffeeberry bask in the sunlight.

At 0.9 miles, the Skyline Trail continues straight, while the Huckleberry Path bears right. (You can extend this hike by taking Skyline another 0.4 miles, then pick up an extension of the Huckleberry Path.) Climb to the right on Huckleberry Path. A few sets of steep stairs quickly ascend through California bay and coast live oak woods to a junction at 1 mile. Walk a few feet to the right, then turn right, following the sign "to 6." The path ascends easily out of the woods to a sunny manzanita barren. On a clear day, views stretch to include Mount Diablo to the east. If you happen to be visiting during the manzanita bloom (generally December through February), hummingbirds and bees are common, gorging on the sweet nectar from the manzanita's small white flowers. Return to the previous junction, then turn right.

The preserve's namesake, huckleberry, dominates the trail, which winds through the towering maze-like hedges of the evergreen shrub. In August, huckleberry plants are crammed with dusky small blueberry-like fruit, a favorite for local birds and even coyotes, who feed from the lower branches. At 1.3 miles, bear right to another manzanita barren, where the brochure assists you in identifying jimbrush and canyon live oak. Retrace your steps back to the main path, then turn right. Chinquapin and silktassel accompany manzanita and huckleberry as the trail continues at a nearly level grade. Douglas irises bloom in clusters along the trail in spring. At 1.7 miles you'll return to the hike's first junction and the end of the loop. Continue straight and return to the trailhead, retracing your steps on the Huckleberry Path.

▶ NEARBY ACTIVITIES

Learn more about Bay Area plants at the East Bay Regional Parks Botanic Garden, located at Wildcat Canyon Road and South Park Drive, in Tilden Park, Berkeley. The garden is open daily from 8:30 a.m. to 5 p.m., except New Years, Thanksgiving, and Christmas days. Phone (510) 841-8732 for more information.

LAS TRAMPAS
REGIONAL WILDERNESS

KEY AT·A·GLANCE INFORMATION

LENGTH: 4.6 miles

CONFIGURATION: Loop

DIFFICULTY: Moderate

SCENERY: Grassland, woods, rock formations

EXPOSURE: Nearly equal parts shaded and exposed

TRAFFIC: Light-moderate

TRAIL SURFACE: Dirt fire roads, trails, and one paved fire road

HIKING TIME: 2.5 hours

SEASON: Muddy in winter, hot in summer, best in spring

ACCESS: No fee

MAPS: The park map is available at the trailhead's information signboard.

FACILITIES: Pit toilets available at the trailhead

SPECIAL COMMENTS: Although Las Trampas is labeled "regional wilderness," the western part of the park has some decidedly domestic inhabitants—cattle, who create muddy conditions during the rainy season. If the described trails are muddy (you'll know right away), the park's eastern section provides good alternative hiking.

▶ IN BRIEF

Las Trampas (Spanish for "the traps") is kind of like two parks in one: from the trailhead at the bottom of a canyon you can hike east to chaparral-coated Las Trampas Ridge, or west to grassy Rocky Ridge. Pick this western loop in spring, after the rains have stopped for a steady climb to Rocky Ridge, where you can enjoy sweeping views and search for wildflowers.

▶ DESCRIPTION

Begin from the parking lot. The paved fire road is the return route—pass through a metal gate, then a cattle gate onto the Elderberry Trail (which may be unsigned) to the left of the paved fire road. At a level grade, the wide trail sweeps across the grassy base of Rocky Ridge, dips to cross a seasonal creek, then runs along a corral on the left. At 0.4 miles you'll reach a junction with a spur leading straight/left to Bollinger Canyon Road. Turn right to remain on the Elderberry Trail. After such an easy-going intro, the subsequent climb is a bit of a shock—the trail shoots uphill, initially through a woodland of California bay, coast live, and black oaks. Even when the Elderberry Trail steps out into grassland, there's still no relief from the sharp grade, which feels especially harsh in summer's heat. As you ascend, there are nice views

▶ DIRECTIONS

Depart San Francisco on the Bay Bridge and use the toll plaza as the mileage starting point. About one-half mile past the toll plaza, bear right onto I-580 East. Drive 1.5 miles, then exit onto CA 24. Drive east 12 miles on CA 24, then exit south onto I-680. Drive south 10 miles and exit onto Crow Canyon Road. Drive west (right) for about 1 mile, then turn right (north) onto Bollinger Canyon Road. Continue about 4.5 miles to the trailhead at the end of the road.

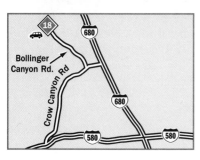

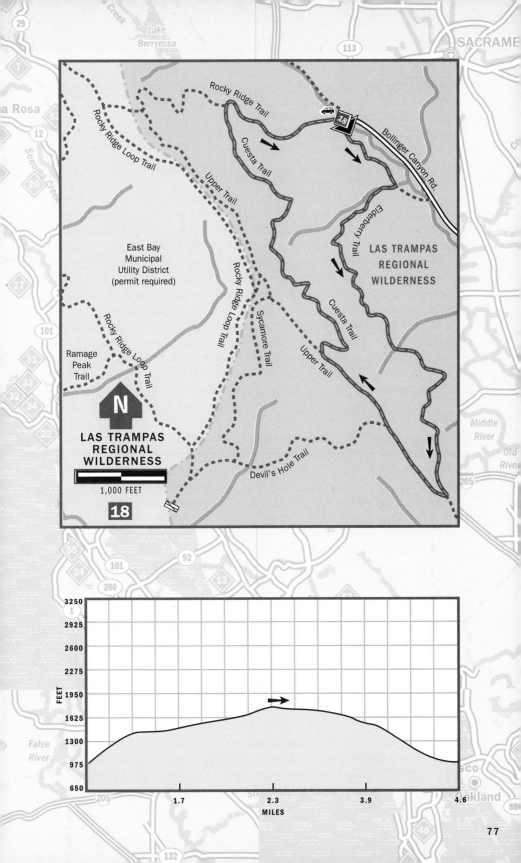

uphill toward the ridge top and across Bollinger Canyon to Las Trampas Ridge. The grade tapers off, then the trail begins a campaign of brief rolling ups and downs. Paintbrush and California poppy are common in spring, blooming in sunny stretches of sagebrush and poison oak. In March, you might catch a few old fruit trees cloaked in a froth of fragrant flowers, as well as areas shaded by California bay, gooseberry bushes in bloom, and buds on maple trees unfurling. Look for newts on the trail after heavy rains in winter or early spring.

Leaving the woods behind, the Elderberry Trail's last stretch is a moderately steep ascent through grassland to the ridge. In mid-March the slope on the right is a kaleidoscope of flowers, including creamcups, California poppy, filaree, and fiddleneck. At 1.8 miles, the Elderberry Trail ends at a junction with the Upper Trail. The segment to the left ends at the park boundary after less than one-half mile. Turn right.

The Upper Trail clings to the ridgeline, ascending in fits and starts at a steep grade through grassland. Wonderful views unfold with every step uphill, to Mount Diablo in the east, and west all the way to the Golden Gate Bridge on clear days. Cattle seem to love this ridge, and there are often lots of cows hanging out up here. On a hike in March one year, I watched an unidentifiable animal running at a fast pace, back and forth on a hillside across the canyon to the left. It was too dark for a coyote, lacked the long tail of a mountain lion, but had a longer tail than a bobcat. What was this mysterious creature? I'll never know, since I forgot my binoculars that day.

Be sure to stop and examine the rock formations along the trail—the seashells are easy to pick out in these remnants of the Orinda Formation. It's hard to believe that this ridge, situated about 30 miles east of the Pacific, originated under the ocean. At 2.2 miles the Devil's Hole Trail departs to the left, looping through the remote part of the park where I saw that mysterious animal. Continue straight. On a breezy day the howling wind is absolutely deafening, but on a hot day you might wish for a little air flow. The Upper Trail drops a bit off the ridgeline, then reaches a junction at 2.6 miles. Turn right onto the Cuesta Trail.

This little path descends moderately through coyote brush, makes a sharp turn left, then levels out a bit, while maintaining a general downhill trend. Like the Elderberry Trail, there is a fair amount of elevation wobble, but it's nothing dramatic. Sheltered from the bulk of the ridge, this is an excellent wildflower trail, despite the best efforts of the park's substantial cow population. In late winter, milkmaids, shooting stars, and buttercups are common and in mid-March, mule ear sunflowers bloom along with California poppies, creamcups, and loads of purple bush lupine, all nicely accented against the green grassland. There are some small pockets of California bay nestled in the crooks of the hillsides, but otherwise the descent is under full sun. Near the 4-mile mark, the Cuesta Trail ends at a junction with a paved fire road, the Rocky Ridge Trail. Turn right (a dirt path across the road is also an option—both lead back to the trailhead).

The descent is moderately steep and steady and is a popular out-and-back route for locals walking with their dogs. Coast live oaks overtake the grassland as the trail winds downhill. After winter rains you may hear and see small rivulets of water draining off the mountain toward Bollinger Creek, downhill to the left. At 4.6 miles the Rocky Ridge Trail ends at a gate back at the parking lot.

With herds of cattle and steady equestrian traffic, most of the park feels a bit like a private ranch, but the wilderness designation rings true in the far western section of Las Trampas and the adjacent property, a massive hunk of land managed by the East Bay Municipal Utility District (EBMUD). You can add on 2.5 miles to the hike described above on a loop to Devil's Hole, through a knob of East Bay Regional Park District (EBRPD) land on the western slope of Rocky Ridge, neighboring the EBMUD watershed. In the watershed proper, trails are open to hikers by advance permit only. With a permit, a car shuttle, and plenty of water, you could hike through Las Trampas and EBMUD lands to the Chabot Staging Area, a nearly 11-mile trek. Get more information from EBMUD at (510) 287-0548 or www.ebmud.com.

LOCH LOMOND RECREATION AREA

KEY AT-A-GLANCE INFORMATION

LENGTH: 4.9 miles

CONFIGURATION: Loop

DIFFICULTY: Moderate

SCENERY: Woods, lake

EXPOSURE: Mostly shaded

TRAFFIC: Moderate near the trailhead and lake, quiet on the trails past the shoreline

TRAIL SURFACE: Dirt fire roads and trails

HIKING TIME: 3 hours

SEASON: March 1–September 15

ACCESS: Pay $4 fee at entrance kiosk, or if the kiosk is unstaffed at the park store

MAPS: Park map is available at the entrance kiosk and park store.

FACILITIES: Rest rooms and drinking water at the trailhead

SPECIAL COMMENTS: Dogs are permitted, but keep them out of the water.

▶ IN BRIEF

A visit to Loch Lomond is like a mini-Sierra getaway. The road to the park is steep and curvy, and a heavily forested canyon nestles a jewel-like lake, just like a remote alpine setting, only Loch Lomond is a short distance from San Jose and Santa Cruz. On this nearly 5-mile hike, you'll follow the shoreline, then climb through a forest to a ridge with lake views, and finally, descend back through the woods.

▶ DESCRIPTION

Since Loch Lomond is open only from March through mid-September, a spring or summer visit is inevitable. That is a good thing, because when the Bay Area's green grassy ridges fade to dull dry brown, it's time to hit the woods. Loch Lomond has forested hillsides and water, essential elements

▶ DIRECTIONS

Drive south from San Francisco on I-280 and use the CA 1/19th Avenue merge as the mileage starting point. Drive south on I-280 about 36 miles, then exit onto CA 85 South. After 7.5 miles, exit onto CA 17 South. Drive south on CA 17 about 17 miles, then exit right onto Mount Hermon Road. Turn right and follow Mount Hermon Road about 3.5 miles into Felton, crossing over East Zayante Road to the junction with Graham Hill Road. Turn left and drive about 0.3 miles to East Zayante Road. Turn left and drive about 2.6 miles to Lompico Road. Bear left onto Lompico and drive about 1.6 miles to West Drive. Turn left and drive carefully uphill on narrow West Drive, following the Loch Lomond signs to the park entrance, about 0.8 miles. Once past the entrance kiosk, continue about 0.6 miles to the parking lot at the end of the road, near the boat launch.

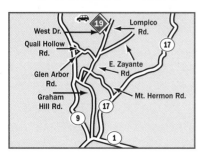

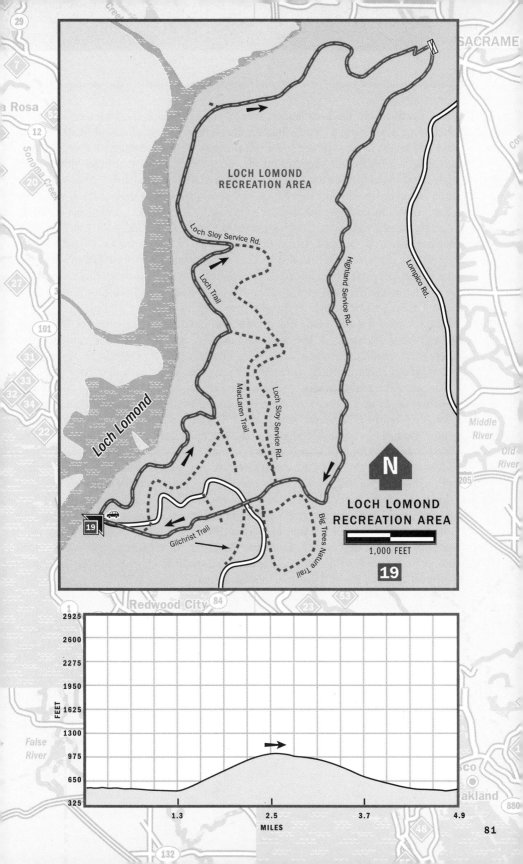

LOCH LOMOND
RECREATION AREA

Loch Lomond

Loch Sloy Service Rd.

Loch Trail

MacLaren Trail

Loch Sloy Service Rd.

Highland Service Rd.

Lompico Rd.

Gilchrist Trail

Big Trees Nature Trail

N

LOCH LOMOND
RECREATION AREA

1,000 FEET

19

FEET

2925
2600
2275
1950
1625
1300
975
650
325

1.3   2.5   3.7   4.9
MILES

for a cool frame of mind, and although one ridge is exposed to full sunlight, it's also commonly breezy.

Starting from the boat launch area on the Loch Trail, hug the shoreline as the trail keeps a level grade. Along this stretch there is usually plenty of fishing activity, and you might need to dodge some tackle boxes. Young redwood, tanoak, madrone, and huckleberry huddle together on the right. Ignore paths that head uphill on the right, leading to picnic areas, and stick to the waterline. Clar Innis Picnic Area on a little island accessible only by boat, is visible to the left. The trail rambles, with some slight elevation changes, through the edge of a forest where California milkwort, Western heart's ease, and trilliums bloom in spring. At 0.9 miles the MacLaren Trail departs uphill on the right. However, continue to the left on the Loch Trail. Wandering a slight distance from the lake, the trail passes through a sparse forest, where poison oak accompanies huckleberry and hazelnut.

The Loch Trail ends at 1.2 miles at a T junction with Loch Sloy Service Road. Turn left. Foot traffic is slight at this distance from the trailhead, and by late spring the broad fire road features a tall strip of grass running down the middle. The lake is kept at a distance by stands of live oak and California bay and with abundant sunlight, there are occasional clusters of understory shrubs, including creambush, toyon, sticky monkeyflower, and lizardtail. Gradually, the fire road drifts back into the woods.

Since the trail is nearly level you'll likely make good time and quickly reach a junction at about 1.7 miles, where a path to the left heads a short distance to Deer Flat. Turn right on Highland Service Road. Under shade from a dense forest of redwood, Douglas fir, tanoak, California bay, live oak, and madrone, Highland Service Road begins to climb. Huckleberry is common here, and you might also see yerba buena and redwood ivy in the understory. At two corners other trails seem to feint off to the left, but the fire road continues to the right each time, always climbing. There's really no break in the ascent until the trail crests at the gated park boundary at about 2.6 miles. The trail veers right and then adopts a course along a ridge where a wide variety of trees mingle, from towering redwoods to more petite specimens of madrone and tanoak. Knobcone pines mix through poison oak, ceanothus, broom, and sticky monkeyflower. Exposed, sunny areas are packed with manzanita, yerba santa, chamise, and toyon, while huckleberry shrubs keep to themselves in the more shaded sections.

After an easy uphill stretch, you'll emerge in a clearing where the hillside drops sharply off to the right. Views to the lake are outstanding—the best of the hike. There are no facilities here, but this is still my favorite spot for a picnic. Just past this spot, the trail begins a roller coaster route, coursing up and down the ridgeline at a mostly steep grade. The forest extends on both sides of the trail, obscuring further views. Faint skid roads, remnants from the logging era, are visible delving into the forest. At the 4-mile mark, the Big Trees Nature Trail crosses the fire road. Turn right (since Big Trees is a loop, the entire trail is an impractical addition to this hike, but if you'd like to take the long way around, turn left here). The trail drops through a beautiful and quiet forest of redwood, madrone, tanoak, Douglas fir, and live oak.

You can follow the guided tour with the Big Trees Nature Trail booklet, but the bulk of the numbered posts are back uphill on the other leg of this trail. Near Glen Corrie Picnic Area the loop reconnects, then the trail ends at about 4.2 miles. Look for a path ascending to the left, before the rest rooms. The Glen Corrie Trail climbs to the park road, crosses it, then heads back into the woods. At a junction just before a bridge, bear right onto the Gilchrist Trail. The trail threads through the forest, descending easily. There are two junctions with minor paths, the first heading back uphill, and a second leading to a picnic area—continue downhill on Gilchrist Trail at each, following the signs for "Lake Picnic Areas." Gilchrist crosses a footbridge, then ends at about 4.7 miles. Turn left and walk down the park road to the trailhead.

▶ NEARBY ACTIVITIES

This hike follows part of the Big Trees Nature Trail, which is a self-guided loop. If you'd like a shorter hike through Loch Lomond, 0.75-mile Big Trees Trail is a fine alternate. Pick up a nature guide at the trailhead and begin at the Glen Corrie Picnic Area.

JACK LONDON STATE HISTORIC PARK

KEY AT-A-GLANCE INFORMATION

LENGTH: 10.9 miles

CONFIGURATION: Out-and-back, with two short loops

DIFFICULTY: Moderate, despite the length

SCENERY: Woods, with some grassland

EXPOSURE: Almost completely shaded

TRAFFIC: Moderate around ranch, light on the upper trails

TRAIL SURFACE: Dirt fire roads and trails

HIKING TIME: 6 hours

SEASON: Autumn is perfect, other seasons are also good.

ACCESS: Pay $5 fee at entrance kiosk.

MAPS: The official park map is available at the entrance kiosk and the park museum.

FACILITIES: Pit toilets and water near the trailhead

SPECIAL COMMENTS: Dogs are not permitted on park trails.

IN BRIEF

This out-and-back Bay Area Ridge Trail segment begins on old ranch roads, then ascends on a narrow path through an unspoiled forest of madrone, black oak, big-leaf maple, buckeye, redwood, and California bay. After 5.5 miles you'll reach the end of the trail, and the return segment is downhill all the way.

DESCRIPTION

Just a stone's throw from the charming wine country village of Glen Ellen, hikers can literally walk up the forested slopes of Sonoma Mountain, following in the footsteps of Jack London, author of *Call of the Wild*. The property, containing London's home and ranch buildings, as well as many surrounding wooded acres, became a state park after London's wife, Charmian, died in 1955. Visitors can tour the "House of Happy Walls," London's grave site, and the remains of Wolf House, London's dream house that was destroyed by fire before it was ever occupied. For many, that's an adequate day trip, but hikers should press on, up the hillsides of Sonoma Mountain and into a gorgeous forest.

This hike clocks in at nearly 11 miles, but the trails are so well graded that it's a moderate

DIRECTIONS

Leave San Francisco northbound on US 101 and use the Golden Gate Bridge toll plaza as the mileage starting point. Drive about 50 miles north on US 101, then exit onto CA 12. Bear right and drive southeast on CA 12 about 15 miles, then turn right onto Arnold Drive. Drive south about 1 mile into Glen Ellen, then turn right onto London Ranch Road. Drive west on London Ranch Road about 1.2 miles to the park's entrance kiosk. Once past the kiosk, turn right and drive less than 0.1 mile to the parking lot.

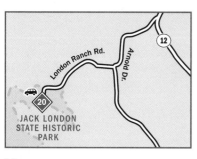

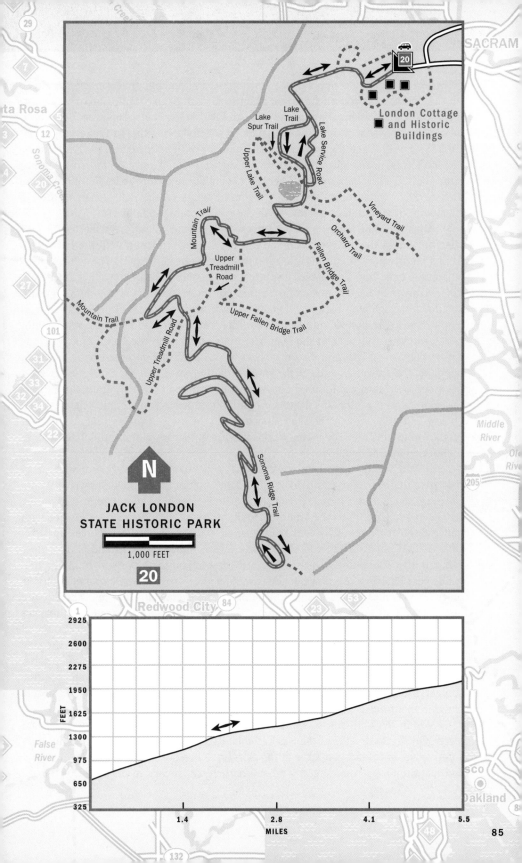

London Cottage
and Historic
Buildings

Lake
Spur Trail

Lake
Trail

Lake Service Road

Upper Lake Trail

Vineyard Trail

Orchard Trail

Mountain Trail

Fallen Bridge Trail

Upper
Treadmill
Road

Upper Fallen Bridge Trail

Mountain Trail

Upper Treadmill Road

Sonoma Ridge Trail

N

JACK LONDON
STATE HISTORIC PARK

1,000 FEET

20

FEET

2925
2600
2275
1950
1625
1300
975
650
325

1.4   2.8   4.1   5.5
              MILES

excursion. The park is a popular stop for summer visitors, but once you get away from the developed areas you might see more squirrels than people. Spring hikes are tempting, but the gentle temperatures and colorful foliage of Indian summer make autumn hikes very enjoyable. Begin from the parking lot, following the Bay Area Ridge Trail (BART) symbol. When the path ends at a T junction with a wide gravel road, turn right. London's cottage and the winery ruins are on your left. If you care to explore them, return back to the ranch road and keep following the signs for the BART and the lake. As you skirt a vineyard on the left, a few more paths on the right depart to the Pig Palace and other old farm buildings. All these are optional side hikes.

After the trail makes a sharp turn with the vineyard still on the left, a gate stretches across the fire road, and you'll reach a signed junction with the Lake Trail. At this point, you will have traveled about 0.6 miles from the parking lot. Turn right, still on the Lake Trail. I surprised a young rattlesnake on this trail on an October hike. The narrow path begins an easy climb through the woods. On sunny days, light filters down to highlight a few stately redwoods nestled in a forest of madrone, big-leaf maple, black oak, tanoak, and Douglas fir. The Lake Spur Trail heads off to the right, taking the long way around the lake. Continue straight on the Lake Trail as it runs within sight of the fire road for a few paces, then veers back into the woods. At about one mile, the Lake Trail ends at the shore of Bathhouse Lake. Here, turn left, walk a few steps, then turn right onto the service road, also known as the Mountain Trail. As the trail swings around the lake, Vineyard Road departs off to the left, with the Quarry Trail following in the same direction after a few steps. Continue to the right on the Mountain Trail. The ascent begins an easy but steady climb through redwoods, California bay, and madrone.

Unless you're visiting on a particularly busy day, the crowds thin with every step past the lake. The fire road reaches a little sloping meadow, known as May's Clearing, at 1.3 miles. Views stretch southeast, as does the Fallen Bridge Trail on the left. Keep going uphill on the Mountain Trail, browsing through a forest crowded with native Bay Area trees: redwood, madrone, coast live oak, big-leaf maple, buckeye, Douglas fir, California bay, and Oregon oak. At 1.5 miles, the other end of the Upper Fallen Bridge Trail returns on the left. Keep climbing on the Mountain Trail. The trail winds past Pine Tree Meadows, really more of a grassy patch mostly overtaken by the pines. At 1.8 miles Upper Treadmill Road breaks off to the left. Continue straight, and just when the ascent seems never ending, the trail dips to cross a creek, then reaches a junction at 2.3 miles. Turn left onto the Sonoma Ridge Trail. Beneath a canopy of California bay, the trail gently ascends through a rocky section. Angling up the side of the mountain, you'll enter a more exposed area where oaks, toyon, and manzanita mingle with Douglas fir. At 2.6 miles, cross the Upper Treadmill Trail and continue straight. The ascent is easy, initially through dense woods of Douglas fir, California bay, and madrone.

Where the trail crosses Asbury Creek, redwoods are especially prominent and lovely. On the south side of the creek, the landscape shifts a bit, making a long transition to the grassland you'll see at the ridgeline. Buckeye, black oak, big-leaf maple, and manzanita are common, and wherever there are breaks in the forest, you'll get views extending far to the north, east, and south. The most prominent landform is 4,304-foot Mount Saint Helena, looming to the north. Switchbacks keep the grade nearly effortless, and the climb passes quickly. Before long you'll find yourself bisecting a grassy slope just under the ridgeline at nearly 2,100 feet. At 5.3 miles, the trail splits into two legs of a loop. Turn left. After less than 0.1 mile, a trail leaves the park on the left. Continue to the right, climbing a little, past giant black oaks sprawled through grassland and fences that guard private property on the park boundary to the left. The loop closes at 5.6 miles. Turn left and retrace your steps back to the junction with the Upper Treadmill Trail at about 8.3 miles. You can shorten the return slightly by taking the Upper Treadmill to the right, but the trail had a badly eroded section on my last visit.

Otherwise continue on the Sonoma Ridge Trail, descend back to the Mountain Trail, then turn right and walk downhill to the junction with the Lake Trail at 9.9 miles. This time, stay to the right on the service road. With plenty of generous curves, the trail sweeps easily downhill through the woods. If you visit after a rainstorm, look for animal footprints in muddy patches. At 10.3 miles, you'll reach the gate and junction with the Lake Trail. Continue straight, retracing your steps back to the parking lot.

▶ NEARBY ACTIVITIES

The park museum, Jack London's grave, and the Wolf House ruins sit within the park. Visit www.parks.sonoma.net/jlpark.html for more information.

LOS VAQUEROS WATERSHED

▶ **IN BRIEF**

You'll start this hike at the County Line Staging Area, and walk uphill on a hiking-only loop through cattle-grazed grassland. From the hike's high point, a ridge, views extend to the reservoir, Mount Diablo, and the suburbs of the San Ramon valley. Bring binoculars to get a better look at the golden eagles that live in the area and are commonly spotted.

▶ **DESCRIPTION**

Constructed in the late 1990s and only filled in early 1999, if you search for Los Vaqueros on a map circa 1998, you won't find it. When this Contra Costa watershed first opened to recreation use, it was an incredibly peaceful place. I expected that when a marina and interpretive center opened it would be packed by fishermen and everyone else in the area looking for a nice picnic spot, but Los Vaqueros is still a very quiet park, particularly the southern area, where trails are open only to hikers. I don't know if it's because of the watershed's steep admission fee, or if hikers don't know about this recreation area, which began receiving visitors in 1999, but these trails are lonely.

The northern trailhead, Walnut Staging Area, has the denser network of multiuse trails

▶ **DIRECTIONS**

Depart San Francisco on the Bay Bridge and use the toll plaza as the mileage starting point. About 0.5 mile past the toll plaza, bear right onto I-580 East. Drive about 16 miles south and, at the CA 238 split, stay to the left on I-580. Continue east about 21 miles, then exit Vasco Road. Turn left and drive north about five miles, then turn left onto Los Vaqueros Road (look for small brown watershed sign), and continue to the County Line Staging Area just past the entrance station.

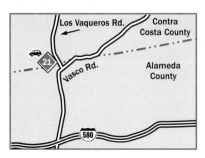

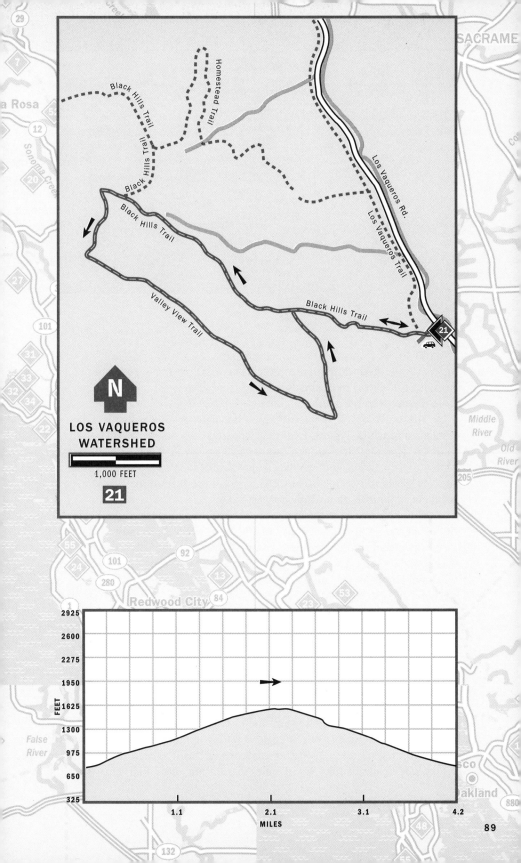

LOS VAQUEROS
WATERSHED

1,000 FEET

21

Los Vaqueros Reservoir from the
Valley View Trail

and the watershed's interpretive center. The southern trailhead, County Line Staging
Area, is off the road to the marina. There is no vehicle through-route inside the park
from the north to the south.

The trails of Los Vaqueros (which translates from Spanish to "the cowboys")
wander through a typical East Bay landscape of oak, grassland, and chaparral
foothills. The watershed property abuts two East Bay Regional Park District preserves,
Morgan Territory and Round Valley. This 4.1-mile loop barely scratches the surface of
the Los Vaqueros watershed, but it is a good introduction, particularly when spring
wildflowers flourish on a windy, treeless ridge.

On my first visit to the park in July 2000, I saw golden eagles before I even got
out of the car. From mid-February to late June, when eagles nest in the watershed's
oaks, some trails are often closed to public use (specific dates and trails change to
accommodate the eagles). Spring is the most pleasant time of year at Los Vaqueros,
with cool temperatures and a variety of wildflowers, but that's the season when trails
are most likely to be closed. If you want a long hike, visit in summer, autumn, or winter, when the connector to Morgan Territory is open. The trails on the hike described
below are not subject to closure during golden eagle nesting. Begin from the parking
lot on the Black Hills Trail. In a damp spot on the right, redwing blackbirds sit atop
mustard and thistles in spring, and squirrels scamper everywhere. After you pass
through a cattle gate and begin climbing on a wide fire road, look for a buckeye and
some oaks in a little draw off the trail to the left—this is as close to a tree as you'll
get on the entire hike.

The grade is moderately steep, and in summer there's not much to look at along
the trail—just an expanse of golden grass rolling uphill to the left and downhill to the
right. You may see a few blooming cardoons (a thistle related to the artichoke) and
yellow star thistle in July. At 0.1 mile, the Los Vaqueros Trail departs on the right,

starting a long, rolling journey along the park road to the marina area. This trail plays a crucial role in longer loops, but unfortunately it's one of the most boring routes in the watershed. Continue uphill on the Black Hills Trail.

In spring, lupine, Ithuriel's spear, filaree, and fiddleneck bloom sparsely in the surrounding grass. As you climb you may come across some of the watershed's cattle. On my last hike, I scattered the herds of cattle each time I came across them. Some stepped toward me, perhaps wondering what I was, but all of them ran (I mean really ran) out of sight before I got within 50 feet. For those of you who are accustomed to the bossy, elitist attitude of bovines at other East Bay parks, these shy cows are a nice contrast.

The Valley View Trail, the return route for the loop, begins to the left at 0.6 miles. Continuing straight on the Black Hills Trail, the grade slackens as the trail passes two small stock ponds on the right. Here are views north to chaparral-covered hillsides stretching past the Cañada Trail, with oak-dotted knolls in the foreground. At 1.5 miles the Black Hills Trail bends right, heading to a junction with the Homestead Trail, then proceeds to the hills above the reservoir in the western part of the watershed, where a trail connects to Morgan Territory. When I visited in spring, the Homestead Trail and the Black Hills Trail from this junction to the Cañada Trail were closed to protect the nesting eagles. Continue straight, now on the Valley View Trail. The fire road heads toward Morgan Territory Road, but then veers sharply left at 1.8 miles, and begins a steep climb. When it's windy (which it seems to be all the time), you'll need to hold onto your hat. Spring brings a few flowers to the trailside grass, including blue-eyed grass, buttercups, and fiddlenecks. The trail crests, turns left, and runs along the ridgeline. Views are expansive, ranging south across the San Ramon Valley to the mountains of Sunol and the Ohlone Wilderness. Northwest, Mount Diablo is visible, and to the northeast you can see the windmills twirling near Altamont Pass.

As you make your way across the rolling ridge, the reservoir comes into view in the heart of the park. With vultures and hawks whipping overhead in the wind, you'll need a quick hand with the binoculars to identify them. Despite the steady winds and the hungry cows, there were plenty of wildflowers on the north slope of the ridge in April, including loads of bluedicks, johnny-jump-ups, California poppy, fiddlenecks, blue and white lupine, Ithuriel's spear, and filaree. Off in the distance to the west, I saw patches of purple owl's clover, bruising lush green hillsides along Morgan Territory Road.

The Valley View Trail drops to a dip, where a worn cow path heads off to the right. Continue straight, climbing and then descending again. The trail curves left and then leaves the ridgeline. After a steady descent, you'll reach the junction with the Black Hills Trail again at 3.5 miles. Turn right and return downhill to the trailhead.

MARIN HEADLANDS:
GERBODE VALLEY LOOP

KEY AT-A-GLANCE INFORMATION

LENGTH: 6 miles

CONFIGURATION: Balloon

DIFFICULTY: Moderate

SCENERY: Coastal scrub, grassland, views of the Golden Gate Bridge, the Pacific, the downtown San Francisco skyline, and Mount Tamalpais

EXPOSURE: Full sun

TRAFFIC: Steady year-round; includes mountain bikers and equestrians

TRAIL SURFACE: Fire roads

HIKING TIME: 3 hours

SEASON: Good all year

ACCESS: Free

MAPS: Obtain NPS's free *Marin Headlands Trail Map* at the Headlands Visitor Center. My favorite map to the area is *A Rambler's Guide to the Trails of Mount Tamalpais and the Marin Headlands*, published by The Olmsted & Bros. Map Co.

FACILITIES: None at the trailhead; rest rooms and water at the visitor center

SPECIAL COMMENTS: Dogs are permitted on some Headlands trails. Check at the visitor center for specifics.

IN BRIEF

The Marin Headlands' soft rolling hills form a picturesque backdrop for travelers driving north across the Golden Gate Bridge, as well as a perfect platform for San Francisco city views that include the world's most beautiful span. You'll begin at the valley floor, climb through coastal scrub along one side of the valley, then crest at the ridgeline and return on the other side of the valley. The entire loop sticks to fire roads and is easy to follow, but expect substantial mountain bike and equestrian traffic.

DESCRIPTION

The Gerbode Valley trailhead is so close to San Francisco that when traffic conditions permit a quick escape, you can make the transition from city mouse to country mouse in 15 minutes. Although the Headlands are a stone's throw from the city and US 101, ridges block traffic noise, and trails are peaceful. The Headlands are laced with a handful of trails and lots of fire roads, some remnants from the land's military past and others part of a development that never happened.

DIRECTIONS

Depart San Francisco northbound on US 101. At the far end of the Golden Gate Bridge, exit onto Alexander Avenue (just past the Vista Point exit). Turn right and drive east toward Sausalito less than 0.1 mile, then turn left onto Bunker Road. Pass under the highway through a one-way tunnel (you may need to wait up to five minutes for your turn). From the other side of the tunnel, drive about 1.2 miles. Turn right onto a small, unmarked dirt road a few feet in front of a "horse crossing" sign (this road is horseshoe-shaped, so if you miss the east end of it, look for the other leg 0.2 miles down the road). After about 0.2 miles, park near the Rodeo Valley Trail sign.

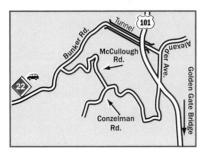

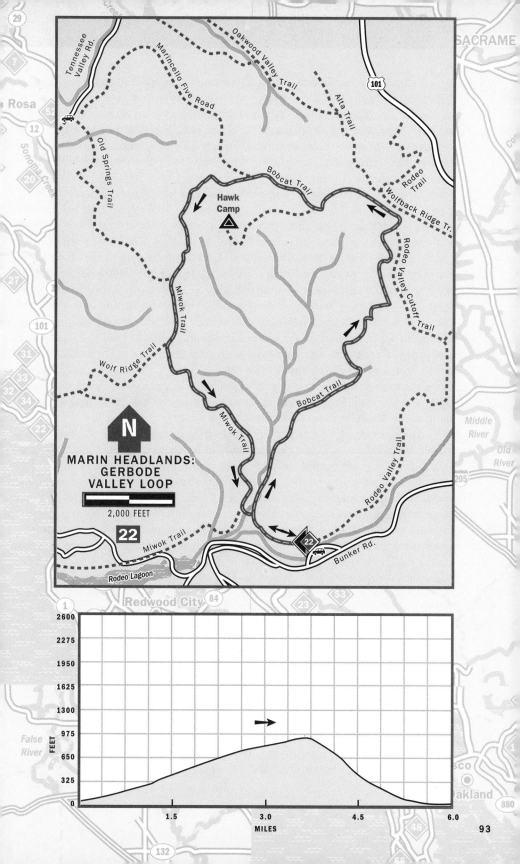

MARIN HEADLANDS: GERBODE VALLEY LOOP

2,000 FEET

22

Just north of the Golden Gate, a military installation occupied the area until the 1960s. After the bunkers and batteries were shuttered, a developer planned to build a massive housing complex called Marincello. Environmental and community activists squelched the development, and the land eventually became part of the Golden Gate National Recreation Area, managed by the National Park Service. It's high-profile open space, exemplifying what Bay Area preservationists and outdoor enthusiasts cherish: broadly accessible land close to urban areas, with tons of elbow-room for animals, wildflowers, and people. Begin at the signed trailhead, marked by a Bay Area Ridge Trail symbol, immediately crossing a little stream crowded by willow and dogwood. Keep an eye open for newts in this area during the rainy season. As the trail curves right, it leave the stream behind and soon reaches a T junction, where you'll turn left onto the Rodeo Valley Trail. Grassy hills rise up to the right, but the broad fire road keeps to a level grade, running along a damp meadow dotted with coyote brush. At 0.4 miles the Rodeo Valley Trail ends at a triangle-shaped junction. Bear right onto the Bobcat Trail. Ascending gradually, the wide dirt fire road follows the course of a creek on the left, where willow and blackberry thrive, and red-winged blackbirds flutter around the fringes of the stream. A stand of tall eucalyptus and a few scattered fruit trees suggest an old settlement in this area. The medicinal eucalyptus aroma mingles with the licorice scent of fennel, which grows with abandon along the trail. As the fire road begins to climb at a more moderate grade, views open up across Gerbode Valley, including glimpses of the Miwok Trail. With each step, more of the ocean becomes visible back to the west.

The sides of the Bobcat Trail are lined with a long list of plants. Coyote brush, purple bush lupine, poison oak, lizardtail, sticky monkeyflower, coffeeberry, sagebrush, and toyon are common coastal scrub plants, but the fog that is often held in this bowl-shaped valley nourishes some plants usually found in less exposed locations, such as creambush, snowberry, and currant. Flowers you might see in bloom range from late winter specialists hound's tongue, milkmaids, and zigadene to spring favorites blue-eyed grass, buttercup, bluedicks, California poppy, iris, paintbrush, checker-bloom, and fringecups. In early April, patches of goldenfields blaze with color on the highest reaches of the ridge. There are very few trees, just a few clusters of some shrubby coast live oak, cypress, and a particularly squat Douglas fir.

After a long, steady ascent, the grade eases, and huckleberry shrubs appear on the left. At 2.3 miles the Rodeo Valley Cutoff Trail begins on the right. This slight path slips over the ridge to the Rodeo Valley Trail, creating another loop option. Continue straight, though, on the Bobcat Trail, which keeps climbing before leveling out at the ridgeline. Fire roads split off to the right at 2.4 miles, with the Wolfback Ridge Trail heading back to the south, and the Rodeo and Alta trails proceeding north toward a pullout along US 101 and the Oakwood Valley Trail. Continue straight on Bobcat. Although this is far from the highest point on the ridgeline, the sweeping views feel well earned. Gerbode Valley slopes down at your feet, and the ocean sparkles to the west. The Bobcat Trail passes under some power lines, then drops to a dip before rising back to follow the ridge. In spring, California poppy, bluedicks, checker-bloom, blue-eyed grass, and buttercups blossom through the grass along the trail. At 2.9

miles a trail leading to Hawk Camp breaks off to the left. Continue straight on Bobcat, which now makes a final push toward the Headlands' second highest hill. The northern Golden Gate Bridge tower peaks out from between two hills to the south, and then the entire ridge of Mount Tamalpais comes into view to the north. Old Marincello Fire Road starts a journey to Tennessee Valley at 3.2 miles on the right. Continue straight on the Bobcat Trail. Still climbing through grassland, the trail finally ends at a junction with the Miwok Trail and two fire roads that service an Federal Aviation Administration navigational antennae perched at the hilltop. Turn right onto Miwok. The fire road descends, sweeping around the hill while offering grand views to the north of Tennessee Valley and Mount Tam. After a brief ascent, Miwok crests. But before heading downhill, take a moment to appreciate the views south. The Bay and Golden Gate Bridges are visible, as are downtown San Francisco skyscrapers, the Sutro tower near Twin Peaks, and farther south, Montara Mountain. If it's not too windy, a little grassy spot off the trail to the left makes a great rest stop. Where the Miwok Trail begins a steep descent, the rest of the journey is all downhill.

A gopher played peek-a-boo with me along the trail once, popping out of a hole, then diving back down. Although this stretch of trail is closed to cyclists, some riders still brave the harsh descent and massive drainage humps known as water bars, so stay alert for traffic. Reach the Old Spring Trail on the right at 4.1 miles, but continue straight on the Miwok Trail. Trailside vegetation is a bit bland compared to the Bobcat's; you'll mostly see coyote brush, with lots of mule ear sunflowers blooming in summer. This is a good trail for raptor watching, though, particularly in autumn when migratory birds pass through, and year-round you'll probably see vultures soaring overhead. Jagged Wolf Ridge rises off to the right, and the trail drops to reach its namesake trail at 4.4 miles. Stay to the left on the Miwok Trail. The descent is relentless, but I always console myself with the thought that at least it's downhill. If you're a bit rusty, your quads will be hollering. As the trail drops back into Gerbode Valley, the vegetation on the hillside to the right becomes more lush, with fern, snowberry, poison oak, purple bush lupine, and sagebrush spread across a hillside of coyote brush. Paintbrush, buttercups, and California poppy are the most common "wild" flowers in early spring, but there's also plenty of non-native Bermuda buttercup, a yellow-blossomed member of the oxalis family related to redwood sorrel. The Miwok finally winds its way back to level ground, meeting the Bobcat Trail at 5.6 miles. Turn left. The trail crosses over a creek where twinberry, a rather bland shrub most of the year, makes a spectacle of itself in spring, putting forth pairs of orange-red flowers which develop into berries in the summer. After about 300 feet, Bobcat veers left at the start of the Rodeo Valley Trail. Turn right and retrace your steps back to the trailhead.

▶ NEARBY ACTIVITIES

The Marin Headlands visitor center is open daily from 9:30 a.m. to 4:30 p.m. From this hike's trailhead, drive west on Bunker Road about 0.7 miles, and where Bunker curves right, continue straight onto Field Road. After less than 0.1 mile, turn right into the visitor center parking lot. Call (415) 331-1540 for more information.

MISSION PEAK
REGIONAL PRESERVE

ℹ KEY AT-A-GLANCE INFORMATION

LENGTH: 6.2 miles

CONFIGURATION: Out-and-back

DIFFICULTY: Strenuous

SCENERY: Grassland, views

EXPOSURE: Almost completely exposed

TRAFFIC: Moderate

TRAIL SURFACE: Dirt fire roads

HIKING TIME: 3 hours

SEASON: Spring is pleasant; winter is muddy; avoid during summer heat waves.

ACCESS: No fee

MAPS: The park map is available at the trailhead's information signboard.

FACILITIES: Pit toilets at the trailhead

SPECIAL COMMENTS: Dogs are permitted in the preserve.

▶ IN BRIEF

On this Mission Peak excursion, you'll begin at the edge of a Fremont residential neighborhood, hike fire roads, then take a little trail straight to the summit—an over 2,000-foot ascent. If you've picked a clear day, the 360-degree views are inspiring, but on windy days you may want to immediately head back downhill to the parking lot.

▶ DESCRIPTION

To get to the Mission Peak trailhead, you turn off a heavily trafficked street, drive one-half mile, then boom, you're there—at the base of a mountain.

Most mountains require long drives. But heck, you can get to Mission Peak by bus! Leaving from the parking lot, the fire road skirts a short, wide hill. The Peak Meadow Trail departs off to the right, but stay to the left on the Hidden Valley Trail. The route ahead really stands out in late winter and early spring when the grass is bright green. There's a brief descent, then the trail crosses Aqua Caliente Creek, bends left, and begins to climb. Ascending at a sharp grade through grassland, you might catch a glimpse of hang gliders drifting downhill from farther up the mountain. The Hidden Valley Trail draws near a wooded canyon and creek on the left, and coast live oaks along the trail offer snatches of shade.

▶ DIRECTIONS

Depart San Francisco on the Bay Bridge and use the toll plaza as the mileage starting point. Just past the toll plaza, bear right onto I-880 South. Drive about 33 miles south, then exit at Warren/Mission Boulevard. Drive northeast on Mission Boulevard, pass under I-680, then turn right on Stanford Avenue. Drive about one-half mile to the trailhead at the end of the street. Park in the lot, not along the side of Stanford Avenue.

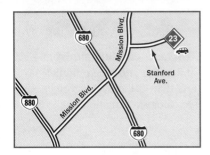

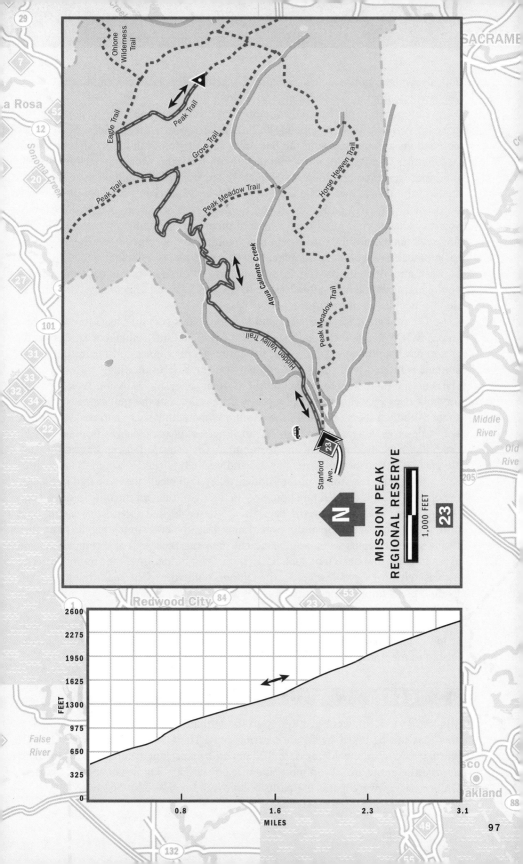

MISSION PEAK
REGIONAL RESERVE

23

1,000 FEET

Stanford Ave.

Ohlone Wilderness Trail

Eagle Trail

Peak Trail

Grove Trail

Peak Trail

Peak Meadow Trail

Aqua Caliente Creek

Horse Heaven Trail

Peak Meadow Trail

Hidden Valley Trail

N

FEET

2600
2275
1950
1625
1300
975
650
325
0

0.8   1.6   2.3   3.1

MILES

You also might notice a few islands of sagebrush, poison oak, and sticky monkeyflower floating in the sea of grassland along the trail.

City noises really fade as you climb, and as things quiet down, don't be surprised if you hear turkeys gobbling back and forth across the hillsides. Wild turkey populations are on the rise in the Bay Area, and Mission Peak has its share of them. At 1.5 miles, the Peak Meadow Trail departs on the right, dropping back toward the trailhead. Continue uphill on the Hidden Valley Trail. Here you'll often come across some of the many cows that graze Mission Peak. Unpleasant cattle–people conflicts do occur in Bay Area parks, and if you think bovines are sweet-tempered creatures, you may change your mind once a herd of them start galloping towards you down a fire road. Sometimes the cattle seem to act completely on caprice, but there are ways to minimize any conflicts. In general, give cattle plenty of room, and do not get between a mother and her calf. Be sure to close all cattle gates you encounter, and if you're hiking with a dog, either leash it or keep it close and under voice control. Cattle, like people, seem friskiest in spring.

The trail grade slackens a bit, and Mission Peak's summit gets closer with every step. You may notice rocks on the sides of the trail, and their numbers increase until, as you reach a junction at 2.2 miles, the entire steeply sloping hillside leading to the summit is littered with rocks and boulders. At the base of the ridge, the Grove Trail starts on the right. Stay to the left on the Hidden Valley Trail. Mission Peak's remaining bulk rises very sharply out of a pretty little valley, but the trail ascends a gentler route. Although the slope under the summit is incredibly sharp and rocky, you may see cattle or goats grazing up there. A small herd of goats, escapees from a domesticated life, have lived elusively on the mountain for years. Still ascending at a moderate grade, the trail sweeps through grassland where fiddlenecks bloom in late winter. At 2.3 miles, the last stretch of the Hidden Valley Trail meets the Peak Trail in the vertex of a big triangle-shaped junction. Stay to the right, then on the other side of a cattle gate, right again, now on the Eagle Trail. The Eagle Trail ascends, sweeping right onto the northeastern side of the peak. Enjoy a nearly level stretch for the final push to the summit begins when you bear right onto the Peak Trail at 2.6 miles. As you ascend the narrow steep trail, look back over your shoulder from time to time to savor increasingly long views east across the Ohlone Wilderness. The Peak Trail jogs to the left and picks through rock outcrops as it ascends, steeply. Finally at 3.1 miles you'll reach the top, elevation 2,517 feet.

From the summit, the entire South Bay seems to sit at your feet. A funny little scope points out prominent natural features within visual range, including Mount Diablo to the north. Return the same way you came back to the parking lot.

▶ NEARBY ACTIVITIES

Mission Peak is the western gateway to the Ohlone Wilderness, a huge 9,156-acre area that can be hiked by advance permit only. The Ohlone Trail makes a 28-mile journey through the wilderness, and there are backpacking campgrounds for hikers making the entire trip. Read more about it on the East Bay Regional Park District's Ohlone page: www.ebparks.org/parks/ohlone.htm, or call (510) 562-PARK.

MONTARA MOUNTAIN

▶ IN BRIEF

Just ten miles south of San Francisco, chaparral-cloaked Montara Mountain rises up from the ocean at Pacifica, offering quick and easy access for hikes with incredible views, interesting vegetation, and frequent animal sightings.

▶ DESCRIPTION

This is a two-for-one hike through attached parks to the highest peaks of the rugged range. McNee Ranch State Park offers fine views attained via steep fire roads. By starting at San Pedro Valley Park you can take advantage of the county park's well-graded trails, cutting the difficulty of the climb considerably, and reducing the overall distance to just under seven miles. Combining the two also permits a peak at Brooks Falls, which drops off the north slope of Montara Mountain.

Montara Mountain has a healthy wildlife population—bobcats are sighted so often that *Lynx rufus* has pretty much become the mascot of San Pedro Valley Park, appearing on sweatshirts sold at the park store. Why are there so many animal sightings in these two attached parks on the outskirts of residential Pacifica? Perhaps because San Pedro Valley Park and McNee Ranch State Park abut the San Francisco Watershed, a massive hunk of land stretching across the southern flanks of the mountain. Although the watershed is mostly closed to public use, plenty of animals enjoy the

▶ DIRECTIONS

Drive south from San Francisco on I-280 and use the CA 1/19th Avenue merge as the mileage starting point. After 1.7 miles, exit onto CA 1 South. Drive 7 miles south into Pacifica, turn left onto Linda Mar Boulevard, and drive two miles east to the end of the road. Turn right onto Oddstad, and almost immediately, make the first left into San Pedro Valley Park.

ⓘ KEY AT-A-GLANCE INFORMATION

LENGTH: 6.9 miles

CONFIGURATION: Balloon

DIFFICULTY: Moderate

SCENERY: Woods, chaparral, waterfall, views

EXPOSURE: Some shade in the first mile, then almost completely exposed until the last mile

TRAFFIC: Light weekdays, moderate weekends

TRAIL SURFACE: Dirt fire roads and trails

HIKING TIME: 4 hours

SEASON: Especially good in January and February for manzanitas in bloom, but nice year-round. Beware of summer fog.

ACCESS: Pay $4 fee at entrance kiosk (self register if unstaffed).

MAPS: The park map is available at the entrance kiosk, and at an information signboard at the trailhead.

FACILITIES: Rest rooms and water at the trailhead

SPECIAL COMMENTS: Fog is very common along this part of the coast; Pacifica can be fogged in while the tip of Montara Mountain is above the fog, or vice versa. I've personally enjoyed this hike in fog so thick I could see only a few feet, but if you're counting on the views, pick a day with clear, stable weather. Dogs are not permitted. Although bikes are not allowed on the trail that connects to McNee Ranch, they are allowed on the state park's fire roads.

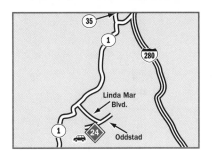

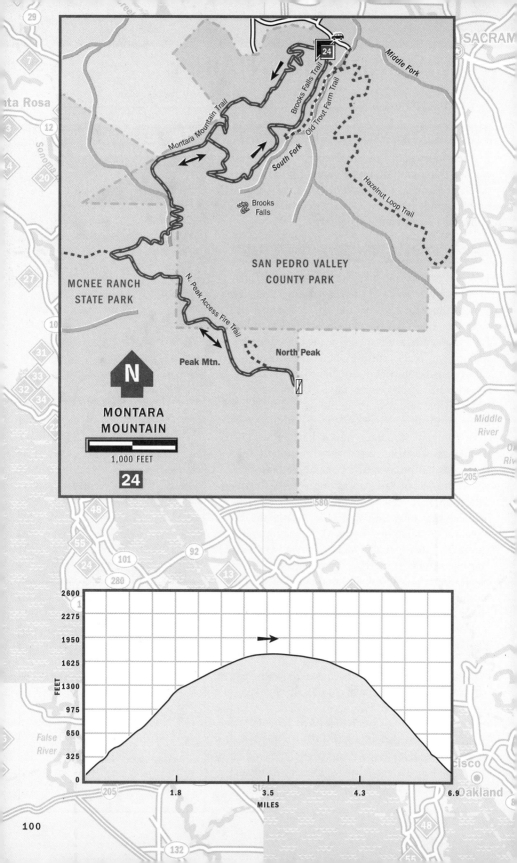

SACRAM

Middle Fork

Brooks Falls Trail

Montara Mountain Trail

South Fork

Old Trout Farm Trail

Brooks Falls

Hazelnut Loop Trail

SAN PEDRO VALLEY
COUNTY PARK

MCNEE RANCH
STATE PARK

N. Peak Access Fire Trail

Peak Mtn.

North Peak

N

**MONTARA
MOUNTAIN**

1,000 FEET

24

Middle
River

Or
Riv

205

580

48

55

24

101

280

92

13

False
River

FEET
2600
2275
1950
1625
1300
975
650
325
0

1.8   3.5   4.3   6.9
MILES

Fsisco
Oakland

132

The Montara Mountain Trail clings to the hillside high above Pacifica.

wildlife corridor, which stretches from Pacifica all the way south to CA 92. Begin near the rest rooms on a path signed to the Montara Mountain Trail and the Brooks Falls Trail. The path ascends about 130 feet, then reaches a T junction where you'll turn right onto the Montara Mountain Trail. After 110 flat feet, the trail crosses a service road and begins to climb through a eucalyptus forest. Zigzagging up a hillside, the sounds of residential Pacifica at first quite loud, begin to fade.

Although in some parts of this forest eucalyptus chokes out all companion plants, there are patches of understory chock-full of natives, including California coffeeberry, hazelnut, toyon, poison oak, creambush, sticky monkeyflower, thimbleberry, currant, ceanothus, and coyote brush. This part of the mountain is not a spring wildflower hotspot, but a few irises, hound's tongue, zigadene, and starflower bloom in spring. When the trail leaves the eucalyptus forest, coffeeberry, ceanothus, and coyote brush linger, bridging the gap between woods and chaparral. Yerba santa is common, and chinquapin and huckleberry appear in a damp shaded spot. A few manzanitas mix through the chaparral and then completely overtake the sides of the trail. Different varieties of this evergreen native bloom in stages during winter—I've seen pure pink blossoms on Montara Mountain manzanita in late November, and waves of more common white flowers around Christmas. Others bloom even later, with flowers persisting into early April. When the manzanitas are in full flower the scent is intoxicating, like honeyed perfume—just ask the hummingbirds. At 1.2 miles the Brooks Falls Trail departs on the left. This is the return leg of the hike—continue straight, but also take a moment to enjoy the ocean view on the right. At an easy ascent, the narrow path squeezes through a dense collection of chaparral. A bench on the left side of the trail is a favorite of mine—I often pause to drink some water and gauge the visibility for the rest of the hike. Although the elevation here is under 1,000 feet on clear days you can see north to both Golden Gate Bridge towers, Mount Tamalpais, and the entire Point Reyes peninsula.

Continuing uphill, you'll pass a solitary cypress commonly surrounded by zigadene in early spring. Manzanita, while still present along the trail, no longer dominates. Silktassel shrubs are conspicuous in winter when they dangle curious catkin-like flowers. In spring when blueblossom ceanothus is in full bloom, bees swarm about, giddy from the abundance of sweet-smelling flowers.

The trail sweeps uphill just off the rounded ridgeline, then begins an ascent up the face of the mountain. Switchbacks ease the climb, but the trail is eroded and rocky, and the plants along this stretch of the Montara Mountain Trail are stunted and windswept. At 1.9 miles with the switchbacking over, you'll pass from the county park into the state park. Just to the right of the transitory sign, walk a few steps out onto a rounded knoll. Views north are awesome—though not as extensive as from the top—you'll likely have this spot completely to yourself.

When I don't feel like continuing to the summit, I consider this the "far enough point." I once watched a chipmunk scampering over the dwarfed vegetation that grows on this granite knoll, and it's also a good vantage point to observe ravens frolicking through the skies, making their odd vocalizations and "wonk wonk" calls. From here it's only 0.3 miles to the fire road, and the trail ascends at a moderate pace, clinging to the steep hillside. At 2.3 miles the Montara Mountain Trail ends, and you'll turn left onto North Peak Access Fire Road where you should be alert for cyclists descending at a rapid rate.

At first the ascent doesn't seem so bad, as the wide fire road climbs through a mix of chaparral over bare swaths of granite. The first hill is reasonable, but the second is one steep climb. Luckily it's a short section and then the fire road adopts a more moderate grade, even throwing in one short downhill. In late winter and early spring, currant shrubs bloom along the trail, presenting dazzling pink flowers to contrast the wide-open blue sky. You also might see California poppy, paintbrush, and purple bush lupine. San Francisco wallflower, a yellow-blossomed plant in the mustard family, is so common in April that you might assume it's just another ordinary plant, but this variety of wallflower is rare.

Where the fire road crests and levels considerably, the area off to the right is scarred with paths and an old crashed car (one of several on the mountain). On the left and straight ahead, coyote brush-coated hillsides ascend to radio towers atop the two tallest points on Montara Mountain. If you've become bored of those terrific views to the north, from the top of the mountain there are new vistas, including the ocean and coastline to the west and Mount Diablo to the east. Goldenfields blaze yellow patches through the grass along the trail in spring.

When the fire road forks, if you want to climb as high as possible, you can walk uphill on the road to the left. Off to the right, North Peak is fenced and inaccessible. If you continue on the fire road to the right, you'll reach the end of the line and the watershed boundary at 3.5 miles. A fence and locked gate fail to screen views south to fire roads traveling across the spine of the ridge. You'll probably want to revel at the summit before heading back downhill, unless it's a windy day; there are plenty of spots suitable for a lunch break. When you're ready, retrace your steps back to the junction with the Brooks Falls Trail (sometimes known as the Brooks Creek Trail) at 5.8 miles, and turn right. Along this trail, you might see rabbits nibbling on the trailside vegetation, which includes coyote brush, yerba santa, poison oak, California coffeeberry, creambush, ceanothus, blackberry, and currant. The initial path is nearly level, and then the Brooks Falls Trail begins to drop into a canyon. In one damp corner, cow parsnip and forget-me-not bloom in spring. There are views back up to the ridge, but you'll want to pay attention to the trail, which has some rocks and roots that are easy to trip over.

Manzanitas return, flourishing in a swale of red soil. A bench on the left is perfect for one last rest stop. When Brooks Falls is running, this is the best viewpoint to the three-tier falls. In all the years I've been hiking at San Pedro, I've never seen a gush to write home about, even when the sound of running water downhill in San Pedro Creek is audible. Most of the time Brooks Falls is just three little trickles, but it's still a scenic and quiet spot and a good place to watch hummingbirds.

As the trail continues downhill, manzanita, huckleberry, chinquapin, and silktassel yield to the eucalyptus forest again. At 6.5 miles a trail doubles back to the right, dropping to follow San Pedro Creek through the remains of an old trout farm on the way back to the trailhead. Either trail is an option, but I usually continue straight on the Brooks Falls Trail, which descends through an unusual mix of coast live oak, redwood, pine, Douglas fir, and dogwood. A picnic area is visible on the right, then the trail ends back at the hike's first junction. Turn right and return to the parking lot.

▶ NEARBY ACTIVITIES

San Pedro Valley Park hosts two other loop trails and one wheelchair-accessible interpretive trail that runs along San Pedro Creek. The visitor center features exhibits about Montara Mountain flora and fauna, and hosts a small store with maps and books.

MONTE BELLO
OPEN SPACE PRESERVE

KEY AT-A-GLANCE INFORMATION

LENGTH: 6.7 miles

CONFIGURATION: Loop

DIFFICULTY: Moderate

SCENERY: Grassland, woods, creek, views

EXPOSURE: Mixed

TRAFFIC: Light-moderate

TRAIL SURFACE: Dirt fire roads and trails

HIKING TIME: 3.5 hours

SEASON: Summer is often very hot; late winter and spring are best.

ACCESS: No fee

MAPS: A park map is available at the trailhead's information signboard.

FACILITIES: Pit toilets available at the trailhead

SPECIAL COMMENTS: Dogs are not permitted.

▶ IN BRIEF

With a 2,800-foot elevation, Black Mountain boasts outstanding 360-degree views. If you want to look down at the Santa Clara valley, you got it. Prefer views of the forested Santa Cruz Mountains? No problem—just turn around! This hike descends to cool, quiet Stevens Creek, then ascends out of a canyon to Black Mountain's summit. The return route is all downhill, through an old walnut orchard and grasslands where flowers riot in spring.

▶ DESCRIPTION

Oddly enough, in a preserve where everything seems supersized, I find myself particularly drawn to Monte Bello's most subtle charms. In this open space preserve the trails are long, the views are long, and hikes are long, but I get lost in the little things—new oak leaves unfolding, hillsides covered with miniature flowers, and water trickling down a tiny waterfall. It's the perfect place for a solo hike-as-meditation.

From the parking lot, walk back toward Page Mill Road, then turn left onto the White Oak Trail. In hot weather beware of rattlesnakes basking along the sides of the trail, which runs along Page Mill Road at a slight ascent. Coyote brush shrubs punctuate the grassland, and an invasive plant, yellow star thistle, will prick your ankles if you stray from the trail—look for blue butterflies here in summer. The White Oak Trail turns left away from the road and preserve boundary and sweeps

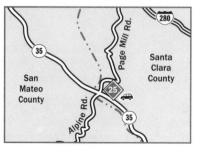

▶ DIRECTIONS

Depart from San Francisco on southbound I-280 and use CA 1/19th Avenue merge as the mileage starting point. Drive south on I-280 about 29 miles, then exit onto Page Mill Road. Drive west on Page Mill Road about 8 miles, and turn left into the preserve parking lot.

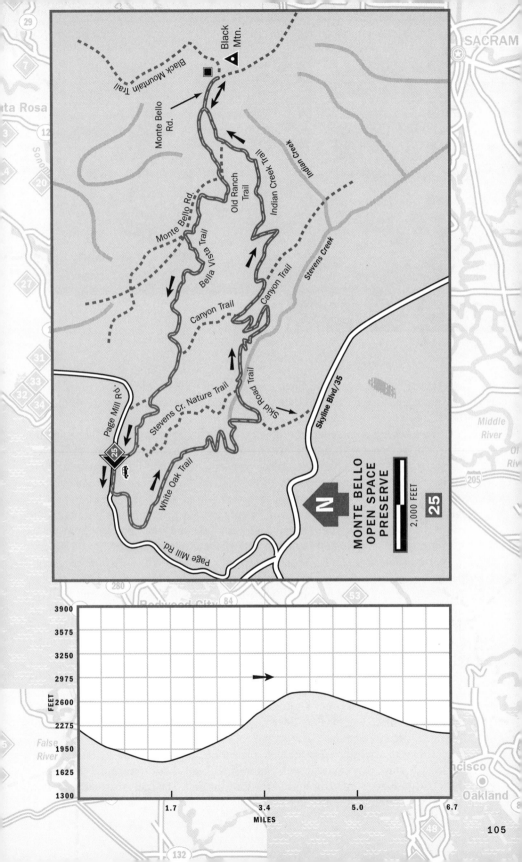

MONTE BELLO OPEN SPACE PRESERVE

Black Mtn.

Black Mountain Trail

Monte Bello Rd.

Monte Bello Rd.

Old Ranch Trail

Bella Vista Trail

Indian Creek Trail

Indian Creek

Canyon Trail

Stevens Creek

Canyon Trail

Canyon Trail

Page Mill Rd.

Stevens Cr. Nature Trail

Skid Road Trail

Skyline Blvd./35

Middle River

White Oak Trail

Page Mill Rd.

25

N

2,000 FEET

25

FEET

3900
3575
3250
2975
2600
2275
1950
1625
1300

1.7   3.4   5.0   6.7

MILES

From the upper reaches of the White Oak Trail, views include the undulating hills of Russian Ridge.

around the base of a knoll. There are views south to Black Mountain, and along the canyon where Stevens Creek flows. At 0.3 miles stay to the left on the White Oak Trail, ignoring another trail heading straight toward Page Mill Road.

Descending moderately, the trail passes a cluster of madrone, then slips into grassland peppered with huge old white oaks. Valley oak and Oregon oak are both classified as white oaks, but Oregon oaks are an unusual find in the South Bay. Some of these gorgeous oaks on the sides of the trail are Oregon oaks, but it takes a practiced eye to tell them apart—oak leaves can vary from tree to tree, and the most telltale distinguishing feature, the acorn, is only around for perusal in autumn (valley oak acorns are slender and long, while Oregon oak's are short and fat). Even though it's tough to identify them, it's easy to admire these venerable oaks.

The White Oak Trail descends, then adopts a series of switchbacks, and the landscape begins to shift as the trail makes its way into a canyon. Mule ear sunflowers bloom along the trail in spring, in the last patches of grassland. As the tree cover thickens, you might notice two oaks of the evergreen variety, coast live and canyon live. Other common plants include California bay, big-leaf maple, gooseberry, Douglas fir, tanoak, wild rose, ferns, and creambush. The springtime flowers, including western heart's ease, trillium, coltsfoot, and pink-flowering currant, are typical to moist dark woods and creekbeds. In the dead of winter the trail is often completely covered with fallen leaves. Following the course of Stevens Creek, the White Oak Trail descends slightly, then rises to a junction at 1.5 miles. The Skid Road Trail climbs to the right on the way to Skyline Ridge Open Space Preserve. Continue to the left, following the sign toward the Stevens Creek Nature Trail.

This wide trail descends through a forest of Douglas fir, tanoak, and California bay. At 1.8 miles the Stevens Creek Nature Trail heads back toward the trailhead on the left. Continue to the right toward the Canyon Trail. The trail crosses, then follows

Stevens Creek. At a second bridge a tributary drops into the creek from the left, creating a small cascade in the wettest months. Thimbleberry, blackberry, and blue elderberry thrive in the damp canyon beneath Douglas fir and California bay, and honeysuckle vines drip from live oaks. Fairy lanterns bloom here in spring. The trail begins to ascend, then makes a sharp turn left, away from the creek. At 2.4 miles the trail ends at a junction with the Canyon Trail. Turn right.

Baby blue-eyes freckle a small grassy meadow in spring. The fire road sweeps uphill through a pocket of woods, then reemerges into grassland and descends to a junction at 2.6 miles. Turn left onto the Indian Creek Trail.

The wide fire road begins to ascend at a sustained, moderate grade. On an August hike, I caught a glimpse of a young coyote sitting in a pocket of sloping grassland near the edge of woods on the right. Gradually, the accompanying vegetation shifts from madrone, oaks, and California bay to a chaparral blend of poison oak, sticky monkeyflower, chamise, toyon, California coffeeberry, ceanothus, and yerba santa. You may also notice clematis, a vine with pretty white flowers in spring and puffy seed clusters in autumn. As the trail ascends, grassland begins to dominate, and graceful displays of popcorn flower, johnny jump-up, chia, owl's clover, fiddleneck, bluedicks, and California poppy appear in spring. At 3.6 miles a path veers off to the left. Continue straight, following the sign toward Black Mountain. The climb continues, then the Indian Creek Trail ends at a T-junction at 3.8 miles. Turn right onto Monte Bello Road.

As if to compensate for the climb, the last stretch to the summit on a broad fire road, is easy. A tangle of California coffeeberry, live oaks, ceanothus, madrone, and pitcher sage blocks views to the east, but just past some communication structures, where a trail begins on the left, and heads at an extremely steep grade downhill into Rancho San Antonio Open Space Preserve, the trees and shrubs yield to grassland. Continue a little further on Monte Bello Road to the top of Black Mountain at 2,800 feet, more of a plateau than an apex. Here, savor views east and south, including Mission Peak and Mount Hamilton. Look for a small boulder field on the right, and follow the unsigned but obvious path into this area. The treeless summit offers exceptional views, particularly of Mount Umunhum to the south and a forested ridge running to the west, much of which is preserved open space, including Portola Redwoods State Park. This is a wonderfully scenic spot for a lunch break. When you're ready, return to the junction with the Indian Creek Trail, then continue straight on Monte Bello Road.

The fire road descends easily, bordered by woods where you might see mournful duskywing butterflies in summer. When the road forks, stay to the left, following the sign for backpack camp. The wide fire road passes Black Mountain Backpack Camp on the right, a small, no-frills camp requiring advance reservations. Continue through the camp to a junction at 4.8 miles, and bear left onto the Old Ranch Trail.

Almost right away, head to the right on a slight path, signed with "no bikes, not a through trail" signs. The path climbs through grassland, then ends at a hilltop with the best views north, extending past San Francisco to Mount Tamalpais on clear days. In spring johnny jump-ups, fiddlenecks, and popcorn flower bloom with abandon through the surrounding grass. Descend back to the Old Ranch Trail, then turn right.

The trail descends downslope from the ridgeline, through grassland dotted with coyote brush. The high reaches of a wooded ravine on the left are packed with poison oak, but thankfully the Old Ranch Trail keeps its distance. Peaking out from spring's lush green grass you might see buttercups, owl's clover, California poppy, and blue and white lupine. Russian Ridge is visible to the northwest, and in the foreground the Bella Vista Trail is conspicuous. At 5.3 miles you'll reach a junction with two paths on the right leading to Monte Bello Road. Stay to the left, now on the Bella Vista Trail.

Beautiful views? Yes indeedy, particularly to the north and west. Bella Vista initially sticks to grassland, but as it descends, trailside vegetation becomes more varied and includes small clusters of creambush, California bay, buckeye, live oaks, and bigleaf maple nestled in creases of the hillside. Painted lady butterflies are commonly glimpsed along the trail in summer. After a steady, moderate descent, the Bella Vista Trail ends at 6.1 miles. Turn right onto the Canyon Trail.

Coyote brush, buckeye, willow, and toyon mix it up along the trail. Activity along the San Andreas Fault, which runs parallel to the fire road, created the little sag pond on the right. The Canyon Trail, keeping to a mostly level grade, passes a spur path on the left, then reaches a junction at 6.3 miles. Turn left, following the sign to Monte Bello parking lot.

The little trail weaves through an old walnut orchard, then sweeps right and ascends slightly. On these grassy slopes high above Stevens Creek, grassland fosters good wildflower displays in spring—on one late April visit, an entire hillside on the left was covered with pink owl's clover. At 6.6 miles, the Stevens Creek Nature Trail enters from the left near a rustic stone bench. Before continuing on the trail heading right, take a moment to gaze south, enjoying one last look at Black Mountain and Mount Umunhum. The final stretch to the parking lot is short and level.

▶ NEARBY ACTIVITIES

Los Trancos Open Space Preserve is just across the street from the Monte Bello parking lot. Los Trancos offers a self-guided nature tour, with an emphasis on earthquakes and geology—the San Andreas Fault runs through both preserves. Read more about Los Trancos on the Midpeninsula Regional Open Space District website www.open space.org.

MORGAN TERRITORY
REGIONAL PRESERVE

Morgan Territory's name whispers of the wilderness, evoking pioneers, wagon trains, and epic journeys. This loop rambles through a lavish landscape of grassland and oaks, drops down off a ridge, then ascends on a narrow path along a creek. Morgan Territory is a good bird-watching and wildflower-spotting preserve, so bring binoculars and field guides.

▶ DESCRIPTION

Begin near the information signboard on the Volvon Trail. After about 150 feet, the Coyote Trail begins on the left—the hike's return route. Stay to the right on Volvon. Sweeping through grassland dotted with oaks, California bay, and buckeye, Volvon is joined by the Bob Walker Regional Trail, and the two paths run together. The trail meets another fire road heading to the park boundary on the right; bear left. At a slight descent, the Volvon Trail meanders through a small bowl-shaped valley, where johnnytuck, California buttercups, fiddlenecks, and bluedicks bloom in spring. Mount Diablo's twin peaks loom in the distance. At 0.6

ⓘ KEY AT-A-GLANCE INFORMATION

LENGTH: 4.7 miles

CONFIGURATION: Loop

DIFFICULTY: Moderate

SCENERY: Grassland and oaks

EXPOSURE: First leg under full sun, last shaded

TRAFFIC: Light

TRAIL SURFACE: Dirt fire road and trails

HIKING TIME: 2.5 hours

SEASON: Summer is often very hot; late winter and spring are best.

ACCESS: No fee

MAPS: The park map is available at the trailhead's information signboard.

FACILITIES: Vault toilets and drinking water are available at the trailhead.

SPECIAL COMMENTS: Dogs permitted

▶ DIRECTIONS

Depart San Francisco on the Bay Bridge and use the toll plaza as the mileage starting point. About one-half mile past the toll plaza, bear right onto I-580 East. Drive about 16 miles south, then at the CA 238 split, stay to the left on I-580. Continue east about 18 miles, then exit onto North Livermore Avenue. Drive north on North Livermore. After about 4 miles, the road makes a sharp left and becomes Manning. Shortly after, turn right onto Morgan Territory Road. Drive about 5.5 miles on narrow, winding, one-lane Morgan Territory Road to the signed park entrance on the right side of the road.

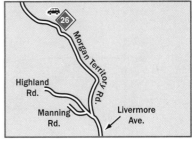

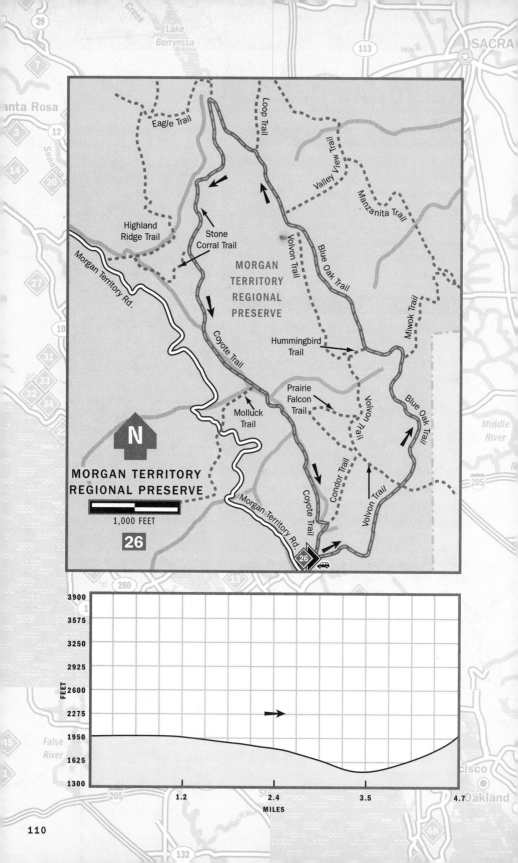

Eagle Trail

Loop Trail

Valley View Trail

Manzanita Trail

Highland Ridge Trail

Stone Corral Trail

MORGAN
TERRITORY
REGIONAL
PRESERVE

Volvon Trail

Blue Oak Trail

Miwok Trail

Morgan Territory Rd.

Coyote Trail

Hummingbird Trail

Prairie Falcon Trail

Blue Oak Trail

N

MORGAN TERRITORY
REGIONAL PRESERVE

1,000 FEET

26

Molluck Trail

Volvon Trail

Condor Trail

Volvon Trail

Morgan Territory Rd.

Coyote Trail

26

3900
3575
3250
2925
2600
2275
1950
1625
1300

FEET

1.2   2.4   3.5   4.7
MILES

miles, a dead-end trail heads off to the right. Bear left, then a few steps later, the Volvon Trail veers left. Turn right onto the Blue Oak Trail.

The fire road winds gently uphill, through graceful old oaks and a few fruit and nut trees. Popcorn flower and filaree, two diminutive spring flowers, sprawl through the grass in early April. In some years there are so many blooming filarees that entire hillsides are tinted light purple. There are more sweeping views of Mount Diablo as the Blue Oak Trail descends easily, but the surrounding landscape is also a visual delight—rolling grassy hills peppered with oaks stretch in every direction. The Miwok Trail breaks off to the right at 1.2 miles, descending toward the Los Vaqueros Watershed. Continue to the left on the Blue Oak Trail. In spring, carpets of goldenfields appear, as blue and valley oaks begin to leaf out. The Hummingbird Trail sets off to the left at 1.3 miles, connecting to the Volvon Trail. Stay to the right on the Blue Oak Trail. Here you can get a close look at the blue oaks lining the trail. The Volvon, a local native American tribe, ground oak acorns into an edible mush using mortar rocks, some of which have been discovered inside this preserve. The other end of the Hummingbird Trail slips off to the left, connecting to the Volvon Trail. Continue straight on the Blue Oak Trail, which gently rises and falls through a more wooded area dominated by oaks and buckeye, where bluedicks and woodland star bloom along the trail in spring. Other than bird cries or soft chattering from squirrels, all is quiet. At 2 miles, the Blue Oak Trail ends at a T-junction. Turn right onto the Volvon Trail again.

After about 400 feet, you'll reach a cattle gate and junction with the Valley View Trail. Continue straight. The trail briefly ascends to a saddle between hills. Views stretch east to the flatlands of the Central Valley. On clear days you may be able to see east all the way to the Sierra. Here, 2.3 miles into the hike, you could extend your journey on a 1.2-mile loop around Bob Walker Ridge to the right. To stay on this 4.7-mile loop, continue to the left on the Volvon Trail, which descends into a narrow valley. At 2.6 miles, the Volvon Trail veers off to the right. Turn left onto the Stone Corral Trail.

The fire road weaves along the valley floor, where rocks are strewn through grassland. The Stone Corral Trail loses some elevation, passes through a cattle gate, and sweeps to the right. Ignore a well-worn path on the left, and ascend a little hill to a signed junction at 3.2 miles. Turn left onto the Coyote Trail.

Initially the narrow path keeps a nearly level grade as it cuts across a meadow, but at a cattle gate, the Coyote Trail heads into the woods and begins to climb along a creek. The trail forks, but the two paths soon rejoin. Big-leaf maple, black oak, coast live oak, and buckeye fill the canyon, with snowberry, poison oak, creambush, and coffeeberry in the understory. Just past a grassy area with some manzanita about halfway up the hill, the Molluck Trail begins on the right. Continue uphill on the Coyote Trail. Although the ascent from the Stone Corral Trail to the trailhead is only about 500 vertical feet, some steep sections of trail are a bit arduous. Chinese houses, royal larkspur, and shooting stars are abundant in early spring. As elevation is gained, views begin to open up back out of the canyon and also to a ridge on the right, crowned with rocky palisades. The Coyote Trail crosses the creek, ascends through a boulder field, then emerges in grassland near a small pond. Bear left and skirt the pond, reaching a junction with the Condor Trail at 4.6 miles. Turn right and follow the Coyote Trail back the remaining 0.1 mile to the Volvon Trail and the parking lot.

MOUNT BURDELL
OPEN SPACE PRESERVE

▶ IN BRIEF

Mount Burdell is a big name for a relatively low Marin County peak. This preserve is backyard wilderness for Novato dog-walkers and runners, and is a great destination for easy to moderate hikes like this one—a loop through oaks and grassland to the high flanks of the mountain and the upper reaches of Olompali State Historic Park.

▶ DESCRIPTION

Two parks occupy the slopes of Mount Burdell: Olompali State Historic Park and Mount Burdell Open Space Preserve. The state park, on the east slope, features a small reconstructed Miwok village and trails that snake uphill through gorgeous oak woods. Unfortunately, traffic noise from US 101 is pervasive in the state park—the open space preserve is quieter and offers more options for loops through oak savanna, with good wildflower displays in spring.

Begin from roadside parking and veer right, entering the preserve through either a V-shaped stile or cattle gate. A shortcut path heads to the right, but follow the access path straight, then begin uphill on San Andreas Fire Road. After 300 feet, San Marin Fire Road begins on the right near a huge coast live oak. Continue on San Andreas Fire Road, ascending past coast live oak and California bay at

▶ DIRECTIONS

Leave San Francisco northbound via the Golden Gate Bridge on US 101; use the Golden Bridge toll plaza as the mileage starting point. Drive north on US 101 20 miles, take the San Marin Drive/Atherton Avenue exit. Drive west on San Marin Drive 2.5 miles, turn right onto San Andreas Drive. Continue uphill for a half mile, then park on the right side of road near the open space gate.

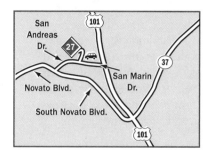

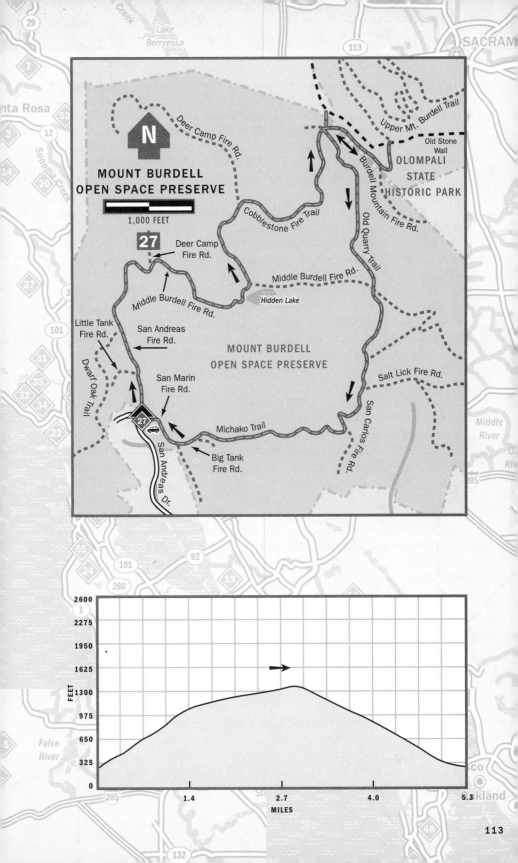

MOUNT BURDELL
OPEN SPACE PRESERVE

N

1,000 FEET

27

Deer Camp Fire Rd.

Deer Camp Fire Rd.

Cobblestone Fire Trail

Upper Mt. Burdell Trail

Old Stone Wall

OLOMPALI STATE HISTORIC PARK

Burdell Mountain Fire Rd.

Old Quarry Trail

Middle Burdell Fire Rd.

Hidden Lake

Middle Burdell Fire Rd.

Little Tank Fire Rd.

San Andreas Fire Rd.

Dwarf Oak Trail

San Marin Fire Rd.

27

MOUNT BURDELL
OPEN SPACE PRESERVE

Salt Lick Fire Rd.

San Carlos Fire Rd.

Michako Trail

Big Tank Fire Rd.

San Andreas Dr.

FEET

2600
2275
1950
1625
1300
975
650
325
0

1.4   2.7   4.0   5.3
MILES

a moderate clip. At 0.2 miles Little Tank Fire Road departs on the left—stick to San Andreas Fire Road and keep climbing. A few black oak and buckeye appear, and in late winter, look for a good display of Chinese houses on the left side of the trail. San Andreas Fire Road crests at the lip of a bowl-shaped valley at 0.4 miles.

The Dwarf Oak Trail heads back downhill on the left—stay to the right on San Andreas Fire Road, ignoring a dead-end fire road heading straight, leading to the park boundary. On an early April hike, the grass in this valley was completely overtaken by the yellow flowers of blooming johnnytuck and California buttercup. Two months later the grassy bowl and oak-dotted slopes ascending out of the valley were a sea of dry, blonde grass. San Andreas Fire Road curves right and ascends again, winding past mature valley oak, California bay, and buckeye, then ends at a fork at 0.7 miles. Deer Camp Fire Road to the left, is a longer option—continue straight, now on Middle Burdell Fire Road.

Bluedicks and popcorn flower bloom along the trail in early spring, preceding a June bonanza of clarkia and elegant brodiaea. Ascending easily, Middle Burdell Fire Road is mostly unshaded, although there is one grove of California bay, coast live oak, and buckeye. At 1.1 miles, you'll reach the edge of Hidden Lake, fenced to keep cows (and dogs) out of this sensitive habitat. In dry months the seasonal pond looks like a damp meadow, but in winter it does hold water. Cobblestone Fire Road begins at 1.2 miles. Turn left.

The fire road initially climbs at an easy to moderate grade, but there is one short, rocky, steeper stretch. Cobblestones were quarried from the upper slopes of Mount Burdell for San Francisco street construction, and as you progress uphill, the trails and hillsides get increasingly rocky. At 1.5 miles Deer Camp Fire Road enters from the left—stay to the right on Cobblestone Fire Road. The trail ascends through grassland, with buckeye, California bay, and oaks standing well back on sloping hillsides. In June, look for yellow mariposa lilies blooming along with California poppy, clarkia, and venus thistle. A rough path sweeps off to the right—supposedly a shortcut—but offers no relief from the climb, so stay to the left. A microwave relay structure is visible to the left, and off to the right, one of the old quarries is conspicuous. Cobblestone Fire Road levels out as it approaches the summit area, then ends at a multiple junction at 2.2 miles. A paved fire road heads west (left) to the microwave relay, and east to the park boundary. The Old Quarry Trail (this hike's return route) departs sharply to the right. Continue straight through the junction, uphill on an unmarked but obvious path.

This little trail ascends through grassland, but beware of a small poison oak shrub crowding the path on the left. The last stretch is very rocky, and the path crests at 2.3 miles at the park boundary, marked by an old stone wall. This rock fence and several others, all built without mortar, were constructed in the late 1800s by Chinese laborers. Return downhill to the paved fire road and turn left.

Burdell Mountain Fire Road keeps a level pace as it winds just downslope from the mountain's highest ridge. There's considerable, if distant, noise from US 101, visible downhill to the east. More scenic are views to Big Rock Ridge and Mount Tamalpais to the south. At 2.6 miles veer left onto an unsigned dirt road, which quickly leads to a fence and entry into Olompali State Park. On my last visit the "gate" was a stretch of barbed wire, looped around an old fencepost, so be careful not to cut your hands. As you enter the state park, a grassy hillside falls steeply to the east, revealing long views of the Petaluma River, upper San Pablo Bay, and the southern tip of the Sonoma Mountains. Two picnic tables here invite a lingering lunch. Follow the trail off to the left through a sparse, grassy forest of California bay to another stone wall crossing the trail at 2.8 miles. If you wanted to extend this hike, you could continue, winding downhill another 3.5 miles to the next junction. Today, retrace your steps back to the junction with Cobblestone Fire Road and the Old Quarry Trail at 3.2 miles. Turn left onto the Old Quarry Trail.

Descending through grassland, the slight path shifts from easy to steep near a pocket of sagebrush and sticky monkeyflower. Coast live oak, California bay, and buckeye nestle in a little creekbed on the right, as the trail descends into a mostly unshaded canyon. Steep grassy slopes on the left are scored with animal paths, and you may see deer browsing in this area of the park, where mule ear sunflowers are common in spring. After the steepest section, littered with loose rock, the Old Quarry Trail eases up in the middle of a California bay grove, then emerges into grassland. At 3.9 miles, the trail reaches a T junction with Middle Burdell Fire Road. Turn left.

After about 300 feet of level strolling, turn right onto the continuation of the Old Quarry Trail. The descent is steep, but less so than the previous segment, and not nearly as rocky. An expanse of grassland stretches off the sides of the trail, punctuated by oaks and buckeye. Just past a gate and stile, the Old Quarry Trail ends at San Carlos Fire Road. Turn right.

The fire road descends easily through coast live oaks, with summer displays of milk thistle. Salt Lick Fire Road sets off to the left at 4.2 miles—stay to the right on San Carlos Fire Road, following an arching curve downhill to the junction with the Michako Trail at 4.5 miles. Turn right.

Note the granary tree at this junction—drilled with holes and stuffed with acorns by birds. At a slight descent, the Michako Trail passes through another cattle gate, then skips across a small creek. In June, large patches of Davy's centaury, a pink flower, bloom in the drying grass, accompanied by sprinkles of elegant brodiaea. The trail forks at another creek crossing—the two legs rejoin shortly. At the 5-mile mark a fire road crosses the trail, leading left to a water tank. Follow the fire road to the right, or continue straight on the trail; the two routes meet at a junction at about 5.1 miles. Veer right, now on San Marin Fire Road.

The waxy, green rock exposed along the trail is serpentine, and this stretch of trail hosts a good display of native flowers in early spring. Nearing the preserve boundary, the trail bends right and descends, then levels out as it approaches the trailhead. Officially, San Marin Fire Road continues to its terminus at San Andreas Fire Road, but a well-worn path shortcuts the route to the left, leading to the entrance gate.

▶ **NEARBY ACTIVITIES**

Tour the east slope of Burdell Mountain from Olompali State Historic Park, accessed off of US 101. Visit the state park's website for more information (www.parks.ca.gov) or call the park at (415) 892-3383.

MOUNT DIABLO STATE PARK:
DONNER CANYON WATERFALL LOOP

▶ IN BRIEF

This hike on Mount Diablo's northeastern slopes is the perfect antidote to the winter doldrums. Spring seems to visit Donner Canyon very early, gracing the rugged hillsides with fresh grass and blooming wildflowers and shrubs, even in February. Choose a clear day after a series of storms and you'll likely see Donner Canyon's waterfalls sparkling in the sunlight.

▶ DESCRIPTION

Rugged Mount Diablo, where temperatures soar to uncomfortable heights in summer, seems an unlikely host to waterfalls. Most of our Bay Area cascades are tucked back in forested canyons, but these falls run out in the open, dropping down rocky, steep chaparral- and pine-covered hillsides. Although the falls in Donner Canyon aren't massive, they are pretty, and you can see them from several different perspectives along this loop. If you can arrange it, drop everything and head for this hike when snowfall accumulates on Diablo's peaks. The road that runs to the top of the mountain is usually closed then, but since snow rarely makes a dent on the lower reaches of

▶ DIRECTIONS

Depart San Francisco on the Bay Bridge and use the toll plaza as the mileage starting point. About one-half mile past the toll plaza, bear right onto I-580 East. Drive 1.5 miles, then exit onto CA 24. Drive east 12 miles on CA 24 to the I-680 split, then exit onto Ygnacio Valley Road. Travel east on Ygnacio Valley Road about 8 miles, and turn right onto Clayton Road. Drive south on Clayton Road (which becomes Marsh Creek Road in Clayton) about 3 miles, then turn right on Regency Road. Drive to the trailhead (simply park at the side of the road) at the end of the road.

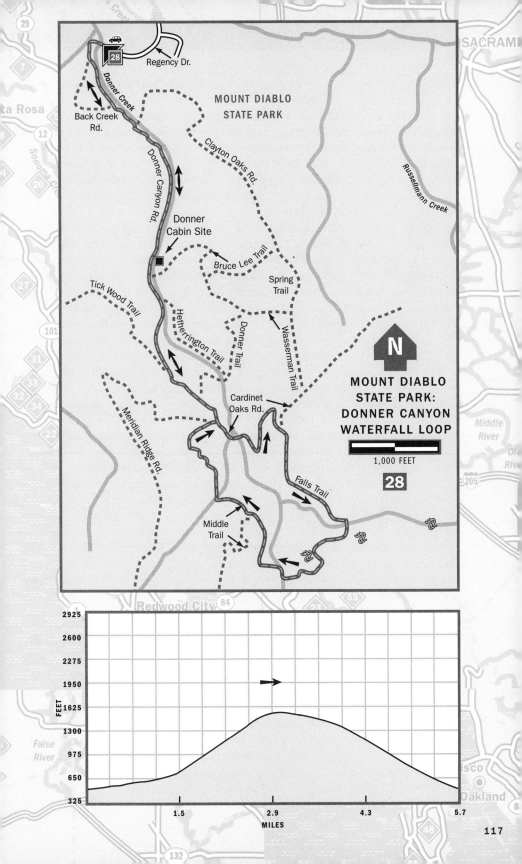

MOUNT DIABLO
STATE PARK

Regency Dr.

Back Creek
Rd.

Donner Creek

Donner Canyon Rd.

Clayton Oaks Rd.

Donner
Cabin Site

Bruce Lee Trail

Spring
Trail

Tick Wood Trail

Hetherington Trail

Donner Trail

Wasserman Trail

N

MOUNT DIABLO
STATE PARK:
DONNER CANYON
WATERFALL LOOP

1,000 FEET

28

Russelmann Creek

Cardinet
Oaks Rd.

Meridian Ridge Rd.

Falls Trail

Middle
Trail

FEET

2925
2600
2275
1950
1625
1300
975
650
325

1.5   2.9   4.3   5.7
MILES

Mount Diablo, you can enjoy views of dusted peaks without having to trudge through the snow.

The end of Regency Road serves as a bare bones trailhead for this hike. From the right side of the street, walk down a gated dirt fire road that ends at a T junction. Turn left. You'll soon reach the gated park boundary, and a junction. Stay to the left on Donner Canyon Road (you can choose either of two side-by-side paths—they converge down the trail). The fire road ascends just slightly, through grassland dotted with oaks and buckeye. At 0.3 miles a trail heads right toward Back Creek Road. Continue to the left on Donner Canyon Road.

Along Donner Creek there are good views uphill to Diablo's highest peaks. Paths split off to the left (crossing the creek) and right (a path not on the map) at 0.4 and 0.5 miles; ignore them and stick to the fire road. You may see buttercups along the trail in February, as well as fresh leaves on buckeye trees. At 0.9 miles a path breaks off to the left, heading to the Donner Cabin site, and a few steps later there's a junction with a path to the Tick Wood Trail (not on the map) on the right. You'll reach yet another junction just around the corner, this one with the Hetherington Loop Trail on the left. Continue straight each time on Donner Canyon Road.

The fire road begins to climb earnestly. After heavy rains the ascent through loose mud seems exaggerated as sticky clumps of mud cling to your boots. Trailside vegetation changes to include manzanita, yerba santa, ceanothus, poison oak, and pine. Shooting stars bloom in the understory in winter. There's another sequence of junctions from 1.1 to 1.3 miles. First the Tick Wood Trail veers right, then the Hetherington Loop Trail goes left. At each junction, keep going straight on Donner Canyon Road. Finally at 1.6 miles you will reach an intersection that matters—Cardinet Junction. A trail to the right sets off toward Meridian Point. Turn left onto Cardinet Oaks Road.

Revealing its true colors right away, the fire road descends somewhat steeply to cross Donner Creek. There is no bridge, so even though the creek is pretty small, when it's full you'll be forced to either get your feet wet or strip off your shoes and plunge through barefoot. When I made the crossing on one February hike the water was shockingly cold and rose up to my ankles. On the other side of the creek Cardinet Oaks Road starts to climb at a steep grade. Switchbacks offer little relief, so if you get winded take some time to stop and look around. There are still pines and chaparral plants along the trail, but patches of grass become more common as the trail ascends, and views back out of the canyon get better with each step. The junction with the Falls Trail is quite a welcome sight at 2.1 miles. Turn right.

This is where an already scenic hike becomes spectacular. The Falls Trail, just a little slip of a path, angles at a slight incline across a hillside of sagebrush, bush lupine, toyon, poison oak, pine, oaks, and grassland. The initial view of the waterfalls, even at a distance, is dramatic; water seems to appear out of thin air and gush out of creases in the hillside across the canyon. As you progress further along the rocky trail you'll have nice views uphill of several falls running down the side of steep Wild Oat Canyon. When the Falls Trail dips to cross the creek at Wild Oat Canyon, check out the broad but short waterfall just a few feet upstream. The trail ascends sharply but then returns to a more moderate grade. Ceanothus, cercocarpus, and pines are common along the path.

Here at the hike's highest elevation, look north for an ideal overview out of Donner Canyon and beyond. The trail descends to cross another creek, just below a small cascade (the water continues downhill to the last fall, but you have to get past it to see it). Climb uphill on the far side of the creek, then look back for my favorite view of the falls—a sheer, frothy drop that's breathtaking when the water flow is heavy. You'll cross one last creek and ascend a bit to a grassy area where hound's tongue blooms in late winter. At 3.6 miles, the Falls Trail ends at a signed junction. The Middle Trail heads uphill to the left, climbing steeply toward Prospector's Gap. Continue to the right on the Middle Trail toward Meridian Ridge Road.

The Middle Trail descends a little, through a thicket of manzanita, which fails to obscure views of the opposite side of the canyon and Mount Diablo's summit. You'll pass through an area with more dense vegetation, including toyon, chamise, and California bay, where chaparral currant blooms along the trail in February. After one last sunny stretch, the Middle Trail ends at 4 miles. Turn right onto Meridian Ridge Road.

Your time on this fire road is brief—less than 0.1 mile down the trail you'll return to Cardinet Junction. Turn left and return to the trailhead on Donner Canyon Road.

MOUNT DIABLO STATE PARK:
FIRE INTERPRETIVE TRAIL LOOP

KEY AT-A-GLANCE INFORMATION

LENGTH: 0.7 miles

CONFIGURATION: Loop

DIFFICULTY: Easy

SCENERY: Chaparral, grassland, views

EXPOSURE: First stretch shaded, the rest exposed

TRAFFIC: Light

TRAIL SURFACE: Initial section is paved and wheelchair accessible, the rest is a narrow dirt path.

HIKING TIME: 0.5 hours

SEASON: Any time of year is good, but the park is hot in summer. When snow dusts the mountain the road to the top is closed.

ACCESS: Pay $4 fee at the entrance kiosk on the way up the mountain.

MAPS: An interpretive guide is available at the trailhead; pick up the official park map at the entrance station or the summit museum (when open).

FACILITIES: Rest rooms at summit

IN BRIEF

The Fire Interpretive Trail offers perspective without perspiration. Less than a mile and at a nearly level grade, the trail makes a circuit just beneath Diablo's summit. The first section of the loop is paved and suitable to wheelchairs and strollers, but the remainder of the trail is a standard rocky mountain path.

DESCRIPTION

A drive to the top of Mount Diablo is a classic Bay Area day trip. A twisty scenic road leads to the mountain's highest peak, which is crowned with a stone observation tower and a little museum. On clear days, Diablo is famous for views that stretch across the San Joaquin Valley to snowcapped Sierra peaks. If you want to supplement a summit

DIRECTIONS

Depart San Francisco on the Bay Bridge and use the toll plaza as the mileage starting point. About one-half mile past the toll plaza, bear right onto I-580 East. Drive 1.5 miles, then exit at CA 24. Drive east 12 miles on CA 24, then exit southward onto I-680. Drive south 6.5 miles, then exit and turn left onto Diablo Road. Following the green "parks" signs, drive east on Diablo Road, which bends right at the junction with El Cerro, then turn left at the (stop sign) junction with Blackhawk onto Mount Diablo Scenic Boulevard. As you enter the park, the road becomes South Gate—drive carefully uphill on this narrow road (watch out for bicyclists) about 7 miles to a stop sign, then turn right onto Summit Road. Pause at the entrance station to pay the day-use fee, then continue all the way to the top. Just before the road splits into two one-way segments near the summit, park in a large paved lot on the right (or continue to the summit, then drive back down to this lot).

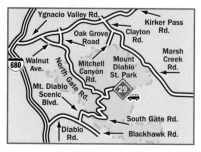

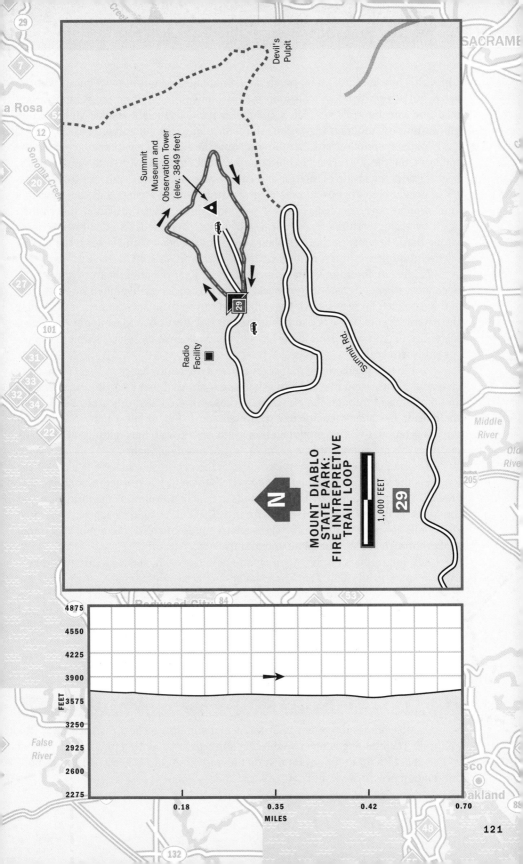

Devil's Pulpit

Summit
Museum and
Observation Tower
(elev. 3849 feet)

Radio
Facility

Summit Rd.

MOUNT DIABLO
STATE PARK:
FIRE INTREPRETIVE
TRAIL LOOP

N

1,000 FEET

29

FEET

4875
4550
4225
3900
3575
3250
2925
2600
2275

0.18   0.35   0.42   0.70

MILES

121

trip with a hike but don't have much time, or are hosting out-of-town guests who are active but not really hikers, this loop trail just down the hill from the summit is perfect. The Fire Interpretive Trail, a 0.7-mile circuit, features awesome views, a self-guided tour of mountain vegetation, and a fraction of the summit crowds.

Walking uphill toward the summit, along the side of the park road, come to the trailhead on the left. The Fire Interpretive Trail, marked with interpretive posts, begins under the shade of interior and canyon live oaks. Post 2 juts out from a cluster of poison oak. This deciduous plant is astoundingly variable, and can grow as a vine, ground cover, or hedge. Here it's a little shrub, naked in winter but clothed again by spring with distinctive "leaves of three." Poison oak's oil, urushiol, is so strong that when any part of the plant comes into contact with clothing, the oil can survive multiple washings, reinfecting the wearer with an itchy rash.

As the Fire Interpretive Trail progresses, you'll move out of the trees into a more open area, where greenstone, greywacke, and chert rocks are identified by Posts 3, 4, and 5. Look left for views north past Mitchell Canyon to Solano County. At 0.2 miles, the pavement ends at a wooden platform. This is a great place to whip out the binoculars. Even if you can't see Mount Lassen, there are great close-up views of Diablo's rugged North Peak.

As the trail bends right, you might notice a dramatic change in vegetation. Here chaparral plants, including ceanothus and cercocarpus, dominate with some live oaks and pines mixed through the evergreen shrubs. A fire ravaged this area in 1977, but the hillside has almost completely recovered and is for the most part covered with thick vegetation. I've seen mountain lion prints on the trail, but sightings of these shy creatures are not commonplace—cougars prowl mostly at night.

The trail crosses an open, rocky hillside, then approaches Devil's Pulpit on the left. This dusky red rock formation, comprised of chert, has resisted weathering that eroded the surrounding earth. Rough paths scramble downhill to the formation and the North Peak Trail, but the Fire Interpretive Trail curves right as sparsely vegetated slopes roll downhill to the south. The summit buildings are visible uphill as the trail snakes through yet another plant community.

Autumn regulars on the mountain are tarantulas, which emerge from their burrows to mate in the fall. The hairy spiders are relatively harmless; their bites are approximately as dangerous as wasp and bee stings. Even if you don't see them on the trails, you may spot a few crossing the park roads. Give them a wide berth and they will ignore you—they've got more important things on their arachnid minds! The last three posts mark juniper, yerba santa, and chamise, which crowd the trail along with some poison oak. At 0.7 miles the trail ends across the street from the trailhead. Turn left and walk back to the parking lot.

▶ NEARBY ACTIVITIES

Summit Museum/visitor center is at the actual summit, a short distance from this trailhead. The building is open Wednesday through Sunday, 10 a.m. to 4 p.m. in the winter, and 11 a.m. to 5 p.m. from spring to autumn. Call (925) 837-6119 for more information or visit www.mdia.org.

MOUNT DIABLO STATE PARK:
MITCHELL CREEK–EAGLE PEAK LOOP

▶ IN BRIEF

This creek to peak Diablo tour begins at Mitchell Canyon and climbs on fire roads, easily then steeply to Murchio Gap. Here the fun really begins on a rollicking single-track excursion over knife-edged Eagle Peak. From the exposed peak top, enjoy views of the park, then continue downhill at an often steep grade, back to the trailhead.

▶ DESCRIPTION

Mitchell Canyon is a popular staging area for long Diablo hikes. From here you can make an all-day excursion to Diablo's summit, a 14-mile round-trip from 590 to 3,849 feet and back again—one of the Bay Area's toughest day hikes. The trek to Eagle Peak does not have the same cache as the bottom-to-top hike, but I prefer the shorter loop. When the long trek to the top of Diablo nears the summit area, you'll commonly cross paths with loads of visitors around Juniper Campground and hear and see cars on a trail running parallel to Summit Road, jarring contrasts to the quiet found on most of the mountain. Eagle Peak is peaceful and lonely, far from the developed parts of the park, and provides excellent hiking with awesome views.

Begin from the trailhead on the signed Mitchell Canyon Trail. As you pass through the

▶ DIRECTIONS

Depart San Francisco on the Bay Bridge and use the toll plaza as the mileage starting point. About one-half mile past the toll plaza, bear right onto I-580 East. Drive 1.5 miles, then exit onto CA 24. Drive east about 12 miles on CA 24 to the I-680 split, then exit onto Ygnacio Valley Road. Travel east on Ygnacio Valley Road about 8 miles, and turn right onto Clayton Road. Drive south about 1 mile, then turn right onto Mitchell Canyon Road. Continue to the trailhead at the end of the road, about 1.5 miles.

ⓘ KEY AT-A-GLANCE INFORMATION

LENGTH: 7.8 miles

CONFIGURATION: Loop

DIFFICULTY: Strenuous

SCENERY: Chaparral, creek, views of the park from Eagle Peak

EXPOSURE: Almost all full sun

TRAFFIC: Moderate around the trailhead and on Mitchell Canyon Road, light farther afield

TRAIL SURFACE: Dirt fire roads and rocky trails

HIKING TIME: 5 hours

SEASON: Any time but summer; exceptional wildflowers in spring

ACCESS: Pay a $2 fee (self-register) at the entrance gate.

MAPS: Obtain the official park map, or better yet, the *Trail Map of Mount Diablo State Park and Adjacent Parklands*, published by Mount Diablo Interpretive Association, at the Mitchell Canyon Interpretive Center (open weekends). No maps are available when the Interpretive Center is closed.

FACILITIES: Rest rooms and drinking water available at the trailhead

SPECIAL COMMENTS: A trekking pole is handy for the Eagle Peak traverse. Check for ticks from late spring through autumn, when the grass is high. Dogs are not permitted.

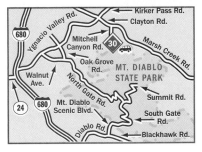

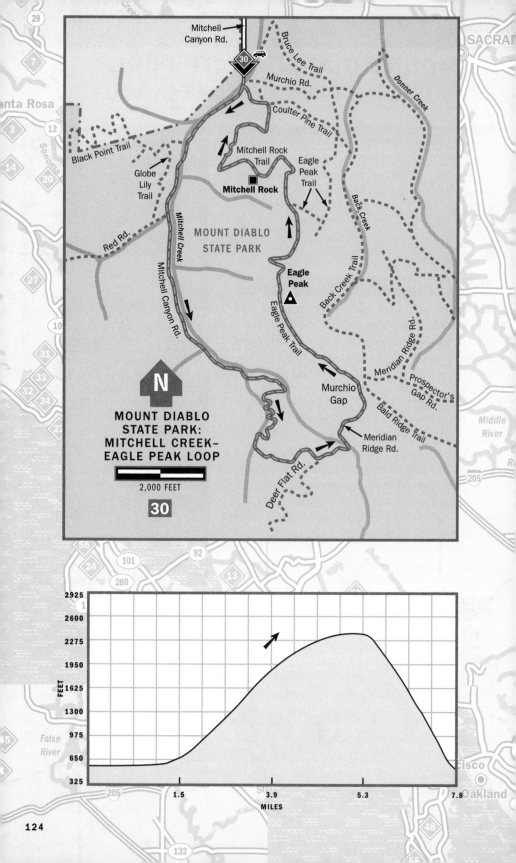

Mitchell
Canyon Rd.

30

Bruce Lee Trail

SACRA

Murchio Rd.

Donner Creek

Coulter Pine Trail

Mitchell Rock
Trail

Black Point Trail

Globe
Lily
Trail

Eagle
Peak
Trail

Mitchell Rock

Red Rd.

MOUNT DIABLO
STATE PARK

Back Creek

Mitchell Creek

**Eagle
Peak**

Back Creek Trail

Eagle Peak Trail

Mitchell Canyon Rd.

Meridian Ridge Rd.

Prospector's
Gap Rd.

Middle
River

205

N

Murchio
Gap

Bald Ridge Trail

MOUNT DIABLO
STATE PARK:
MITCHELL CREEK-
EAGLE PEAK LOOP

Meridian
Ridge Rd.

2,000 FEET

30

Deer Flat Rd.

Santa Rosa

55

24

101

280

92

13

False
River

FEET

2925				
2600				
2275				
1950				
1625				
1300				
975				
650				
325				

1.5   3.9   5.3   7.8

MILES

Oakland

cisco

205

124

gate, pick up the *Mitchell Canyon Trail Interpretive Guide,* an excellent accompaniment to the first 2 miles of this hike. The broad fire road starts out climbing gently through grassland dotted with blue, coast live, and valley oak. At 250 feet, Mitchell Rock Trail begins on the left, the return leg of this loop. Continue straight on Mitchell Canyon Trail. In spring you may see sticky monkeyflower, Chinese houses, paintbrush, and Ithuriel's spear in bloom along the trail, blended through a mixture of oaks, pines, and chaparral plants, including sagebrush, California coffeeberry, poison oak, and pitcher sage. At 0.6 miles, the Black Point Trail departs on the right. Continue on the Mitchell Canyon Trail, where the trail's namesake creek runs along the left side of the fire road, and pockets of riparian trees willow and alder are common. Swallowtails were out in abundance on my May hike, along with variable checkerspots and mylitta crescents, flitting to and fro. In spring look for Mount Diablo fairy lanterns, a yellow globe lily found only on and around Mount Diablo. On other Diablo hikes I had seen a few of these fairy lanterns, but all along the length of the Mitchell Canyon Trail I saw dozens and dozens of them, as well as staggering amounts of wind poppy, a beautiful four-petaled orange flower.

On the right, Red Road drops down from Black Point at 0.9 miles—once again, continue on the Mitchell Canyon Trail. As the canyon broadens slightly, views begin to unfold uphill to the left of rocky, steep-sided Eagle Peak. The fire road begins to climb with a bit more purpose, somewhat shaded by coast live oaks and a few big-leaf maple, buckeye, and California bay. At about the 2-mile mark the grade picks up significantly, and although there are some nearly level stretches, the climb is a long, sustained one. Stay alert for cyclists descending. On warm days every bit of shade and cooling breeze are welcome. With the creek left behind in the low reaches of the canyon, the surrounding slopes are dry, and host many chaparral plants, with coulter pine, sagebrush, ceanothus, goldenbush, cercocarpus, poison oak, toyon, sticky monkeyflower, and black sage prominent. There's plenty to look at along the trail, particularly in spring, when a variety of flowers bloom, including linanthus, paintbrush, lupines, onions, mule ear sunflower, and clarkia. Views continue to open up to Eagle Peak on the left, and out of the park back to the north.

The ascent, following a series of sweeping curves, seems never-ending, but abruptly the grade tapers off slightly, then the fire road sweeps right and reaches a flat on the right at 3.4 miles. Two picnic tables provide welcome rest spots. When you're ready, press on uphill at a moderate pace through oaks and pine to the Deer Flat junction at 3.5 miles. Deer Flat Road continues to climb toward the summit on the right, but our route, Meridian Ridge Road, swings left.

The fire road descends through oaks, pine, poison oak, and California hoptree, offering a break from all that climbing. The relief is short-lived though for once the trail crosses Deer Flat Creek it begins to ascend steeply. The Deer Flat Creek Trail (not shown on the map) slips off to the left at 3.8 miles, offering an alternate route to Murchio Gap. Continue on Meridian Ridge Road, ascending past a grassy slope on the right, where California poppies bloom in big patches in April. The trailside vegetation shifts to chaparral, with lots of yerba santa, manzanita, pine, and chaparral pea enjoying the sunny exposure. The climb ends at Murchio Gap at 4.2 miles, where trails depart in every direction: the Deer Flat Creek Trail doubles back to the left, and traveling clockwise, the Eagle Peak Trail begins next; then the Back Creek Trail, the continuation of Meridian Ridge Road; and the little Bald Ridge Trail, across the road to the right. Turn left onto the Eagle Peak Trail.

The slight path skirts a rock outcrop, climbing through ceanothus, chamise, yerba santa, black sage, goldenbush, and hoptree. As the Eagle Peak Trail starts to descend, loose rock on the path presents a challenge—if you've brought a trekking pole you'll definitely be glad. When you reach the saddle there's a brief level respite as the trail punches through thickets of chamise. Look to the left for a view of the Mitchell Canyon Trail's snaking uphill route, and back to the right for views of Diablo's summit area. As the trail begins to climb again, you'll enter a rocky and grassy area, where juniper and pine are common, and in early May, tons of clarkia, buckwheat, and jeweled onion brighten the grass as it begins to fade to gold. The ascent over these exposed slopes is sharp, with a couple of very rocky sections. Finally at 5 miles, you'll arrive at the top, 2,369 feet (unsigned, but obvious). There's remarkably little real estate here, and the peak slopes drop sharply off this knife-edge ridge. You'll surely want to pause and enjoy the views, which encompass the entire northern part of the mountain, including the summit and North Peak, as well as rolling ridges on the right and left, and hills well off into the distance. In winter, with strong binoculars you might be able to see the waterfalls dropping out of Donner Canyon. On my May hike I observed a horned lizard that scampered a few feet from me, almost perfectly camouflaged in the surrounding tan pebbles. Birdwatchers and butterfly enthusiasts could spend some time on this peak, watching hawks and swallowtail butterflies soaring or fluttering overhead.

The trail clings to the ridge top, then drops off to the left, beginning a descent. There are more steep rocky patches to traverse, as the Eagle Peak Trail swings through some shaded areas where you might notice currant blooming in winter. Mostly the hillsides are cloaked in an army-green coat of chamise, black sage, and toyon. Continuing down the sloping ridgeline, a second peaklet is crossed, and the trail just keeps dropping. At 5.9 miles the Eagle Peak Trail swings sharply right, descending off the east side of the mountain. Here, continue straight, now on the Mitchell Rock Trail.

The narrow path rises, then drops to the side of a red outcrop on the right. Some pine shade the trail as you make a transition into a mixture of grassland and chaparral. Look for a good variety of flowers in spring, including California poppy, coyote mint, butterfly mariposa lily, Chinese houses, paintbrush, milkweed, owl's clover, and blue-eyed grass. Although the trend is firmly downhill, there are a few short easy uphill stretches. The trail veers off the ridgeline into pure grassland, and other than a few forays through chaparral patches, stays that way all the way downhill. You'll pass Mitchell Rock, a pillow basalt outcrop, on the left. By mid-May, thigh-high grass crowds the trail as it weaves downhill, reaching a junction with the Coulter Pine Trail at 7.6 miles. Turn left, continuing on the Mitchell Rock Trail. After a few feet you'll reach a junction with a trail on the right leading to the Bruce Lee Trail. Continue straight on the Mitchell Rock Trail, and descend through blue oaks and grassland to a junction with the Mitchell Canyon Trail at 7.8 miles. Turn right and return to the trailhead.

MOUNT TAMALPAIS: PHOENIX LAKE

▶ IN BRIEF

How do I love thee? Let me count the trails . . . Mount Tamalpais has many trailheads and a lifetime's worth of paths. The options for hikes from here are staggering, and you can't really take a wrong step, but this gorgeous route through woods and grassland, with great views to Tam's summit, thrills me each time.

▶ DESCRIPTION

This northwestern flank of Mount Tam is Marin Municipal Water District land, preserved for the primary purpose of providing domestic water supply to Marin County. The hiker's benefit is a network of many trails and fire roads that connect to Mount Tamalpais State Park and a few small Marin County Open Space District preserves. I've loved this hike from my first visit, and it's a particularly good choice for late winter and spring, when wildflowers bloom everywhere.

From the parking lot, begin walking uphill on a broad fire road. This trail provides access to many destinations farther up the mountain and is heavily used by cyclists and runners. At an easy grade, the trail ascends through a mixed woodland of madrone, coast live oak, buckeye, California bay, and one unpopular non-native plant called broom. Early spring flowers include California

▶ KEY AT-A-GLANCE INFORMATION

LENGTH: 4.9 miles

CONFIGURATION: Balloon

DIFFICULTY: Easy

SCENERY: Grassland, woods, lake

EXPOSURE: Nearly equal parts shade and sun

TRAFFIC: Moderate weekdays, busy weekends

TRAIL SURFACE: Dirt fire roads and trails

HIKING TIME: 2.5 hours

SEASON: Good any time, although trails are muddy in winter

ACCESS: No fee. The dirt road to the parking lot, in Natalie Green Park, is often closed to vehicles after heavy winter storms. In that case, parking is restricted to a very few side-of-the-road spots along Lagunitas Road, 1 mile from the parking lot, near the junction with Glenwood. Mind the "no parking" signs.

MAPS: *A Rambler's Guide to the Trails of Mount Tamalpais and the Marin Headlands,* published by The Olmsted & Bros. Map Co., and *Mount Tam Trail Map,* by Tom Harrison Maps; no maps available at the trailhead

FACILITIES: Pit toilets at the trailhead and at Phoenix Lake

SPECIAL COMMENTS: Dogs permitted

▶ DIRECTIONS

Leave San Francisco via the Golden Gate Bridge on northbound US 101 and use the Golden Bridge toll plaza as the mileage starting point. Drive north on US 101 about 11 miles, then exit Sir Francis Drake/San Anselmo. Drive west on Sir Francis Drake about 3.5 miles to the intersection with Lagunitas Road (at the Marin Art and Garden Center), turn left onto Lagunitas, and drive about 1 mile to the parking lot at the end of the road.

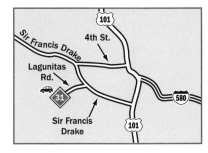

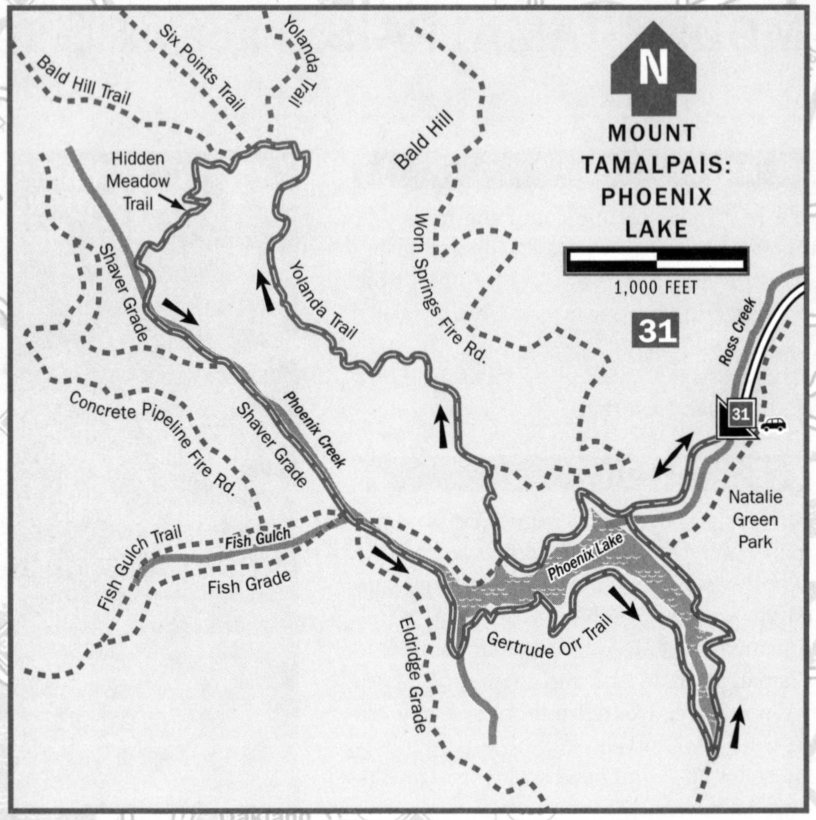

MOUNT TAMALPAIS: PHOENIX LAKE
1,000 FEET
31
Six Points Trail
Yolanda Trail
Bald Hill Trail
Bald Hill
Hidden Meadow Trail
Shaver Grade
Yolanda Trail
Worn Springs Fire Rd.
Ross Creek
31
Phoenix Creek
Shaver Grade
Concrete Pipeline Fire Rd.
Natalie Green Park
Phoenix Lake
Fish Gulch Trail
Fish Gulch
Fish Grade
Gertrude Orr Trail
Eldridge Grade

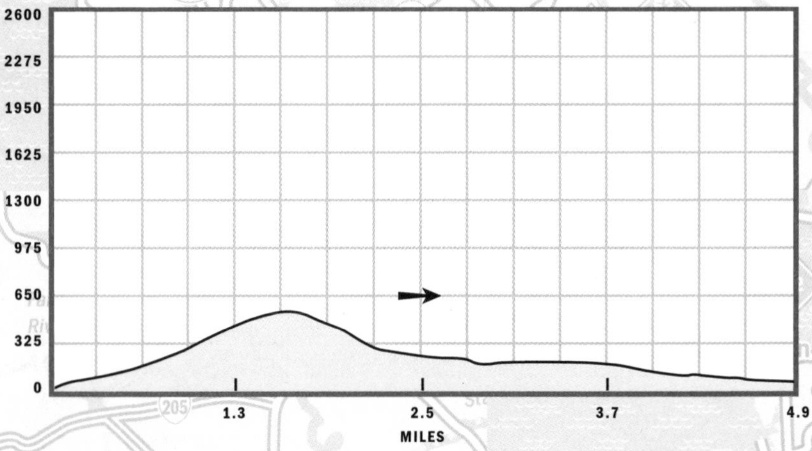

2600
2275
1950
1625
1300
975
650
325
0
1.3
2.5
3.7
4.9
MILES

buttercups, milkmaids, and Welsh onion (another non-native). In winter months, the water rushing downhill from Phoenix Lake is a melodious accompaniment. The fire road passes the spillway and crests at 0.3 miles. Another fire road heads off to the left; this is the return route for the hike, so continue straight. After one last little hill, the fire road levels out. On the left, Phoenix Lake stretches its arms into the creases of a wooded canyon. Mature buckeye, black oak, coast live oak, and California bay provide partial shade but still permit views to the lake. The Worn Springs Fire Road departs from a small cluster of redwood on the right at 0.4 miles, offering a steep route to Bald Hill. Continue on the tour around Phoenix Lake to the next junction, at 0.6 miles, then turn right onto the Yolanda Trail. This diminutive trail begins to climb at a moderate grade along a creekbed, through madrone, black oak, coast live oak, and California bay. Wildflowers emerge in these woods as early as January, when you might see hound's tongue, milkmaids, and shoot-

Redwoods nestle in the creases of Phoenix Lake along the Gertrude Orr Trail.

ing stars. In early spring, bluedicks, buttercups, and irises are common. Yolanda crosses the creek and winds uphill into a more grassy area, somewhat overgrown with a young forest of broom. On a morning hike here I got a little wake-up jolt when a jackrabbit came barreling down the trail toward me.

At 0.7 miles, after you pass a spur path signed only with a "no horses" symbol, the trail levels out for a few feet in a saddle between two hills, then skirts a knoll and begins a slight ascent across the flanks of Bald Hill to the right. Little pockets of shaded California bay, coast live oak, buckeye, and madrone are interspersed with long sunny stretches through grassy chaparral, with chamise, sticky monkeyflower, sagebrush, toyon, and coyote brush enjoying the western exposure.

After rainstorms in winter, mini waterfalls gush down the slopes of Bald Hill at nearly every little fold in the hillside. A March or April hike on this stretch of the Yolanda Trail is usually a very good place for wildflower viewing. On early spring visits I've seen larkspur, bluedicks, shooting stars, paintbrush, popcorn flower, California poppy, blue and white lupine, and blue-eyed grass. During those soft days of late spring, grassy knolls, which extend off the trail on the left, invite a sunny snooze.

Continuing, as the trail travels northwest, there are unobstructed views of Tam's summit ridgeline. The Yolanda Trail then descends a bit through cool woods where a pint-sized waterfall flows well into summer. It's such a spectacular journey that I always feel a little sad to reach Six Points Junction at 1.9 miles. The Yolanda Trail continues to the right. Then, moving counterclockwise, there's the Six Points Trail, the Bald Hill Trail, and the Hidden Meadow Trail. Take Hidden Meadow Trail to the left. As the trail starts to descend through oaks and then grassland, the panorama revealed on the left side of the trail is one of my favorite Tam vistas. From Bald Hill to East Peak and everything in between, it's all beautiful. After a foray through grassland, the trail descends into a mixed woodland, where broom is the dominant understory plant (a bunch of it has been manually uprooted, but there's still plenty). A few short, tight switchbacks descend to cross a creek as it enters Hidden Meadow, a small level grassy shelf running between a creek and an ascending hillside. A forest of buckeye, California bay, and oaks surround the meadow, and the trail winds among a few large oaks and buckeyes. Great colonies of hound's tongue linger at the fringes of the meadow in late winter.

The trail crosses another creek, then turns to accompany the water flow toward Phoenix Lake. Some young redwoods are mixed through the forest. At 2.6 miles the Hidden Meadow Trail ends at a junction with Shaver Grade. Here, turn left onto the fire road. The fire road follows Phoenix Creek at an easy downhill grade. Be alert for bicycle traffic along this well-traveled route. The surrounding forest, where I've heard turkeys yodeling back and forth, is mostly California bay, redwood, madrone, big-leaf maple, and buckeye. At 3 miles, Shaver Grade ends at a multiple junction. Fish Grade and Fish Gulch climb off to the near right, and Eldridge Grade sets off to the far right. Continue straight, then after about 300 feet, veer off to the right onto the Gertrude Orr Trail (signed with generic water district "hiking only" symbols but not named at this junction). Tall hazelnut shrub tower above the trail, welcoming visitors into a redwood forest. The trail follows Phoenix Creek for about 150 feet, then reaches a junction just before a bridge. Turn right and cross the creek. The Gertrude Orr Trail runs along Phoenix Creek, which soon empties into the lake. Redwoods are common in the fingerlike extensions of the lake, accompanying ferns, hazelnut, creambush, and trilliums and milkmaids that bloom in early spring. In slightly sunnier stretches uphill from the shoreline, you might notice madrone, California bay, coast live oak, big-leaf maple, and black oak. The trail alternates level sections with some undulating areas where steps keep the path stable. Just past an area heavily colonized by tanoak, the trail rises, drops on a graceful flight of curving stairs, and then ends at 4.1 miles. The Bill Williams Trail heads deeper into the mountain, to the right. Turn left onto a fire road. This broad fire road ascends at a barely noticeable rate, along the eastern shore of Phoenix Lake. On the right, look for a short but pretty waterfall, active during the rainy season with redwood, big-leaf maple, madrone, and California bay lining the trail. At 4.2 miles, The Harry Allen Trail sets off on the right, but continue on the fire road. Blossoms on broom and ceanothus shrubs through here draw hoards of bees in early spring, filling the air with a drowsy buzzing sound. A bench a short distance off the trail to the left is a good spot to enjoying views stretching across the lake to the crest of Bald Hill.

The fire road levels out above the dam, and a path leading back to Lagunitas Road departs on the right at 4.5 miles. The shallows off to the left of the trail host many somewhat-tame ducks that often waddle over to quack for snacks along the shoreline. At 4.6 miles you'll return to a familiar junction, above the spillway. Turn right and walk back downhill on the fire road.

▶ NEARBY ACTIVITIES

Natalie Green Park, just off the parking lot, hosts some picnic tables and pretty creekside scenery.

MOUNT TAMALPAIS STATE PARK:
MATT DAVIS AND STEEP RAVINE LOOP

▶ IN BRIEF

This loop really showcases the best the Bay Area offers to hikers. While there are many other parks with more of a wilderness vibe, Mount Tamalpais is a short drive from many parts of the north and east bay, and San Francisco residents flock to the mountain, particularly on sunny weekends in spring.

▶ DESCRIPTION

In the heart of summer weekends there are so many visitors on the trails around Mount Tamalpais, Pantoll area that you might feel like a pint of blood trying to squeeze through a clogged artery. Travel is sluggish, particularly on the Steep Ravine Trail, a narrow route that doesn't tolerate crowds well. Try to plan this hike for a weekday or early in the day during off-season. The best possible time may be the thin overlap between late winter and early spring, particularly if it's been a wet winter. During that window wildflowers bloom everywhere, and the waterfalls are plump with runoff.

The Steep Ravine Trail departs from a signed trailhead at the southern edge of the parking lot. The sign warns of a 10-foot ladder, an unusual trail element, but if you are up for a 7-mile hike, descending on a little ladder shouldn't scare you.

▶ DIRECTIONS

Leave San Francisco on northbound US 101 and use the Golden Gate Bridge toll plaza as the mileage starting point. Drive north on US 101 about 5.5 miles, then exit at CA 1/Mill Valley/Stinson Beach and drive on Shoreline Highway to the junction with Almonte (look for the CA 1 sign) for about 1 mile. Turn left on CA 1 and drive about 2.5 miles to the junction with Panoramic Highway. Turn right on Panoramic and drive about 5.5 miles to the junction with Pantoll Road. With caution, turn left into the parking lot.

ⓘ KEY AT-A-GLANCE INFORMATION

LENGTH: 7.3 miles

CONFIGURATION: Loop

DIFFICULTY: Moderate

SCENERY: Grassland, woods, and waterfalls

EXPOSURE: Equal parts sun and shade

TRAFFIC: Moderate, heavy on the trails near Pantoll Ranger Station

TRAIL SURFACE: Dirt fire road and trails

HIKING TIME: 4 hours

SEASON: Good any time; late winter (for waterfalls) and spring (for flowers) are best

ACCESS: Pay $4 fee at ranger station.

MAPS: The official park map is available at the ranger station (when open). Another choice is *A Rambler's Guide to the Trails of Mount Tamalpais and the Marin Headlands*, published by The Olmsted & Bros. Map Co.

FACILITIES: Rest rooms and drinking water at trailhead

SPECIAL COMMENTS: This trailhead packs 'em in, particularly during the summer tourist season, so arrive early. If you don't want to tote a lot of stuff with you, plan for a lunch break in Stinson Beach, where you can either eat in a cafe or pick up lunch supplies. Dogs are not permitted.

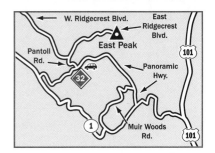

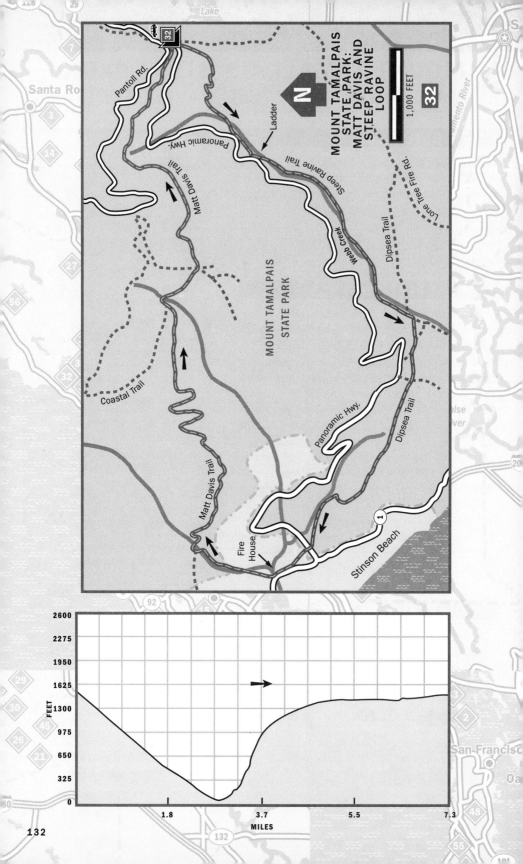

MOUNT TAMALPAIS
STATE PARK:
MATT DAVIS AND
STEEP RAVINE
LOOP

32

N

1,000 FEET

Ladder

Pantoll Rd.

Panoramic Hwy.

Matt Davis Trail

Coastal Trail

Steep Ravine Trail

Webb Creek

Dipsea Trail

Lone Tree Fire Rd.

MOUNT TAMALPAIS
STATE PARK

Panoramic Hwy.

Matt Davis Trail

Fire
House

Dipsea Trail

Stinson Beach

1

2600

2275

1950

1625

1300

975

650

325

0

FEET

1.8   3.7   5.5   7.3

MILES

Without any prelude, the narrow trail begins to drop into a canyon. After a few switchbacks across a steep hillside, the Steep Ravine Trail hooks up with Webb Creek and follows the stream as it makes its way through a lush forest of redwood, California bay, ferns, tanoak, and Douglas fir. Little bridges channel hikers back and forth across the creek a few times along the route.

Spring wildflowers here include plants that adore moist environments, like trillium, coast fairy bells, and stream violets. At 0.8 miles, you'll reach the ladder. The wood can be slippery, so take it slow—I prefer descending it facing the ladder, rather than facing out. The little waterfall running beside the ladder, one of a couple along the trail, burbles with a soothing sound. Below the ladder, trailside vegetation seems to become even more lush. Redwoods uprooted or snapped off by winter storms lie across the trail and in the streambed in places; one tree is notched for passage. At 1.7 miles, the first of two junctions with the Dipsea Trail departs on the left. Continue straight another 0.1 mile, then bear right, following the sign toward Stinson Beach. As the Dipsea Trail begins a slight climb, a connector back to Steep Ravine veers to the left, but you keep going straight. The narrow trail climbs through some young Douglas fir and toyon, then reaches a junction where you'll continue straight and emerge at the edge of a meadow and another junction with a fire road. Cross the fire road, remaining on Dipsea and watch as incredible views unfold to the north! On a clear day you'll see Stinson Beach, Bolinas Lagoon, and the forested hills of the Point Reyes peninsula.

While it's hard to top the enchantment of Steep Ravine, a spring hike through here boasts verdant grass and pockets of California poppy, checkerblooms, and blue and white lupine. The Dipsea Trail descends steadily, through a little coastal scrub and then a pocket of woods stretching along a creek. Gnarled moss-covered buckeyes are the star here, although California bays are more common. At 2.9 miles Dipsea reaches Panoramic Highway. Carefully cross the road and pick up the trail on the other side.

Descending toward the town of Stinson Beach, traffic and neighborhood noise is abundant. At 3 miles, where the Dipsea Trail meets CA 1, you can add an optional out-and-back to this hike by continuing across the highway, and walking on city streets to the Dipsea Trail's terminus at the beach. Otherwise, carefully turn right and walk along the side of CA 1 (the other side of the street may be a better alternative, but you'll have to cross the road twice—if you're looking for lunch or a store to buy water, walk past the fire house to Stinson's commercial district). After less than 0.1 mile, turn right, at the fire house, onto Belvedere Avenue. Walk up this street and, just past the "wrong way" sign, turn right onto the signed Matt Davis Trail.

Back in the woods, this narrow trail winds uphill. When you reach an unsigned T junction, turn left, then cross a creek and at a second junction, bear right. This is the last junction for the next 2.3 miles. Sounds of town life fade away as the trail rises through a forest of buckeye and California bay. A bridge crosses a descending stream with less gush than Webb Creek, but the setting is incredibly pretty, year-round.

After a set of steps and a switchback, the Matt Davis Trail bisects a patch of chaparral. Glancing over purple-flowered lupine bushes, already there are views to the ocean. The sunny interlude is short, and soon you'll ascend through a shaded woodland. The trail climbs relentlessly, but at a moderate pace. Just past another bridge a long series of steps may be the toughest stretch of the trail, especially if you have short legs.

With Table Rock Creek tumbling downhill on the left, the trail skirts a huge boulder. California bays mix through a forest of massive Douglas firs, and ferns are a perennial star of the understory, with trilliums, iris, forget-me-nots, and milkmaids making special appearances in spring. Still ascending, negotiate a few broad switchbacks and then step out of the woods into grassland. The transition is startling, particularly in late winter, when the grass is so green it practically throbs with life.

The Matt Davis Trail ascends gently downslope from the ridgeline, through grassland and little pockets of trees that linger in hillside creases. Framed by tall Douglas firs, views west take in the ocean. In late winter and spring, peruse the sides of the trail for blue-eyed grass, California buttercups, California poppy, and bluedicks. At 5.7 miles, the Coastal Trail swings off to the left, from a signed junction. Bear right to remain on the Matt Davis Trail.

With the worst of the climbing behind you, this next segment is a pleasurable stroll at a gentle incline across the sloping grassy hillside. Bypass two quick junctions, the first with an ascending trail and the second with a descending trail, and continue straight, following the symbols for the Bay Area Ridge Trail. Prepare for some more sweeping views, this time south, extending past the Headlands to San Francisco and the San Mateo County coast. You may also be able to spot Northern harriers hunting from overhead.

Follow the Matt Davis Trail, leaving the grassland for woods once more. Dense stands of California bay, redwood, Douglas fir, and live oaks filter the sun, creating shade that sustains a little flower favored by native plant enthusiasts, the Calypso orchid. I saw dozens of the delicate purple flower along the trail on one late March hike, along with red larkspur, hound's tongue, and milkmaids.

The trail's elevation remains nearly level through here and, although trees block any views, they fail to screen the sound of traffic on Pantoll Road, just uphill to the left. You probably will cross paths with a steady flow of hikers on this part of the trail, a signal that the trailhead is growing closer with each step. Pass through an open rocky area marked with soaring Douglas firs, where ceanothus and chamise line the trail. The Matt Davis Trail breaks off to the left, continuing toward Mountain Home Inn. Here, bear right, descend a few steps, and carefully cross the street to the Pantoll parking lot.

MOUNT TAMALPAIS STATE PARK:
MOUNTAIN HOME TO MUIR WOODS LOOP

▶ IN BRIEF

This hike starts from a parking lot across from Mountain Home Inn, descends on a paved service road, then winds through woods on a narrow footpath. At Van Wyck Meadow, you'll begin a steep descent following creeks into Redwood Canyon and Muir Woods, where you'll mingle with the crowds on the park's main trail. After only 0.3 miles, the hike veers off into Fern Canyon and relative solitude. A long set of steps ascends through woods into grassland and a nearly level path makes for a quick return to the trailhead.

▶ DESCRIPTION

Steep-sloped Redwood Canyon escaped the flying axes of the Bay Area's gold rush boom and today preserves some of the oldest and most majestic redwoods in the Bay Area. To prevent logging, William Kent began buying canyon property in 1905, then donated the land to the federal government for protection. The woods became a national monument in 1908, named in honor of conservationist John Muir. Although Muir Woods proper is quite small, the land is surrounded by Mount Tamalpais State Park and Golden Gate National Recreation Area property, forming a

▶ DIRECTIONS

Leave San Francisco on northbound US 101 and use the Golden Gate Bridge toll plaza as the mileage starting point. Drive north on US 101 about 5.5 miles, then exit onto CA 1/Mill Valley/Stinson Beach and drive on Shoreline Highway to the junction with Almonte (look for the CA 1 sign), about 1 mile. Turn left and drive about 2.5 miles on CA 1 to the junction with Panoramic Highway. Turn right on Panoramic Highway and drive about 2.5 miles to a large parking lot on the left side of the road, across from Mountain Home Inn.

ℹ KEY AT-A-GLANCE INFORMATION

LENGTH: 4.7 miles

CONFIGURATION: Loop

DIFFICULTY: Moderate

SCENERY: Redwoods, forested canyon, and creeks

EXPOSURE: Mostly shaded

TRAFFIC: Moderate around trailhead, very heavy in the heart of Muir Woods

TRAIL SURFACE: Two short paved sections, dirt trails, and lots of steps on the Lost Trail

HIKING TIME: 3 hours

SEASON: Any time is good, but summer is the busy season; autumn is gorgeous.

ACCESS: No fee at this trailhead; entrance to the main Muir Woods trailhead requires a fee

MAPS: There are two outstanding maps to the area: *A Rambler's Guide to the Trails of Mount Tamalpais and the Marin Headlands*, published by The Olmsted & Bros. Map Co., and *Mount Tam Trail Map*, published by Tom Harrison Maps. No maps are available at the trailhead.

FACILITIES: Vault toilets and drinking water are available at the trailhead.

SPECIAL COMMENTS: Dogs are not permitted. Arrive very early for parking in summer.

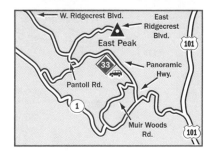

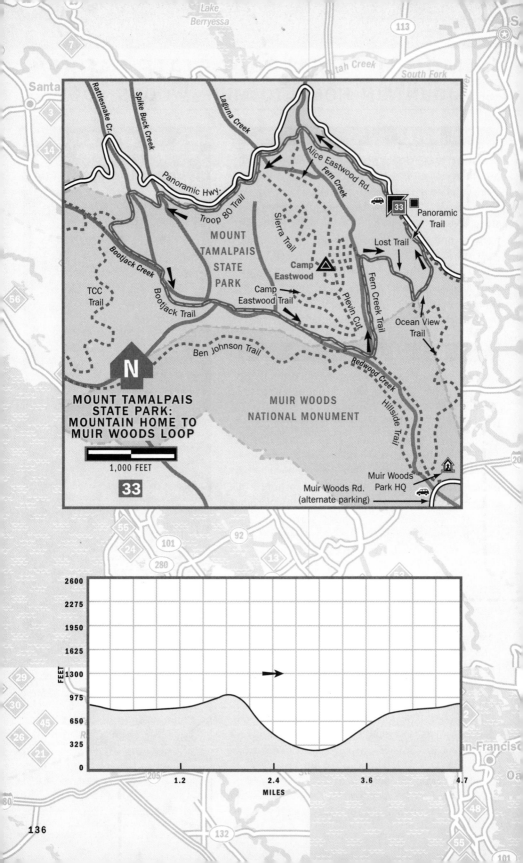

MOUNT TAMALPAIS
STATE PARK:
MOUNTAIN HOME TO
MUIR WOODS LOOP

1,000 FEET

33

huge greenbelt of protected redwood canyons, creeks, coastal grassland, and mixed woodland that stretches from the Golden Gate Bridge to the northern flanks of Mount Tam.

Whether you're a Bay Area visitor or a permanent resident, a trip to Muir Woods is mandatory—everyone should visit this awesome redwood monument at least once. With so many people pouring into one small canyon, Muir Woods always seems crowded, but there are ways to tour the park and still have a few quiet moments; this hike makes the most of an alternate trailhead.

Begin at the north end of the parking lot on the Trestle Trail, entering Mount Tamalpais State Park. This little path drops down a flight of steps, then ends at Camp Eastwood Road. Turn right. Descending easily, the paved road, which accesses a group camp, winds through sundrenched slopes where bush poppy and chaparral pea bloom in spring. Broom, chamise, toyon, and manzanita are common, but as the trail drops into a cool canyon redwood, California bay, and Douglas fir take over. At 0.4 miles where the road crosses Fern Creek and swings left, turn right onto the Troop 80 Trail.

The narrow trail, built by Boy Scouts in 1931, ascends along Fern Creek, then veers left and climbs at an easy pace. Redwoods, Douglas fir, and tanoak completely shade the trail, and one pocket of young redwoods is so densely packed that there is virtually no understory. At 0.8 miles the Sierra Trail heads downhill on the left. Continue straight on the Troop 80 Trail. Running downslope from Panoramic Highway, the forest screens views of the road, but traffic noise is steady, especially on summer weekends. The Troop 80 Trail crosses creeks and damp seeps on a series of pretty bridges, winding through huckleberry patches, woods, and occasional sunny stretches of chaparral, where you might see pitcher sage and chaparral pea in bloom in spring, accompanying manzanita, coffeeberry, and chinquapin. There are occasional views south, encompassing forested hillsides rising from Redwood Canyon.

The trail forks at 1.7 miles, with the path on the right heading to the Bootjack trailhead. Continue straight another tenth of a mile, through a display of false lupine (in spring) to Van Wyck Meadow. Meadow is a big word for the little grassy spot, but everyone seems to get a kick out of the misspelled sign that reads "Van Wyck Meadow pop. 3 Stellar Jays." The meadow is a good place for a short rest before continuing into the canyon. When you're ready, head downhill to the left, on the Bootjack Trail.

Stone steps begin the descent, dropping the narrow trail to the side of Bootjack Creek. Redwoods tower overhead, mixed through a lush forest of Douglas fir and tanoak, with ferns in the understory. Look for trilliums and starflower blooming in spring. Some sections are nearly level, but the overall trend is quite steep and somewhat rocky in areas. Deer are common in this quiet part of the park, and you might see them clinging to the steeply sloped canyon walls like mountain goats, calmly munching vegetation. Bootjack Creek joins Rattlesnake Creek, plumping the stream with added water, which cascades merrily downhill.

As the Bootjack Trail progresses down into the canyon, you may notice big-leaf maple, and elk clover and thimbleberry in the creekbed. The trail sweeps left and crosses a confluence of streams on a curving bridge, supported in the middle by a large boulder. Still following the creek, the grade slackens to a slight descent. At 3 miles a path breaks off on the left, on the way to Camp Eastwood. Continue straight, following the sign toward Muir Woods. Trail traffic picks up, and increases to a fever pitch as the Bootjack Trail leaves the state park and ends at 3.1 miles at the main Muir Woods trail. Stay to the left, on the wide paved path, as it meanders beneath huge redwoods on the canyon floor. A trail to Camp Eastwood bends left at 3.2 miles, but continue a bit further, to the signed junction with the Fern Creek Trail. Turn left.

With a course along the banks of Fern Creek, the trail gets quieter with every step, weaving slightly uphill through redwoods and ferns, with redwood sorrel a common understory plant. At 3.6 miles you'll reach a junction with a trail to the left leading to Camp Eastwood. Turn right onto the Lost Trail.

The trail starts out on an easy grade, ascending out of the canyon, but the climb soon stiffens. On a long sequence of steps you might come to the conclusion that the Lost Breath Trail would be a more appropriate name for this route. Redwoods give way to live oaks, Douglas fir, and California bay, then the Lost Trail ends at 4.1 miles. Turn left onto the Ocean View Trail.

Now keeping to an easy uphill grade, the Ocean View Trail departs the wooded canyon and emerges in grassland just below Panoramic Highway. There are views north to Tam's peaks, and west toward the Pacific, though the only ocean I've ever seen here is a sea of trees. Stay to the left near a boulder, and when the Ocean View Trail ends at 4.4 miles, turn left onto the Panoramic Trail.

The nearly level trail winds through grassland dotted with broom and acacia, two non-native plants, and coyote brush, one of the most common native shrubs in the Bay Area. Lizards scamper along the path in summer. At 4.6 miles the Panoramic Trail ends at the top of Camp Eastwood Road. You can return to the parking lot down Camp Eastwood Road to the Trestle Trail, or by simply walking the less than 0.1 mile along the side of Panoramic Highway to the left.

▶ NEARBY ACTIVITIES

Instead of visiting Redwood Canyon and Muir Woods, you can begin at this trailhead and hike to the top of Mount Tam, via easily graded fire roads that follow the route of an old railroad. Gravity Car Grade begins across the street from the parking lot, and Old Railroad Grade makes the final push to the top, although you can take alternate routes on several minor footpaths.

MOUNT TAMALPAIS STATE PARK:
ROCK SPRING AND POTRERO MEADOWS LOOP

 IN BRIEF

One of the most compelling assets of Mount Tamalpais is the broad variety of possible hikes. Like a San Francisco burrito, you can have your hike hot or mild, small or grande, just with rice and beans, or with "the works." This 5.2 mile loop is one of the mountain's wildest, with only three short segments on fire roads and the rest on trails. Some of these paths are well marked and easy to follow, while others are secondary trails, with ambiguous routings. All have rocky sections that provide a bit more scrambling than the average trail.

 DESCRIPTION

This entire loop is a tour de force of the mountain's magic: you'll see stands of redwoods, dense forests of madrone and Douglas fir, chaparral, rushing creeks, and meadows. In fact the hike begins at a meadow, on the edge of the Rock Spring trailhead. Follow the trail signs toward the Cataract Trail, then after 0.1 mile, bear right onto the Benstein Trail. This little path skips across a creek, then ascends slightly through grassland where blue and white lupines bloom in May.

DIRECTIONS

Leave San Francisco on northbound US 101 and use the Golden Gate Bridge toll plaza as the mileage starting point. Drive north on US 101 about 5.5 miles, then exit at CA 1/Mill Valley/Stinson Beach and drive on Shoreline Highway to the junction with Almonte (look for the CA 1 sign), about 1 mile. Turn left and drive on CA 1 about 2.5 miles to the junction with Panoramic Highway. Turn right on Panoramic and drive about 5.5 miles to the junction with Pantoll Road. Turn right onto Pantoll and drive another 1.5 miles to the Rock Spring Trailhead, which is at the junction of East and West Ridgecrest Boulevards.

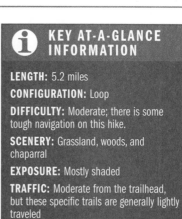

KEY AT-A-GLANCE INFORMATION

LENGTH: 5.2 miles

CONFIGURATION: Loop

DIFFICULTY: Moderate; there is some tough navigation on this hike.

SCENERY: Grassland, woods, and chaparral

EXPOSURE: Mostly shaded

TRAFFIC: Moderate from the trailhead, but these specific trails are generally lightly traveled

TRAIL SURFACE: Dirt fire road and trails

HIKING TIME: 3 hours

SEASON: Muddy after heavy rains; good in late winter for waterfalls and blooming manzanitas and in spring for flowers

ACCESS: No fee; Pantoll Gate is locked at sunset

MAPS: The official park map is available at the Pantoll Ranger Station (when staffed). A better choice is *A Rambler's Guide to the Trails of Mount Tamalpais and the Marin Headlands*, published by The Olmsted & Bros. Map Co.

FACILITIES: Pit toilets at trailhead

SPECIAL COMMENTS: Dogs are not permitted.

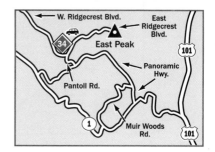

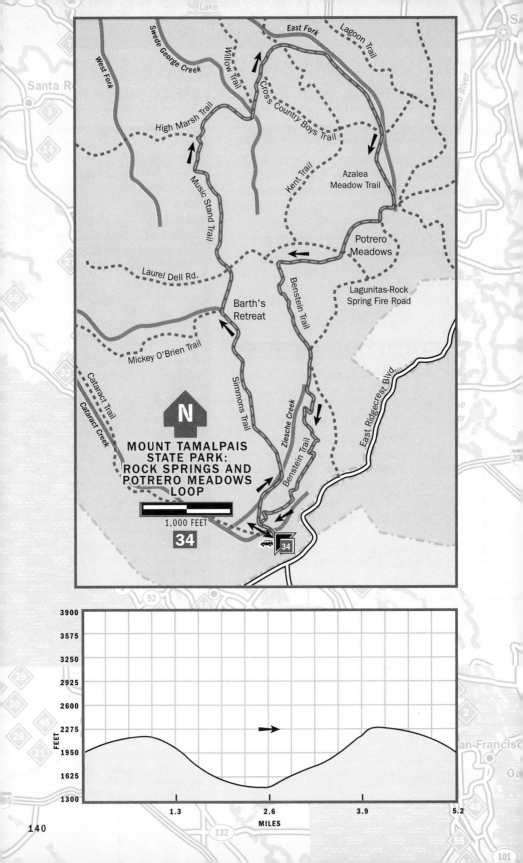

A massive, sprawling madrone on the Benstein Trail

At 0.2 miles, Benstein veers right. Continue straight, now on the Simmons Trail. Look down low for shooting stars along the trail in March.

Almost immediately the trail enters a forest of Douglas fir, tanoak, redwood, and California bay, following along Ziesche Creek. After crossing the creek on a wooden bridge, the trail begins to climb, at a moderate grade. Abruptly, like a curtain opening, the forest ends in a very rocky area dominated by chaparral plants. The Simmons Trail picks its way uphill through ceanothus, manzanita, and chamise, into a thin collection of Sargent cypress trees. Stay to the left at a vague fork—the trail does become easier to follow as you progress uphill.

At the crest, admire surprisingly long views north into Sonoma County, and then descend, veer right, and take a quick tour through a shaded section of woods. While descending at a fairly easy pace, the Simmons Trail continues to wind through chaparral and woods that lead to Barth's Retreat and a junction at 1.1 miles. Though no retreat remnants remain, the area is named for a mountain old-timer who built himself a solitary camp near here. The Mickey O'Brien Trail heads toward Laurel Dell, on the left. Continue straight, on a widened course through serpentine rock and chaparral.

At 1.2 miles the Simmons Trail ends at Laurel Dell Fire Road. Cross the fire road and begin downhill on the Music Stand Trail. Linanthus, a native plant that prefers serpentine soil, blooms along the trail in May. Chamise and manzanita give way to Douglas fir as the trail enters woods. A stream accompanies the trail, which keeps a moderate downward grade, although footing can be tricky along the narrow, sometimes slippery route. Look for an unsigned but obvious path breaking off to the left. This little spur leads to Music Stand, one of the mountain's oddities. As the name promises, there's a music stand, sitting in a small clearing. Mountain visitors often leave small trinkets in the area.

Return on the spur to the main trail, then continue downhill as the grade steepens. You'll emerge in a crowded sunny area, where pitcher sage, creambush, sticky monkeyflower, and ceanothus threaten to completely obscure the trail. This is one place where you can't see the woods for the shrubs. After crossing the creek, the trail skirts a big boulder and then becomes one with the stream for a few confusing yards. Keep following the path, back and forth across the creek, until the Music Stand Trail ends, at an unsigned junction at about 1.7 miles on the left side of the creek. When you reach the fork look for a massive boulder sitting in the crook of the Y junction and then bear right onto the High Marsh Trail.

Contouring across a forested slope, the High Marsh Trail is initially fairly level. Since the area is moist and almost completely shaded by chinquapin, Douglas fir, and madrone, it can be chilly in winter. There are a few stretches where manzanita is common, and other areas where huckleberry thrives and moss covers every rock in sight. Iris blooms along the trail in May.

The High Marsh Trail descends into a canyon surrounding Swede George Creek, where small waterfalls cascade downhill in the wettest months of the year. On the far side of the creek, at about 2 miles, you'll reach two tricky unsigned junctions with the Willow Trail (also know as the Swede George Trail). The first leg of the Willow Trail doubles back to the right then climbs along the creek. Willow and High Marsh run together for a few feet, then Willow departs to the left. Be sure to stay to the right; the trail begins to climb at this point. The forest thins a bit as the trail enters the High Marsh area.

High Marsh, on the left, is a little pond ringed with cattails, coyote brush, and Douglas fir. In winter the trail, too, becomes a bit swamped, but by summer's end both the pond and the trail are dry. The Cross Country Boys Trail departs to the right here, at about 2.2 miles. Continue straight as the High Marsh Trail heads back into the woods. At 2.4 miles reach a major junction and cross the Kent Trail. Continue straight, now on the Azalea Meadow Trail.

After crossing a creeklet and passing through a flat area often muddy in winter, Azalea Meadow veers right and begins to ascend on the right bank of the east fork of Swede George Creek. The going is steep on this narrow trail, but the surroundings are very scenic and peaceful. Madrone, Douglas fir, tanoak, and live oaks comprise the forest, with creambush, huckleberry, and ferns in the understory. At 3 miles there's a two-part junction with the Cross Country Boys Trail. Stay to the right, then the left, and continue uphill on the Azalea Meadow Trail. The trail's namesake meadow is off to the left just before the junction—azaleas, native relatives of rhododendrons, bloom here in June.

There's no flat or downhill relief on the remaining ascent, which is a shade tougher than moderate. Tree cover persists all the way to the end of the trail at 3.3 miles, where you'll turn right onto Lagunitas-Rock Spring Fire Road.

If you're ready for a lunch break, there are some picnic tables off to the left at Rifle Camp. However if it's a sunny day you may want to press on to scenic Potrero Meadows that is just uphill. Lagunitas-Rock Spring Fire Road is an important route for long treks on horseback, bicycle, or foot—the fire road extends from Lake Lagunitas to East Ridgecrest Boulevard. Practical as it is, it's a bit dull, so when the fire road crests at 3.4 miles, and veers left, continue straight on a slim footpath, marked "to picnic area," that meanders along the edge of Potrero Meadows.

This wide, open basin, an oasis of grassland surrounded by a forest, is one of Mount Tam's special places. On a winter weekday it can be surprisingly lonely, but in the thick of spring and summer you'll likely see plenty of people in and around the meadow. The area's name may annoy grammar sticklers; it's redundant, since potrero means meadow in Spanish. Little carpets of flowers brighten the grass in May, when you might see buttercups, goldenfields, California poppy, and linanthus in bloom. I like to sit right on the side of the trail if I'm lunching by myself, but there are picnic tables a bit further on, in a separate meadow, if you're with a crowd.

Proceed to the far edge of the meadow. Where a little seep crosses the trail (most obvious in winter), a path continues to the right toward the picnic area. Continue though to the left, where the path ends at a signed junction with Laurel Dell Fire Road at 3.5 miles. Turn right.

The wide fire road descends gently, through live oaks, Douglas fir, and tanoak. A second route to the picnic area is signed on the right. At 3.8 miles, turn left onto the Benstein Trail.

Right away the trail begins to climb. The initial section is very rocky and can be slippery when wet. Nestled in the woods here is a little chaparral pocket of Sargent cypress and manzanita. But as the Benstein Trail ascends, a very dense forest of tanoak, chinquapin, Douglas fir, and madrone surrounds it—it's so dense that there is little understory vegetation. The going is steep, but the trail soon levels out a bit to the left of a manzanita thicket. At 4.3 miles, Benstein feeds into Lagunitas-Rock Spring Fire Road. Go with the flow to the right, then abandon the fire road for the path as Benstein veers off to the right.

This well-cared for segment of trail is delightful. At an easy descent, Benstein drifts downhill through madrone, Douglas fir, and live oaks. Some switchbacks drop the trail away from a previous route through a serpentine meadow. Milkmaids and hound's tongue are common late winter flowers, but should you be hiking in March or April, you might also see calypso orchid, a stunning pink flower only about two inches tall. You may hear Ziesche Creek rushing in winter; the two tiny streams you'll cross are headed downhill to the bigger creek. The Benstein Trail ducks under a massive multitrunked madrone I call the octopus, then continues downhill through a very rocky area. At 5 miles Benstein again meets the Simmons Trail. Turn left and retrace your steps back to the trailhead.

PINNACLE GULCH
COASTAL ACCESS

IN BRIEF

There is plenty of public beach access along the Sonoma County coast, but this short downhill hike through a gorge to the beach is a bit hidden in the middle of a posh golf-based housing development. This hike is easy enough that just about anyone will find it doable, but remote enough for some solitude.

DESCRIPTION

Cross the street from the parking lot and begin on a narrow path tucked beneath cypress trees. The trail runs parallel to the road for a short distance, then, in a clear spot at the top of the gulch, turns right. Some steps and switchbacks ease the trail downhill. Hilltops on either side of the gorge are grassy and crowned with houses, but as the slopes slip steeply down into the gulch, they adopt a covering of coastal scrub. A creek bed on the left is lined with willow and salmonberry, and the sound of rushing water is a pleasant accompaniment to the hike.

The trail keeps to an easy downward trend, but there are a few short undulations. Ignore the

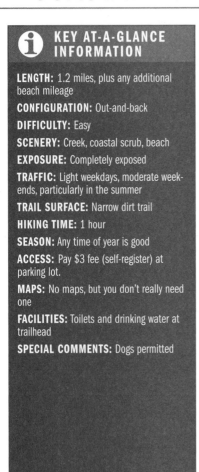

DIRECTIONS

Leave San Francisco on northbound US 101 and use the Golden Gate Bridge toll plaza as the mileage starting point. Drive about 43 miles north on US 101, then exit onto CA 116 West. Turn left and drive 8 miles to downtown Sebastopol, then turn left at a traffic light onto Sebastopol Avenue, following the sign to Bodega. Sebastopol Avenue becomes Bodega Highway. Continue west 11 miles to the T-junction with CA 1. Turn right and drive 3.5 miles, then turn left onto South Harbor Way. Where the road forks after less than 0.1 mile, turn left onto Heron Drive, proceed about 0.8 miles, then turn left onto Mockingbird Road. After less than 0.1 mile, turn left into the parking lot.

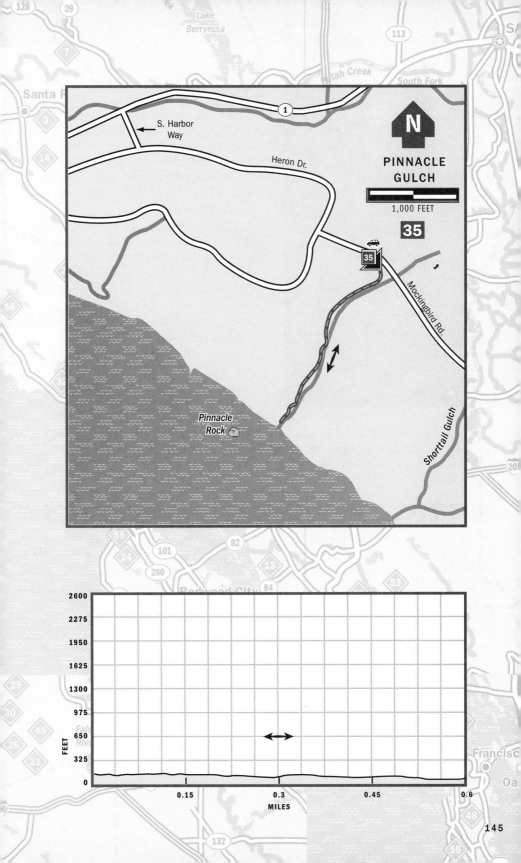

N

PINNACLE
GULCH

1,000 FEET

35

S. Harbor
Way

Heron Dr.

Mockingbird Rd.

Shorttail Gulch

Pinnacle
Rock

2600			
2275			
1950			
1625			
1300			
975			
650			
325			
0			

FEET

0.15   0.3   0.45   0.6

MILES

The Pinnacle Gulch Trail follows a creek downhill to the ocean.

assortment of paths departing uphill to the right and left; they pass into private property. Before spring breaks many wildflowers bloom along the trail, including paintbrush, California poppy, fringecups, scorpionweed, checkerlily, bluedicks, cow parsnip, milkmaids, and great clusters of iris. Later in the season you might see buckwheat, bush lupine, and yarrow.

Some small wooden bridges support the route as it descends. Look for a hedge of poison oak that frames the trail on the left. As the trail follows the curve of the creek, the ocean comes into view. The creek spills onto the beach at 0.6 miles, and the trail follows. From this sandy expanse there are views north past Pinnacle Rock, usually crowded with birds to Bodega Head. Look south for a surprising view of Point Reyes, including Tomales Point and the peninsula's western coastline. You can walk for short distances in either direction along the coast here, but access depends on the tides. If you scramble over rocks, note that a return route can disappear as the tide rolls back in. The safest bet is to linger on the beach near the trail. When you're ready, retrace your steps back to the trailhead.

▶ NEARBY ACTIVITIES

Experience more of the Pacific coastline between Bodega Bay and Jenner from more than a dozen coastal access points comprising the Sonoma Coast State Beaches. To find these beaches from the Pinnacle Gulch Trailhead, return to CA 1, then turn left (north). Once past the town of Bodega Bay, CA 1 runs right along the ocean on a high bluff. Simply pull off into any of the parking areas (some signed, some not; all obvious) and start exploring. Many of these staging areas provide beach access, where you can stroll along the ocean or explore tidal pools. Find out more at the state parks website: www.parks.ca.gov.

You can make a nice loop back to Sebastopol along the redwood-lined Russian River by driving north to Jenner on CA 1, then turning east onto CA 116. Follow CA 116 through Forestville south back to Sebastopol, then continue south to US 101.

POINT REYES NATIONAL SEASHORE:
BEAR VALLEY TO ARCH ROCK

▶ IN BRIEF

Departing from the Bear Valley Visitor Center, a nearly level fire road ushers you through woods, a meadow, and coastal grassland. At a bluff called Arch Rock, the turnaround point, there are beautiful views of the ocean and shoreline. The hike returns on the same route, although more ambitious hikers can opt for a loop to the top of Mount Wittenberg.

▶ DESCRIPTION

Like Muir Woods, Big Basin, and Mount Tam's Pantoll area, there are some trailheads that bustle with visitors from sunup to sundown. Every day of the year, Point Reyes' Bear Valley is inundated with nature lovers, many who come just for this trail. But you can beat the crowds by arriving very early, or choosing a weekday, particularly in winter, the park's quietest season.

Although there are a few trails that begin near the visitor center, it's not too hard to find the Bear Valley Trail, which starts at the south edge of the parking lot—look for the steady stream of people. The initial section of trail runs along the edge of a meadow, but it quickly veers right and into shade. The Bear Valley Trail is level with very

▶ DIRECTIONS

Leave San Francisco on northbound US 101 and use the Golden Gate Bridge toll plaza as the mileage starting point. Drive 11 miles north on US 101, then exit at San Anselmo/Sir Francis Drake. Drive west on Sir Francis Drake about 20 miles to the junction with CA 1. Turn right on CA 1 and drive about 0.1 mile, then turn left onto Bear Valley Road. Drive about 0.4 miles, then turn left at the "seashore information" sign just past the red barn. Drive about 0.2 miles to the parking lots at the end of the road.

ⓘ KEY AT-A-GLANCE INFORMATION

LENGTH: 8.8 miles

CONFIGURATION: Out-and-back

DIFFICULTY: Moderate, due to length

SCENERY: Douglas fir forest, coastal bluff, and ocean views

EXPOSURE: Mostly shaded

TRAFFIC: Heavy

TRAIL SURFACE: Dirt fire roads and trails

HIKING TIME: 4.5 hours

SEASON: Good all year—beat the crowds with a winter visit

ACCESS: No fee

MAPS: The official park map is available at the visitor center.

FACILITIES: Rest rooms and drinking water at the visitor center

SPECIAL COMMENTS: Dogs are not permitted.

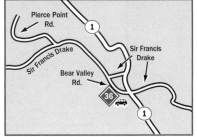

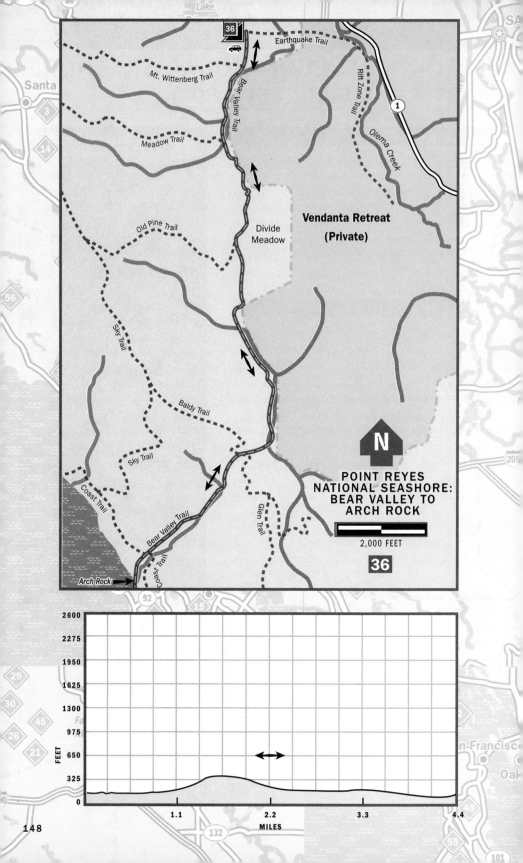

Lake

36

🚗

Earthquake Trail

Mt. Wittenberg Trail

Bear Valley Trail

Rift Zone Trail

Olema Creek

1

Meadow Trail

Vendanta Retreat
(Private)

Divide
Meadow

Old Pine Trail

Sky Trail

Baldy Trail

Sky Trail

Coast Trail

N

**POINT REYES
NATIONAL SEASHORE:
BEAR VALLEY TO
ARCH ROCK**

2,000 FEET

36

Bear Valley Trail

Glen Trail

Coast Trail

Arch Rock →

2600		

FEET

2600
2275
1950
1625
1300
975
650
325
0

1.1   2.2   3.3   4.4
MILES

148

few blips in elevation along its length. The moist environment shelters Douglas fir, California bay, tanoak, elk clover, creambush, red elderberry, and hazelnut.

After 0.2 miles the Mount Wittenberg Trail departs on the right, on the way to Point Reyes' tallest spot, a whopping 1,407 feet. Stick to the Bear Valley Trail at this junction and the next, with the Meadow Trail at 0.8 miles. After a tour through the woods, the trail emerges at the edge of Divide Meadow at 1.6 miles. The sunny sloping meadow, rimmed with Douglas fir, is the turnaround point for many visitors, but more scenic delights wait for hikers down the trail. The Old Pine Trail veers off uphill near the rest rooms on the right. Continue toward the ocean on the Bear Valley Trail.

The next 1.5 miles has no junctions and is a quiet part of the park. The trail descends briefly into a little shaded canyon tucked between ascending forested hillsides. At 3.1 miles you'll reach a multiple junction. The Baldy Trail begins on the right, and the Glen Trail starts on the left. The Bear Valley Trail in the middle shrinks from a fire road to a trail. Cyclists who want to continue on Bear Valley must leave their bikes at a rack.

Past this junction, the woods become even more lush. Coast Creek murmurs on the left side of the trail, and ferns cascade off the sloping hillsides. In the summer months, you might see foxglove blooming here. Moisture-loving buckeyes sprinkled through dense stands of Douglas fir completely shade the trail, and when you step out of the woods on a sunny day you'll be blinking like a newborn kitten. Along the trail, young Douglas fir tower above coyote brush, sticky monkeyflower, sagebrush, and bush lupine.

The Bear Valley Trail ends at a junction at 4 miles. The Coast Trail picks up the baton for the final stretch to the ocean, now partially visible straight ahead. Stay to the left, following the sign for Arch Rock. At 4.2 miles the Coast Trail slips off to the left, almost unnoticed when the grasses are high in summer. The path to Arch Rock continues straight, ascending gently through a pretty mix of coastal plants, including paintbrush and lizardtail. Views open up to the ocean. At 4.4 miles, you'll reach Arch Rock and the end of the trail. This little bluff, jutting out over the ocean, has unfenced drop-offs, so use caution.

On a sunny day, is there a better spot for lunch anywhere in the Bay Area? If you love ocean breezes, the sound of crashing waves, the calls of sea birds, and sweeping seashore views, I think you'll be pleased. This bluff is also an excellent location for seal watching. I lingered on my last hike, transfixed by a harbor seal bobbing up and down in the water while looking right at me.

When you're ready, return to the Bear Valley Trailhead. If you hanker for a more strenuous hike, as you return up the Bear Valley Trail, turn left on either the Old Pine or the Meadow Trail, then ascend on the Sky Trail to the Mount Wittenberg Trail, which returns to Bear Valley Trail 0.2 miles from the parking lot. The views from Mount Wittenberg are mostly obscured by a young forest of Douglas fir, but the trails are pretty, and you may see the remnants of an exotic white deer herd.

▶ NEARBY ACTIVITIES

Three short interpretive trails begin at the Bear Valley trailhead, exploring the region's history, vegetation, and the effects of the 1906 earthquake.

POINT REYES NATIONAL SEASHORE:
ESTERO TO DRAKE'S BAY

KEY AT-A-GLANCE INFORMATION

LENGTH: 8 miles (8.4 miles if you continue to the "beach")

CONFIGURATION: Out-and-back

DIFFICULTY: Moderate

SCENERY: Coastal

EXPOSURE: Almost entirely unshaded

TRAFFIC: Light

TRAIL SURFACE: Dirt trails

HIKING TIME: 4 hours

SEASON: Good all year; muddy in winter

ACCESS: No fee

MAPS: The official park map is available at the Bear Valley Visitor Center.

FACILITIES: Pit toilets at trailhead

SPECIAL COMMENTS: Dogs are not permitted.

▶ IN BRIEF

Point Reyes has creeks, ocean and bay coastline, a lagoon, waterfalls, ponds and lakes, and an estuary, which lends its name to this trailhead, Estero. You'll descend through coastal scrub and a pocket of pines to a little bridge, then climb to a bluff where you can see the other three bays that also feed into Drake's Estero. After a bit of roller coastering, the trail drops to ocean level, and although the official end of the trail is near the mouth of Drake's Estero, if the tide is low you can continue another quarter mile over mudflats to glimpse Drake's Bay.

▶ DESCRIPTION

The solitary Estero Trail departs from the parking lot through grassy coastal scrub, with coyote brush and blackberry brambles punctuating the landscape. Irises flower along the trail in spring, along with some blue-eyed grass and California buttercup. Off to the east, a steady slope rises to crest at Mount Vision. The Estero Trail skirts a rounded hill, then leans right, descends, and cuts through the corner of a pine forest, where you'll hear, if not see, many birds.

▶ DIRECTIONS

Leave San Francisco on northbound US 101 and use the Golden Gate Bridge toll plaza as the mileage starting point. Drive 11 miles north on US 101, then exit onto San Anselmo/Sir Francis Drake. Drive west about 20 miles on Sir Francis Drake to the junction with CA 1. Turn right and drive about 0.1 mile, then turn left onto Bear Valley Road. After about 2 miles, Bear Valley Road ends at Sir Francis Drake; turn left. Continue on Sir Francis Drake about 7.5 more miles, and turn left at the sign "Estero Trail." Drive slowly (there may be cows) for another mile to the trailhead on the right side of the road.

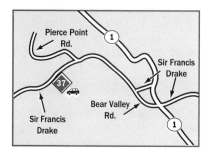

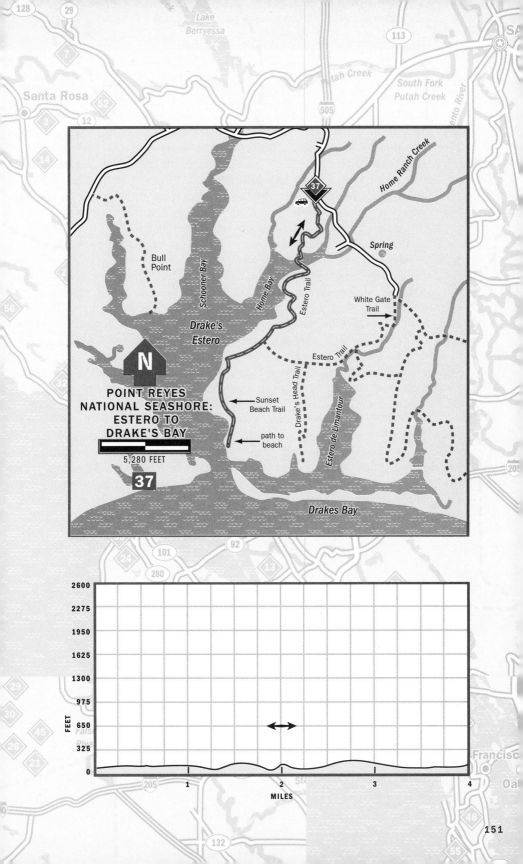

Bull
Point

Schooner Bay

Home Bay

Drake's
Estero

Home Ranch Creek

37

Spring

Estero Trail

White Gate
Trail

Estero Trail

Drake's Head Trail

Estero de Limantour

N

**POINT REYES
NATIONAL SEASHORE:
ESTERO TO
DRAKE'S BAY**

5,280 FEET

37

Sunset
Beach Trail

path to
beach

Drakes Bay

This pocket of woods has an unnatural feeling to it, probably because it was planted as a grove many years ago. Although I've hiked through it several times, I always have a slight feeling of foreboding in these woods, which remind me of the scary forest in *The Wizard of Oz*. As the trail leaves the pines, it adopts a gentle downhill course, through more pines, coyote brush, blackberry, wild rose, and a few twinberry bushes. The Estero Trail bends left and crosses the confluence of a freshwater pond and Home Bay on a pretty little bridge.

Since Drake's Estero empties into the ocean, and the entire estuary is affected by sea tides, the amount of water in the bay varies from slim forked threads to deep pools. On some occasions, I am happy to go no farther than the benches at the middle of the bridge. On one of my visits here, a pair of egrets perched like sentinels on opposite sides of the viewing platform on the middle of the bridge.

At the other end of the bridge, the trail turns right and begins to climb. Quail and rabbits are commonly spotted, rushing from one cluster of vegetation to another—the sides of the trail are tangled with a variety of plants, and you might be able to identify coyote brush, toyon, huckleberry, bush lupine, ceanothus, blackberry, sticky monkeyflower, and sagebrush. At the first crest, there are impressive views of Drake's Estero, but the trail doesn't linger. Instead it drops to the shores of a tiny pond, which contributes its share of water into the estuary, a few boards cross the drainage channel. (This area is commonly muddy in winter, and trail conditions can be terrible if the cattle that range through here have clomped through recently.)

The trail climbs again, through coyote brush, and reaches a fence stretched across the trail (it may be open, depending on the season). Squeeze through the V-shaped stile and ascend to a hill topped with a eucalyptus tree, where daffodils bloom in late winter. The Estero Trail descends again to another small pond. It's not much of a surprise at this point to begin climbing once more, but after another fence and stile the trail levels out and reaches a junction at 2.5 miles. Here, where the Estero Trail bends left, continue straight onto the Sunset Beach Trail.

The trail sweeps south through coyote brush (short enough to allow views back toward the trailhead) and across the estero to feeder bays to the west. In late summer, bright yellow goldenrod flowers seem especially showy among the drab tan and green brush. There's a descent, but this time it's easy. After you pass through one last cattle fence and stile, the trail reaches the edge of a small pond. According to the park maps, this is the official end of Sunset Beach Trail at about four miles. From here you can see Drake's Estero emptying into Drake's Bay, but there are better views (and a little beach) if you continue south.

A slight path veers left, squeezes through coyote brush, poison oak, bush lupine, and sagebrush, then sets off across mudflats. If it's not too muddy, you can continue another quarter mile to a narrow beach at a sandy point across from Limantour Spit. You may be able to see Chimney Rock from here. This is one of the quietest and loneliest places in the Bay Area where little waves lap against the shoreline and sand sings as it blows across the beach. When you're ready, retrace your steps back to the trailhead.

POINT REYES NATIONAL SEASHORE:
TOMALES POINT

▶ IN BRIEF

Animal sightings are not uncommon in the Bay Area, but there are a few locations where you are nearly assured of a peek at undomesticated creatures. One of the best spots is Point Reyes' Tomales Point. This hike is a 9.5-mile out-and-back trek on a remote peninsula where tule elk roam through coastal scrub and birds paddle in the ocean and soar through the skies. Bring binoculars, a hat, and a windbreaker.

▶ DESCRIPTION

At its northwestern edge Point Reyes tapers to Tomales Point. Pierce Point Ranch occupied the area until 1973, and the farm buildings, now historically preserved, stand near the Tomales Point trailhead. A self-guided tour through the ranch is a fine way to begin (or end) a hike. In 1978, a herd of 10 tule elk were reintroduced to the point, which was then fenced off from the rest of Point Reyes. The elk have multiplied, and the population at last count (in 2000) was over 400. Other creatures you may see on the point are a variety of birds, coyote, bobcat, and (although sightings are

▶ DIRECTIONS

Leave San Francisco on northbound US 101 and use the Golden Bridge toll plaza as the mileage starting point. Drive north on US 101 about 11 miles, then exit onto Sir Francis Drake/San Anselmo. Drive west on Sir Francis Drake about 20 miles to the junction with CA 1, turn right, and drive about 0.1 mile, then turn left onto Bear Valley Road. After about 2 miles, Bear Valley Road ends at Sir Francis Drake; turn left. Continue on Sir Francis Drake about 5.5 miles, then turn right onto Pierce Point Road. Drive about 9 miles on Pierce Point Road to the signed Tomales Point Trailhead, a short distance from McClures Beach at the end of the road.

ⓘ KEY AT-A-GLANCE INFORMATION

LENGTH: 9.5 miles

CONFIGURATION: Out-and-back

DIFFICULTY: Moderate

SCENERY: Coastal scrub and grassland

EXPOSURE: Full sun

TRAFFIC: Steady nearly year-round

TRAIL SURFACE: Broad sandy fire road and meandering paths, with some loose sand

HIKING TIME: 5 hours

SEASON: Spring and autumn are best.

ACCESS: Free

MAPS: Pick up the free official Point Reyes trail map at the Bear Valley Visitor Center, or purchase *Trail Map of Point Reyes National Seashore,* by Tom Harrison Cartography.

FACILITIES: None at the trailhead; there are pit toilets at nearby McClures Beach

SPECIAL COMMENTS: Dogs are not permitted.

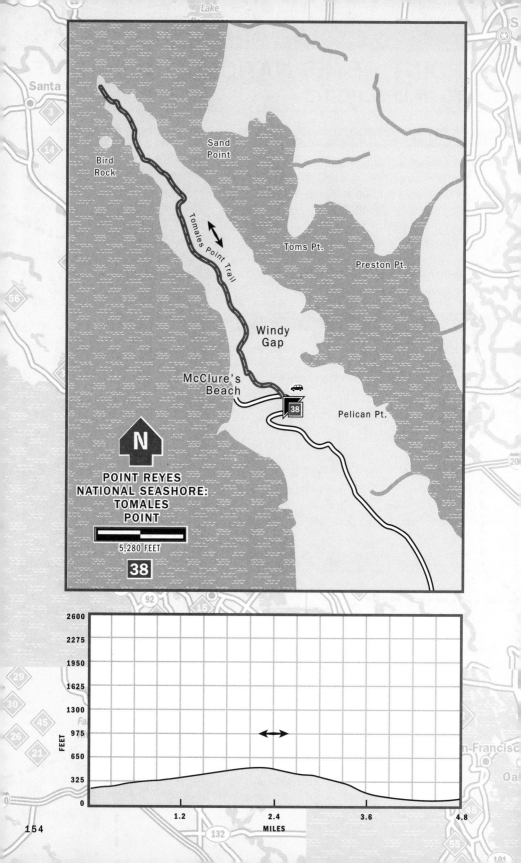

POINT REYES
NATIONAL SEASHORE:
TOMALES
POINT

5,280 FEET

38

Bird
Rock

Sand
Point

Tomales Point Trail

Toms Pt.

Preston Pt.

Windy
Gap

McClure's
Beach

38

Pelican Pt.

2600
2275
1950
1625
1300
975
650
325
0

FEET

1.2   2.4   3.6   4.8
MILES

rare) mountain lion. The weather plays a big part in enhancing (or ruining) hikes along the coast, and Tomales Point is no exception. Attempt a hike during one of the Bay Area's famous foggy summer days, and not only will the views be completely obscured, but the wind can chill you thoroughly. Spring and autumn are the best seasons for a visit, and note that when the elk rut (from July to November), males are more aggressive and you should give them an extra wide berth.

The trail starts at a level grade, skirting the ranch buildings before heading into a grassy coastal scrub plant community, dominated by coyote brush. In early spring, wild radish covers the knoll on the left, presenting a lavish display of white and lavender blossoms. Northern harriers seem to favor the Point, and you might see one or two fluttering in place a few feet above the ground, looking for a meal. As the trail travels north it offers views of the coastline, which past McClure's Beach gradually ascends to steep rocky bluffs. The Tomales Point Trail drifts downhill to aptly named Windy Gap. If you haven't already seen elk, the sloping valley on the right is one of their favorite spots. A brief moderate ascent brings the trail up to the grassy ridgeline, dotted in some spots with wind-sculpted coyote brush. Look to the left for ocean views and right to enjoy the hills of Bolinas Ridge rolling up from Tomales Bay. The trail descends to Lower Pierce Point Ranch, now a site marked by a handful of cypress trees often occupied by raptors. A few salmonberry shrubs mingle through stinging nettles in a damp spot on the right.

Once again the trail begins to climb, but here vegetation begins to crowd the route. Somewhat abruptly, the path dissolves to sand at about 3.8 miles—some more firm patches of terra are ahead, but this is the trend for the rest of the trail. Navigating becomes a bit tricky, as elk paths score the area, so try to stick close to the ridgeline and keep heading northwest. Elk scat is common everywhere, and you stand a very good chance of observing *Cervus elaphus nannodes* if you keep your noise level down. On the other hand, if you are too quiet, you might come across a loner mostly camouflaged by the tall thick stands of lizardtail and yellow bush lupine. Even if you don't see them, you'll hear them—elk bellows are unlike any other animal vocalization I've ever heard. I can only describe the sound as similar to a loud high-pitched door squeak.

The trail finally begins to descend slightly, signaling that the first leg of the hike is near its end. Be careful of unannounced sheer drop-offs on the left—the views are incredible, but the ground can be unstable near the edge. This is one of the most isolated and quiet hiking destinations on the coast, where the only sounds are the crash of the surf, bird cries, and the peal of a buoy near the mouth of Tomales Bay. At about 4.8 miles there's a bare spot, kind of a sandy bowl, that is a bit sheltered from the wind and makes a decent rest stop, especially if you're in a group. Beyond that a tiny path drops straight down to the tip of the point, but I don't recommend this option. After you've had your fill of this coastal gem, backtrack to the trailhead.

▶ NEARBY ACTIVITIES

From this trailhead (or from a second parking lot 0.1 mile to the west) it's a 0.8-mile round-trip hike to McClure's Beach.

PORTOLA REDWOODS STATE PARK

KEY AT-A-GLANCE INFORMATION

LENGTH: 7.4 miles

CONFIGURATION: Loop, with two short out-and-back segments

DIFFICULTY: Moderate

SCENERY: Redwoods, creek

EXPOSURE: Mostly shaded

TRAFFIC: Autumn through spring: moderate weekends, quiet weekdays; moderate/heavy in summer

TRAIL SURFACE: Dirt fire roads and trails

HIKING TIME: 4 hours

SEASON: In winter, park staff remove bridges crossing Pescadero Creek, restricting access to a few trails; summer is the best season.

ACCESS: Pay $5 fee inside the Ranger Station, or self-register out front if it's unstaffed.

MAPS: The park map is available at the Ranger Station.

FACILITIES: Rest rooms and drinking water at the trailhead

SPECIAL COMMENTS: The park is sometimes closed after heavy storms, so during winter, check trail conditions with park staff before leaving home. From October to the end of the rainy season, bridges are removed from trails that cross Pescadero Creek. If the bridges are out and the creek is high, start your hike on the Iverson Trail, across from the Madrone Picnic Area parking lot, and omit the trip to Tiptoe Falls. Dogs are not permitted.

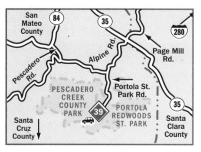

IN BRIEF

Choosing the best hike at Portola Redwoods is like choosing a favorite child. This gorgeous park is packed with quiet woods, redwood canyons, and rushing creeks, and you could easily spend a three-day camping holiday here and still not hike every trail.

DESCRIPTION

Portola Redwoods State Park is a perfect tree lover's park, with forests of mostly second-growth redwoods, mature tanoaks, madrones, and Douglas fir extending as far as the eye can see. Tucked in canyons on the Santa Cruz Mountain's western slope, this remote and sheltered location is a haven for hikers and campers who seek refuge from noisy city living and summer heat. This 7.4-mile hike hits many of Portola's high points: Pescadero Creek, Tiptoe Falls, and forests of redwood. The last segment is an out-and-back trip to

DIRECTIONS

Depart San Francisco on southbound I-280 and use the CA 1/19th Avenue merge as the mileage starting point. Drive about 29 miles south on I-280, then exit onto Page Mill Road. Drive west on Page Mill Road about 9 miles to the junction with Alpine Road and CA 35/Skyline Boulevard. Continue straight through the intersection onto Alpine Road and drive west about 3 miles on this narrow road (be especially careful for bicycle and motorcycle traffic on weekends). Turn left onto Portola State Park Road, and drive on the tiny and winding road the remaining 3 miles to the entrance kiosk. Continue another 0.4 miles to the parking areas near the ranger station. If possible, park in the Madrone lot (to the left just before the Ranger Station), or in the spots past the Ranger Station and across the bridge, on the right side of the road.

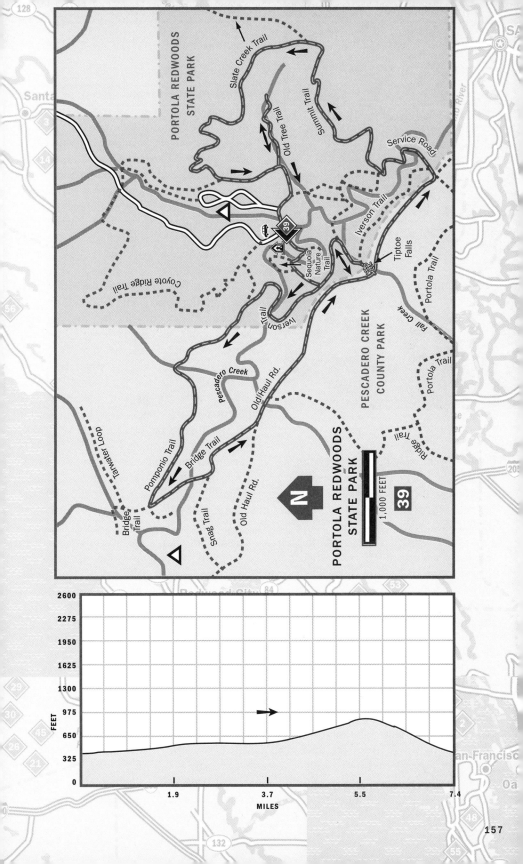

PORTOLA REDWOODS
STATE PARK

PORTOLA REDWOODS
STATE PARK

PESCADERO CREEK
COUNTY PARK

Slate Creek Trail

Old Tree Trail

Summit Trail

Service Road

Iverson Trail

Tiptoe Falls

Portola Trail

Fall Creek

Sequoia Nature Trail

Coyote Ridge Trail

Iverson Trail

Pescadero Creek

Old Haul Rd.

Ridge Trail

Portola Trail

Pomponio Trail

Bridge Trail

Old Haul Rd.

Snag Trail

Tarwater Loop

Bridge Trail

N

1,000 FEET

39

39

FEET				
2600				
2275				
1950				
1625				
1300				
975				
650				
325				
0	1.9	3.7	5.5	7.4

MILES

157

A bench nestled in a scenic redwood grove on the Slate Creek Trail

an old-growth redwood. If you're worried that this hike is too tough, you can easily break the hike into two loops and traverse them separately. Portola Redwoods abuts two other parks, Pescadero Creek County Park and Long Ridge Open Space Preserve. Hikers have the opportunity to start at Portola and hike for miles, but many visitors are content to make short treks on two popular park trails, a short loop near Pescadero Creek and an out-and-back path to an old-growth redwood.

Begin from the side of the Ranger Station, on the signed Sequoia Nature Trail. The path descends slightly, through redwood, tanoak, and huckleberry, then bends right and drops to the banks of Pescadero Creek. Use the bridge to cross the creek, then walk along the bank until the trail ascends a few steps and soon reaches a junction at 0.2 miles. Bear left, following the sign toward the Iverson Trail. Where the other leg of the Sequoia Nature Trail feeds in from the right, stay to the left. The trail rises a bit to a T-junction with the Iverson Trail at 0.3 miles. There, turn left onto Iverson and ascend through a forest of redwood, tanoak, madrone, and huckleberry. The hillside drops sharply off to the left where the trail runs high above Pescadero Creek, so step carefully. At one-half mile, where a path heads off to the left and down to the creek, stay to the right. This area can be bogged down by winter rains; then somewhat overgrown in summer. The Iverson Trail steps over a stream, then reaches a junction at 0.6 miles where you'll turn right and climb briefly and easily to Tiptoe Falls. Although the falls cascade only a few feet before spilling into a pool, Tiptoe Falls seems to charm those who visit. It's a pretty and calm place that can relax and rejuvenate you in the way that only rushing water can. When you're ready, retrace your steps back to the junction with the Iverson Trail and the connector to the Sequoia Nature Trail at 0.9 miles. Continue straight, remaining on the Iverson Trail. The trail descends gently to wander along the forest floor. Some wildflowers that bloom here throughout spring include starflower, redwood sorrel, milkmaids, and trillium. The trail drops to the shores of Pescadero Creek and, once again, you'll cross on a bridge. On the other side, the trail ascends a bit on some steps, then reaches a junction at 1.2 miles. Turn left onto the Pomponio Trail. At a nearly flat grade, the Pomponio Trail follows the general course of Pescadero Creek, although the distance precludes views of the water. The forest understory is particularly dense here, with huckleberry thickets squeezing the trail in areas. Huckleberry is an evergreen shrub common to redwood canyons. Its fruit, which somewhat resembles blueberries, ripens in some parts of the Bay Area by late summer. Along this trail they aren't usually edible until October—the seasons seem to arrive late at Portola.

With a transition marked by signs facing both directions, the Pomponio Trail leaves the state park and enters Pescadero Creek County Park. In summer you might see fairy lanterns along the trail, and by autumn, honeysuckle berries dangle from vines twined through trees and shrubs. Madrone, California bay, creambush, toyon, ceanothus, and wild rose succeed huckleberry as the trail widens and passes through a slightly sunnier area. Where there are breaks in the forest, you can actually see the surrounding forest of Douglas fir and redwood towering above the trail. At 2.2 miles the Pomponio Trail ends at a junction with the Bridge Trail. The path straight across leads to Tarwater Trail Camp.

Turn left onto a broad fire road that is level until it drops a short distance to cross Pescadero Creek. Tanoak, redwood, Douglas fir, and big-leaf maple line the trail, which begins a moderate climb. At 2.5 miles, pass the Snag Trail on the right and continue straight on the Bridge Trail. Now nearly level again, the Bridge Trail passes a damp tree-lined meadow on the right, then ends at 2.8 miles. Continue straight/left, now on Old Haul Road. Almost right away, the Ridge Trail begins on the left. The trail climbs about 1,500 feet in a little over 2 miles, then leaves the county park and heads toward Big Basin Redwoods State Park via an easement trail connection. For now, keep an easy pace straight ahead on Old Haul Road. On the high south bank of Pescadero Creek, Old Haul Road passes through redwood, huckleberry, creambush, Douglas fir, and tanoak. In winter months, you'll likely hear water rushing, as feeder creeks flow downhill on the way to Pescadero Creek. The largest of these streams, Fall Creek, tumbles into Tiptoe Falls a short distance off to the left but is inaccessible from the fire road. At 4.1 miles the Portola Trail and Iverson Creek drop to the fire road from the right, and a service road descends on the left. Turn left onto the service road. Now back in the state park, you'll begin a somewhat steep descent. The Iverson Trail begins on the left, but this segment of the trail has been perennially plagued with landslides. Although a reroute is planned, as of this writing it was impossible to reach Tiptoe Falls from this end of the trail. Slightly downhill from the junction with Iverson sits the remains of Iverson's cabin. This little redwood structure was built in the 1860s and remained intact until the 1989 earthquake toppled it.

The service road winds downhill to a junction at 4.5 miles. If you're already tired, this is your opportunity to bale on the remaining hike. Simply follow the service road back to the trailhead. Otherwise, turn right onto the Summit Trail. Initially, the Summit Trail is a broad fire road, but once past a pair of water tanks, the trail shrinks to a footpath. At a moderate grade, the trail ascends through an assortment that by now should be familiar: Douglas fir, redwood, tanoak, madrone, and huckleberry. If you arrive in late winter hoping for wildflowers, you'll probably be disappointed; on my last visit in early March, I saw nary a flower on this trail, although there were still some exotic colored mushrooms. Wild rose is really the only understory plant here besides huckleberry to make a statement.

Curve left with the Summit Trail as it travels across the sloping walls of a canyon. At one point, the trail crosses over the top of a tiny ridge, then continues to contour across the hillside. A pretty wooded knoll extends off to the right. What's marked on the map as "the summit," the highest point on this loop, doesn't quite live up to its name. You'll know you're there when you spot a handful of chamise and manzanita shrubs. There are no views, and this tiny hilltop has barely enough room for a group of three to sit. However, it's a peaceful spot to pause and listen to the wind sweep through the trees. The Summit Trail descends, curves left, then levels out on a ridge and ends at 5.3 miles. At this junction bear left onto the Slate Creek Trail, which leads back to the ranger station. An easy descent commences through the same combination of madrone, Douglas fir, and redwood, with slightly more tanoak. In some places, redwood needles and tanoak leaves cover the trail in a cushy carpet. Many tree trunks here are charred from a long ago fire. Yellow banana slugs, if you happen to encounter them, really stand out in this forest of brown and green.

Continuing a loop around the canyon, the Slate Creek Trail weaves through a quiet forest where birdcalls filter through the air. Just past a memorial grove sign, look on the right for a bench nestled in the middle of a redwood fairy ring—an excellent lunch stop. Soon after, at 6.2 miles, a path to the campground departs on the right. Continue to the left on the Slate Creek Trail, traverse a short steep downhill section on some stairs, and then return to a gentle grade. Moss-covered tree stumps and evergreen plants create an incredibly lush atmosphere. Also look for redwood violets and milkmaids in late winter. The Slate Creek Trail passes through a massive fallen redwood, then reaches a junction at 6.6 miles, where you'll turn left onto the Old Tree Trail for a short out-and-back. With a huge fallen tree on the right, the Old Tree Trail makes its way into the heart of the canyon at an easy incline, following along a seasonal creek. Western wood anemone bloom here in late winter. At 6.9 miles, you'll reach the end of the trail and the trail's namesake, an old tree. Cradled in a deep canyon, this redwood has a circumference of over 12 feet and seems to scrape the sky. When you're ready, walk back to the junction with the Slate Creek Trail, then continue straight. The wide path descends gently, then ends at 7.3 miles at the park road. Turn right and walk the remaining 0.1 mile along the road to the Ranger Station.

PURISIMA CREEK REDWOODS OPEN SPACE PRESERVE

▶ IN BRIEF

This loop initially follows Purisima Creek upstream into a canyon, then breaks off through wooded Soda Gulch. You'll wind uphill through chaparral, then descend rapidly on a moderately steep fire road, which returns to the creek, redwoods, and trailhead.

▶ DESCRIPTION

Large-scale logging was a commonplace occurrence in the Santa Cruz Mountains, with redwood lumber widely used as a building material for San Francisco structures. By the early 1900s, most of the redwood giants had been cut and hauled out of the canyons and steep hillsides. Although some small virgin groves of redwoods still stand throughout the Santa Cruz Mountains, usually tucked in hard-to-reach canyons, most of the redwood forests are second-growth woods. Purisima Creek Redwoods is no exception, although when wooded canyons are this gorgeous, I really find myself transfixed by the trees rather than by the stumps. Life along Purisima Creek and the surrounding canyons changes with the seasons. In early winter, redwood needles pad the trails, and after rainstorms, newts can be spotted making their way to the creek to breed. Late winter and spring bring wildflowers to brighten the floors of the darkest canyons. Summer's abundant daylight

▶ KEY AT-A-GLANCE INFORMATION

LENGTH: 7 miles

CONFIGURATION: Loop, with a very short out-and-back segment

DIFFICULTY: Moderate

SCENERY: Redwoods, creek, chaparral

EXPOSURE: Nearly equal parts shade and sun

TRAFFIC: Moderate weekends, quiet weekdays

TRAIL SURFACE: Dirt fire roads and trails

HIKING TIME: 3.5 hours

SEASON: Cool in summer if you get an early start; good year-round

ACCESS: No fee

MAPS: The park map is available at an information kiosk a short distance from the parking lot.

FACILITIES: Pit toilets near the trailhead

SPECIAL COMMENTS: Dogs are not permitted.

▶ DIRECTIONS

Drive south from San Francisco on I-280 and use the CA 1/19th Avenue merge as the mileage starting point. Drive 14 miles on I-280, exit onto CA 92 west, and drive 8 miles to the junction with CA 1. Turn south (left) onto CA 1 and drive about 1 mile, then turn left onto Higgins-Purisima Road. Drive on this narrow, winding road about 4.5 miles to the trailhead on the left side of the road (just past the tiny white bridge).

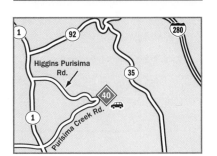

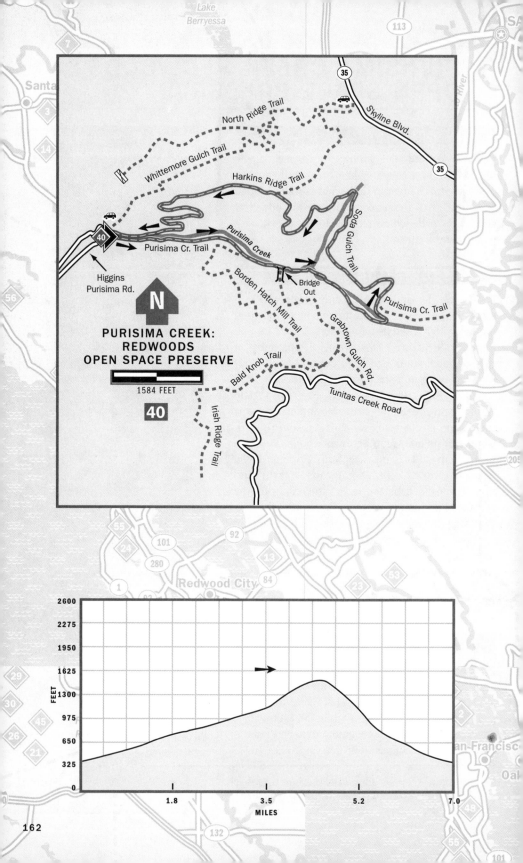

North Ridge Trail

Whittemore Gulch Trail

Harkins Ridge Trail

Skyline Blvd.

35

Purisima Cr. Trail

Purisima Creek

Soda Gulch Trail

Purisima Cr. Trail

Higgins
Purisima Rd.

40

N

**PURISIMA CREEK:
REDWOODS
OPEN SPACE PRESERVE**

1584 FEET

40

Borden Hatch Mill Trail

Bridge
Out

Grabtown Gulch Rd.

Bald Knob Trail

Tunitas Creek Road

Irish Ridge Trail

FEET			
2600			
2275			
1950			
1625			
1300			
975			
650			
325			
0	1.8	3.5	5.2	7.0

MILES

encourages day-long hikes through chaparral spiced with the aroma of blooming native shrubs. As you make your way from the parking lot into the preserve, almost immediately you can feel and see the cooling influence of Purisima Creek and the redwoods. The canyon wall on the right is a tangle of moisture-loving plants, including thimbleberry, alder, red elderberry, and fern. Near the pit toilets and information signboard, the Whittemore Gulch Trail departs to the left. Continue straight on the Purisima Creek Trail. Running above the banks of Purisima Creek, the broad trail is nearly flat and almost completely shaded by redwoods. Banana slugs are often sighted curled up on logs and plants, although occasionally you might see one or two in the middle of the trail. These mollusks are important composters, chewing fallen leaves, needles, and mushrooms, and expelling fresh fertile soil. After 1 mile of easy walking, you'll reach a junction with the Borden Hatch Mill Trail. Continue straight on Purisima. The grade picks up a

The Soda Gulch Trail weaves through a forest of redwood with fern and redwood sorrel in the understory.

bit but still remains easy. Huckleberry makes an appearance in an understory where trillium, starflower, and California larkspur bloom in June. The Purisima Creek Trail enters a flat, open area that is somewhat overgrown. This is the junction with the Grabtown Gulch Trail. A severe winter storm washed the bridge out, leaving the Grabtown Gulch Trail inaccessible, stranded on the opposite bank of the creek. A new bridge and slight reroute are planned, reopening the Grabtown Gulch and Borden Hatch Mill loop.

The Purisima Creek Trail presses on uphill, delving further into the redwood-lined canyon. A little bridge marks the confluence of Soda Gulch and Purisima Creek. You'll cross Soda Gulch again later on in this hike. After one more bridge routing the trail back across to the south side of the creek, the trail begins to climb with more purpose. At a sharp bend left, you'll leave Purisima Creek behind and, after one last hill, reach a junction at 2.3 miles. The Purisima Creek Trail continues uphill toward Skyline Boulevard. Turn left onto the Soda Gulch Trail to continue the journey through the darkest part of the canyon. This Bay Area Ridge Trail segment is a stunner. The narrow path winds through redwoods, angling across the steep sides of a canyon. Ferns cascade off the hillsides and nestle on the shores of a little creek crossed by a small wooden bridge. Winter storms uproot trees pretty much every year, forcing ad hoc reroutes or short scrambles over or around the fallen giants. There's a "wow" around nearly every corner, including a surprising grassy spot where a few coast live oaks and ceanothus shrubs permit views west.

The Soda Gulch Trail crosses its namesake creek on another pretty little bridge. The sound of water is supremely refreshing on a hot summer day. Finally, as the trail begins to climb, you'll slalom through a very dark patch of redwoods and then emerge on the sun-drenched slopes of the mountain, blinking in the sudden sunlight. Views here stretch to the ocean.

Switchbacks route the trail through ceanothus, coyote brush, toyon, coffeeberry, and lizardtail. Paintbrush, monkeyflower, and cow parsnip are just a few of the wildflowers that linger into summer, thriving under a coastal influence that keeps the hillsides here green when inland parks' wildflowers are already dry and brown. A few madrones and coast live oaks shade the trail occasionally, which you'll likely appreciate around noon on a sunny day. At 4.9 miles, where the Soda Gulch Trail ends at a junction with the Harkins Ridge Trail, turn left. The contrast between the Harkins Ridge Trail, a wide steep fire road, and the intimacy of hiking-only Soda Gulch Trail is illuminated immediately. Harkins Ridge sets off downhill like it means business, through towering Douglas fir and an understory of creambush, hazelnut, huckleberry, yellow bush lupine, and coyote brush. Watch out for cyclists zipping down the steepest sections, where the sharp grade might give hikers with unstable knees a pause. Since views were mostly obscured by the redwoods until this part of the hike, the trail compensates for the steep descent with lots of stunning vistas. To the right you can see North Ridge, and the high eastern flanks of Montara Mountain. Dead ahead to the west, hills undulate all the way to the ocean.

The trail soon veers left and begins a series of broad switchbacks, heading down into the canyon. As redwoods exert their influence, look also for hazelnut and currant. The Harkins Ridge Trail ends at a junction with the Whittemore Gulch Trail at 7 miles. Turn left, cross Purisima Creek for the last time, turn right, and retrace your steps back to the parking lot.

▶ **NEARBY ACTIVITIES**

You can also begin a Purisima hike from the preserve's main trailhead on CA 35, 4 miles south of CA 92.

RANCHO SAN ANTONIO OPEN SPACE PRESERVE

▶ IN BRIEF

After a mile of gentle strolling, you'll leave the crowds behind and climb through oaks and grassland to a vista point. Then press on uphill, through chaparral where coyotes have been spotted. The hike then descends to a shaded canyon and follows a creek back toward the farm, but a bypass route skirts the area and returns to the trailhead through woods and grassland.

▶ DESCRIPTION

Once you've nailed down a parking space, you'll start this hike with the masses, walking to Deer Hollow Farm. Begin from the parking lot near the rest rooms and cross Permanente Creek on a footbridge (not the sturdy vehicular bridge on the other end of the parking lot). On the far side of the bridge, turn right onto the Permanente Creek Trail, following the sign toward Deer Hollow Farm. This broad dirt trail runs along the creek, through a flat grassy area.

Once past a massive California bay and some tennis courts, the trail ends at a multiple junction. Turn left, cross a paved path and the road, and you'll arrive at the boundary with the open space preserve. Pick up a map from the signboard and continue on the Lower Meadow Trail, a wide dirt path through a pretty swatch of grass dotted with coast live oaks and California bays. Orange fiddlenecks bloom along the trail here in late winter, preceding mule ear sunflowers.

ⓘ KEY AT-A-GLANCE INFORMATION

LENGTH: 6 miles

CONFIGURATION: Figure eight

DIFFICULTY: Easy/moderate

SCENERY: Grassland, woods, creek

EXPOSURE: Nearly equal parts shaded and exposed

TRAFFIC: Busy, busy, busy—365 days a year

TRAIL SURFACE: Dirt fire roads and trails

HIKING TIME: 2.5 hours

SEASON: Good any time

ACCESS: No fee

MAPS: Midpeninsula Regional Open Space District's Rancho San Antonio map is available from an information signboard 0.3 miles inside the park.

FACILITIES: Rest rooms and water at the trailhead

SPECIAL COMMENTS: Arrive early on weekends for parking. The eastern hunk of this vast preserve is actually a Santa Clara park, but is managed by the Midpeninsula Regional Open Space District. Trail signs can be a bit confusing near the trailhead, and maps aren't up for grabs until you get into the open space preserve part of the complex. Dogs are not permitted.

▶ DIRECTIONS

Drive south from San Francisco on I-280 and use the CA 1/19th Avenue merge as the mileage starting point. Drive south on I-280 about 36 miles, then exit at the Foothill Expressway. Turn right and drive south on Foothill Boulevard and take the first right on Cristo Rey Drive. Drive about 1 mile and turn left into the park.

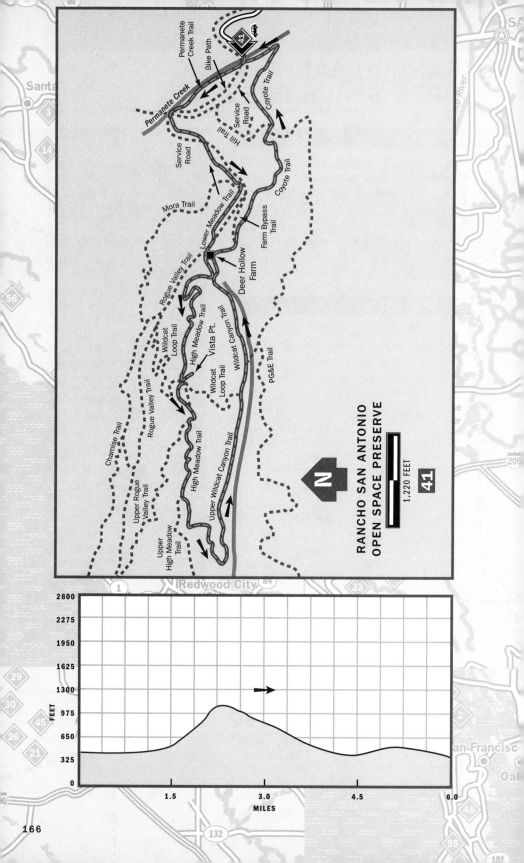

RANCHO SAN ANTONIO
OPEN SPACE PRESERVE

N

1,220 FEET

41

FEET

2600
2275
1950
1625
1300
975
650
325
0

1.5   3.0   4.5   6.0
MILES

The Coyote Trail is one of the many Rancho San Antonio trails favored by runners.

When the Lower Meadow Trail meets the paved road, cross the street and skirt a permit parking area, then pick up a continuation of the trail. You'll cross a creek, then walk on a level grade parallel to the park road. At 0.8 miles, a multiple junction sends trails scattering in every direction. Across the paved road to the left, the Farm Bypass Trail loops around Deer Hollow Farm. The other two routes, the paved road and a path straight ahead, proceed to the farm. The Mora Trail to the right, avoids the area altogether, climbing up to a grassy ridge. Continue straight, following the sign marked "foot traffic."

This little path rolls gently up and down on the edge of grassland. At 0.9 miles, the trail sweeps left and feeds into the paved road. Turn right toward Deer Hollow Farm. The buzz of activity surrounding Deer Hollow Farm includes excited kids, vocalizing animals, and the hum of farm equipment. Along with farm buildings that date back to the 1850s, mature persimmon, pomegranate, and other fruit trees create an old-time, bucolic atmosphere. Although the farm is not open to the public every day, you can still enjoy watching goats and cows from the trail side of the fence and peer into a pretty garden of flowers and vegetables. Wild animals seem ridiculously comfortable near the farm, and you might see deer or quail along the trail. Just past a barn which wears a historical patina, the Rogue Valley Trail heads off to the right. Stay to the left, though, heading toward the Wildcat Canyon Trail.

A few steps past some pit toilets, you will pass the Farm Bypass Trail, which enters from the left. Continue straight through a damp area where willow, bigleaf maple, buckeye, ninebark, and blackberry brambles form a dense wall of vegetation. At 1.1 mile, the Wildcat Canyon Trail continues straight, while a path to the Coyote Trail sets off to the left. Turn right onto the High Meadow Trail.

An assortment of plants line this broad trail, including silktassel, sagebrush, sticky monkeyflower, poison oak, pitcher sage, coast live oak, buckeye, and toyon. The High Meadow Trail curves up the outside of a hill at a moderate grade, then turns left and begins a series of long switchbacks, softening the ascent. As the trail meets the lower reaches of a sloping grassy meadow, blue oaks and coast live oaks appear. Coast live oaks are evergreen and enjoy each other's company, while deciduous blue oaks stand in more solitary formations. Blue oaks are easy to pick out in autumn, when their leaves are at their bluest, and in late winter, when they leaf out. Mule ear sunflowers bloom along the trail in abundance as early as March, and if you visit in late May or early June, you might see a few butterfly mariposa lilies.

The trail continues uphill on the edge of the sloping grassy hillside, passing coast live oak, toyon, and a few cercocarpus. Look for several venerable valley oaks that grace the grassland to your left.

At 1.9 miles, moving clockwise at a multiple junction, the first path heads to a vista point, the Wildcat Loop Trail descends to Wildcat Canyon Trail, then the High Meadow Trail, and the last is the other segment of the Wildcat Loop Trail. Turn left for a short out-and-back, on the path to the vista point.

The trail ascends quickly then ends at a belvedere. Straight ahead, the sloping grassy meadow peppered with oaks descends to the south, framing a view across Silicon Valley to peaks of the Mount Hamilton range. Return downhill to the previous junction, then resume uphill on the High Meadow Trail.

After a few steps, the trails split. Either route is an option, but the path on the right is less steep than the fire road, so bear right.

Angling across the hillside, the trail enters a shaded area where California bays mix with coast live oak, sticky monkeyflower, poison oak, and toyon. After a switchback, the path meets and crosses the other steep fire road. The difference between the two sides of the hill are remarkable. On these sunny slopes, chamise basks in the sun along with sagebrush and toyon. There are good views to the northwest of Black Mountain, which tops out at 2,800 feet. At 2.2 miles, the two legs of the High Meadow Trail rejoin for good at a junction where the Upper Rogue Valley Trail drops off the ridge on the right. Continue to the left on the High Meadow Trail.

The trail ascends slightly through chaparral, then reaches a junction at 2.5 miles. The Upper High Meadow Trail continues uphill straight ahead, presenting a good option for extending this hike 2 miles, on a loop through one of the most remote parts of the preserve, but for today's hike bear left onto the Upper Wildcat Canyon Trail.

Descending, the Upper Wildcat Canyon Trail winds through madrone, toyon, silktassel, chamise, California coffeeberry, pitcher sage, and coast live oak. As the trail drops into Wildcat Canyon, a forest of California bays completely overtakes the landscape, then the trail bends left and runs along a creek. It's hard to believe that this quiet section of the park is less than 2 miles from the farm area. With steep hills rising up to the right and left, this trail really captures the essence of a canyon, and in the heat of summer the sound of water and total shade are welcome. In October and November, big-leaf maples create a gorgeous autumnal tableau, releasing their colorful leaves to drift slowly down to the trail and creek. The trail descends gently to a junction at 3.8 miles with the Wildcat Loop Trail. Continue to the right, now on the Wildcat Canyon Trail.

Creambush, coast live oak, California bay, and blackberries tangle along the trail, accompanying a large colony of western leatherwood. Early wildflowers include trillium, hound's tongue, and milkmaids. A connector to the PG&E Trail departs to the right at 3.9 miles, but continue left on the Wildcat Canyon Trail.

As you make your way out of the heart of the canyon, the trail crosses the creek on tiny bridges under arching graceful California bays. At 4.4 miles you'll reach a familiar junction with the High Meadow Trail. Continue straight a few feet, then bear right toward the Farm Bypass Trail.

Buckeyes dominate the landscape as the narrow trail ascends easily. You might notice California bay, poison oak, and pitcher sage, as well as trilliums in late winter. The Farm Bypass Trail breaks off to the left at 4.6 miles, but continue to the right on the Coyote Trail.

Runners favor this trail for its easy grade and abundant shade. In this fairly open woodland, the limited understory vegetation makes it easy to find wildflowers such as woodland star and mission bells. When the trail enters a sunny area, look for clematis, a trailing vine, draped over shrubs. Gooseberry, ceanothus, sagebrush, poison oak, and sticky monkeyflower are common here. Just past some blue oaks, the trail ends at 5.3 miles. The PG&E Trail doubles back to the right, and the Hill Trail descends on the left, past a water tank. Make a soft right, following the sign "to county park."

Vetch covers much of the hillside on the right, and coast live oak, California bay, buckeye, and blue oak are scattered about. Where the trail descends to a junction near the equestrian parking at 5.8 miles, turn left. The perfectly flat path accompanies Permanente Creek, on the right, screened by willows. At 6 miles you'll reach a junction with a paved bike path and the park road. Turn right and cross the bridge to return to the parking lot.

REDWOOD REGIONAL PARK

LENGTH: 4.1 miles

CONFIGURATION: Loop

DIFFICULTY: Easy

SCENERY: Redwoods and a mixture of grassland and shrubs

EXPOSURE: Shaded in the canyon, partial sun on the ridges

TRAFFIC: Moderate/heavy

TRAIL SURFACE: Dirt fire roads and trails

HIKING TIME: 2 hours

SEASON: Nice every season, although trails are muddy in winter

ACCESS: Free from this trailhead; main park staging area requires a fee

MAPS: The park map is available at the trailhead.

FACILITIES: Pit toilets are available at the trailhead.

SPECIAL COMMENTS: Dogs permitted

▶ IN BRIEF

The next time you find yourself gazing east from Mount Tamalpais or the Marin Headlands, think of this—towering above the East Bay hills in the 1800s was a row of redwoods so tall that ship captains used them to navigate through the Golden Gate into San Francisco. Although the giant trees were logged by the turn of that century, second-growth redwoods now fill canyons where rainbow trout spawn and ladybugs hibernate in the winter, wildflowers bloom in spring, and other wild creatures scamper through the woods year-round. This easy 4.1-mile loop drops into a redwood canyon and then climbs back to a nearly level trail which returns to the trailhead.

▶ DESCRIPTION

Redwood is really one big canyon, and although there are some neighborhood access points, most people enter from either end of the park. There are many loop options, so hikers can mix and match on canyon and ridge trails. Hikers, equestrians, dog walkers, runners, and cyclists frequent Redwood trails, but it's still easy to find peace and quiet, particularly on the paths closed to cyclists.

▶ DIRECTIONS

Depart San Francisco on the Bay Bridge and use the toll plaza as the mileage starting point. About 0.5 miles past the toll plaza, bear right onto I-580 East. Drive 1.5 miles, then exit onto CA 24. Drive east 3.5 miles on CA 24, then exit onto CA 13 south. After about 3 miles, exit at Joaquin Miller. At the foot of the exit ramp, make a left, then take the next left, and then go straight onto Joaquin Miller. Drive uphill about 1 mile, then turn left at a light onto Skyline (there's a brown park sign before the turn). Drive about 3 miles (past the Chabot Space Center), and turn right into the parking lot and staging area.

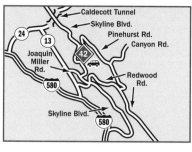

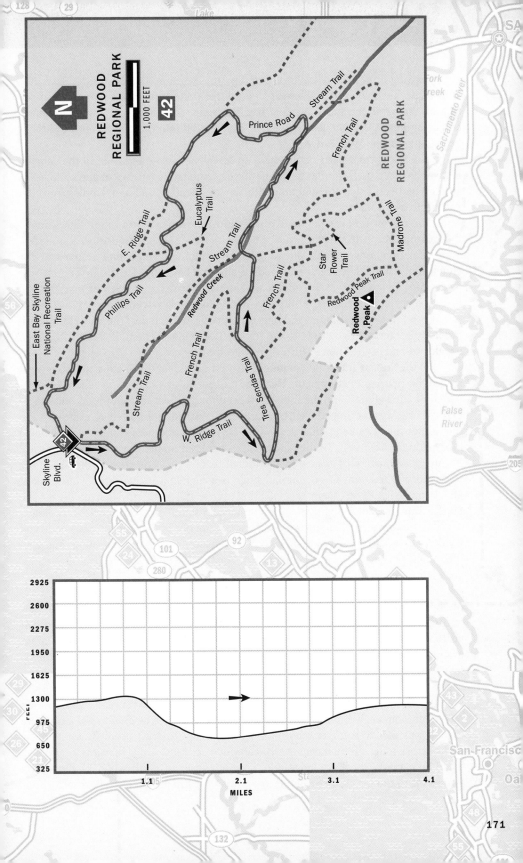

REDWOOD
REGIONAL PARK

N

1,000 FEET

42

Lake

Prince Road

Stream Trail

French Trail

REDWOOD
REGIONAL PARK

North Fork Creek

Sacramento River

E. Ridge Trail

Eucalyptus Trail

Stream Trail

Star Flower Trail

Madrone Trail

East Bay Skyline National Recreation Trail

Phillips Trail

Redwood Creek

Stream Trail

French Trail

French Trail

Tres Sendas Trail

Redwood Peak Trail

Redwood Peak

W. Ridge Trail

Skyline Blvd.

42

False River

2925				
2600				
2275				
1950				
1625				
1300				
975				
650				
325				

FEET

1.15   2.1   3.1   4.1

MILES

San-Francisco

Starting from the Skyline Gate Staging Area, begin on the West Ridge Trail. At a level grade, the wide fire road sweeps past some eucalyptus into a more natural setting of chaparral currant, California bay, madrone, coast live oak, toyon, hazelnut, and creambush. At 0.6 miles, the French Trail sets off into the canyon on the left, but keep going on the West Ridge Trail.

The sea of trees parts occasionally to reveal views southeast out of the canyon. Redwoods creep up from the canyon in places, contrasting patches of grass and chaparral. When you reach the junction with the Tres Sendas Trail at 1.1 miles, turn left and begin a descent.

The narrow trail can get quite muddy in winter when storm runoff filters downhill, plumping a little stream. It doesn't take long to make the transition at a moderate grade, from ridge to canyon. In just a few minutes you'll find yourself in the clutches of a gorge filled with redwoods, California bays, and ferns. The French Trail feeds into Tres Sendas at 1.5 miles, and the two paths run together briefly, until French veers off to the left. Continue on Tres Sendas as it descends deeper into groves of redwood. Look for trilliums blooming in spring. At 1.8 miles, the Star Flower Trail heads uphill on the right. Stay to the left on Tres Sendas. The trail crosses Redwood Creek and ends at 1.9 miles. Turn right onto the Stream Trail.

As the Stream Trail follows along Redwood Creek, fences line the trail to protect the fragile riparian environment. Here in the heart of the canyon, it is almost completely shaded all day, and the trailside vegetation is a lush tangle of ferns and blackberry vines. Moss is draped over boulders and swathed around redwood trunks. On one winter hike I came upon thousands of ladybird beetles (also known as ladybugs) hibernating. The orange beetles looked like a pile of maple leaves from a distance, but up close I marveled at how they huddled together on branches and leaves of the understory vegetation. Observing ladybugs is a highlight of Bay Area winter hikes, and I have since seen them several other times, but never in such quantity. The Stream Trail descends slightly to a junction at 2.3 miles. Turn left onto Prince Road.

As the broad trail climbs at a moderate grade out of the canyon, redwoods and California bays give way to coast live oak and madrone; then the trees thin, and coyote brush, poison oak, and blackberry dot grassland. Prince Road ends at 2.7 miles. Turn left onto the East Ridge Trail.

The wide fire road follows along the park boundary at a nearly level grade. Coyote brush, pine, coast live oak, and madrone seem to stand off from the trail, permitting views back across the canyon to the west ridge. Although dogs are frequent visitors to the park, there are plenty of wild animals that live here, and you might examine the sandy trail surface for telltale animal signs. Bobcat prints are decidedly feline, though their feet are considerably larger than domesticated cats. Coyote leave spade-like prints and are fond of marking their territory at junctions, leaving piles of scat as calling cards for other coyotes where deer trails and paths cross. Deer are the most common hoofed animal in the Bay Area, and their crescent-shaped prints are easy to pick out. In summer months, when the trails are dry, you might see squiggly paths across trails left by traveling snakes, which are most active in warm weather. At the 3-mile mark, the East Ridge Trail continues to the right, while Phillips Loop swings off to the left. Either route is an option, but I prefer Phillips. Bear left.

The trail undulates a bit through coyote brush, pine, and madrone. You might hear (and see) hawks perched on tall trees nearby. The Eucalyptus Trail crosses Phillips at 3.3 miles, but continue straight. Eucalyptus trees, imported in the 1800s from Australia, are a common fixture in East Bay parks. Timbermen hoped the fast-growing trees would provide profitable lumber crops, but their wood turned out to be unsuitable for building purposes. Another exotic plant you might notice along the trail is cotoneaster, a landscaping shrub with glossy leaves and red berries. Unlike toyon, a native shrub which also bears red berries, cotoneaster's fruit is poisonous, although birds eat the berries. The Phillips Trail runs downslope from the ridge on the right until the trail merges into the East Ridge Trail at 3.9 miles. The trail straight across the junction leaves Redwood Park and heads north into Huckleberry Preserve on the East Bay Skyline National Recreation Trail, a 31-mile path that runs through six East Bay parks. Bear left and follow the East Ridge Trail another 0.2 miles back to the trailhead.

▶ NEARBY ACTIVITIES

Sibley Regional Volcanic Preserve, a few miles north of Redwood Regional Park, hosts a self-guided loop through the remains of a volcano. Read more about Sibley at www.ebparks.org/parks/sibley.

RING MOUNTAIN
OPEN SPACE PRESERVE

KEY AT-A-GLANCE INFORMATION

LENGTH: 2 miles

CONFIGURATION: Balloon

DIFFICULTY: Easy

SCENERY: Rock-strewn grassland

EXPOSURE: Mostly unshaded

TRAFFIC: Moderate

TRAIL SURFACE: Dirt fire roads and trails

HIKING TIME: 1 hour

SEASON: Good year-round; Tiburon mariposa lilies usually bloom from mid-May to early June

ACCESS: No fee

MAPS: The park map is available at an information signboard inside the preserve.

SPECIAL COMMENTS: Due to the rare plants that thrive here, take special care to stay on the trails at Ring Mountain. Dogs are permitted.

▶ IN BRIEF

There's a dramatic backdrop to the incredible views hikers enjoy on Ring Mountain. Although small and totally contained by Tiburon residential neighborhoods, the preserve hosts Native American petroglyphs and an incredibly rare flower.

▶ DESCRIPTION

This 405-acre preserve sits on ultraprime real estate. A short drive from US 101, Ring Mountain offers views of San Pablo Bay, Mount Tamalpais, and San Francisco. The property was never developed because of a single flower, the Tiburon mariposa lily, which grows in a small section of Ring Mountain and nowhere else in the world.

There's no parking lot but plenty of street parking along Paradise Drive. Access the preserve from an open space gate and stop at an information signboard for a map, which also contains the self-guided tour key. These lower reaches of Ring Mountain are dominated by a damp basin, fed from little streams.

To begin, access the Phyllis Ellman Trail, skirt through a marshy area, and begin to climb through rocky grassland. In winter, look on the left for oso berry, a slight deciduous shrub, which produces clusters of little white nodding flowers.

▶ DIRECTIONS

Leave San Francisco on northbound US 101 and use the Golden Gate Bridge toll plaza as the mileage starting point. Drive north on US 101 9 miles, then exit at Paradise Drive/Tamalpais Drive. Turn right, drive east a short distance, and bear right onto San Clemente (before The Village shopping center). After a few blocks, San Clemente dumps into Paradise Drive. Continue on Paradise past Westward Drive to the preserve gate on the right side of the road. It's about 1.5 miles from US 101.

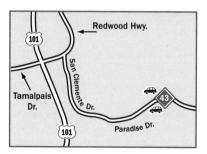

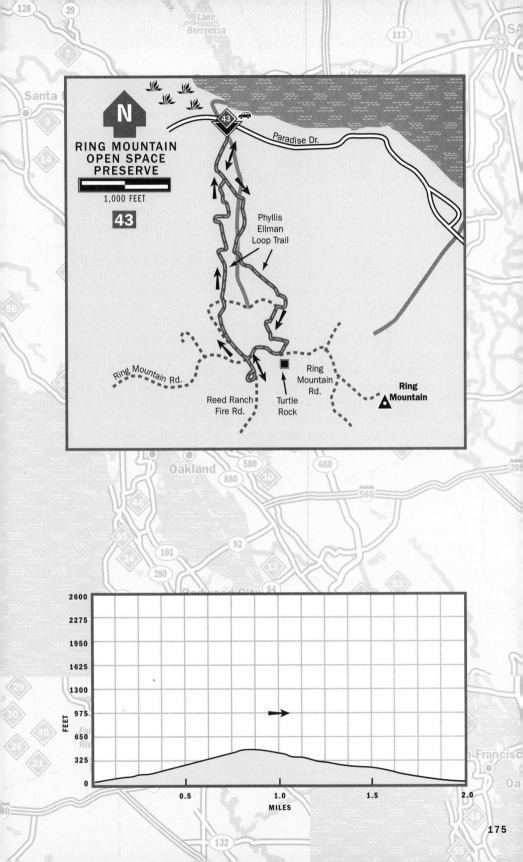

N

RING MOUNTAIN OPEN SPACE PRESERVE

1,000 FEET

43

Paradise Dr.

Phyllis Ellman Loop Trail

Ring Mountain Rd.

Reed Ranch Fire Rd.

Turtle Rock

Ring Mountain Rd.

Ring Mountain

At 0.2 miles the trail splits; you can hike the loop in either direction, but to follow the self-guided tour, turn left. Keeping to an easy grade, the trail travels laterally across the hillside. Toyon, coyote brush, young California bays, and some poison oak dot the grassland. Wildflowers are sprinkled across these sloping grassy hillsides from February through late summer. The first arrivals are often milkmaids and buttercups, followed by blue-eyed grass, lupine, Ithuriel's spear, and later still, tarweeds.

In spring, where a little footbridge crosses the creek, look to the right for ninebark, a shrub with leaves that resemble blackberry and currant. Like those edible berry-producing plants, ninebark is a member of the rose family and prefers a moist yet exposed environment. Ninebark's bracts of red flowers set it apart from its kin berry plants.

At post 7, stay to the right, avoiding a well-trampled path heading left and steeply uphill toward the ridge. At the next unsigned split a short distance from post 7, stay to the left or you'll shortcut the loop. The trees get bigger and more impressive on this part of the mountain, despite their exposed location. Post 8 points out a massive coast live oak and, near post 9, the trail winds through an incredible multi-trunked California bay—one of the magical spots on the mountain.

As the trail presses on uphill, Mount Tamalpais's east peak pops up to the west. Past the creek's headwaters, the trees fade away and grassland returns, although you'll wind through one last cluster of bays near the crest. Where the first leg of the Phyllis Ellman Trail ends at a junction with a fire road at 0.9 miles, you'll surely want to pause and savor the views south, which extend past Richardson Bay to San Francisco. The big lunk of a rock just off the trail on the left is Turtle Rock. Turn right onto Ring Mountain Fire Road. As the fire road follows the bare ridgeline, there are dead-on views to Mount Tam. After a brief downhill stretch and when you reach a saddle where trails stretch out in each direction, turn left. A few steps down Reed Ranch Fire Road, a little unsigned path veers off to the right. Follow this trail a short distance to Petroglyph Rock. An interpretive sign explains that the carvings still plainly visible on the boulder were made by Miwok Indians centuries ago. Where the path ends after skirting around the rock, turn left and walk back uphill on the fire road to the previous junction, then continue straight, back on the Phyllis Ellman Trail. Returning downhill, the long views north may distract you from the trailside display of flowers. The trail splits near post 14 but joins again shortly. A high concentration of rocky soil along the trail sustains native wildflowers, including the Tiburon mariposa lily.

Continuing downhill, San Quentin State Prison is visible, perched on the edge of its namesake point. A gracefully canopied buckeye tree sits alone in the grassland on the right, producing sweet-smelling blossoms in May and chestnut-sized nuts (which are poisonous, so don't eat them) in winter. Where the split path rejoins, a trail heads right and bisects the loop. Continue downhill, following the route highlighted by a couple of arrow signs. In winter before rains transform the hillsides into a green verdant canvas, toyon shrubs loaded with cheerful red berries become a favorite of small birds. Where the loop closes at about 1.8 miles, stay to the left and retrace your steps back to the trailhead.

ROCKVILLE HILLS COMMUNITY PARK

▶ IN BRIEF

Solano County's Rockville Hills Community Park is dominated by blue oak savanna, but also hosts a Bay Area Ridge Trail segment, rock formations, little lakes, and chaparral. Rockville can be incredibly hot in summer, but winter and spring hikes are sublime. This is a tour through my favorite parts of Rockville, visiting grassland, blue oaks, and Upper Lake.

▶ DESCRIPTION

Rockville has many fire roads and paths, and only some of them are signed. The park map is helpful, but you might also approach Rockville with a spirit of adventure and just ramble around. It's easy to navigate based on your relative position to overhead power lines, which run north to south through the park.

At the trailhead paths, feel free to explore off to the right and left, but begin this hike uphill on the main route, a broad fire road named the Rockville Trail. The fire road starts climbing at a moderate pace, but soon loses steam and adopts an easier grade as it ascends through buckeye, blue and coast live oak, and a grassland understory. Many different flowers bloom on the sides of the trail in spring, and you might see clarkia, Chinese houses, buttercups, lupines, bluedicks, owl's clover, and Ithuriel's spear in April and May. Some

▶ KEY AT-A-GLANCE INFORMATION

LENGTH: 3.1 miles

CONFIGURATION: Balloon

DIFFICULTY: Easy

SCENERY: Grassland, oaks, lake

EXPOSURE: Almost entirely exposed

TRAFFIC: Moderate weekends, quiet weekdays

TRAIL SURFACE: Dirt fire roads and trails

HIKING TIME: 2 hours

SEASON: Muddy in winter, hot in summer, best in spring

ACCESS: No fee

MAPS: A park map is available at the trailhead's information signboard.

FACILITIES: None

▶ DIRECTIONS

Depart San Francisco on the Bay Bridge and use the toll plaza as the mileage starting point. Stay to the left, on northbound I-80. Drive north on I-80 about 33 miles into Solano County, then exit onto Suisun Valley Road (just before Fairfield). Turn left and drive north on Suisun Valley Road about 1.5 miles, then turn left at a traffic light onto Rockville Road. Drive about 0.7 miles and turn left into the parking lot.

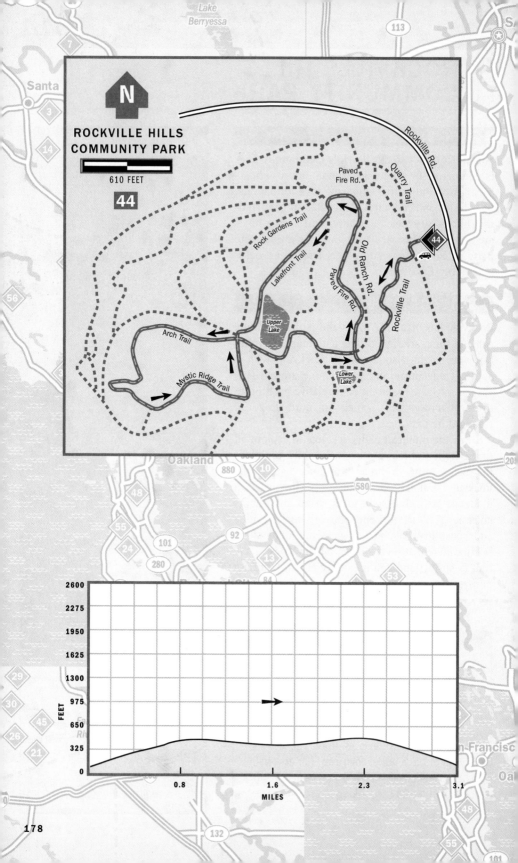

stretches of the trail traverse exposed rock—not much of a surprise at a park named Rockville. As the trail gains elevation, look off to the left for a view of a big palisade rock formation. At 0.4 miles, crest at the edge of a pretty valley and turn right onto a paved fire road signed "to North Trailhead."

The Bay Area Ridge Trail segment ascends easily, between the edge of a valley and a wooded knoll. Most of the trees along the trail are spectacular specimens of blue oak. The leaves on these deciduous trees hardly look blue in spring, when they produce bright green new leaves, but by autumn, just before they drop, the leaves shift to a decidedly blue color. Side trails depart to the left and right on a regular basis, but stay on the paved trail. A few manzanitas bloom in winter, preceding the spring splendor of linanthus, goldenfields, owl's clover, blue larkspur, and johnny-jump-ups. At a crest about 0.7 miles into the hike, turn left onto Old Ranch Road (a footpath) as it crosses the pavement, just before the paved road descends and passes a bench on the

Oaks dot grassy hillsides along the Mystic Ridge Trail.

left. The path winds through blue and coast live oaks, then reaches a T-junction. Turn left.

As the broad fire road sweeps downhill through oak and buckeye, look to the right for a view of rock formations pockmarked with holes. At 0.9 miles, the fire road joins another trail feeding in from the right. The two run together through an oak-dotted valley, with a wall-like rock formation on the right. Lots of lupine bloom in patches around Easter, accompanied by less organized displays of popcorn flower, blue larkspur, johnny-jump-ups, and linanthus. After less than 0.1 mile, bear right onto the first path departing from the fire road, the Lakefront Trail.

The slight Lakefront Trail makes its way toward the north edge of Upper Lake, an area that can be hard to navigate. Aim for the shoreline to the right of the lake, but stay to the left of the power lines. In spring, goldenfields really favor the shoreline area, and on one mid-April visit, huge patches of the sunny little flowers rimmed the lake like the yellow ink from a highlighter. Just before the trail reaches a picnic table, turn right at about 1.3 miles. After ascending a few feet, the path reaches a T-junction. Turn left and walk a few feet to a multitrail junction, signed with a Bay Area Ridge Trail symbol on a post. The first trail clockwise to the left heads back toward the trailhead, the second (heading uphill) is the return route for the hike, the third is the Arch Trail, and the fourth is the Fire Trail. Bear right onto the Arch Trail.

This diminutive trail cuts across a grassy hillside, dodging blue oaks. I've always seen plenty of flowers along this trail in early spring, including big patches of lupine and, in April, sprinklings of bluedicks, woodland star, buttercups, linanthus, popcorn flower, and owl's clover. All but the lupines and buttercups usually persist through mid-May, when the grass begins to dry out. A shortcut (not on the map) veers sharply uphill to the left at 1.4 miles, but continue on the Arch Trail. The path curves left, and then on a little shaded stretch, squeezes through a gap between hillsides so small that to call it a canyon would be an exaggeration. You may see Chinese houses in bloom here in May. The Arch Trail ends just before a major junction at 1.8 miles, where you'll turn left onto the Mystic Ridge Trail.

The early stages of the trail are rough going, with the rocky path ascending steeply under oaks. The tough part ends when the Mystic Ridge Trail steps out to a grassy plateau and then adopts an easy ascent that fades to level. California poppies begin to bloom through here in April just as the height of the grass threatens to obscure all flowers. This is my favorite trail segment at Rockville. A few gorgeous blue oaks stand in a sea of grass along this wide ridge, where views extend out of the park to neighboring Solano County lands still ranched and farmed, although every year there seem to be more houses on the surrounding hillsides.

A trail doubles back to the right at 2 miles, heading to the Upper Mystic Ridge Trail, but continue to the left and then ignore a path departing left that leads to the shortcut off the Arch Trail. The Mystic Ridge Trail bends right and forks. Either way is an option, because both lead to the same place, but the last feet of the right fork are rocky and steep, so bear left. Whenever I hike through here in spring, I always look for a good display of owl's clover blooming along the trail. The Mystic Ridge Trail ends under a power tower at 2.2 miles. Turn left onto a wide fire road (Fire Trail on the park map) that drops down to the north, offering fine views of Upper Lake (especially if you can mentally "ignore" the power lines). At 2.3 miles, you'll return to the lake area and again meet with the Arch Trail. Turn right. Following the southern shoreline of Upper Lake, continue on the fire road as you pass two trails that head off to the right, which join together to loop past Lower Lake. This part of the park gets a lot of use, and not just from people; cattle graze right up to the waterline.

The fire road veers left, continuing to follow the shoreline, but then at 2.5 miles, the trail takes a sharp turn right. At a nearly level grade, you'll pass through more of the park's oak population. This is one of Rockville's main routes, so expect traffic from cyclists and folks heading to the lake. Another path breaks off to the right toward Lower Lake, but keep going straight until you reach a junction with the paved road at 2.7 miles. Walk to the right for a few feet, then turn left and return down the Rockville Trail to the parking lot.

ROUND VALLEY
REGIONAL PRESERVE

IN BRIEF

Round Valley's single trailhead is on a lonely country road that winds through Mount Diablo's eastern foothills, a good distance from any freeway. Hikers can take long out-and-back or shuttle hikes through this preserve and the neighboring Los Vaqueros Watershed, but this is the sole official loop at Round Valley, a three-creek, 4.1-mile tour through the preserve's rolling hills of oak woods and grassland.

DESCRIPTION

Hikes at Round Valley scratch that peace-and-quiet itch. You may hear an occasional plane overhead, but traffic noise is nonexistent once you leave the trailhead, and the flanks of Mount Diablo block views of suburban sprawl to the west. This is one of those backyard getaway spots that makes Bay Area life bearable for folks who love the outdoors.

Round Valley is part of a little-known mini greenbelt. The East Bay Regional Parks District–managed Round Valley and Morgan Territory preserves abut Mount Diablo State Park and Los

DIRECTIONS

Depart San Francisco on the Bay Bridge and use the toll plaza as the mileage starting point. About one-half mile past the toll plaza, bear right onto I-580 East. Drive about 16 miles south and, at the CA 238 split, stay to the left on I-580. Continue east about 21 miles, then exit onto Vasco Road in Livermore. Turn left and drive north on Vasco Road about 14 miles to the junction with Camino Diablo Road. Turn left onto Camino Diablo Road, drive about 3.5 miles, then continue straight/left onto Marsh Creek Road. Drive west on Marsh Creek Road about 1.5 miles to the preserve entrance on the left side of the road.

KEY AT-A-GLANCE INFORMATION

LENGTH: 4.1 miles

CONFIGURATION: Loop

DIFFICULTY: Easy

SCENERY: Grassland and oaks

EXPOSURE: Some full sun, some partial shade

TRAFFIC: Light

TRAIL SURFACE: Dirt fire road and trails

HIKING TIME: 2 hours

SEASON: Summer is often very hot. Autumn and late winter are best.

ACCESS: No fee

MAPS: The park map is available at the trailhead's information signboard.

FACILITIES: Vault toilets and drinking water at trailhead

SPECIAL COMMENTS: No dogs are allowed in the preserve.

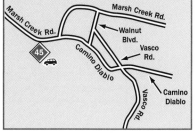

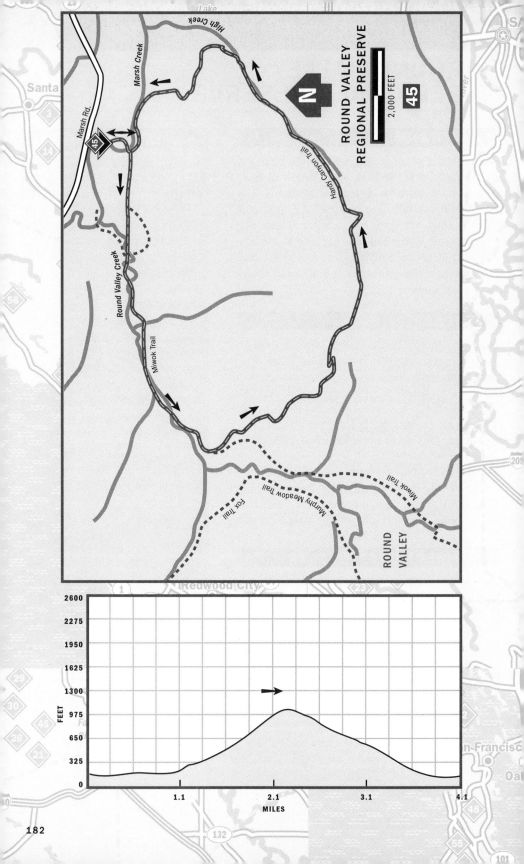

ROUND VALLEY
REGIONAL PRESERVE

N

2,000 FEET

45

High Creek

Marsh Creek

Santa

Marsh Rd.

45

Round Valley Creek

Miwok Trail

Hardy Canyon Trail

Murphy Meadow Trail

Fox Trail

Miwok Trail

ROUND
VALLEY

FEET	
2600	
2275	
1950	
1625	
1300	
975	
650	
325	

1.1   2.1   3.1   4.1

MILES

Vaqueros Watershed (owned and run by the Contra Costa Water District), creating a huge protected block of land. The wildlife viewing is exceptional through all these parklands; Round Valley is protected habitat for the San Joaquin kit fox, and golden eagle sightings are frequent.

From the trailhead, follow the obvious route over a bridge to a gate and junction with the Hardy Canyon Trail, the other end of the loop, but stay to the right on the Miwok Trail. This fire road begins a moderate climb along the preserve boundary, downslope from an oak-studded hillside. After a short dip, as the trail rises again, veer right onto an unsigned but well-worn path, which shortcuts a roller-coaster stretch best suited to equestrians. The path descends and feeds back into the fire road, which meets a dead-end trail at one-half mile. Stay to the left on the Miwok Trail.

The trail now follows along Round Valley Creek at an easy grade. Hills rise up to the right and left, marked with many lovely trees, including blue and coast live oak and buckeye. There are usually quite a few squirrels scuttling about in the grassy areas off the trail, and you might see hawks sitting in trees near squirrel burrows. I've seen golden eagles soaring above this part of the preserve in autumn. The Miwok Trail ascends a bit and reaches a junction at 1.2 miles. The valley stretches south from here.

Turn left onto the Hardy Canyon Trail, a narrow path that ascends through grassland and blue oak. Cattle that graze throughout the preserve seem to prefer the valley basin, but you might come across a few up in these hills as well. During the wettest months of the year, rain cascades downhill in the creases of the hillsides, where buckeyes thrive. Look for coyote and bobcat prints on the trail—since dogs are not permitted at Round Valley, all prints are most likely from wild residents of the area.

Although the grade never increases beyond moderate, you might want to stop occasionally to enjoy the views back to the northwest, which extend beyond the boundaries of the preserve to include Mount Diablo's main and north peaks, an unusual perspective of the East Bay's tallest mountain.

The Hardy Canyon Trail sticks to a course downslope from the hilltop, effectively looping around the hill. As you progress uphill, the oaks thin a bit and grassland dominates the landscape. The trail jogs left, then right, on a little switchback around a long thin rock formation that resembles a sloping wall. There's one last gentle ascent through grassland, and then the trail reaches a slight saddle. A rough path veers right, but the official trail almost immediately starts downhill to the left. You never reach the hilltop; but then again, with views this nice, you don't need to.

The preserve boundary is a short distance to the right, and the adjacent property is the Los Vaqueros Watershed. The two properties don't connect here, but if they did, it would create a great hiking loop opportunity (you can enter the watershed from a gate on Miwok Trail at the south end of Round Valley). As the Hardy Canyon Trail descends to the east, scattered cow paths (one leading to a watering trough) make navigation a bit tricky. Aim for the crease between this hill and another to the right. Gradually you'll enter an area with a high concentration of blue and coast live oaks. There's a little steep scramble down and up near a slide area, then the trail adopts a course along the banks of High Creek. Here, as in other parts of the park where water runs in winter and spring, buckeyes grow clustered together.

The Hardy Canyon Trail climbs slightly, then descends back toward the creek. Since the creek is dry by autumn, previous ranchers maximized the flow by constructing a little dam, which still stands today, to hold back a little pool of water year-round.

At 3.3 miles, you'll reach a crucial junction, which may be unsigned. Be sure to bear left and cross the creek—the path to the right heads into private property. As you make your way gently uphill through oaks and grassland, an occasional vehicle on Marsh Creek Road may be audible. Hawks are very common in this part of the preserve, using the trees to scope out small mammals in the adjacent meadow to the right.

The trail descends into grassland, then sweeps left to reach a gate. On the other side you'll follow along yet another waterway, Marsh Creek, where cottonwood and sycamore share their autumnal-tinted leaves in November. At 4 miles the trail rises up to meet the Miwok Trail back at the hike's first junction. Turn right and return to the parking lot.

▶ NEARBY ACTIVITIES

In spring the sides of Marsh Creek Road host a better wildflower display than the preserve, which is grazed by flower-eating cows.

RUSH RANCH

▶ IN BRIEF

Just a few miles from Solano County's bustling suburbia, the largest contiguous estuarine marsh in the Lower 48 unfolds. Suisun Marsh has over 100,000 acres of grassland, bays, sloughs, and tidal wetlands teaming with wildlife, including elk, otters, birds, and fish. Rush Ranch, a tiny oasis in the northern part of Suisun Marsh, is the most user-friendly destination to explore the area.

▶ DESCRIPTION

Pick up a South Pasture Trail Guide from the visitor center, then begin on the south side of the ranch, following the sign for the South Pasture Trail. If you're visiting in April, you might catch lilac bushes in bloom beside a house on the right. The trail begins near a water tower, windmill, and walnut grove in the middle of a display of old ranching equipment, all surrounded with a white fence. You can take the loop in either direction, but the tour progresses counterclockwise, so continue straight from the trailhead. Past the windmill, the trail heads toward Spring Branch Creek through some grassland and marsh plants, including pickleweed and alkali heath. This area is a transitory zone between Rush Ranch's lowland marsh and higher, dry pasture. In spring, some owl's clover, butter and eggs (johnnytuck), and vetch bloom along the trail; in late summer, yellow star thistle accompanies willowherb, a tall delicate

ⓘ KEY AT-A-GLANCE INFORMATION

LENGTH: 2.2 miles

CONFIGURATION: Loop

DIFFICULTY: Easy

SCENERY: Grassland, marsh

EXPOSURE: Entirely exposed

TRAFFIC: Light

TRAIL SURFACE: Dirt trails

HIKING TIME: 1 hour

SEASON: Muddy in winter, good other seasons—trail can be hard to follow in winter and spring

ACCESS: No fee

MAPS: The park map is available at the trailhead's information signboard.

FACILITIES: Portable toilets are located at the trailhead.

SPECIAL COMMENTS: Dogs are permitted on one trail only.

▶ DIRECTIONS

Depart San Francisco on the Bay Bridge and use the toll plaza as the mileage starting point. Stay to the left, on northbound I-80. Drive north on I-80 about 35 miles, then exit onto CA 12 East. Drive about 4 miles east on CA 12, then turn right onto Grizzly Island Road. Drive about 2.5 miles south on Grizzly Island Road, then turn right into the preserve.

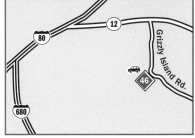

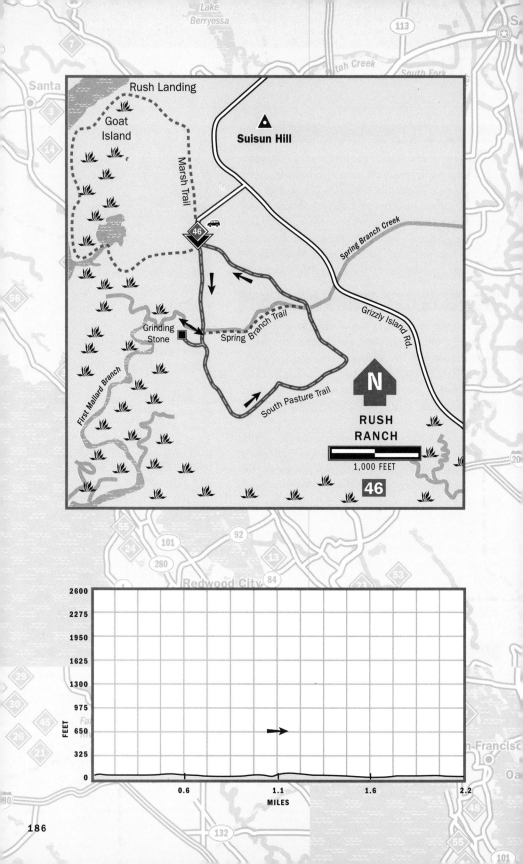

plant with tiny pink flowers. According to the ranch's trail guide, the little notched hill off to the right was a "barrow pit." Just before the trail ascends a slight rise at 0.3 miles, the Spring Branch Trail breaks off to the left, shortcutting the loop. Continue straight to the hilltop, then turn right, following a sign "to Indian grinding rock."

The path descends easily. On one hike, I flushed a northern harrier off a fencepost and watched it fly away, searching for a quieter hunting spot. At about one-half mile, you'll reach the grinding rock, a bedrock mortar used by Patwin Indians. Continue back to the South Pasture Trail, then turn right. After a few feet, pass through a cattle gate, then turn right. In spring this part of the ranch is tough to navigate, since there are cow paths everywhere—look for the numbered posts if you wander off the trail. While in late summer the pasture is an unbroken expanse of dry golden grass, there are quite a few wildflowers in spring, including blue-eyed grass, butter and eggs, and lupines. Acres of flat land and marsh to the south accentuate views of Mount Diablo. As the South Pasture Trail sweeps left you may notice military aircraft taking off or landing at Travis Air Force Base, just over the Potrero Hills to the east. Near a water tank and trough, the trail again becomes hard to follow, since the area is muddy and traced with cattle paths. A post off to the left seems to be a decoy—the trail goes between the tank and trough. Once out of the area, you should be aimed toward the hills. Tall willowy wild radish plants sway with the breeze in spring along the trail. At 1.4 miles, be on the lookout for an important junction, signed by a post. Here the trail seems to continue straight, but the hike's route bends left.

Descending through a lumpy area, a little seep makes things muddy in the wet months. On a hike in September through dry grass, every step dislodged a cloud of grasshoppers. The South Pasture Trail approaches a fenceline and junction. Although most fences in cattle country feature squeeze-through stiles, this one is a climb-over kind. In summer and autumn, try to avoid jabs from the yellow star thistle plants around the fence. The Spring Branch Trail heads back to the left. Continue straight.

The South Pasture Trail drops into the Spring Branch Creek basin. In summer and autumn the area is a bone-dry bowl, while winter and spring restore a seasonal flow. I've seen the creek as a wispy waterway small enough to jump over, but the trail guide suggests that heavy rains create a river 50 feet across and up to 2 feet deep. An elevated walkway helps keep your feet dry in the wetter months. The trail curves left around a hillside where vetch stains the grass purple in April. As you pass a small pond on the left, the ranch buildings come back into view. There's another cattle fence, this one with a proper gate. On the right, in March, a level meadow is overtaken by carpets of butter and eggs, a little cream-colored flower properly named *Triphysaria eriantha*. At 2.2 miles, you'll pass through one last gate and return to the trailhead.

▶ NEARBY ACTIVITIES

Unlike the Grizzly Island Wildlife Area, which comprises the bulk of the publicly-accessible land, Rush Ranch does not permit hunting or fishing, is open year-round, and offers self-guided hikes and interpretive programs. There are three options at Rush Ranch: an out-and-back path that climbs into the Potrero Hills across from

Rush Ranch's entrance; one loop exploring the marsh; and a second loop, described above, a mellow circuit through the preserve's pasture area.

Grizzly Island Wildlife Area, 6.5 miles farther south on Grizzly Island Road, is one of the best spots in the Bay Area for birdwatching and also boasts populations of elk and otter. Grizzly Island's marshes and wetlands can be experienced quite well on a leisurely drive or hike, but the area is only open for nature exploration from mid-winter to mid-summer, and again briefly in autumn. When Grizzly Island closes for nature exploration, it opens to hunting, and the dates fluctuate every year, so call (707) 425-3828 for exact dates or more information.

RUSSIAN RIDGE
OPEN SPACE PRESERVE

▶ IN BRIEF

When spring in all its glory graces the Bay Area, Russian Ridge is one of the top destinations to enjoy swaths of green grass, gentle breezes, and wildflowers. This loop showcases the best of the preserve on an easy circuit through grassland and clusters of venerable live oaks.

▶ DESCRIPTION

Russian Ridge Open Space Preserve sprawls over one of the Santa Cruz Mountains' rare treeless ridges, so the views are incredible. And since the trailhead is right off CA 35, Russian Ridge is easy to get to and easy to hike—it takes just 10 minutes of walking to reach the ridgeline. If you're on a wildflower mission, you might go no further than an out-and-back jaunt along the ridge. Here, usually peaking in early May, a dramatic blossom extravaganza unfolds with some massive carpets of lupines shading the grass purple and plenty of liberal multihued sprinklings. In addition to the lupines, you'll likely see tidytips, owl's clover, California poppy, creamcups, and johnny-jump-ups. Although Russian Ridge is renowned as a wild-flower destination, the preserve offers good hike possibilities year-round.

From the trailhead, begin walking uphill on the Ridge Trail. The first stretch runs parallel to CA 35, but soon the trail passes a cluster of buckeye

ⓘ KEY AT-A-GLANCE INFORMATION

LENGTH: 3.6 miles

CONFIGURATION: Balloon

DIFFICULTY: Easy

SCENERY: Grassland, oaks, wildflowers

EXPOSURE: Mostly unshaded

TRAFFIC: Moderate weekends, quiet weekdays, busy during wildflower peak

TRAIL SURFACE: Dirt trails and fire roads

HIKING TIME: 2 hours

SEASON: Good any time, amazing in spring

ACCESS: No fee

MAPS: Park map is available from an information signboard in the parking lot.

FACILITIES: Pit toilets at the trailhead

SPECIAL COMMENTS: Dogs are not permitted.

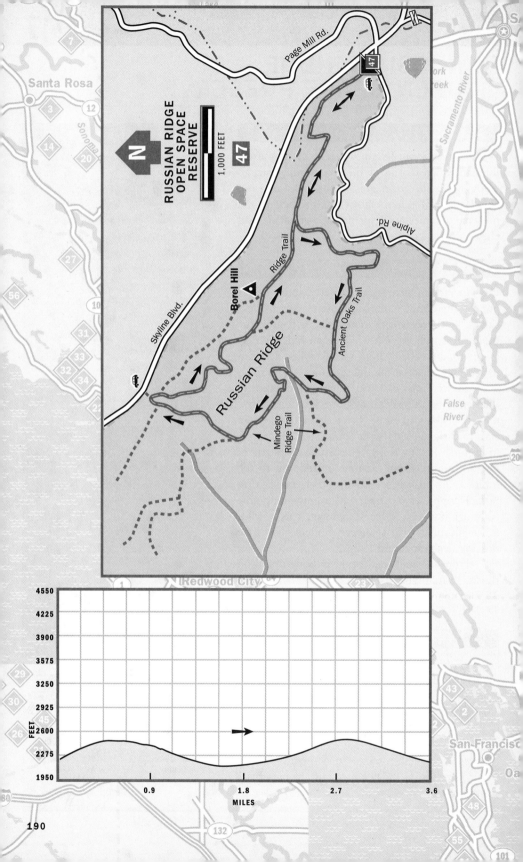

RUSSIAN RIDGE OPEN SPACE RESERVE

N

1,000 FEET

47

Page Mill Rd.

Santa Rosa

Skyline Blvd.

Borel Hill

Ridge Trail

Russian Ridge

Ancient Oaks Trail

Alpine Rd.

Mindego Ridge Trail

False River

Redwood City

San Francisco

FEET

4550
4225
3900
3575
3250
2925
2600
2275
1950

0.9   1.8   2.7   3.6
MILES

and jogs left, cushioning the noise from the road. The trail turns again and now begins to follow the ridgeline, gaining elevation at an easy pace. Grassland sprawls on both sides of the trail and, as you head northwest, the trail stretches out straight ahead into an inviting ribbon. At 0.6 miles, bear left, following the sign "to Ancient Oaks Trail."

Sweeping south downslope from the ridge, the trail passes through some pockets of California bays and oaks. You'll likely hear vehicles on Alpine Road, partly visible in some places on the left. At 0.9 miles, ignore a spur trail that heads straight, ending shortly at the road, and turn right onto the Ancient Oaks Trail.

Pass buckeyes cuddled up in the creases of the hillside on the left, as the narrow trail crosses through grassland and descends slightly. On clear days there are long views west to the ocean, as well as to Mindego Ridge, a volcanic formation. California poppy and blue and white lupine dot the grassland through here in spring. You might also see gopher snakes sunning themselves on the trail. Where the Ancient Oaks Trail steps into the woods and reaches a junction at 1.2 miles, continue to the left/straight on the Ancient Oaks Trail.

Although gorgeous live oaks play a starring roll along the trail, you might also see madrone and Douglas fir. In the shaded understory, look for hound's tongue in spring. The trail winds downhill, taking a brief foray through grassland before returning to woods again. Creambush and hazelnut mingle with ferns to create a lush atmosphere, particularly in winter after a rainstorm, when you might catch newts crossing the trail. At 1.6 miles the Ancient Oaks Trail ends. Turn right onto the Mindego Ridge Trail and begin to climb out of the woods, skirting the base of the grassy ridge. In summer, look for painted lady and red admiral butterflies near a wet seep on the right. The Mindego Ridge Trail ends at a 3-way junction at 1.9 miles, and there is an opportunity to extend this hike an additional 1.3 miles, via the Hawk Trail to the left. Bear right, though, following the signage for vista point parking.

Ascend easily through quiet grassland. At 2.2 miles, follow the trail as it crests and reaches a junction. The trail continuing straight ends at Skyline Boulevard, across from a small vista point parking area. The Bay Area Ridge Trail extends to the left and right. Turn right onto the Bay Area Ridge Trail, and, after a few steps, the path splits (both trails reconnect after about one-half mile), but stay to the right.

Small rock outcrops sit off the sides of the trail, which ascends slightly through grassland just off the ridgeline. This is a good segment to look for coyotes, active residents of the preserve. Views west are outstanding. Flowers are sprinkled through the grass in spring, a visual snack for the main course still to come. At 2.7 miles a path connecting to the Ancient Oaks Trail departs on the right, but continue straight on the Ridge Trail. A few feet farther uphill, the other leg of the Ridge Trail feeds in from the left. Stay to the right.

Now hugging the spine of the ridge, the trail enters an area legendary with Bay Area wildflower enthusiasts. During the peak of the season, usually early May, flowers pop (literally and figuratively) out of the lush green grass along the trail. These are "common" wildflowers, including johnny-jump-ups, owl's clover, blue and white lupine, California poppy, tidytips, creamcups, clarkia, and blue-eyed grass, but the display's frequency and urgency are what knock your socks off. Marvel at your leisure, but take care to stay on the trail, and of course, don't pick the flowers! If you follow the change of seasons at Russian Ridge, you'll note that while in spring the grass is short and verdant, by midsummer the hillsides are cloaked in thigh-high grass, and the only flowers still in bloom are usually a few tired-looking tidytips and mule ear sunflowers.

Continuing, the Ridge Trail descends gradually, offering views south to the hills of Monte Bello Open Space Preserve, topped by 2,800-foot Black Mountain. When you reach the junction with the path to the Ancient Oaks Trail again at 3 miles, continue straight, retracing your steps back to the parking lot.

▶ NEARBY ACTIVITIES

Yerba Buena Nursery sells a broad variety of native plants and features a gorgeous garden. The nursery is down a dirt road 3 miles north of the Russian Ridge trailhead —look for a large sign on the west side of CA 35 at 19500 Skyline Boulevard. Phone (650) 851-1668 for more info, or visit www.yerbabuenanursery.com.

SAN BRUNO MOUNTAIN COUNTY PARK

▶ IN BRIEF

Sprawling just south of the San Francisco County line, San Bruno Mountain is the perfect park for a quick get-out-of-town hike. This 3.5-mile loop climbs through coastal scrub to a ridge, where views include the mountains of Marin and San Mateo counties. After cresting near the mountain's summit, the hike descends back to the trailhead, offering San Francisco and Mount Diablo views all the way downhill.

▶ DESCRIPTION

One of the Bay Area's most important urban-fringe open spaces, San Bruno Mountain has evaded development plans since the 1960s. One group wanted to shave land off the top of the mountain to fill the bay near San Francisco Airport, and many developers eyed the land for housing tracts. Development plans were firmly squelched in 1976, when the rare Mission Blue butterfly, which lives only on San Bruno Mountain and San Francisco's Twin Peaks, was placed on the U.S. Fish and Wildlife's endangered species list. Although houses have crept up the sides of the mountain and communications equipment protrudes from the summit area, over 2,000 acres of San Bruno Mountain is protected. The mountain, surrounded by densely populated neighborhoods, feels like an island.

▶ DIRECTIONS

From US 101 in San Francisco County (just north of the San Mateo County border), exit at Third Street/Cow Palace. Drive south on Bayshore Boulevard about 2 miles, turn right on Guadalupe Canyon Parkway, and drive uphill about 2 miles to the park entrance on the right side of the road. Once past the entrance kiosk, follow the park road under Guadalupe Canyon Parkway to the trailhead near the native plant garden on the left.

ℹ KEY AT-A-GLANCE INFORMATION

LENGTH: 3.5 miles

CONFIGURATION: Loop

DIFFICULTY: Easy

SCENERY: Coastal scrub, views

EXPOSURE: Nearly all full sun

TRAFFIC: Moderate; the loop is popular in spring.

TRAIL SURFACE: Dirt trails

HIKING TIME: 2 hours

SEASON: Perfect in spring, but bring a jacket in case it's windy

ACCESS: Pay $4 day-use fee at entrance kiosk.

MAPS: Park map is available at the entrance kiosk and trailhead.

FACILITIES: Rest rooms and water near the entrance kiosk

SPECIAL COMMENTS: Dogs are not permitted.

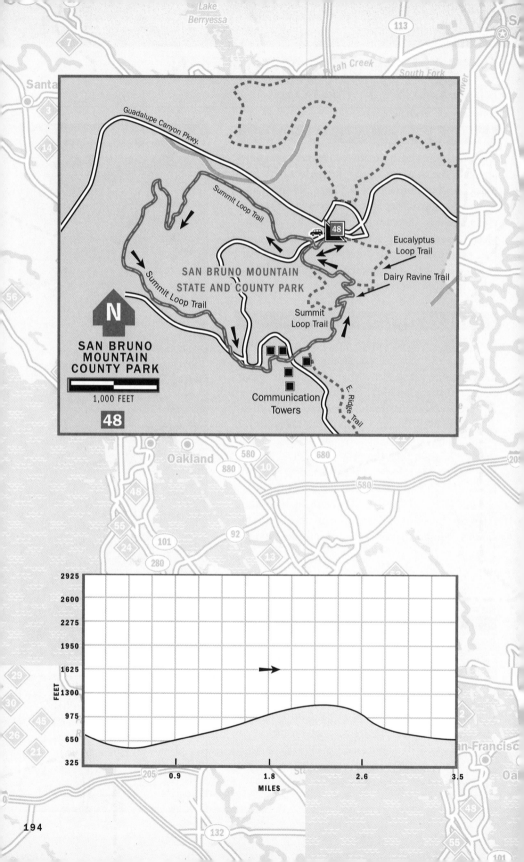

Guadalupe Canyon Pkwy.

Summit Loop Trail

48

Eucalyptus
Loop Trail

Dairy Ravine Trail

SAN BRUNO MOUNTAIN
STATE AND COUNTY PARK

Summit
Loop Trail

Summit Loop Trail

N

SAN BRUNO
MOUNTAIN
COUNTY PARK

1,000 FEET

48

Communication
Towers

E. Ridge Trail

FEET	MILES
2925	
2600	
2275	
1950	
1625	
1300	
975	
650	
325	

0.9   1.8   2.6   3.5

Removal of invasive vegetation has been a long-term volunteer project for San Bruno Mountain advocacy groups. Eucalyptus, cotoneaster, ivy, and broom thrive in some areas, but the shrub gorse probably covers the most terrain. The area of the park north of Guadalupe Canyon Parkway is largely overrun with the plant—you can get a first-hand view of the problem from the eastern leg of the Summit Trail in spring, when entire hillsides in the north part of the park flush yellow with blooming gorse. Even with so much non-native vegetation, there are plenty of native plants a hiker might see on just one San Bruno Mountain visit. There is an abundance of common flora, but you'll see lots of unusual and some endangered plants, including a wallflower, an owl's clover, and a few varieties of manzanita. April and May are the peak times for wildflowers.

The San Bruno Mountain loop begins at a large trail sign in front of the native plant garden. Follow the arrow pointing right to the Summit Loop Trail, and you'll wind through the garden, then reach a signed junction with the Eucalyptus Loop Trail. Bear right onto the Summit Loop Trail, then after a few steps, cross the road.

The Summit Loop Trail begins a slight descent through an area where eucalyptus, ivy, and cotoneaster thrive near a creek. On the right, a damp bowl-shaped meadow fosters willows. Scorpionweed, blue-eyed grass, checkerbloom, fringecups, and cow parsnip bloom in spring, tangled through coyote brush, coffeeberry, and lizardtail. Guadalupe Canyon Parkway is visible and audible to the north, but the trail soon bends left, crosses April Brook, then starts climbing south on a few switchbacks. As you reach the ridgeline, the grade tapers off and plants along the trail seem to hunker down, keeping a low profile against winds that regularly whip across the mountain. Oregon grape nestles in rock outcroppings, while sprinkled through sagebrush, annual wildflowers include paintbrush, johnny-jump-up, and varieties of owl's clover.

On clear days, views extend north to the Point Reyes Peninsula and Mount Tamalpais. The Summit Loop Trail veers left off the ridgeline and runs downslope. Cottontails can be glimpsed at the edge of the trail, but on approach they dive into thickets of coastal scrub comprised of coyote brush, lizardtail, sticky monkeyflower, twinberry, and poison oak. A cluster of hummingbird sage near a kink in the trail puts forth bold, bright pink flowers in spring.

On the final push toward the summit, the trail crosses a paved service road, then snakes uphill not far from the park road. In spring, stands of iris bloom in a community of stunted-looking sagebrush, coyote brush, and lizardtail. Tiny-leaved yerba buena trails along the ground, within sight of downtown San Francisco—an appropriate proximity since this plant lent its name to the village which became the city of San Francisco in 1847.

Some shortcuts and one unsigned spur off to the right make the trail a little hard to follow, but just keep heading uphill toward the communications towers. Looking west, the Farallon Islands are often visible if it's not too foggy. At 2.4 miles the Summit Loop Trail crosses a paved road. You'll likely want to hurry through this area, marred with ugly communications buildings, dishes, and towers (but I did have my first ever coyote sighting near this junction). After a few steps, a gorgeous blend of coastal scrub signals a return to a more natural setting.

Just as the trail begins to descend, the East Ridge Trail departs on the right. Continue straight on the Summit Loop Trail. At an easy pace, the trail drifts downhill towards a bench off to the right where hikers can gaze north to San Francisco or across the bay to Mount Diablo. In spring, goldenfields occupy grassy patches off the trail like an invading army. At 2.6 miles you'll reach a signed junction. Turn right onto the Dairy Ravine Trail, although either of the opposing flanks of Dairy Ravine will return to the trailhead.

On long fluid switchbacks through coastal scrub, the Dairy Ravine Trail descends. I've seen wildflowers blooming along the trail here as early as mid-January, and during the peak season you'll likely see plenty of scorpionweed, blue-eyed grass, bluedicks, seaside daisy, California poppy, and paintbrush. Soon, the Dairy Ravine Trail ends at a signed junction at 3 miles. Again, although either trail is an option, bear left onto the Eucalyptus Loop Trail.

Following a slight descent, the trail levels as it passes through a stretch of invasives. Three of the park's problem plants—eucalyptus, ivy, and cotoneaster—all grow together in a small colony of exotics. Here, the Eucalyptus Loop Trail drops easily back to a junction with the Summit Loop Trail at 3.2 miles, where you'll continue straight/right.

The two loops run together downhill, then split at 3.4 miles. Turn right at the split and walk back through the garden to the trailhead.

SIERRA AZUL
OPEN SPACE PRESERVE

IN BRIEF

The biggest Bay Area preserve you've never heard of may be Sierra Azul. With over 16,700 acres, this massive preserve sprawls over the flanks of Mount Umunhum, in the Sierra Azul range just southwest of San Jose. There are plenty of long, hard hikes to experience here, but this short out-and-back stroll is the preserve's easiest—a nearly level hike through chaparral to a grassy knoll where views extend far to the southeast.

DESCRIPTION

The Sierra Azul Open Space Preserve has a long and colorful history. The preserve's highest point, Mount Umunhum, was a sacred peak to native Ohlone Indians, who graced the rugged peak with this melodius name, which translates as "the resting place of the hummingbird." In the 1950s the Air Force constructed a radar station at the top of Umunhum, and until 1979, the facility scanned the coast for potential Russian threats. When the station closed, the Air Force left behind crumbling buildings, contaminated property, and an oddly shaped six-story structure at the top of the mountain, which still stands today. Locals have fond

KEY AT-A-GLANCE INFORMATION

LENGTH: 1.4 miles

CONFIGURATION: Out-and-back

DIFFICULTY: Very easy

SCENERY: Chaparral, grassland, views

EXPOSURE: Entirely unshaded

TRAFFIC: Light

TRAIL SURFACE: Dirt fire road

HIKING TIME: 1 hour

SEASON: Very hot in summer, but good any time

ACCESS: No fee

MAPS: None at this trailhead. Stop at the Jacques Ridge trailhead (on Mount Umunhum Road just a few feet from the Hicks Road intersection) for a map.

FACILITIES: None at this trailhead—there's a vault toilet at the Jacques Ridge trailhead

SPECIAL COMMENTS: The only parking is a small rough pullout on the right side of the road, just before a gate across Mount Umunhum Road—don't block the gate. Dogs are permitted on some preserve trails, but not this one.

DIRECTIONS

Drive south from San Francisco on I-280 and use the CA 1/19th Avenue merge as the mileage starting point. Drive south on I-280 about 36 miles, then exit onto CA 85 south. After 10 miles, exit at Camden Avenue. Stay in either of the two left lanes, and at the end of the exit ramp, turn left onto Camden. Drive 2 miles, then turn right onto Hicks Road. Drive 6 miles, and turn right onto (probably unsigned) Mount Umunhum Road (if you get to Almaden Road, you've gone too far). Drive uphill 1.7 miles to a small pullout just before the gate stretching across Mount Umunhum Road.

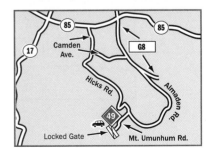

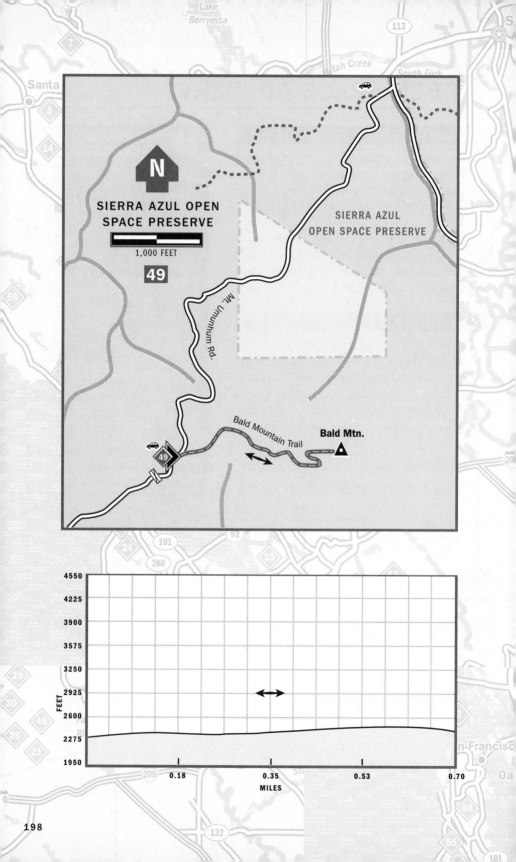

memories of (mostly illegal) trespasses on the slopes of Mount Umunhum, and bittersweet feelings about the prominent sugar cube–shaped mountaintop building that was made inaccessible more than 20 years ago. The Midpeninsula Regional Open Space District began purchasing Sierra Azul property in the 1980s, and like a jigsaw puzzle, a series of relatively small additions have resulted in one huge, but somewhat fragmented, preserve. Many areas are still off-limits to the public while other parcels are surrounded by private inholdings, and the battle to clean up the top of Umunhum has raged for years. It's now hoped that federal funds can be channeled to the area, so that the dangerous conditions at the summit can be rectified, and the top reopened.

Most of the preserve trails are long fire roads that ramble up and down the hillsides at steep grades, making Sierra Azul a favorite with experienced mountain bikers and equestrians. Hikers can make all-day treks along rolling ridgelines, like the 11-mile (one-way) trip from Lexington Reservoir to the Jacques Ridge Trailhead on Mount Umunhum Road. Sierra Azul rivals some of the largest state parks in the Bay Area for sheer size and diversity, preserving chaparral, redwood groves, mixed woodlands, headwaters, and grassy slopes, all just a short drive from San Jose.

Start from the parking lot on the wide fire road departing to the southeast, called the Bald Mountain Trail. As the trail skirts a hill to the left, on the right the hillside drops steeply into a canyon, permitting long views to the southern leg of the ridge, including 3,806-foot Loma Prieta. The name Sierra Azul translates to blue range, and in winter months the hillsides off to the south do indeed look blueish-green. The fire road keeps a level pace as it makes its way east, leaves chaparral for grassland, and begins an easy ascent. The trail sweeps uphill, through grass overtaken with flowers in spring, including concentrated pockets of blue-eyed grass and California poppy. The trail curves left and after following a short circuitous route, reaches the top of Bald Mountain at 0.7 miles. Views east and south are excellent—there is a particularly good overview of Almaden Quicksilver County Park, as well as a long look to the Mount Hamilton Range. Back to the west, there's a superb view to Mount Umunhum's conspicuous summit. On a winter hike, I spent some time watching a northern harrier hunt just off the trail—these medium-sized hawks often flutter in place while scanning the ground for prey. Adult males are light gray, with dark-rimmed wings, while adult females are brown above, and mottled brown beneath. When you're ready to return, retrace your steps back to the trailhead.

▶ **NEARBY ACTIVITIES**

You can begin a moderate 4.2-mile out-and-back Sierra Azul trek from the Jacques Ridge Trailhead on the lower section of Mount Umunhum Road: follow the above directions, but as soon as you turn off Hicks Road, look for a small parking and gate SA06 on the right. This hike is a pleasant ascent through chaparral on a fire road, with many nice views of Umunhum's summit. The turnaround point is the trail's junction with Barlow Road, although you could continue to the right, still on the Woods Trail toward El Sombroso (elevation 2,999 feet). View current preserve information and a comprehensive map on the MROSD website at www.openspace.org.

SKYLINE RIDGE
OPEN SPACE PRESERVE

KEY AT-A-GLANCE INFORMATION

LENGTH: 3.8 miles

CONFIGURATION: Loop, with a short out-and-back segment

DIFFICULTY: Easy

SCENERY: Ponds, grassland, chaparral, views

EXPOSURE: A few pockets of shade, otherwise, full sun

TRAFFIC: Moderate

TRAIL SURFACE: Dirt fire road and trails

HIKING TIME: 2 hours, plus any additional time spent lollygagging around the ponds

SEASON: Good all year—nice wildflowers in spring

ACCESS: No fee

MAPS: The "South Skyline Region" map is available at the trailhead.

FACILITIES: A vault toilet at the trailhead, and another near Alpine Pond

SPECIAL COMMENTS: Dogs are not permitted.

▶ IN BRIEF

If you enjoy the quiet tranquility of little mountain lakes, I recommend this short but stunning Skyline Ridge hike. This loop skirts Horseshoe Lake, climbs to a chaparral-covered ridge, then descends through grassland to Alpine Pond. The return route ascends through live oaks to the ridge, then drops through woods and grassland back to the trailhead.

▶ DESCRIPTION

There are quite a few open space preserves and parks sprawled on the crest of the Santa Cruz Mountains, but Skyline Ridge is a favorite of mine. Not only are there sweeping views, grassland, chaparral, and woods, but the preserve also is home to two small man-made lakes which were created to ensure a steady supply of water for former ranches. Horseshoe Lake is partly rimmed with Douglas fir and Christmas tree farm escapees, while Alpine Pond, tucked in the far northern corner of the preserve, hosts Skyline Ridge's nature center. Stretched between the two ponds, there's a ridge comprised of grassland and chaparral, where views extend far to the west, south, and east. This is a good hike for families with kids, because it's fairly short and there's good wildlife viewing at the ponds. You will likely

▶ DIRECTIONS

Depart from San Francisco on southbound I-280 and use the CA 1/19th Avenue merge as the mileage starting point. Drive south on I-280 about 29 miles, then exit onto Page Mill Road. Drive west on Page Mill Road about 9 miles to the junction with CA 35/Skyline Boulevard. Turn left onto Skyline Boulevard and drive south about 0.8 miles, then turn right into the preserve. Stay to the right, and follow the park road to the northern parking lot.

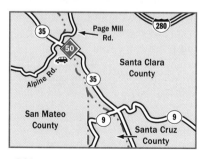

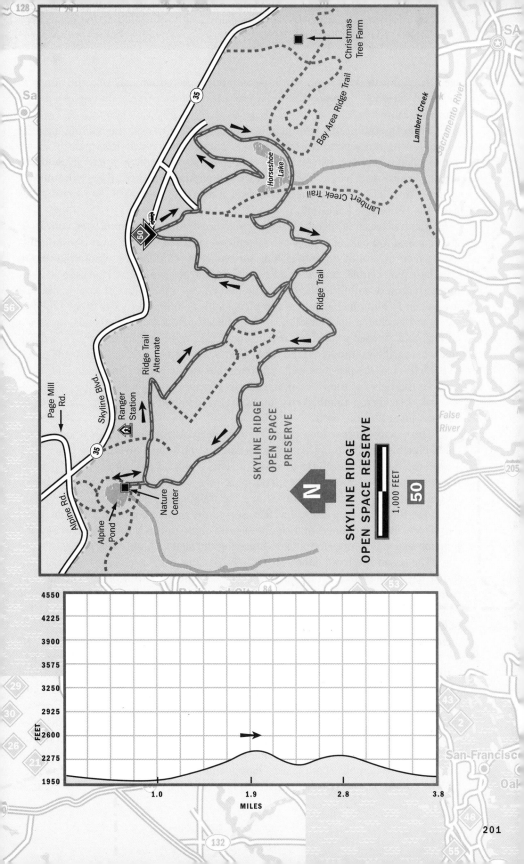

see plenty of waterfowl here, but less-commonly spotted animals visit the ponds as well—on one hike I came within 10 feet of a bobcat completely engrossed in a shoreline hunt.

From the trailhead's information signboard a few feet off the parking lot, bear left, following the sign to Horseshoe Lake. This narrow, nearly level path bisects a sloping damp meadow, where coyote brush is mixed through a few yellow bush lupine shrubs. At 0.1 mile, the path reaches a parking lot reserved for handicapped visitors. Turn left, walk up the access road a few feet, then bear right onto a slim path, the Horseshoe Lake Trail.

The trail ascends slightly, leaving coyote brush for a grassland dotted with Douglas fir, coast live oak, and a few other conifers—a Christmas tree farm is a short distance off to the south. In spring, look for blue and white lupine, California poppy, blue larkspur, clarkia, and Ithuriel's spear. You'll get a peek at Horseshoe Lake's northern arm, downhill to the right. The trail crests in the midst of a grove of coast live oak and California bay, where two picnic tables on opposite sides of the trail provide good, secluded spots for lunch. The Horseshoe Lake Trail descends, crosses a culvert, and reaches a junction at 0.6 miles. Turn right, and pass through a damp area where willows huddle on the right. After a few steps, a second trail heads uphill to the left—like the previous trail, this one leads to the equestrian parking lot. Continue to the right, as the Horseshoe Lake Trail passes through a lush area, with poison oak, blackberry, thimbleberry, and buckeye dominating. The south arm of the lake sits just off to the right.

Once across a tiny footbridge, the trail curves right, leveling in woods where columbine blooms in spring. At 0.8 miles you'll reach a junction with the Ridge Trail. Stay to the right, and reach the shore of the lake. From here you'll have nice views of the entire pond—if you want to spend more time on the shoreline, there's a bench on the right. At 0.9 miles the Horseshoe Lake Trail bends right. Continue straight on the Ridge Trail, and then after a few feet, stay to the right at a junction with the Lambert Creek Trail. The Ridge Trail climbs slightly, through pines and coyote brush to a junction at 1 mile. Turn sharply left, following the sign to Alpine Pond.

The broad fire road climbs moderately, passing a few live oaks, buckeye, California bay, and madrone on the way into grassland. White brodeia, clarkia, and yarrow bloom along the trail in early June. When the Ridge Trail bends right, enjoy views of forested ridges off to the west, including Portola Redwoods State Park. At 1.4 miles, the Ridge Trail meets its alternate route (the return leg of this hike), which continues straight. The path to the right returns to the trailhead. Turn left.

A sign warns of entry into an area inhabited by rattlesnakes. I've never seen any rattlesnakes on this trail, but should you encounter one, here's the protocol. If the snake is stretched out on a trail with plenty of real estate surrounding it, you can probably just gingerly walk around it, keeping yourself as far as possible from its head. If the rattlesnake is coiled, that means it's stressed. Back off a good distance and wait for it to chill out, uncoil, and slither away. Gopher snakes are also common in this and all parts of the Bay Area, and these snakes resemble rattlesnakes, although they are non-venomous. Both snakes have a similar cream, tan, and brown pattern, but the easiest way to tell them apart (from a safe distance, of course!) is by head shape. Gopher snakes have no distinction from their "necks" to their heads, but rattlers have diamond-shaped heads. Both, by the way, make noises to warn off predators—rattlesnakes by shaking their rattles, and gopher snakes by vibrating their tails against the ground.

Climbing easily through grassland, views south and west continue to impress. Although this hillside is infested with invasive yellow star thistle, spring wildflowers are still quite good, with an abundance of owl's clover, clarkia, and California poppy blooming in May. Later, in June, look for yellow mariposa lilies, blended through the tall grass with dandelions. As the trail veers right and runs downslope from the ridge, the trailside vegetation shifts to chaparral, with chamise, manzanita, ceanothus, and yerba santa common, as well as a few shrubs of silktassel and pitcher sage. A pocket of coast live oak provides some unexpected shade. At 1.8 miles, the Ridge Trail squeezes past a boulder on the right, then reaches a junction with an unnamed trail heading right to the top of the ridge. Continue straight.

The next section is dominated in late spring by orange-blossomed sticky monkeyflower shrubs, overshadowing neighboring sagebrush and lizardtail. Descending easily, the Ridge Trail offers views to the grassy shoulders of Russian Ridge to the north. The trail leaves grassland and enters woods, where California bays are dwarfed by some positively massive old live oaks. Now nearly level, the Ridge Trail reaches a junction at 2.3 miles, with a (still somewhat) paved trail. Cross the pavement and continue on the Ridge Trail segment, winding through Douglas fir, pine, California bay, and buckeye to the south shore of Alpine Pond at 2.4 miles. At the Daniel's Nature Center (open weekends) there are exhibits about the preserve's history and wildlife, but even when the nature center is closed, you can enjoy the pond's shoreline, where I've seen crawfish meandering through mud in the driest months of the year. A wheelchair-accessible pond viewing station is set up on the side of the building. When you're ready, return to the previous junction with the paved trail, and turn left (you can also make a loop around the lake, but the trail's proximity to Skyline Boulevard and Alpine Road makes the walk a bit noisy).

The sides of this paved but crumbling wide trail host good displays of Chinese houses and fairy lanterns in spring. Ignore a path breaking off to the right, signed "not a through trail," and continue easily uphill to a T-junction with a paved road at 2.5 miles. Turn left, and after a few feet, just before the ranger station compound, turn right, following the sign to Horseshoe Lake.

White poplars, non-native trees with silvery leaves, are conspicuous on the right. The broad trail passes an old tennis court, then sweeps sharply right and begins to climb, bordering a forest of interior live oak, Douglas fir, and tanoak on the left. At 2.8 miles, turn left, continuing on the Ridge Trail alternate. Climbing at a moderate grade, the trail weaves through the woods, then leaves the trees behind and reaches a crest and junction at 3 miles with an unnamed (and unsigned trail). Continue straight. Slightly downslope from the ridgeline, there are sweeping views east to Monte Bello Open Space Preserve's Black Mountain. In the middle of a sandstone patch, a second trail heads off to the right, but once again, continue straight. From here, it's all downhill, as the trail drops through coyote brush and grassland to a familiar junction at 3.3 miles. Turn left.

The trail steps into woods comprised of big-leaf maple, live oaks, Douglas fir, California bay, and hazelnut. Descending past a cluster of buckeye, you'll reemerge in grassland, where elegant brodeia, yellow mariposa lilies, and clarkia bloom in early June. At 3.8 miles the trail ends, back at the trailhead.

▶ NEARBY ACTIVITIES

At Skyline Ridge's neighboring preserve, Long Ridge, you can hike through woods to a grassy hilltop where a stone bench memorializes Wallace Stegner, an author and preservationist who lived the last years of his life in nearby Portola Valley. Read more about Long Ridge, and view maps of the preserve, at www.openspace.org.

SKYLINE WILDERNESS PARK

▶ IN BRIEF

This hike starts near Skyline Wilderness's RV park, but you'll quickly leave the trappings of civilization behind on a fire road ascending through grassland and oaks to shaded woods near Lake Marie. From here a narrow path skirts sunny slopes above the lake, then you'll follow a series of paths wandering up and down grassland dotted with oaks and buckeyes.

▶ DESCRIPTION

When the Napa State Hospital decided to unload some surplus property in 1979, this land on the outskirts of Napa could easily have been developed. Local residents lobbied to preserve the property and proposed a unique plan: a volunteer-run park. Volunteers, always a huge asset to perennially budget-strapped parks and preserves, manage Skyline Wilderness Park with the assistance of a few paid, part-time employees. The result is a one-of-a-kind destination with miles of trails, an archery range, disk golf course, and small RV park.

   Begin on a trail starting at the edge of the parking lot, beneath a big coast live oak. A small RV park is off to the left, but the Martha Walker Native Habitat Garden creates a buffer between the

▶ DIRECTIONS

Leave San Francisco via the Bay Bridge and use the toll plaza as the mileage starting point. Drive north on I-80 26 miles, then exit onto CA 37. Drive west on CA 37 2.5 miles to the junction with CA 29. Turn right and drive north on CA 29 7.5 miles, then stay to the right at the junction with CA 221 (signed towards downtown Napa and Lake Berryessa). Drive north on CA 221 (signed as the Napa-Vallejo Highway) 3 miles, then turn right onto Imola Avenue. Drive east 2.3 miles, then turn right into the park.

ℹ KEY AT-A-GLANCE INFORMATION

LENGTH: 5.8 miles

CONFIGURATION: Balloon

DIFFICULTY: Easy

SCENERY: Grassland, chaparral, lake, oaks

EXPOSURE: Some pockets of shade, but largely exposed

TRAFFIC: Light

TRAIL SURFACE: Dirt fire road and rocky trails

HIKING TIME: 3 hours

SEASON: Very hot in summer, but good any time

ACCESS: Pay a $4 fee at the entrance kiosk.

MAPS: Pick up a trail map at the entrance kiosk.

FACILITIES: Rest rooms and drinking water available at the parking area

SPECIAL COMMENTS: Dogs are not permitted.

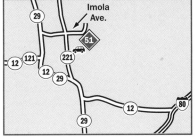

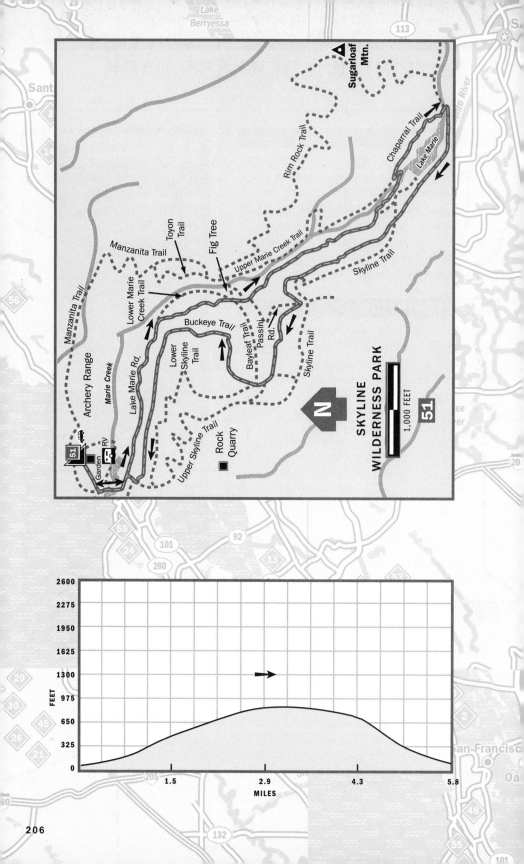

SKYLINE WILDERNESS PARK

1,000 FEET

51

Sugarloaf Mtn.

Rim Rock Trail

Chaparral Trail

Lake Marie

Manzanita Trail

Toyon Trail

Fig Tree

Upper Marie Creek Trail

Skyline Trail

Lower Marie Creek Trail

Manzanita Trail

Buckeye Trail

Bayleaf Trail

Passini Rd.

Skyline Trail

Archery Range

Marie Creek

Lake Marie Rd.

Lower Skyline Trail

Upper Skyline Trail

Rock Quarry

Garden

RV

51

N

trail and the campground. After passing some fruit and nut trees and climbing a few stairs, the trail seems to disappear in the middle of a picnic area. Stay to the right here (if you reach the Social Hall you're headed the wrong way), passing a row of elevated concrete stands. On the far side of the picnic area, a wide trail swings in from the right, reaching a crossroads with a gravel road. Veer left onto signed Lake Marie Road.

Coast live oaks, snowberry shrubs, and blackberry vines strain against a fence which closely borders both sides of the broad dirt road. The trail sweeps left onto pavement briefly, then darts off to the right as the paved road continues straight into privately held Camp Coombs. At a level grade Lake Marie Road skirts at a distance, small lakes to the left and right, then reaches a junction at 0.3 miles. The road to the right leads to Buckeye and Skyline trails. Continue straight on Lake Marie Road.

With a grassy hillside dotted with blue oak and buckeye on the right, the fire road begins an easy climb. On a summer hike, I craned my neck to watch a hummingbird zip past overhead, then noticed a hawk soaring higher in the sky. Wild turkeys and quail also live here and are regularly spotted, even on trails and roads around the RV park. As the fire road ascends, the terrain becomes increasingly rocky, and views open up to include steep-sided Sugarloaf Mountain, the park's highest peak (not to be confused with Sugarloaf Ridge State Park, well north of Skyline Wilderness Park). Near a horse watering trough on the left, there's a cave on the right—this is one of several mysterious old ruins throughout the park, remnants that may predate Napa State Hospital's ownership, which began in the 1870s. Easy-to-miss Marie Creek Trail begins on the left, slipping down to run along the stream toward Lake Marie—continue straight on Lake Marie Road. Off in the distance to the left, look for a well-preserved stone fence dropping down the flanks of Sugarloaf Mountain, one of several stone walls in the park, constructed at an unknown date, perhaps by Chinese or Italian immigrants. Manzanita share the hillsides with chamise and toyon as the fire road dips to a quick series of junctions at 1.2 miles.

The Bayleaf Trail is the first to depart on the right. Continue straight a few more steps where an immense fig tree on the left, swollen with fruit in late summer, is barely contained by a fence constructed to protect it. Here, an unsigned path begins on the left, leading to Lower and Upper Marie Creek trails, the Manzanita Trail, and the Rim Rock Trail. Continue uphill on the Lake Marie Trail, past Passini Road on the right and a path to an outhouse on the left. At a slight incline, the Lake Marie Trail ducks under the shade of California bays, accompanied by varieties of fern, hazelnut, poison oak, creambush, madrone, and sticky monkeyflower. In July, you might see red-flowered Indian pink, one of the latest blooming woodland wildflowers. On the right, the trail passes exposed rock ribs jutting out from the hillside—since no written records were kept preserving the history of the park property, it's difficult to imagine what purpose these served.

At 2 miles, just past a muddy seep beneath a wall of rock on the right, Lake Marie Road rises, and an unsigned but obvious trail departs to the left. Follow this connector trail downhill, and when it climbs to kiss Lake Marie Road goodbye one last time, stay to the left again. The trail descends through dense woods of California bay, passes a few picnic tables on the right, then climbs to Lake Marie's spillway. Here, a rustic log bench, surrounded by blooming paintbrush in spring, makes for a good lunch stop with views down to the water, where there are almost always ducks and birds to watch. This reservoir was constructed in 1908 to supply water for the hospital. Continue from the top of the dam, following the sign to the Chaparral Trail, doubling back parallel to the connector from Lake Marie Road. The path runs along a thin berm, then dips to cross a creek bed and reaches a junction with Chaparral and Upper Marie Creek trails. Turn right.

The Chaparral Trail begins in the shade of coast live oak and California bay, but soon leaves these woods for sun-baked hillsides dotted with buckeye, sagebrush, sticky monkeyflower, poison oak, chamise, and coyote brush. Except for one short foray through a pocket of woods, there are continuous views downhill to the lake. Partly over exposed rock, the Chaparral Trail turns right and begins a descent over a short series of switchbacks. In July, you might notice red-jewel-toned berries on spiny redberry shrubs, a low-growing evergreen bush often confused with ceanothus. Near the far end of the lake, the trail returns to shade beneath California bay, then reaches a T-junction with the Skyline Trail at 2.7 miles. The trail to the left leads to the Rim Rock Trail and the park boundary. Turn right.

After crossing a feeder creek to Lake Marie, the Skyline Trail begins to rise through California bay and coast live oak to a sunnier mix of buckeye, sticky monkeyflower, thimbleberry, and creambush. A connector to Lake Marie Road drops off to the right at 3.1 miles, but continue straight on Skyline, passing an old chimney and the remains of a stone house on the right. At 3.2 miles, another path heading to Lake Marie Road departs on the right, but again, stay to the left, climbing slightly to a junction with the Buckeye Trail at 3.3 miles. The Skyline Trail, a Bay Area Ridge Trail segment, continues uphill, keeping a course parallel to Buckeye but at a higher elevation. Bear right.

The Buckeye Trail quickly climbs into grassland, then tapers off. If you visit in summer, yarrow and California poppy, as well as any last lingering wildflowers, will be long gone, but colorful dragonflies and butterflies, including California sister and common buckeye, are abundant, fluttering above golden grassland. To the right there are views across Marie Creek to Sugarloaf Mountain, Napa Valley, and the rugged ridges that encircle Lake Berryessa. Along the trail, a variety of trees stand in grassland, including buckeye, Oregon oak, blue oak, and coast live oak. The trail forks at 3.7 miles—stay to the right and descend through partial shade to a junction at 3.9 miles. Turn right onto Passini Road briefly, then veer off to the left, onto the signed continuation of the Buckeye Trail. Mostly keeping to exposed grassy slopes, the Buckeye Trail climbs easily. The trail's namesake trees begin to shed their leaves in summer, part of an action-packed lifecycle that includes bare branches and dangling poisonous chestnut-like seedpods in winter, new leaves in late winter, and sweet-smelling white blossoms in spring. At 4.3 miles, the Buckeye Trail follows a stone fence, then merges into an unsigned path from the left, connecting to the Skyline Trail. Stay to the right, pass through a break in the fence into a grassy meadow, then reach a fork with a trail leading left to the Skyline Trail. Veer right and descend a few yards to yet another junction, a roughly elongated X-shaped interchange with the Bayleaf Trail. Turn left, then bear right, remaining on the Buckeye Trail.

The trail passes through a pretty meadow, then ascends slightly to a rocky, rambling route. You may hear noise in this part of the park from a quarry operation, out of sight over the ridge to the west. Deciduous oaks (blue, Oregon, and black) accompany coast live oak, California bay, and buckeye, as the trail sweeps across the hillsides above Lake Marie Road, occasionally visible on the right. At a steady descent, the Buckeye Trail's final stretch runs parallel to Lake Marie Road, ending at 5.4 miles. Turn right.

A fire road descends through blue oaks, passing the River to the Ridge Trail as it heads toward the Napa River on the left, before returning to the junction with Lake Marie Road at 5.5 miles. Turn left and retrace your steps back to the trailhead.

▶ NEARBY ACTIVITIES

Skyline Wilderness Park's habitat garden is a must stop for native plant enthusiasts. This garden began in 1985 and, carefully tended by volunteers, has expanded to a small, impeccably maintained oasis with numerous small fountains and abundant shade that make it the perfect place to cool off after a hike. There are all kinds of native plants, and benches secreted away in leafy alcoves are perfect vantage spots from which to spy on the many birds visiting the garden. I saw about 20 quail and several other birds in one visit—if you're interested in providing habitat for birds and animals in your own garden, this is an inspiring place.

ROBERT LOUIS STEVENSON
STATE PARK

KEY AT-A-GLANCE INFORMATION

LENGTH: 11.2 miles

CONFIGURATION: Out-and-back

DIFFICULTY: Strenuous

SCENERY: Mixed woods, chaparral, views—the highest accessible mountaintop in the Bay Area

EXPOSURE: First half mile is shaded; the rest is exposed.

TRAFFIC: Moderate

TRAIL SURFACE: Badly eroded trail and dirt fire road

HIKING TIME: 5 hours

SEASON: Any time unless it's hot

ACCESS: No fee

MAPS: The Robert Louis Stevenson map (printed along with the Bothe-Napa Valley map) is available at Bothe-Napa Valley State Park, 3.5 miles south of Calistoga on the left side of Highway 29.

FACILITIES: None

SPECIAL COMMENTS: Dogs are not allowed on the park trails.

IN BRIEF

Mount St. Helena is the Bay Area's highest publicly accessible peak, topping out at 4,304 feet. This trek begins uphill on a short, eroded trail, then continues to the summit on a long, sinuous, well-graded fire road. There's very little challenge here, just a steady climb to the top, where views unfold, spanning the distance from the San Francisco skyline to Mount Lassen (on a clear day).

DESCRIPTION

This long hike begins on the west side of CA 29 at the Stevenson Memorial trailhead. A few steps bring the trail up into a small grassy meadow dotted with a few picnic tables, then the climb begins through a mixed woodland of California bay, Douglas fir, tanoak, madrone, and live oaks. You might see red larkspur and columbine blooming in late spring, preceding pink flowers on wild rose shrubs. Visitors have worn ugly shortcuts into the hillsides between the switchbacks here—for anyone considering following their lead, consider the erosion you will cause, as well as the copious amounts of poison oak along the trail. After ascending through woods and a few pockets of manzanita, chamise, and pine, the trail reaches the Stevenson Memorial spot at about 0.7 miles. Author Robert Louis Stevenson and his wife spent

DIRECTIONS

Leave San Francisco via the Bay Bridge and use the toll plaza as the mileage starting point. Drive north on I-80 26 miles, then exit onto CA 37. Drive west on CA 37 2.5 miles to the junction with CA 29. Turn right and drive north on CA 29 38 miles to the junction with CA 128. Turn right, and continue another 9 miles east on CA 29 into Robert Louis Stevenson State Park, where there's roadside parking on the left side of the road (there's a larger dirt lot on the right).

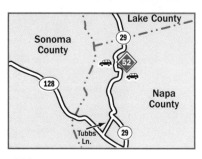

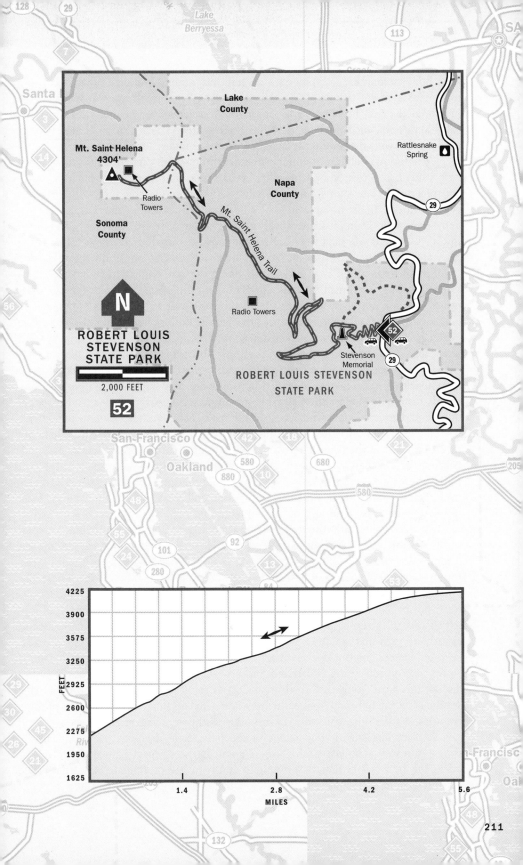

Lake
Berryessa

Lake
County

Mt. Saint Helena
4304'

Radio
Towers

Sonoma
County

Napa
County

Rattlesnake
Spring

N

ROBERT LOUIS
STEVENSON
STATE PARK

2,000 FEET

52

Mt. Saint Helena Trail

Radio Towers

Stevenson
Memorial

52

ROBERT LOUIS STEVENSON
STATE PARK

San Francisco

Oakland

4225

3900

3575

3250

2925

2600

2275

1950

1625

FEET

1.4   2.8   4.2   5.6
MILES

their honeymoon here, sleeping in a decrepit old mining building. Stevenson's slim memoir, *Silverado Squatters,* is a vivid description of their adventures. Just past the memorial the trail becomes badly eroded with several steep sections over exposed rock. Manzanita and knobcone pine line the last steep stretch, then the trail ends at a T-junction with the Mount St. Helena Trail at 0.8 miles. Turn left.

The fire road climbs at a modest grade, through sun-drenched hillsides packed with canyon live oak, knobcone pine, yerba santa, and manzanita. Bush poppy is conspicuous in late spring, when its straggly branches are crammed with gorgeous yellow flowers. Traffic noise from CA 29 is audible, but fades as the trail bends right and heads west. Even at this relatively low elevation there are sweeping views down to Calistoga, and you might see hot air balloons floating through Napa Valley in the early morning hours. Big rock formations are visible, jutting out of the mountainside uphill, and there are piles of little rocks lining the trail with virtually no topsoil in sight. In spring, deerbrush (a white-flowered ceanothus), sticky monkeyflower, paintbrush, iris, and purple bush lupine bloom along the trail. Later, in early summer, look for red-flowered California fuschia, a native annual flower often found in rocky areas. When in *Silverado Squatters* Stevenson wrote about chaparral "thick with pea-like blossoms," he's describing chaparral pea, a shrub with vibrant magenta flowers.

At the base of a rock formation the trail bends sharply right, the first of three switchbacks on the eastern side of the mountain. You might see chipmunks and lizards scampering across the trail and birds of prey flying overhead—be on the lookout for peregrine falcons, which nest in the park. The Mount St. Helena Trail curves left on the second switchback, all the while gaining elevation gradually. There are nice views east to the Palisades area of the park, distinguished by dramatic dark red, volcanic rock formations. After the third switchback the fire road heads north. When I hiked here on an unfortunately hot May day, I appreciated every tiny patch of shade from the occasional knobcone pine, Douglas fir, and cluster of canyon live oak; most of the vegetation is comprised of chaparral shrubs.

At the 4-mile mark, the trail reaches a saddle and unmarked junction. Look off to the right here for a peek of Lake Berryessa. The fire road doubling back to the left leads to South Peak. Continue straight on this fairly level stretch with good views toward North Peak. The trail descends gently, passing through knobcone pine, chinquapin, manzanita, toyon, and California coffeeberry. Some of the manzanita shrubs were still in bloom a few days after Memorial Day. The Mount St. Helena Trail jogs left (ignore the steep path worn by shortcuts, heading straight) and begins to ascend again. Although this is a quiet part of the park, far from civilization and paved roads, keep an eye out for trucks that travel the fire roads to service the communications equipment on top of the North and South peaks. The fire road crests at 5.1 miles, and an unsigned, rough fire road breaks off to the left. Continue to the right. This spot may be the only Bay Area parkland where you can stand at the junction of three counties: Napa to the southeast, Lake to the northeast, and Sonoma to the west.

Descending slightly downslope of the hillside on the left, North Peak finally comes into view. The last push to the summit is the steepest part of the hike, but offers the best views from the mountain south to the prominent Bay Area peaks, Mounts Diablo and Tamalpais. Even though it was a bit hazy on my hike, I could make out downtown San Francisco skyscrapers. The steep climb is over quickly, and at 5.6 miles you'll reach the top. With communications structures sprawling over the mountaintop, there is surprisingly little room to explore—an exposed rocky area is probably the best perch to gaze north, where I was stunned to see all the way to snow-topped Mount Lassen. When you're ready, retrace your steps back to the parking lot.

▶ NEARBY ACTIVITIES

Learn more about the history of the Calistoga area at the Sharpsteen Museum, 1311 Washington Street, Calistoga. Call (707) 942-5911 or visit their website, www.sharp steen-museum.org.

Old Faithful Geyser is a good detour on the way back to Napa Valley. Return toward Calistoga on CA 29, turn right onto Tubbs Lane, and drive about one-half mile to the entrance on the right. Read more about the geyser at www.oldfaithful geyser.com, or call (707) 942-6463.

I highly recommend combining a Mt. St. Helena hike with an overnight stay in one of Calistoga's mineral springs resorts. There are a variety of lodging choices, from basic motels to luxurious inns—just be sure to pick a place with a heated mineral pool to soak your tired legs after climbing the mountain.

SUGARLOAF RIDGE STATE PARK

KEY AT-A-GLANCE INFORMATION

LENGTH: 6.2 miles

CONFIGURATION: Loop

DIFFICULTY: Moderate

SCENERY: Grassland, oaks, views, chaparral, creeks

EXPOSURE: Mostly full sun

TRAFFIC: Light

TRAIL SURFACE: Dirt fire roads, rocky trails, and one paved fire road

HIKING TIME: 3.5 hours

SEASON: Spring is best; it's muddy after rains, and hot in summer.

ACCESS: Pay a $4 fee at the entrance kiosk.

MAPS: The park map is available at the visitor center or entrance kiosk (when staffed).

FACILITIES: Portable toilet located at the trailhead

SPECIAL COMMENTS: Dogs are not permitted on park trails. After rains, you'll get your feet wet crossing the Sonoma Creek. Start this hike early, since there's no shade on the final push to the summit.

IN BRIEF

Sugarloaf Ridge's Bald Mountain holds bragging rights to one of the prettiest and serene viewpoints in the Bay Area. From a relatively diminutive height of 2,729 feet, views include every significant wine country peak and valley. This hike starts at the edge of a sloping meadow, and climbs steadily through a mixture of grassland, chaparral, and mixed woodland for 2.5 miles to the summit. The return route travels along a quiet ridge, drops steeply through gray pines and chaparral to cross Sonoma Creek twice, then wanders through a meadow on the way back to the trailhead.

DESCRIPTION

At Sugarloaf Ridge every step seems like a gift. From the get-go the trails are quiet and the scenery is gorgeous—views from the top of Bald Mountain are icing on the cake. There's so much variety at Sugarloaf that every season has its charm. Sonoma Creek's headwaters originate here, and in winter, streams gush downhill at such a rate that you may feel transported from dry California to lush Washington state. Spring flowers are pretty and the temperatures are hospitable. Summer (if you can endure the heat)

DIRECTIONS

Leave San Francisco on northbound US 101 and use the Golden Gate Bridge toll plaza as the mileage starting point. Drive about 50 miles north on US 101, then exit onto CA 12. Drive east on CA 12 toward Sonoma for 1.5 miles, then turn left on Farmer's Lane. After about 1 mile, turn right onto Fourth Street/CA 12, drive southeast about 8 miles, and turn left onto Adobe Canyon Road. Drive east 3 miles to the entrance kiosk, pay the fee, and then continue a short distance to the parking lot on the left.

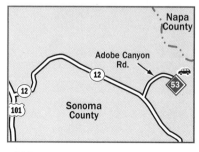

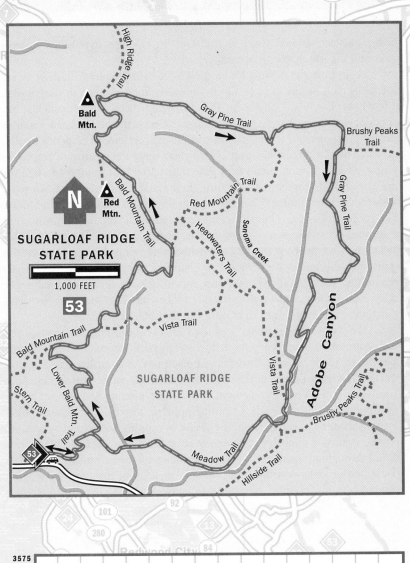

SUGARLOAF RIDGE STATE PARK

N

1,000 FEET

53

Bald Mtn.

Red Mtn.

High Ridge Trail

Gray Pine Trail

Brushy Peaks Trail

Gray Pine Trail

Red Mountain Trail

Bald Mountain Trail

Headwaters Trail

Sonoma Creek

Vista Trail

Bald Mountain Trail

Lower Bald Mtn. Trail

Stern Trail

SUGARLOAF RIDGE STATE PARK

Vista Trail

Adobe Canyon

Brushy Peaks Trail

Meadow Trail

Hillside Trail

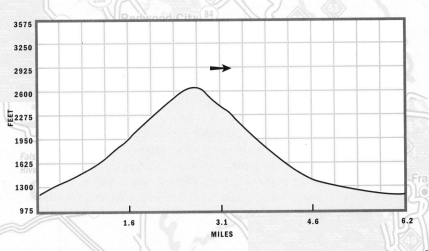

FEET	
3575	
3250	
2925	
2600	
2275	
1950	
1625	
1300	
975	

1.6   3.1   4.6   6.2

MILES

brings hillsides stacked with fragrant blooming chamise. In autumn, foliage on black oaks and big-leaf maples is stunning.

Begin from the parking lot on the Lower Bald Mountain Trail. At an easy grade, the rocky path begins to ascend from the valley floor, winding through grassland past a few coast live oak, Douglas fir, and manzanita. Look for goldenfields, buttercups, shooting stars, iris, bluedicks, and blue-eyed grass in spring. A few small ceanothus shrubs growing close to the ground suggest the presence of serpentine soil—while it may not be obvious in this part of the park, there are significant serpentine swales visible off Bald Mountain and Gray Pine trails. After a short foray through some trees, the Lower Bald Mountain Trail returns to grassland and reaches a two-part junction with the Meadow Trail at 0.2 miles. Stay to the left on the Lower Bald Mountain Trail. The grade picks up as the path climbs into an open woodland mostly comprised of madrone, coast live oak, California bay, and manzanita. On an April hike I saw jackrabbits hopping up the trail. Switchbacking uphill between two creekbeds, the trail gradually makes a transition to chaparral, where chamise, toyon, scrub oak, ceanothus, sticky monkeyflower, and poison oak are the most notable plants. The deep umber color of the trail surface is adobe clay. This rocky segment ends at a T-junction at 0.8 miles. Turn right onto the Bald Mountain Trail.

The trail—a wide, paved road used to access communications equipment atop Red Mountain—ascends at a moderate, steady pace. Vegetation ranges from chamise, manzanita, toyon, monkeyflower, and poison oak to coast live oak and madrone. In spring, flowering purple bush lupine brightens the sides of the trail. At about the 1-mile mark, the Vista Trail departs on the right, offering an early out for hikers who are discouraged by the grade. Continue uphill on the Bald Mountain Trail.

In winter and early spring, the sound of running water from a creek out of sight on the right will probably accompany your hike. The Bald Mountain Trail sweeps uphill through an open area where ceanothus and coyote brush are common. At one corner, water spills downhill from the left, then drops into a ravine where buckeyes nestle. California poppies, blue and white lupine, and scorpionweed bloom along the trail in May. The trail still climbs, and trailside vegetation reflects the change in elevation and exposure—there's lots of chamise, ceanothus, cercocarpus, and scrub oak. At about 1.6 miles, if you pause and look south you will already be able to see Mounts Diablo and Tamalpais. The Red Mountain Trail breaks off to the right at 1.7 miles, headed toward the Gray Pine Trail. Continue straight on the Bald Mountain Trail.

In the shadow of Red Mountain the trail is lined with black oak, big-leaf maple, California bay, and live oaks. Buttercups are common in spring. After a swing into grassland, you'll reach a junction and saddle at 2 miles. Straight ahead the hillside drops, then gradually rises to the flanks of Mount Hood. The pavement curves left on a dead-end spur to Red Mountain. Turn right, remaining on the Bald Mountain Trail.

Now a dirt fire road, the trail adopts a moderately steep course uphill through grassland. You may notice bluish serpentine, exposed on a rock cut on the left. The grassy hillside on the right gently slips away, offering expansive views south. On an April visit, blooming popcorn flowers painted huge white swaths in spring's still-green grass. As you follow the Bald Mountain Trail, sweeping around the very top of the mountain, ignore any side trails and persist to a signed junction at 2.4 miles. The

High Ridge Trail heads left on a dead-end journey. Turn right onto the Gray Pine Trail. After just a few feet, Gray Pine veers left. Turn right and walk uphill a few more feet to the summit. Interpretive signs assist you in identifying the surrounding sites: in the immediate area you can see Napa Valley, Sonoma Valley, the steep hillsides of Jack London Park, and the more gently graded hillsides of Annadel State Park. On an April hike the top of Mount St. Helena to the north, hid in a puffy white cloud.

When the visibility permits, you may also see Mount Wittenberg, the highest peak on Point Reyes (33 miles west); Snow Mountain (65 miles north, and since it is well-named, easy to pick out); Mount Diablo (51 miles southeast); Mount Tamalpais (37 miles southwest); the Golden Gate Bridge (44 miles southwest); and even Pyramid Peak in the Sierra (a whopping 129 miles east). The bench at the grassy summit offers a perch for one of the most quiet and gorgeous lunch breaks in the entire Bay Area. Save for an occasional airplane, there's no outside noise. When you're ready to start moving again, return to the Gray Pine Trail and begin to descend.

The first section of this trail seems poorly named, as there is nary a pine in sight. On the left some towering black oak make a big impact in autumn, but in spring, train your gaze to the grass on the sides of the trail where bird's eye gilia bloom. The fire road follows just about smack on the line dividing Napa and Sonoma counties as it descends, generally following the ridgeline. You'll see more manzanita, California bay, Douglas fir, coyote brush, chamise, and toyon. In early April, blue-blossom ceanothus flowers, followed a bit later by clematis, a trailing vine with white flowers, which drapes itself over shrubs. Although the route is downhill, there is one short uphill section. At 3.2 miles the Red Mountain Trail ventures off to the right—you could make an alternate return on Red Mountain, Headwaters, and Vista trails. Continue straight on the Gray Pine Trail.

Descending at a slightly steep pitch, look for woodland star, buttercups, and blue-eyed grass in spring. Black oaks, chaparral, and grassland continue to line the trail, but the first of the gray pines appears as well. After one last hill climb, you'll reach the junction with the Brushy Peaks Trail at 3.6 miles. Turn right, remaining on the Gray Pine Trail.

By now the trailside blend of chamise, cercocarpus, ceanothus, scrub oak, manzanita, and monkeyflower should be familiar. Tall and spindly gray pine (also known as ghost pine) tower above the trail here and there—if you're hiking when it's a bit breezy, you may want to pause and enjoy the sound of the wind whispering through the pines. Descending off the ridge, the grade is steep, and some sections are very rocky. The Gray Pine Trail leaves its namesake trees behind and arcs through a grassy area, where wet-weather runoff flows down off the hillsides and muddies the trail.

Now following a branch of Sonoma Creek, still descending but at an easy grade, madrone and coast live oak appear. After a sharp turn left, you'll cross another feeder creek. Look along the sides of the trail for golden fairy lanterns in late April and early May. Wandering along the creek through this flat creek basin during a spring hike with the sounds of rushing water everywhere, I felt like I was on an alpine vacation. The Gray Pine Trail makes its first creek crossing—in the warmest months of year you can hop over whatever water is left in the creek bed, but from winter through spring the water level is high enough that your feet (and ankles) will likely get wet. I took off my shoes and socks and waded across the cool water, and my feet felt like they had been given a whole new lease on life. (Park management is exploring the addition of footbridges to this segment, so you may not have the option of wading across in the future.) Buckeye, alder, and California bay stand near the creek, enjoying the reliable water source. At 4.8 miles the Vista Trail feeds in from the right. Continue to the left on Gray Pine to the second creek crossing with generally even deeper water to ford. A gorgeous mature big-leaf maple graces the stream here—if you're here in spring when the tree is clothed in fresh green leaves, you'll have to imagine it lit up with autumn foliage. The Gray Pine Trail ends at 5 miles. Turn right onto the Meadow Trail.

From here on out, the grade is very easy—a relaxing stroll, really. Once more you'll cross Sonoma Creek (this time on a bridge), then pass through groves of maples. A curious "Saturn" sign on the left is part of the Planet Walk interpretive hike that originates at Ferguson Observatory. The creek veers off to the left, continuing its journey toward Sonoma Valley, but the trail leaves the streamside to make its way through a meadow. Some chaparral thrives in a serpentine patch on the right, but grassland soon overtakes the landscape. The meadow is yet another super scenic Sugarloaf spot—this would be a good location for a bench, since both grass and trail are often damp in winter and spring. At 5.7 miles the Hillside Trail breaks off to the left, heading back over Sonoma Creek toward the park's campground. Continue straight, through or around a gate, where you'll emerge in a parking lot. Veer right, passing Ferguson Observatory, and pick up the continuation of the Meadow Trail. On a slight ascent through a rocky area, another feeder creek descends on the left. Goldenfields make a big impact along the trail in spring, when they form sunny carpets in the grass. In patches of serpentine with sparse grass, you likely see more bird's eye gilia. Here on my April hike I had another jackrabbit sighting. At 5.8 miles you'll reach a two-part, triangle junction with the Lower Bald Mountain Trail. Stay to the left, and retrace your steps back to the trailhead.

▶ NEARBY ACTIVITIES

Sugarloaf abuts Hood Mountain, a Sonoma County park with a peak 1 foot higher than Sugarloaf's Bald Mountain. Some Hood Mountain trails are shown on Sugarloaf's map, but for more information visit the Sonoma County Parks website at www.sonoma-county.org/parks/pk_hood.htm, or call (707) 565-2041.

SUNOL REGIONAL WILDERNESS

▶ IN BRIEF

Sunol's jagged peaks and grassy ridges are surrounded by open space, cushioning the impact from nearby East Bay towns and highways. There's a lot of real estate here with natural wonders that include rock formations, creeks, and even small waterfalls in winter and spring. This loop just scratches the surface of Sunol, climbing along a creek to a grassy ridge with rock formations and views galore, then descending through grassland back to the trailhead.

▶ DESCRIPTION

Does every rose have its thorn? You may wonder at Sunol, where the bucolic splendor of rolling hills, waterfalls, and creeks is dampened by a marauding band of spunky cattle. It's easy enough to dodge their patties, and in fact it's best to avoid them altogether—these cows can be dangerous when they're annoyed, and they seem to get upset at the drop of a hiking boot. Some people stay away from Sunol, preferring to hike through cow-free parks, but I put up with the bovines, because

▶ DIRECTIONS

Depart San Francisco on the Bay Bridge and use the toll plaza as the mileage starting point. About one-half mile past the toll plaza, bear right onto I-580 East. Drive 1.5 miles, then exit onto CA 24. Drive east 12 miles on CA 24, then exit onto I-680 south. Drive south about 25 miles, then exit onto Calaveras/CA 84. Follow the brown "parks" signs: stay in the left lane of the exit ramp, turn left, drive under the freeway, and then stay in the left lane through a stop sign to remain on Calaveras. Drive south on Calaveras about 4 miles to the junction with Geary, and turn left. Continue on Geary almost 2 miles to the park entrance kiosk, then continue past the visitor center to an unmarked dirt lot on the left.

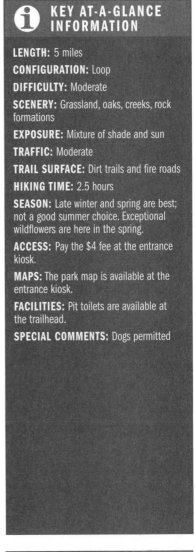

ⓘ KEY AT-A-GLANCE INFORMATION

LENGTH: 5 miles

CONFIGURATION: Loop

DIFFICULTY: Moderate

SCENERY: Grassland, oaks, creeks, rock formations

EXPOSURE: Mixture of shade and sun

TRAFFIC: Moderate

TRAIL SURFACE: Dirt trails and fire roads

HIKING TIME: 2.5 hours

SEASON: Late winter and spring are best; not a good summer choice. Exceptional wildflowers are here in the spring.

ACCESS: Pay the $4 fee at the entrance kiosk.

MAPS: The park map is available at the entrance kiosk.

FACILITIES: Pit toilets are available at the trailhead.

SPECIAL COMMENTS: Dogs permitted

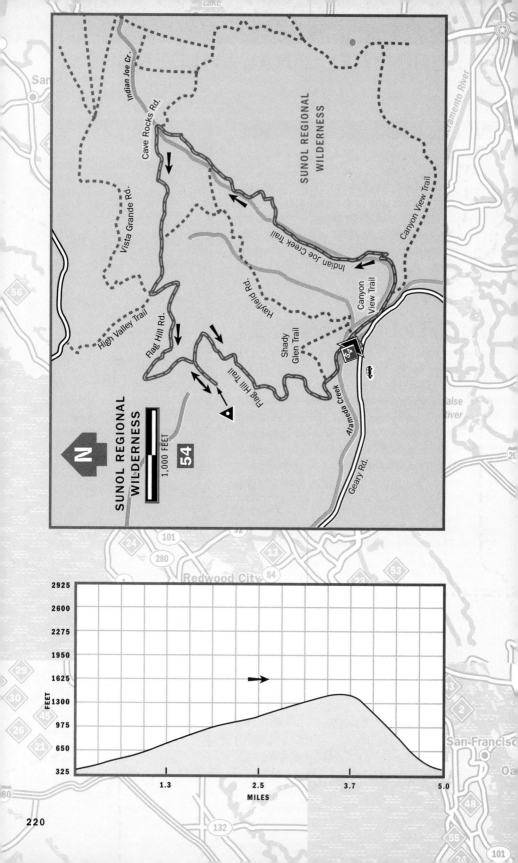

SUNOL REGIONAL WILDERNESS

Indian Joe Cr.

Cave Rocks Rd.

Vista Grande Rd.

SUNOL REGIONAL WILDERNESS

Canyon View Trail

Indian Joe Creek Trail

High Valley Trail

Flag Hill Rd.

Hayfield Rd.

Flag Hill Trail

Shady Glen Trail

Canyon View Trail

Alameda Creek

Geary Rd.

SUNOL REGIONAL WILDERNESS

1,000 FEET

54

N

Sunol is that good, particularly in early spring when flowers bloom everywhere, soft breezes undulate fields of grass, and temperate weather encourages hikes. March through the end of May is the optimal time to visit Sunol—arrive earlier and you'll face sloppy mud; later, and the heat can be stifling. I hiked this loop once in early June and it was so hot that I had to stop and rest on a downhill stretch!

Begin by walking across Alameda Creek on a pretty footbridge. At the far side of the creek, turn right onto the Canyon View Trail. This flat path follows the creek through a sparse population of buckeye, coast live oak, sycamore, and big-leaf maple. Hayfield Road sets off uphill on the left at 0.1 mile—continue on the Canyon View Trail to a signed junction at 0.2 miles, then turn left onto the Indian Joe Creek Trail.

The narrow path climbs slightly. Coast live oaks line the way on the left, while on the right side of the trail clusters of sagebrush frame views of oak-studded hills to the west. This little stretch features a premium blend of spring wildflowers, including wind poppy, Chinese houses, California larkspur, yellow mariposa lily, and elegant clarkia. Just before the trail bends left at about 0.4 miles, there's another connection to the Canyon View Trail on the right. Stay to the left on the Indian Joe Creek Trail.

Crowded by toyon, the path descends toward the banks of Indian Joe Creek. On one April hike I saw an unlikely pair of wildflowers together—sturdy mule ear sunflowers seemingly employed as bodyguards to a huddle of delicate fairy lanterns. In autumn, thickets of snowberry dangle their ghostly white berries in the shade of coast live oaks. The trail crosses through a cattle gate and begins to climb slightly, beginning the journey out of the canyon. Sycamores appear occasionally, but coast live oaks are more common, and you might also see sagebrush, sticky monkeyflower, and California coffeeberry. As the trail cuts across a sloping, grassy hillside, there are views uphill to the park's highest ridge. The Indian Joe Creek Trail crosses back and forth from one side of the creek to the other, then abruptly begins a somewhat steep ascent. Stands of coast live oak and California bay shade some of the route, while other stretches pass through little patches of grassland dotted with sagebrush. In the hottest days of summer, some of the park's cattle seek refuge from the harsh sunlight under the trees. At about the 1.8-mile mark, a trail heads left toward Hayfield Road. Continue uphill on the Indian Joe Creek Trail.

Just off the left side of the trail, sycamores and buckeyes ring a basalt rock formation known as Indian Joe Caves. The trail presses on uphill, alternating some level stretches with steep ones. Finally, at 2.2 miles the trail ends at a junction with a fire road. Turn left onto Cave Rocks Road.

You'll cross Indian Joe Creek one last time, then begin an easy stroll through grassland on a high plain. Look for turtles in a little pond on the right. Some huge solitary valley oaks stand off to the sides of the trail, where in spring popcorn flowers and Ithuriel's spear bloom throughout the grass. Cave Rocks Road descends to a junction at 2.6 miles with Hayfield Road dropping past a barn, part of High Valley Group Camp on the left. Continue straight to the next junction at 2.8 miles, marked by a huge eucalyptus which positively dwarfs a couple of nearby valley oaks. Turn left onto Flag Hill Road.

The fire road sweeps uphill through grassland. There are competing views— look back to admire High Valley from a different perspective, and gaze off to the right for excellent views of Maguire Peaks, two rocky spires at the northern edge of the park. If you can tear yourself away from the long views, check out the sides of the trail for spring wildflowers. I've seen blue-eyed grass, fiddlenecks, lupines, and California buttercups, mostly on the downslope to the right. Flag Hill Road makes a sharp turn left and levels out considerably. If you're hiking in early June take some time to look for butterfly mariposa lily, a stunning wildflower that looks like it was hand-painted by a watercolor master. Beetles and spiders love them, and you might see a half dozen tiny insects crawling in the bowl of each flower. At 3.6 miles the Flag Hill Trail begins on the left. This will be the return route back downhill, but first continue straight on an unmarked but obvious path.

The trail winds along this little ridge, through rocky grassland where coyote mint, California poppy, lupines, and owl's clover bloom in spring. You'll reach the end of the path and a rock formation at about 3.7 miles. Carefully scramble onto the rocks. Once you get up there, you'll see why caution is in order: there's a steep drop-off, but the views are simply out of this world. The entire eastern section of the park seems to sit at your feet, and it's common to see vultures and hawks soaring below your perch—an unusual experience. Needless to say, this is the day's lunch break destination.

When you're ready to move on, walk back to the previous junction, and turn right onto the Flag Hill Trail. If you're suffering from a post-lunch stupor, this tiny path may be a bit of an affront. There are rocky sections and overall the descent is quite steep. The scenery is mostly grassland with a few coast live oaks here and there. Once through a cattle gate, oaks are clustered closer together, yielding more shade. The descent is steady, and soon you'll arrive at a junction and another gate at about 4.9 miles. The Shady Glen Trail goes off to the left. Bear right, remaining on the Flag Hill Trail.

After a short downhill section, the trail ends at the banks of Alameda Creek. Turn left and follow the creek back to the bridge at 5 miles. Turn right and retrace your steps to the parking lot.

▶ NEARBY ACTIVITIES

Nearby Del Valle Regional Park offers a similar, slightly tamer terrain of rolling oak savanna, plus a lake for swimming, boating, and fishing. Visit the East Bay Regional Parks District website at www.ebparks.org/parks/delval.htm, or call (510) 562-PARK for more information.

SWEENEY RIDGE

▶ IN BRIEF

Although the Sweeney Ridge trailhead is just minutes from San Francisco, and begins at the edge of a residential neighborhood, a climb of less than an hour on a paved fire road through coastal scrub leads to a quiet ridge with sweeping views. Once at the ridge, this hike meanders past the Portola Discovery site, reaches a turnaround point at the boundary with water district lands, then loops past a little meadow and returns to the ridge, where you'll retrace your steps back to the trailhead.

▶ DESCRIPTION

In many ways, Sweeney Ridge exemplifies the past, present, and future of Bay Area open space. In 1769, Spanish explorer Portola had his first glimpse of San Francisco Bay from the ridge. From 1956 to 1974, Sweeney Ridge was home to a Nike missile site, the remains of which are still visible. Currently, Sweeney Ridge is the gateway to Peninsula Watershed property which stretches from the edge of Sweeney Ridge across Montara Mountain to CA 92. The Bay Area Ridge Trail Council has worked for years to allow public access into the water district lands, and in 2003 docents started leading hikes through the watershed, beginning at Portola Gate (the southern terminus of the Sweeney Ridge Trail).

Begin from the parking area at the end of Sneath Lane, and squeeze through the V-shaped

▶ DIRECTIONS

Depart San Francisco on southbound I-280 and use the CA 1/19th Avenue merge as the mileage starting point. Drive about 5.5 miles south on I-280, then exit onto Sneath Lane (just before the I-380 exit). At the base of the exit ramp, turn left onto Sneath Lane, and drive west 2 miles to the trailhead at the end of the road.

ⓘ KEY AT-A-GLANCE INFORMATION

LENGTH: 5.9 miles

CONFIGURATION: Out-and-back with a short loop

DIFFICULTY: Easy–moderate

SCENERY: Coastal scrub, views

EXPOSURE: Except for a few tiny pockets of shade, exposed

TRAFFIC: Heavy on the Sneath Lane Trail, lighter farther afield

TRAIL SURFACE: Paved fire road, dirt fire road, dirt trail

HIKING TIME: 3 hours

SEASON: Good all year—at its best from late winter through spring. Stay away on a foggy day (unless you like that kind of thing).

ACCESS: No fee

MAPS: None at the trailhead. A good map to the area is Pease Press's *Trails of the Coastside and Northern Peninsula.*

FACILITIES: None

SPECIAL COMMENTS: Dogs are permitted. Get up-to-date information about the Bay Area Ridge Trail segment through water district lands at www.ridgetrail.org.

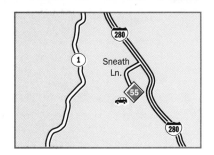

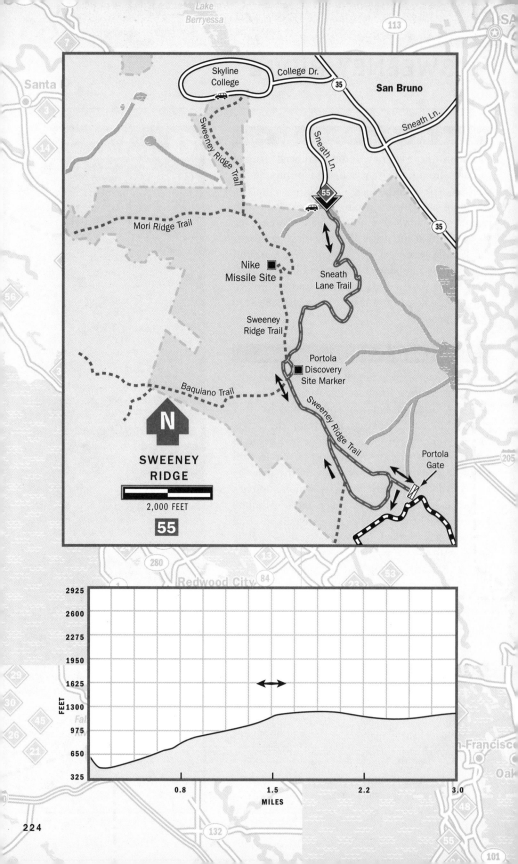

Skyline College

College Dr.

35

San Bruno

Sneath Ln.

Sweeney Ridge Trail

Sneath Ln.

55

35

Mori Ridge Trail

Nike
Missile Site

Sneath
Lane Trail

Sweeney
Ridge Trail

Portola
Discovery
Site Marker

Baquiano Trail

Sweeney Ridge Trail

Portola
Gate

N

**SWEENEY
RIDGE**

2,000 FEET

55

2925
2600
2275
1950
1625
1300
975
650
325

FEET

0.8   1.5   2.2   3.0

MILES

stile onto the Sneath Lane Trail. This old paved road descends slightly through a damp area where dogwood, coyote brush, twinberry, California coffeeberry, and toyon tangle together. In late spring, mustard, wild radish, and fennel are common. Just past a junction with a gated water district fire road on the left, the trail passes through a cluster of eucalyptus and begins to climb at a modest grade. The sides of the Sneath Lane Trail are lined with coastal scrub plants, most notably coyote brush, ceanothus, creambush, poison oak, sagebrush, lizardtail, and sticky monkeyflower. Shrubby willows soak up moisture in the draws of the hillsides, accompanied by currant and gooseberry. In early spring, I often make this part of the hike at a near crawl, scanning the right side of the trail for a variety of wildflowers, including milkmaids, fringecups, iris, hound's tongue, and woodland star. Even in early summer you are likely to see a multitude of paintbrush in bloom, as well as California poppy, California larkspur, and the last lingering fairy lantern blossoms. Three edible favorites fruit along the trail in June: strawberry, thimbleberry, and blackberry. If you hike quietly you might see cottontail rabbits browsing on vegetation along the trail. Many locals use the Sneath Lane Trail as a daily exercise route, so expect traffic from cyclists, joggers, and walkers.

As the trail winds up the hillside, a yellow fog line joins the journey. This line down the middle of the trail may seem unnecessary on a clear day, but when thick, fiercely blowing wet fog descends on the ridge creating white-out visibility, the fog line assists hikers and cyclists on the journey back toward the trailhead. Just beyond the start of the fog line, the trail curves right and ascends moderately steeply. At the end of this stretch, you may want to stop at a bench on the right and enjoy the views north and east, which encompass San Francisco, Mount Tamalpais, San Bruno Mountain, and San Francisco Bay. Traffic (and noise) from planes is steady. The grade slackens back to moderate, and continues to taper off as the trail presses on uphill, through the upper reaches of a eucalyptus grove. Look downhill to the left for a good view of San Andreas Lake, one of the reservoirs that make up the Peninsula Watershed. At 1.7 miles the trail crests at a junction with the Sweeney Ridge Trail, a Bay Area Ridge Trail segment. Turn left.

About 100 feet down the dirt fire road, bear left onto an unsigned but obvious trail. The path cuts through coastal scrub, then reaches the Portola Discovery site, marked by a small monument. Adjacent to the marker, there's a "mountain finder," with the prominent landforms visible from Sweeney Ridge etched onto a granite cylinder. On clear days you might be able to make out Mount Hamilton to the southeast, but even in the smog of summer views include Montara Mountain and the Pacifica coastline to the west. From this clearing, walk a few steps to the right, returning to the fire road at the junction with the Baquiano Trail, which travels west to the park boundary. Turn left and resume hiking south on the Sweeney Ridge Trail.

The fire road descends easily, through dense shrubs of coyote brush, lizardtail, and California coffeeberry. Here, a knoll on the left blocks noise from the east, and bird song fills the void quite nicely. Iris, buttercup, mission bells, and blue-eyed grass, all early spring flowers, bloom through the coastal scrub, but goldenfields commonly flower clustered together in pockets of grassland, forming bright yellow patches. In early June look for annual lupines, checkerbloom, paintbrush, and yarrow in bloom. At 2.2 miles an unnamed and unsigned path, known to most as the Meadow Loop Trail, departs to the right, across from a BART symbol marking the Sweeney Ridge Trail. This is the return route—for now, continue straight. In a saddle, traffic noise from I-280 drifts up to the ridge, where twinberry, ceanothus, and a few huckleberry shrubs mingle through the scrub. Views west to Montara Mountain continue to impress. The Sweeney Ridge Trail ascends slightly, and the Portola Gate comes into view. At 2.8 miles the other end of the Meadow Loop Trail feeds in from the right, then the Sweeney Ridge Trail ends at Portola Gate. This is the trailhead for watershed hikes. Walk back down the Sweeney Ridge Trail the short distance to the Meadow Loop Trail at 2.9 miles, and turn left.

The little trail drops through coastal scrub on a rocky course. Fire roads in the adjacent water district property are visible on the left, but as the trail nears the park boundary, it sweeps right and levels out in a bowl-shaped meadow. In the wettest months of the year the trail may be swamped with mud, and by June you'll be wading through knee-high grasses. A seasonal wetland so high on the ridge is rare, and park staff urge you to stay on the trail, preserving the area. Since there is slightly more grass on this part of the ridge, look for plenty of wildflowers in spring, including blue-eyed grass, California poppy, and California buttercup. At 3.4 miles a trail departs on the left, heading off the ridge to a stable on private property. Stay to the right.

The next section is somewhat overgrown—beware of poison oak mixed through ceanothus, sagebrush, and coyote brush. On a June hike through here butterflies floated overhead and quail made their distinctive "chi-ca-go" call somewhere close by but out of sight. Ascending easily, the trail squeezes through the coastal scrub, then returns to the Sweeney Ridge Trail at 3.7 miles. Turn left, return to the Sneath Lane Trail, then descend on the pavement back to the trailhead.

▶ **NEARBY ACTIVITIES**

Explore the northern part of Sweeney Ridge from the Skyline College trailhead: from Skyline Boulevard (less than 1 mile north of Sneath Lane), turn west onto College Drive. Turn left at the college entrance, then park in lot 2. From the College trailhead, the Sweeney Ridge Trail extends 2.3 miles south, past the old Nike missile site area to the junction with the Sneath Lane Trail. You can extend this hike on an out-and-back excursion west along the Mori Ridge Trail, but to avoid a steep uphill return, turn back before the last sharp drop to Shelldance Nursery.

SAMUEL P. TAYLOR STATE PARK

▶ IN BRIEF

From an ease-of-hiking standpoint, this 6.5-mile Barnabe Mountain loop is close to perfect—like taking the escalator up and the elevator down. An easily graded path starts along a creek where salmon spawn some winters, makes a short detour to a waterfall, then ascends through wooded canyons to the grassy high slopes of Barnabe Mountain. From a viewpoint with sweeping views of Point Reyes, Mount Tamalpais, and Bolinas Ridge, you'll return downhill on a moderately steep fire road through grassland back into woods.

▶ DESCRIPTION

Samuel P. Taylor State Park's Barnabe Mountain hides in plain sight. Although the 1,466-foot peak is bare at the summit, the lower reaches of this mountain are heavily forested, obscuring views from the bottom to the top. The park's campground, picnic sites, and ranger station sit in a canyon alongside Papermill Creek, where hillsides covered with redwood and Douglas fir forest ascend to Bolinas Ridge (out of the park, but part of the Golden Gate National Recreation Area). Across Sir Francis Drake on the low slopes of Barnabe Mountain, redwood groves thrive near the creek, while Douglas fir, California bay, and coast live oak woods fill steep-sided canyons where small waterfalls run in winter and spring.

▶ DIRECTIONS

Leave San Francisco via the Golden Gate Bridge on northbound US 101 and use the Golden Bridge toll plaza as the mileage starting point. Drive north on US 101 about 11 miles, then exit onto Sir Francis Drake/San Anselmo. Drive west on Sir Francis Drake 15 miles, then continue past the main park entrance 1 more mile to a big dirt pullout on the left side of the road, just past the Devil's Gulch sign on the right.

ℹ KEY AT-A-GLANCE INFORMATION

LENGTH: 6.5 miles

CONFIGURATION: Loop

DIFFICULTY: Moderate

SCENERY: Douglas fir, California bay, big-leaf maple, and coast live oak woods, creek, waterfall, grassland, views

EXPOSURE: The start and finish are shaded, the middle section is under full sun.

TRAFFIC: Light from autumn through spring, moderate during summer camping season

TRAIL SURFACE: Dirt fire roads and trails

HIKING TIME: 3.5 hours

SEASON: Muddy after rains—best in winter for the waterfall, and spring for the flowers

ACCESS: No fee

MAPS: Pick up the park map at the ranger station (when staffed), 1 mile back down Sir Francis Drake.

FACILITIES: None at the trailhead; there are pit toilets at Devil's Gulch horse camp

SPECIAL COMMENTS: Dogs are not permitted.

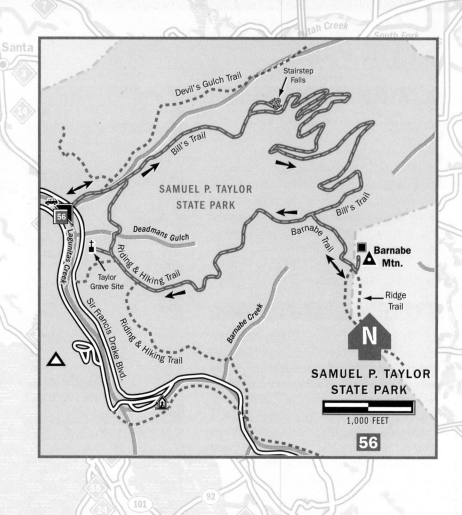

Stairstep Falls

Devil's Gulch Trail

Bill's Trail

SAMUEL P. TAYLOR STATE PARK

Deadmans Gulch

Bill's Trail

Barnabe Trail

■ △ Barnabe Mtn.

Ridge Trail

Laguinitas Creek

Taylor Grave Site

Riding & Hiking Trail

Riding & Hiking Trail

Barnabe Creek

Sir Francis Drake Blvd.

N

SAMUEL P. TAYLOR STATE PARK

1,000 FEET

56

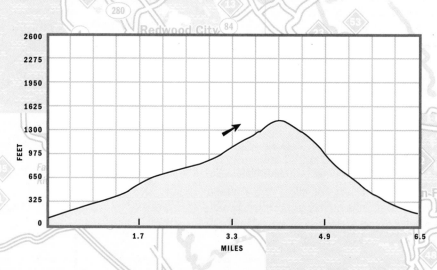

FEET

2600
2275
1950
1625
1300
975
650
325
0

1.7   3.3   4.9   6.5

MILES

At the top, near a Marin County fire lookout, wildflower displays brighten the grassland in spring.

From the pullout, carefully cross Sir Francis Drake and begin walking down a paved, gated service road signed for Devil's Gulch Horse Camp. This level road runs along one of the feeder streams for the largest waterway in the park, Lagunitas Creek. The sides of the trail are lined with buckeye, California bay, redwood, Douglas fir, big-leaf maple, and California nutmeg with wild rose, poison oak, hazelnut, and blackberry in the understory. After about 0.1 mile, veer right onto a path signed simply "trail." The first of two interpretive signs explains that coho salmon and steelhead trout arrive in this creek when the water level is high enough for them to spawn, generally from October through March. I've never visited when the creek was full, but in spring I always scan the water, just in case. The little path weaves around some massive coast live oaks, then at about 0.2 miles, reaches a junction I call "Redwood Fork," for the huge tree just off the trail. A path to the left leads to the horse camp. Cross the bridge to a T-junction. Turn left onto Bill's Trail.

Now on the opposite bank of the creek, the trail starts a slight climb. In spring, look for columbine, woodland star, fringecups, iris, starflower, and bleeding hearts peeking out from a lush landscape of ferns, hazelnut, Douglas fir, and California bay. This sheltered canyon is home to some very large, old trees, including some graceful mature big-leaf maples and a little cluster of eucalyptus. At 0.9 miles, the trail forks. Veer left to visit Stairstep Falls.

The path descends gradually at first just barely clinging to the hillside. In the wettest months you'll hear the gush of water long before the path curves right and ends at the falls at about the 1-mile mark. Stairstep, as the name suggests, is a tiered waterfall with three drops totaling about 35 feet. When ready, return to Bill's Trail and turn left.

A long series of drawn-out switchbacks begins, keeping the grade incredibly easy. The first time I hiked this loop, it was so windy that tree branches crashed to the ground continuously, and I felt lucky to escape without a beaning. Usually, these woods are almost totally quiet, except for the sound of the wind through the trees and bird song. Wildflowers begin to bloom along the trail as early as February, when the first blossoms on pink-flowering currant and milkmaids appear. Hound's tongue and checkerlily are usually the next to bloom, in March, and later still, you might see varieties of iris, lots of woodland star, fringecups, starflower, and California larkspur. Banana slugs creep across the trail, in the shade of Douglas fir, coast live oak, big-leaf maple, and California bay. Evergreen California nutmegs are very common and easy to pick out when bearing fleshy, olive-shaped arils (eaten by birds, but not edible for humans)—much different from redwood and Douglas fir cones. Beware of poison oak, which crowds the trail in many areas. As the trail ascends you'll cross pretty bridges and pass through woods and a few small grassy knolls. Near the end of the trail the grassy patches are more common and bigger. Finally at 4.1 miles, after bridge 7, Bill's Trail emerges from the woods and ends at a fire road. Turn left.

After miles of easy hiking, the moderately steep uphill grade of the Barnabe Trail is less than ideal, but the setting makes up for the climb. To the west, rolling grassy hills, dotted in spring with California poppy, buttercup, and clarkia, drift downhill and meet on the other side of the canyon by a forest of evergreens, thickly covering the ascending slope. Ahead, the fire lookout at the mountaintop is conspicuous, so with the goal in site, trudge on uphill, winding through grassland and small pockets of California bay. At 4.4 miles you'll reach a junction at a fenceline and the park boundary. The Ridge Trail continues to the right, descending steeply along a grassy ridge to a redwood forest. Walk a bit up the hill to the left toward the fire lookout, then turn and gaze south for a rare glimpse of Kent Lake's spillway, most evident when the runoff is heavy. It's generally accepted as permissible to continue uphill to the summit near the lookout, but don't stray any further into private property. Views are outstanding, particularly to the northwest, of Tomales Bay, the entire Point Reyes Peninsula, and Bolinas Ridge.

If you're hiking solo or with one other person, there's a perfectly-sized little rock outcrop on the west side of the summit, offering protection from the winds that commonly buffet the peak. When I visited on a May hike, bees buzzed through huckleberry growing around the rock, and a single lizard sat unaffected beside me while I ate my lunch. If you're here in spring, you may want to look through the grass downhill near the junction for wildflowers including creamcups, California poppy, clovers, fiddlenecks, clarkia, and checkerbloom with the display at its best in early May. When you're ready, retrace your steps back downhill past the junction with Bill's Trail, continuing on the fire road.

The Barnabe Trail drops moderately steeply with the upper reaches of a forested canyon on the right and grassland on the left, then swings left away from the canyon into grassland and coyote brush. In spring look for paintbrush, sticky monkeyflower, blue-eyed grass, and buttercup. Other than one short uphill stretch, this is a quad-working downhill segment. At 5.9 miles the Riding and Hiking Trail departs on the left. Continue to the right. A white picket–fenced plot is visible ahead—this is Taylor's grave site, and the path leading to it breaks off to the left at 6 miles, a 0.1-mile out-and-back spur. Taylor was a gold rush entrepreneur who bought the area now preserved as this park and built a paper mill along the creek. It's widely reported that he named the tallest peak on his property after his mule Barnabe (bet his wife loved that).

Past the gravesite path, the fire road returns to woods in Deadman's Gulch, an area often very muddy after rains. At 1.7 miles the trail bends left with an old routing, now closed, still visible on the right. At a level grade, the narrow path sweeps around the base of a hill. On a May hike, butterflies fluttered everywhere, landing on buttercups and blue-eyed grass flowers strewn through the grass. The path veers left back onto the fire road, which commences its moderately steep descent through the woods. At 6.3 miles you'll reach the first bridge and junction with Bill's Trail again. Turn left and retrace your steps back to the trailhead.

▶ NEARBY ACTIVITIES

From the park headquarters trailhead you can make a 3-mile loop through redwoods on the Pioneer Tree Trail. Read more about the park at www.parks.ca.gov.

TOMALES BAY STATE PARK

IN BRIEF

Most people are drawn to Tomales Bay in summer, particularly to Heart's Desire Beach, which sits just off one of the state park's parking lots. There are three other beaches that can be reached only by foot. Hike to one busy and one quiet beach on this 2.8-mile loop through a gorgeous woodland and along the coast.

DESCRIPTION

This little park is largely ignored by tourists who flock to the Point Reyes peninsula. Since it's a state park, it's off the National Park Service (NPS) radar, and Tomales Bay's trails don't even appear on NPS's Point Reyes maps. The park, though, is no secret with West Marin locals, who favor it for beach parties, picnics, and hikes. Tomales Bay, a body of water that separates Point Reyes from the rest of West Marin, sits directly above the San Andreas Fault. Tomales Bay's beaches are more

DIRECTIONS

Leave San Francisco via the Golden Gate Bridge on northbound US 101 and use the Golden Bridge toll plaza as the mileage starting point. Drive north on US 101 about 11 miles, then exit at Sir Francis Drake/San Anselmo. Drive west on Sir Francis Drake Boulevard about 20 miles to the junction with CA 1, turn right, and after about 0.1 mile make the first left onto Bear Valley Road. After about 2 miles, Bear Valley Road ends at Sir Francis Drake; turn left. Continue on Sir Francis Drake about 5.5 miles, then turn right onto Pierce Point Road. Drive about 1.2 miles to the park entrance on the right side of the road. Turn right and drive down the park road about 0.7 miles to the ranger station, stop and pay the fee (if staffed), then continue about 0.9 miles to the parking lot at the end of the road (not the Heart's Desire lot).

KEY AT-A-GLANCE INFORMATION

LENGTH: 2.8 miles

CONFIGURATION: Loop with a short out-and-back segment

DIFFICULTY: Easy

SCENERY: Woods, beach

EXPOSURE: Mostly shaded

TRAFFIC: Light during off season, moderate in summer, heavy near Heart's Desire Beach

TRAIL SURFACE: Dirt trails

HIKING TIME: 1.5 hours

SEASON: Good all year; peaceful from autumn to spring

ACCESS: Pay $4 entrance fee at Ranger Station.

MAPS: Park map is available at the Ranger Station.

FACILITIES: Rest rooms and drinking water at trailhead

SPECIAL COMMENTS: Dogs are not permitted.

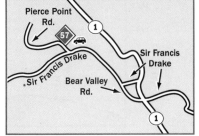

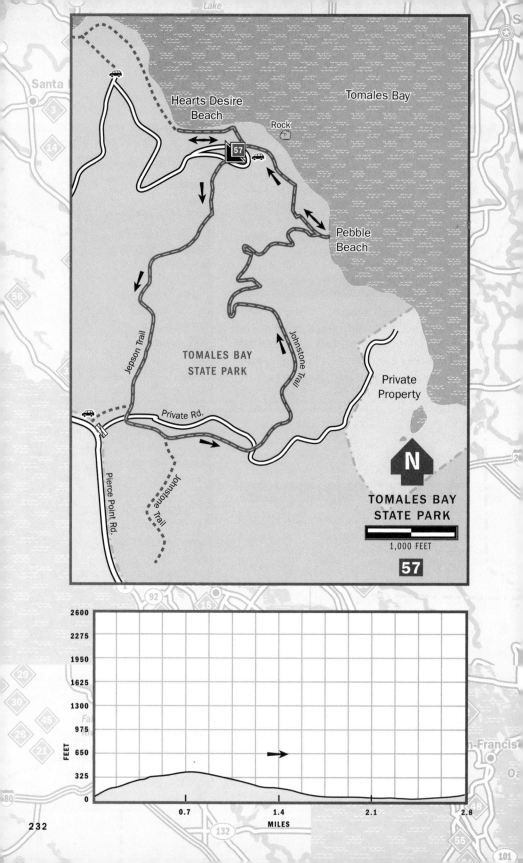

Hearts Desire Beach

Tomales Bay

Rock

57

Pebble Beach

Jepson Trail

Johnstone Trail

TOMALES BAY
STATE PARK

Private
Property

Private Rd.

Johnstone Trail

Pierce Point Rd.

N

TOMALES BAY
STATE PARK

1,000 FEET

57

FEET

2600
2275
1950
1625
1300
975
650
325
0

0.7   1.4   2.1   2.8
MILES

Graceful coast live oaks on the Jepson Trail

sedate than the Pacific coastline and appeal to families with kids. With beaches this pretty, it's tough to tear yourself off the sand. Perhaps that's why Tomales Bay State Park trails can be a quiet refuge even when the beaches are crowded.

Trails depart from the parking lots in a couple of different locations. Begin at the Jepson Trailhead, about midway through the upper parking lot. Immediately the scenery is incredibly lush with huge coast live oaks covered in moss, while ferns, huckleberry, and California coffeeberry crowd the narrow trail. The ascent is steady but easy. You may hear deer crashing through the woods, but the foliage is so thick that it's hard to see more than a few feet into the forest.

In late spring look for tiny white flowers on yerba buena, a native herb that creeps close to the ground. Gradually bishop pines and madrones muscle their way into the woods. In the understory a variety of berry-producing native plants provide food for local birds and small mammals. Some of these berries, from thimbleberry, huckleberry, and currant, are palatable for humans as well. If you notice masses of a glossy-leaved shrub that seem familiar yet out of place, that's salal, a plant often used in floral arrangements. In April you might catch salal in bloom. At 0.9 miles, a path heads off to the right toward a parking area on Pierce Point Road. Continue straight on the Jepson Trail.

Although there's a break in tree cover, dense stands of toyon, coyote brush, and coffeeberry still obscure any views. At 1 mile the Jepson Trail crosses a paved road which leads to a private beach. Continue straight. The same familiar vegetation lines the trail, although poison oak seems especially assertive. Honeysuckle vines dangle from shrubs, producing fragrant pink blossoms in June and pretty red berries in autumn. The Jepson Trails ends at about 1.1 miles, where you'll turn left onto the Johnstone Trail.

The grade remains close to level as the Johnstone trail winds through bishop pine, coffeeberry, huckleberry, coast live oak, hazelnut, and tanoak. At 1.3 miles the private road is crossed for the last time, and the trail begins to descend easily. A bench on the left offers somewhat screened views of the bay. Madrones and manzanitas grow together in one area, inviting a comparison between these two related plants of the Heath family that are common throughout the bay area.

Manzanitas usually grow no larger than other chaparral shrubs, while madrones can attain stately heights. Both feature reddish peeling bark, white urn-shaped blossoms, and red berry-like fruit. Since height comparisons can be deceiving (some manzanitas can reach 30 feet), a crucial difference is the plants' leaves. While manzanita leaves average about 1 inch in length, the madrone's are much larger, about 5 inches long.

The Johnstone Trail reaches the slopes of a little canyon that drains to a creek, and you may notice some moisture-loving plants along the trail, including alder, chinquapin, ferns, huckleberry, and salmonberry. Labrador tea, a shrub that looks a bit like azalea, blooms in June. A few switchbacks ease the descent, but expect some mud here in all but the driest parts of the year. Where the Johnstone Trail levels and reaches a junction with a path to Pebble Beach at 2.2 miles, turn right. The path descends briefly, then ends at the beach. Not surprisingly, given the name, Pebble Beach is rocky, but it's also much quieter than sandy Heart's Desire Beach. Look across the bay for views of a series of low rolling grassy hills. Return to the previous junction and turn right, back onto the Johnstone Trail.

Back on the main trail, California bay, coast live oak, madrone, huckleberry, ferns, and creambush line the trail. At about 2.5 miles the Johnstone Trail steps out of the woods at rest rooms near the trailhead. If you don't want to make the trip to Heart's Desire Beach, turn left and walk back to the parking lot; otherwise, continue straight.

After passing under some huge coast live oaks, the trail bisects a pretty group-picnic area. When the area is vacant, you can have your pick of tables, but I prefer to snack on a wooden bench overlooking the bay on the right. Keep hiking and drop down a set of steps to reach Heart's Desire Beach at about 2.7 miles. On a hot day, you may want to take a dip in the bay, or at least cool off your toes. When you're ready, retrace your steps back to the junction near the rest rooms, then turn right and return to the parking lot.

▶ NEARBY ACTIVITIES

If you want to check out a nearby Pacific Ocean beach, the Abbotts Lagoon trailhead is another 1.8 miles north on Pierce Point Road. From the parking lot, a nearly level path travels west along a butterfly-shaped lagoon. After 1 mile, in a gap between the two lagoon wings, the trail disintegrates in loose sand, leaving the route to the ocean up to you.

UVAS CANYON
COUNTY PARK

▶ IN BRIEF

Uvas Canyon Park has a premium waterfall-to-mileage quotient. Most bay area waterfalls require substantial hikes, but that's not the case at Uvas, where three of the falls can be reached with very little effort. The fourth requires a bit more grunt, but is still an easy trek. With four waterfalls on four different creeks, you can visit them all on this 4 mile hike on a tour through the canyon's woods and chaparral.

▶ DESCRIPTION

Uvas hikes are all about waterfalls. It's no wonder, given the park's location tucked back in a canyon. Steep hillsides channel runoff to a series of creeks that flow with the greatest intensity after sequential winter rainstorms. However, if you enjoy autumn foliage (such as it is in the Bay Area), you might make a special trip to Uvas in October or November, when the leaves on

▶ DIRECTIONS

Drive south from San Francisco on I-280 and use the CA 1/19th Avenue merge as the mileage starting point. Drive south on I-280 about 36 miles, then exit onto CA 85 south. After about 12 miles, exit at Almaden Expressway. Stay in the ramp's right lane, make the first left, then the next right onto Almaden Expressway. Drive about 5 miles to the end of Almaden Expressway, and turn right onto Harry. Almost immediately, turn left onto McKean. Drive south on McKean, which turns into Uvas Road after about 6.5 miles. Continue on Uvas for another 3.7 miles, then turn right onto Croy (there's a brown county park sign before the turnoff). Drive about 3.8 miles to the park entrance at the end of the road. *Note:* The last stretch of Croy passes through the Swedish private community of Sveadal. Drive slowly.

ⓘ KEY AT-A-GLANCE INFORMATION

LENGTH: 4 miles

CONFIGURATION: Balloon with two very short spurs

DIFFICULTY: Easy

SCENERY: Woods, waterfalls, chaparral

EXPOSURE: Mostly shaded

TRAFFIC: Light except in summer, when campers increase trail traffic

TRAIL SURFACE: Dirt trails and fire roads with some rocky stretches along Swanson Creek

HIKING TIME: 2 hours

SEASON: Best in winter for waterfalls

ACCESS: Pay $4 fee at entrance station.

MAPS: The official park map is available at the entrance station and the start of the waterfall loop.

FACILITIES: Rest rooms and drinking water at trailhead

SPECIAL COMMENTS: Dogs are permitted on most trails.

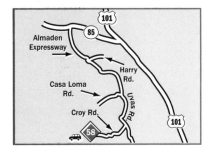

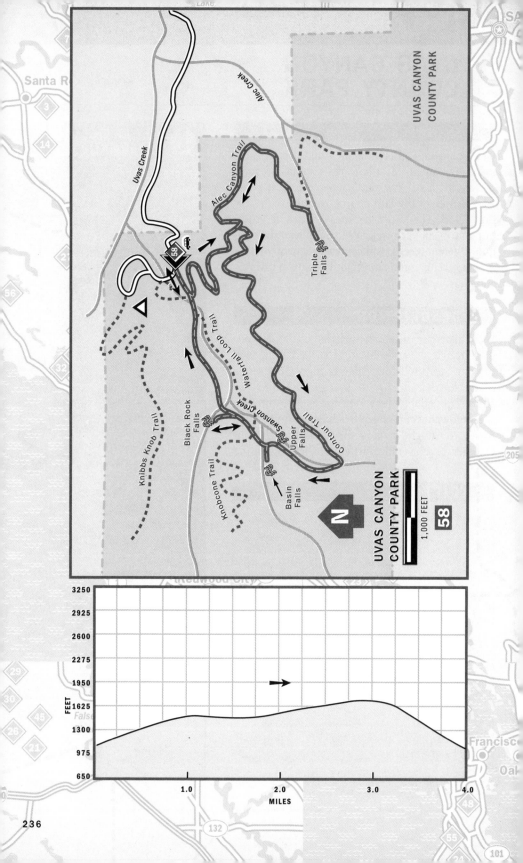

UVAS CANYON COUNTY PARK

N

58

1,000 FEET

UVAS CANYON
COUNTY PARK

Alec Creek

Uvas Creek

Santa R

Alec Canyon Trail

Triple Falls

Waterfall Loop Trail

Contour Trail

Swanson Creek

Knibbs Knob Trail

Black Rock Falls

Knobcone Trail

Upper Falls

Basin Falls

FEET

3250
2925
2600
2275
1950
1625
1300
975
650

1.0   2.0   3.0   4.0
MILES

park's many big-leaf maple trees flush orange and drift slowly down onto the creekbeds and trails.

Part of Uvas's charm is that the journey to the park is such a pleasant prelude to a dayhike. Once you get off the highway, backroads travel through bucolic country, a landscape of rolling hills studded with oaks. This part of Santa Clara County has largely escaped the era of the tech boom, when developers dug up orchards and installed acres of tilt-up buildings. There are few mega-mansions, but there are still lots of old horse ranches and lonely stretches where you might see wildlife. On my last visit to Uvas, I spotted a huge bobcat along the side of McKean Road, walking through the far reaches of a golf course.

The trailhead for this hike is at the end of the Black Oak Group Area, a reservable picnic spot. Leave the parking spaces adjacent to the area for picnickers, and park in the day use lot just uphill and around the corner from the park entrance and the ranger station. From the lot ascend a flight of steps toward the rest rooms, then walk up the park road and where it forks, bear left, following signage for the Waterfall Loop. Begin hiking at the gated start of a dirt fire road, about 0.1 mile from the day-use parking lot. Check the wooden box on the right for the self-guided nature trail brochure and a map. After a short easy stretch, the Waterfall Loop begins on the right. Continue straight on the Alec Canyon Trail.

The fire road winds uphill on a series of broad switchbacks, through a forest of California bay, madrone, tanoak, and Douglas fir. The grade fluctuates between easy and moderate. A bench on the side of the trail is a good spot for a rest, as there is a break in the vegetation that permits good views east. In 2002, the Croy Fire burned over 3,000 acres north and south of the park. The surrounding hillsides will remain charred and bare for a few years, and from the viewpoint you can see where the flames rushed up from the canyon floor and scorched steep hillsides. Just uphill from the bench, the Alec Canyon Trail meets Contour Trail at one-half mile. You'll return to the Contour Trail, but for now continue straight on the Alec Canyon Trail.

The trail ascends gently out of the woods and through a stretch of chaparral. In February, when toyon shrubs still are weighted down with clusters of red berries, you might see buckbrush in bloom. At about 0.7 miles, the Alec Canyon Trail crests and reaches Manzanita Point. Silktassel, toyon, and manzanita sprawl on the hillside downslope from a rest bench. There are more sweeping views east out of the canyon. On a steady but easy descent, the trail passes through a chaparral plant community dominated by chamise, where you might also see coyote mint and hollyleaf cherry. Buckeyes mark a transition into a more damp area, and then California bays and redwoods come into view along the steep banks of a creek.

Look for a sign pointing right and uphill to Triple Falls at about 1 mile, and follow the narrow path along the creekbed to the falls. It's not far, only 0.2 miles, but the trail is pretty steep, and damp leaves on the path can make the ascent a bit slippery. California nutmeg makes an appearance along the trail. This native tree with evergreen needles can be confused with a young redwood or Douglas fir, until you touch the tip of a needle. Redwood and Douglas fir needles are rounded, but nutmeg needles are quite sharp! Native Americans are said to have used these needles for tattooing. At the end of the spur you'll reach Triple Falls, the most remote of Uvas's waterfalls. This little redwood canyon is a quiet place, where the burble of the creek competes with the steady rush of the fall, a three-stage procession of water dropping about 35 feet in total. With the first waterfall visited, return back to the junction with Alec Canyon and Contour trails at about 1.8 miles. Turn left onto the Contour Trail.

The narrow path cuts across a steeply walled canyon, mostly under the shade of madrone, Douglas fir, coast live oak, tanoak, and California bay. There's a fair bit of elevation wobble, but only in short stretches. Two nooks and crannies are crossed with the aid of a plank and a little wooden bridge. It's interesting to note the contrast between the woodsy damp ravines and the sunny patches of chaparral. Sunlight rarely punctuates the dark creases of the canyon, but the parts of the mountain that jut out get enough sunshine to sustain manzanita and toyon shrubs. The sound of rushing water grows ever louder, until the trail drops to the banks of Swanson Creek at about 3 miles. Except for two very short spurs to visit waterfalls, it's all downhill from here, as you follow the creek back toward the trailhead. The flow rate can seem a bit tame this far up the canyon, but a low water level permits the trail to cross over to the opposite bank here. Use caution descending and crossing the creek, especially when the rocks are wet. The ground is less rocky on the other side, and the descent is easy through Douglas fir, California bay, and big-leaf maple. You may notice a little path ascending on the left, heading to an old hothouse site. Along the trail tiny facets of broken glass twinkle on the hillsides surrounding a length of pipe. On a short set of steps, the trail descends through an area prone to landslides, then reaches Upper Falls, Swanson's Creek's largest drop. Just past Upper Falls, the path to Basin Falls departs at about 3.3 miles. Turn left.

It's an easy and brief ascent to the falls, a 15-foot cascade that creates a charming pool before continuing down the canyon to join Swanson Creek. Return to the main trail, and continue downhill. In a little flat area, two other trails head off—the Knobcone Point Trail to the left and the Waterfall Loop Trail to the right. You'll also find a few picnic tables with good creek views. The ground cover that pervades the area is vinca, a non-native. Continue straight on Waterfall Loop Fire Road. Less than 0.1 mile down the trail, veer left onto the path to Black Rock Falls.

The path ascends slightly, then curves left into a steeply walled canyon. This waterfall, a little taller than Basin Falls, may be my favorite at Uvas. It's an incredibly lush setting, where moss covers big-leaf maple trunks and giant boulders with abandon. Milkmaids bloom here and there in winter. When you return to Waterfall Loop Fire Road, if you have brought along the nature trail guide, now's the time to fish it out and follow along. Buckeye, big-leaf maple, sycamore, canyon live oak, and California bay may be spotted and identified with the aid of the guide. The trail descends at a moderate grade. In winter you might see scores of ladybugs hibernating on the trailside vegetation. This curious natural phenomenon is one of the benefits of Bay Area winter hiking, as this is only time of year theses ladybird beetles can be seen in such concentrated colonies. The Waterfall Loop Trail rejoins the fire road, and the two run together, crossing the creek one last time just downstream from what's left of an old retaining pond. Stay to the right as a trail veers off toward the campground, and at about 4 miles you'll return to the junction with the Alec Canyon Trail. Turn left and walk back to the parking lot.

WILDER RANCH
STATE PARK

IN BRIEF

Considering how much of Santa Cruz County is coastline, it's surprisingly tough to find a park that offers ocean views and extensive hiking options. This loop begins near some historic ranch buildings, travels under CA 1 via a tunnel, climbs steadily through grassland, then descends back toward the trailhead with ocean views nearly the entire way.

DESCRIPTION

Wilder Ranch State Park, just north of Santa Cruz, features bluff-top paths right along the ocean and a large trail network on grassy hillsides ascending from the coast. The park is a popular mountain bike destination, but as long as you remember to stay alert for traffic, Wilder Ranch is a great place to hike.

Begin from the parking lot, following the signs toward the historic buildings. A paved path gently eases downhill, then ends at a service road. Turn right. After a few feet you'll reach the ranch complex—turn left. As the paved path winds at a level grade through the complex, you can poke around the buildings and farm, where historical interpretive programs are often underway. These structures, most of which date from the late 1800s, were built by the Wilder family, who worked the land that now bears their name. Although there is almost always a great deal of

DIRECTIONS

Drive south from San Francisco on I-280 and use the CA 1/19th Avenue merge as the mileage starting point. Drive 1.7 miles, then exit CA 1 and drive 63 miles south, to the park entrance on the right side of the road (about 6.5 miles south of Davenport). Turn right into the park and proceed past the entrance kiosk to the parking lot.

KEY AT-A-GLANCE INFORMATION

LENGTH: 7.2 miles

CONFIGURATION: Balloon

DIFFICULTY: Moderate

SCENERY: Grassland, coastal views

EXPOSURE: Almost entirely exposed

TRAFFIC: Moderate

TRAIL SURFACE: Dirt fire roads and trails

HIKING TIME: 4 hours

SEASON: Good all year—can be muddy. Trails may be closed because of storm damage in winter and early spring.

ACCESS: Pay $5 fee at entrance kiosk.

MAPS: The park map is available at the entrance kiosk—ask for the full color map with topography.

FACILITIES: Rest rooms and drinking water at trailhead

SPECIAL COMMENTS: Dogs are not permitted in the park.

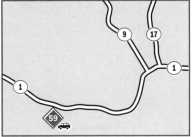

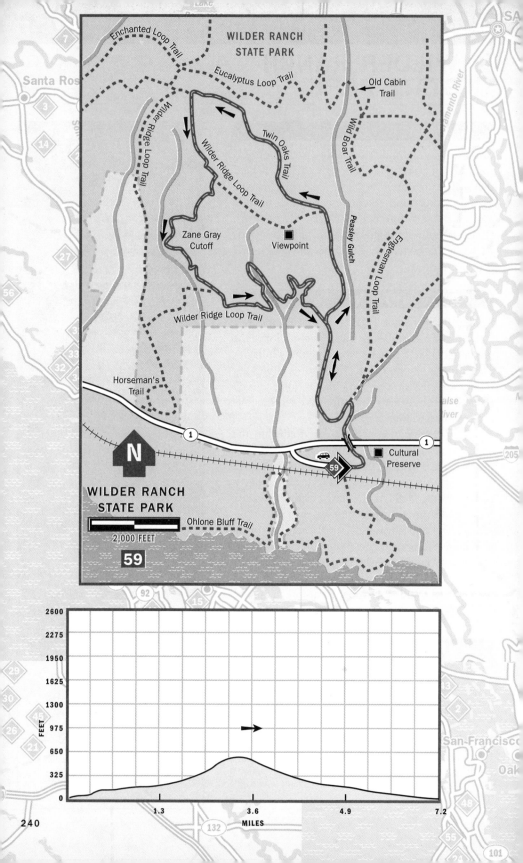

WILDER RANCH
STATE PARK

Enchanted Loop Trail

Eucalyptus Loop Trail

Old Cabin Trail

Twin Oaks Trail

Wilder Ridge Loop Trail

Wild Boar Trail

Wilder Ridge Loop Trail

Zane Gray Cutoff

Viewpoint

Peasley Gulch

Engelsman Loop Trail

Wilder Ridge Loop Trail

Horseman's Trail

Cultural Preserve

N

WILDER RANCH
STATE PARK

2,000 FEET

59

Ohlone Bluff Trail

240

activity in this part of the park, I had a bobcat sighting here once—perhaps it was eyeing the farm's chickens. The trail passes vegetable gardens and rows of apple trees, then meets a paved bike trail heading east. Continue straight, through a tunnel under CA 1, and emerge in the park's "backcountry." At the base of a grassy hillside, you'll pass some more ranch buildings and a corral on the right. Stay to the left as the route splits, then reach a junction at one-half mile. Take the fire road doubling back to the left, the Wilder Ridge Loop Trail.

The trail curves uphill around the hillside, already offering some nice ocean views to the left. By late spring the grass on the sides of the trail is tall, dried to a crisp, and ugly Italian thistle is common; but in April or May you might see annual lupines and elegant brodiaea, a blue-purple flower, blooming close to the ground. As the trail levels out, you'll have good views of grassy hills rising up to the north— ancient ocean terraces pushed uphill by thousands of years of seismic movement. To the right, ribbons of evergreen mark gulches where creeks flow toward the ocean. At 1.3 miles the Wilder Ridge Loop Trail forks. Continue to the right.

The grade picks up as the fire road weaves between clusters of coyote brush, California coffeeberry, and poison oak. Coffeeberry, an evergreen shrub, produces delicate tiny flowers and small purple-red drupes favored by coyotes and birds—as the berries dry they shrivel and darken, slightly resembling coffee beans (some say the name was prompted by the shape of the seed). Upslope from a steep-sided ravine, the Wilder Ridge Loop Trail passes through a pocket of Douglas fir and California bay, tangled with hazelnut and thimbleberry. Just past this shaded interlude near the 2-mile mark, the loop trail swings left. Bear right onto the Twin Oaks Trail.

Squeezing through coyote brush and poison oak with madrone, coast live oak, and Douglas fir just off the path, the narrow trail starts a slight climb. There's very little long-range visibility here, so be alert for bicycles. After dipping to cross a creek, the trail rises into a meadow, where ferns sprawl through the grass. White brodiaea, flax, and blue-eyed grass bloom here in May, but by mid-June the dominant flower is a common dandelion. Train whistles from Roaring Camp and Big Trees Railroad trains (running a few miles east) compete with the whisper of the wind in this quiet part of the park. The Twin Oaks Trail climbs easily on a trail re-route constructed in 2003, which moved the path from the low point of a basin-like meadow, slightly up onto the shoulder of a sloping hill. Path staff hopes this re-route will permit year-round passage on this trail, which previously became bloated with runoff after winter rains. At 2.7 miles the trail forks at an undersigned junction. To the right, the path heads into a pretty pocket of woods, then returns to grassland at a junction with the Euca-lyptus Loop Trail—a nice option, but one that requires navigating two very confusing junctions. Instead, continue to the left. The Twin Oaks Trail rises through grassland, then meets a fenceline on the right. Ahead on the left, twin coast live oaks—the trail's namesake—stand near a cluster of tall redwood. The Twin Oaks Trail ends at an undersigned junction at 2.9 miles with the Wilder Ridge Loop Trail. Turn left.

The broad fire road now begins an easy descent through grassland. Although by late spring most of the wildflowers are gone, colorful butterflies are everywhere, including swallowtails and buckeyes. You might also see snake tracks, undulating across the sandy trail. At 3.4 miles you'll reach a junction with Zane Gray Cutoff. The

Wilder Ridge Loop Trail continues another half mile, returning to the junction with the lower part of the Twin Oaks Trail, an option for shortening the hike. Turn right onto Zane Gray Cutoff.

The slight trail meanders along a grassy plateau, then curves right and begins a descent. On a clear day, look southeast for views stretching across Monterey Bay to the mountains of Los Padres. Some noise from a landfill off to the right is steady, but the trail bends left and leaves it behind, passes through a damp shaded area near a creek, and then ends at 4.3 miles. Bear left onto the Wilder Ridge Loop Trail. With very little elevation change, the narrow trail winds through grassland in a basin around Old Dairy Gulch. This is a good location for wildflower spotting, and I've seen dozens of golden brodiaea blooming along the trail in May, along with blue-eyed grass and yellow mariposa lily. Clusters of poison oak, sticky monkeyflower, and coyote brush pepper the landscape. The Wilder Ridge Loop Trail returns at 5.9 miles to a T-junction. Turn right and retrace your steps back to the trailhead.

▶ NEARBY ACTIVITIES

If you're a fan of Bonny Doon wine, consider making a brief detour off CA 1 to their tasting room. Staff provide samples of their award-winning wines, and it's a fun place to visit (and less than 4 miles from CA 1). Call the tasting room for directions, (831) 425-4518, or visit their website at www.bonnydoonvineyard.com.

WINDY HILL
OPEN SPACE PRESERVE

▶ IN BRIEF

Windy Hill showcases the micro and the macro sides of nature. From the highest reaches of this preserve, there are excellent views from the ocean to East Bay; on narrow winding paths that climb through quiet woods, there are spectacular displays of wildflowers and autumn foliage. At Windy Hill you can see the woods for the trees, and then some. This loop begins at the edge of Portola Valley, then ascends through woods to the top of Windy Hill. The return leg is a fast descent on a fire road with a quick detour around Sausal Pond.

▶ DESCRIPTION

I have enjoyed many magical hikes at Windy Hill over the years, in every season. In summer the woods are cool, spring brings tons of flowers, in autumn maple leaves blaze with color, and winter is lonely with starkly naked oaks and nearly deserted trails. The preserve has two major trailheads at the top and bottom of the mountain. I like to start in Portola Valley, get the climbing out of the way first, and cruise downhill back to the trailhead, but if you prefer to face the ascent on the return, begin at the CA 35 trailhead, but note that the Spring Ridge Trail is significantly steeper than the Hamms Gulch Trail.

The lower trailhead sits just off Portola Road, a parking lot next to the Sequoias, a retirement community. Begin on a connector trail that winds through oaks, buckeye, poison oak, and

▶ KEY AT-A-GLANCE INFORMATION

LENGTH: 7.4 miles

CONFIGURATION: Loop

DIFFICULTY: Moderate

SCENERY: Grassland, woods, pond

EXPOSURE: Nearly equally shaded and exposed

TRAFFIC: Moderate weekends, quiet weekdays

TRAIL SURFACE: Dirt fire roads and trails

HIKING TIME: 4 hours

SEASON: Good any time, although the Spring Ridge Trail is very hot in summer

ACCESS: No fee

MAPS: Park map is available at the trailhead's information signboard.

FACILITIES: Pit toilets at the Portola Valley trailhead, as well as at the CA 35 trailhead

SPECIAL COMMENTS: Dogs are permitted on specified trails only.

▶ DIRECTIONS

Drive south from San Francisco on I-280 and use the CA 1/19th Avenue merge as the mileage starting point. Drive south on I-280 about 27 miles, then exit Alpine Road. Head west on Alpine Road about 3 miles, then turn right onto Portola Road. Drive about 1 mile and turn left into the preserve parking lot.

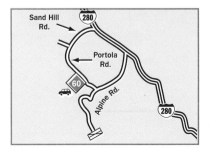

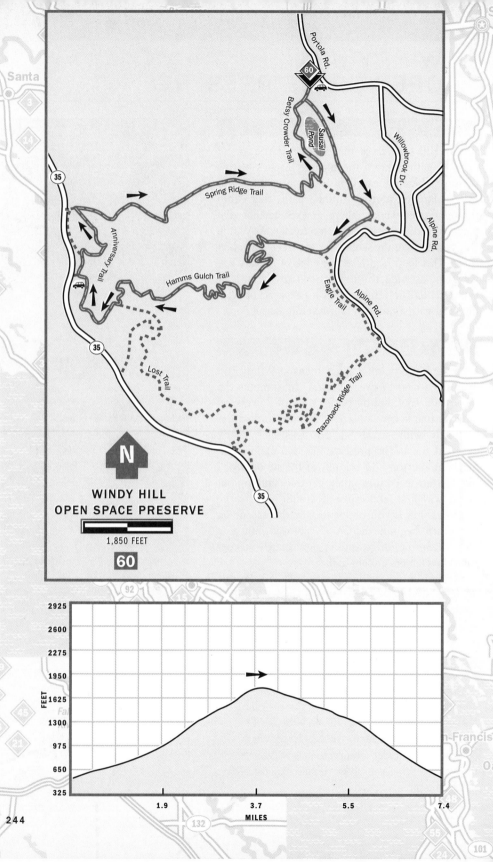

N

WINDY HILL
OPEN SPACE PRESERVE

1,850 FEET

60

Majestic oaks in grassland along the
lower portion of the Hamms Gulch Trail

coyote brush. After about 300 feet, you'll reach a junction near Sausal Pond. Turn left onto the Spring Ridge Trail.

At a level grade, the broad trail creeps along the preserve boundary. As they grow, young planted native shrubs including currant and toyon should help to block the noise from the Sequoias complex, visible on the left. Sausal Pond sits off to the right behind tangles of blackberry, poison oak, and young coast live oak. The Spring Ridge Trail begins to ascend a bit, passing huge old valley oaks. You may see or hear red-winged blackbirds and quail in this area. At 0.6 miles, the Spring Ridge Trail curves right and heads uphill, and a path leaves the preserve on the left. Continue straight, following the sign toward Alpine Road.

Madrone, coast live, black, and valley oaks, California bay, and big-leaf maples shade the level trail, where hound's tongue and buttercups blooms in late spring. In autumn you might notice delicate-leaved shrubs with marble-sized white berries—the aptly named snowberry plant. Quite a few hawthorne shrubs blend into the vegetation on the right. Hawthorne is not a plant commonly spotted in natural areas in these parts, and it's easy to pick out in autumn, when red berries dangle from toothed-leaved branches. You'll reach an important junction at about 0.8 miles—first the trail crosses a paved private road, then a trail leads left to Alpine Road. An old connector to Spring Ridge is unsigned but still somewhat visible on the right. Continue straight onto the Hamms Gulch Trail. A few steps later, a new re-route of the connector to the Spring Ridge Trail, now named the Meadow Trail, departs to the right. Continue straight.

In the grassy understory beneath gorgeous black and valley oaks, bluedicks and blue-eyed grass bloom in early spring. Watch out for poison oak, which is common along this slim path. The Hamms Gulch Trail enters the woods. A creek runs slightly downslope to the left, and this riparian microclimate hosts plants which prefer a damp environment, including currant, California bay, and buckeye, plus trilliums and milkmaids in late winter. The Eagle Trail begins on the left at about 1.2 miles. Stay to the right on the Hamms Gulch Trail. The trail dips to cross a creek, then abandons the waterway and begins to climb. In early March, hound's tongue is usually very prolific, blooming in giant colonies along the length of the trail, but you'll also likely see many other wildflowers, including shooting stars, trilliums, and milkmaids. The forest is a pretty mix of madrone, oaks, California bay, and some maple, redwood, and Douglas fir. Hazelnut, creambush, poison oak, currant, and gooseberry comprise the bulk of the understory. The Hamms Gulch Trail is well graded with many switchbacks, and except for a few short steeper sections, makes for an easy climb. Occasionally there are breaks in the forest, revealing views across the gulch to the Spring Ridge Trail. In a sunny patch of chaparral, nearly hidden in thick stands of coyote brush, look for western leatherwood, an extremely rare shrub that is easiest to spot when yellow blossoms appear in late winter. After another foray through the woods, the Hamms Gulch Trail skirts the edge of a sloping grassy meadow—the only significant grassland on the trail. Benches placed here and there along the trail are a welcome site for weary hikers. The trail just keeps climbing, and you may begin to notice some incredibly large Douglas fir mixed through tanoak, big-leaf maple, oaks, and madrone. At 3.8 miles the Hamms Gulch Trail ends at a T-junction. Turn right onto the Lost Trail.

The Lost Trail makes its way out of the forest, then runs along the edge of the woods, allowing good close ups views of those giant Douglas firs. On the left side of the trail coyote brush dominates with some currant mixed in. This level stretch is a nice intermission between the ascent of Hamms Gulch and the descent of Spring Ridge. Within audible range of CA 35 on the left, the Lost Trail cuts across grassland on the high flanks of Windy Hill. Blue-eyed grass, mule ear sunflowers, fiddlenecks, and California poppy are common in early spring. Views east extend to Mount Diablo. At 4.2 miles you'll reach a picnic area on the left, near the CA 35 trailhead. More than once I've seen hikers sprawled on top of the picnic tables, resting at either the mid-point or end of their journeys. Continue straight past the trailhead, now on the Anniversary Trail, built and named to commemorate the 10th anniversary of Windy Hill's preservation. The trail follows CA 35, then veers right and makes the brief ascent to the hilltop. There are no formal trails to the actual top, but you can easily pick one of the paths that rise a few feet to the crest. If you have been wondering why the preserve is named Windy Hill, visit on a breezy day and the mystery will be revealed—air rushes unimpeded east from the ocean to this prominent Santa Cruz Mountains hilltop. A 360-degree panorama encompasses the Santa Clara Valley, Mounts Hamilton and Diablo, and soft grassy hills descending to the ocean. Once past the crest at 4.9 miles, the trail drops through coyote brush to a junction near a roadside parking area and CA 35. Turn right onto the Spring Ridge Trail.

The broad fire road descends somewhat steeply through grassland with pockets of cypress standing off the left side of the trail near the preserve boundary. Look for blue-eyed grass, California poppy, lupines, and popcorn flower blooming in early spring. In the first stages of the descent, little huddles of coast live oak provide the only shade, but as the Spring Ridge Trail heads downhill, woods begin a gradual squeeze toward the trail. The connector to the Hamms Gulch Trail sets off on the right at 6.5 miles. In April, blue and white lupines put on a good show in the grass on both sides of the trail at this junction. Continue to the left on the Spring Ridge

Trail. The grade thankfully eases to moderate as the trail winds through madrone, coast live oak, California bay, toyon, buckeye, and poison oak. California coffeeberry dangle red and black berries in late autumn to the delight of Windy Hill's bird and coyote population. The Spring Ridge Trail emerges in an area dominated by coyote brush and offers some views east. The quad-aching descent finally ends at 6.8 miles at a junction with the Betsy Crowder Trail. Turn left.

This gentle grade is welcome after Spring Ridge's descent. The trail is named in honor of Betsy Crowder, a guidebook author and Midpeninsula Regional Open Space District board member who died in 2000. Although she was in her 70s at the time of her death, Betsy was a vibrant and strong woman who worked tireless on preservation issues. Whenever I saw her at outdoor volunteer projects I was amazed at her youthful spirit. Her namesake trail drifts through a grassy meadow favored by deer, then drops into a forest of California bay, madrone, buckeye, hazelnut, coffeeberry, and coast live oak. Sausal Pond is barely visible. In early spring look for the dregs of blooming hound's tongue, plus trilliums, and bluedicks. The path curves right around a few massive eucalyptus and draws near a road outside the park boundary. Vinca, a non-native ground cover, sprawls through the understory. If you peer through the trees on the right you may notice a tall, level berm, which contains the north side of Sausal Pond. At 7.4 miles the Betsy Crowder Trail ends. Turn left and return to the trailhead on the connector trail.

60 Hikes within 60 MILES

SAN FRANCISCO
INCLUDING SAN JOSE, OAKLAND, AND SANTA ROSA

APPENDICES
& INDEX

APPENDIX A: HIKING CLUBS AND INFORMATION SOURCES

Bay Area Outdoor Adventure Club
1750 Montgomery Street, Suite 1119
San Francisco, CA 94111 (415) 954-7190
www.sfoac.com

Bay Area Ridge Trail Council
1007 General Kennedy Avenue, Suite 3
San Francisco, CA 94129 (415) 561-2595
www.ridgetrail.org/activ.htm

Berkeley Hiking Club
P.O. Box 147
Berkeley, CA 94701
www.berkeleyhikingclub.pair.com

California Alpine Club
Eva Libien, Hike Coordinator
(415) 383-5184
calalpine.org/hikes/index.htm

Cal Hiking and Outdoor Society (CHAOS)
www.uc-hiking-club.berkeley.ca.us

Confused Outdoor Club
www.confusedclub.com.

East Bay Regional Park District
2950 Peralta Oaks Court, P.O. Box 5381
Oakland, CA 94605-0381 (510) 562-PARK
www.ebparks.org/events/bytheme/hikes.htm

Greenbelt Alliance
631 Howard Street, Suite 510
San Francisco, CA 94105 (415) 543-6771
www.greenbelt.org/getinvolved/outings
   index.html

Henry W. Coe State Park
Park office 408-779-2728
www.coepark.org/programs.html

Hiking North of SF Bay
www.hikenorthbay.com

Intrepid Northern California Hikers (INCH)
www.rawbw.com/%7Esvw/inch/

Marin County Open Space District
3501 Civic Center Drive, Room #415

San Rafael, CA 94903 (415) 499-6387
www.marinopenspace.org/os_walks.asp

Midpeninsula Regional Open Space District
330 Distel Circle
Los Altos, CA 94022-1404 (650) 691-1200
www.openspace.org/hikes_and_
   activities/calendar_of_activities.html

Mount Diablo Interpretive Association
P.O. Box 346
Walnut Creek, CA 94597-0346
(925) 927-7222
www.mdia.org/events.htm

Mount Tamalpais Intrepretive Association
www.mttam.net/

Pacific Trail Society
www.geocities.com/pacifictrailsociety

Santa Clara County Parks
298 Garden Hill Drive
Los Gatos, CA 95032 (408) 355-2200
www.parkhere.org/channel/0,4770,chid%253
D16221%2526sid%253D12761,00.html

Santa Cruz Mountain Trail Association
P.O. Box 1141
Los Altos, CA 94023
www.stanford.edu/%7Emhd/trails.

Sierra Club/Loma Prieta chapter
3921 East Bayshore Road
Palo Alto, CA 94303 (650) 390-8411
lomaprieta.sierraclub.org/outingsmain.html

Sierra Club/San Francisco chapter
2530 San Pablo Avenue, Suite I
Berkeley, CA 94702-2000 (510) 848-0800
sanfranciscobay.sierraclub.org/hiking.
*Information on the Hiking Section is available
from Eva Libien (415-383-5184). Information on
the Hiking Schedule is available from Bob Muller*
(925) 631-0751

Stanford Outing Club
www.stanford.edu/group/outing/index.html

APPENDIX B:
PLACES TO BUY MAPS

Any Mountain
www.anymountain.net
2777 Shattuck Avenue
Berkeley, CA 94705 (510) 665-3939

20640 Homestead Rd.
Cupertino, CA 95014 (408) 255-6162

4906 Dublin Avenue
Dublin, CA 94568 (925) 875-1115

71 Tamal Vista Blvd.
Corte Madera, CA 94925 (415) 927-0170

The Willows 1975 Diamond Boulevard
Concord, CA 94520 (925) 674-0174

928 Whipple Avenue
Redwood City, CA 94063 (650) 361-1213

Berkeley Map Center
1995 University Avenue, Suite 117
Berkeley, CA 94704 (510) 841-6277

Lombardi Sports
www.lombardisports.com
1600 Jackson Street
San Francisco, CA 94109 (415) 771-0600

Marin Outdoors
www.marinoutdoors.com
935 Andersen Drive
San Rafael, CA 94901 (415) 453-3400

2770 Santa Rosa Avenue
Santa Rosa, CA 95407 (707) 544-4400

3900A Bel Aire
Plaza Napa, CA 94558 (707) 256-1680

REI
www.rei.com
1338 San Pablo Avenue (near Gilman)
Berkeley, CA 94702 (510) 527-4140

213 Corte Madera Town Center
Corte Madera, CA 94925 (415) 927-1938

1119 Industrial Road, Suite 1-B
San Carlos, CA 94070 (650) 508-2330

The Willows Shopping Center
1975 Diamond Boulevard, Suite B-100
Concord, CA 94520 (925) 825-9400

43962 Fremont Boulevard
Fremont, CA 94538 (510) 651-0305

400 El Paseo de Saratoga
San Jose, CA 95130 (408) 871-8765

2715 Santa Rosa Avenue
Santa Rosa, CA 95407 (707) 540-9025

840 Brannan
San Francisco, CA 94103 (415) 934-1938

2598 Taylor Street
San Francisco, CA 94133 (415) 345-8080

1160 Blossom Hill Road
San Jose, CA 95118 (408) 264-5553

Westgate Mall 1600 Saratoga Avenue
San Jose, CA 95129 (408) 871-1001

1342 Broadway Plaza
Walnut Creek, CA 94596 (925) 977-9090

Sonoma Outfitters
www.sonomaoutfitters.com
145 Third Street
Santa Rosa, CA 95401
(707) 528-1920 or (800) 290-1920

G & M Sales
www.gmoutdoors.com
1667 Market Street
San Francisco, CA 94103 (415) 863-2855

Wilderness Exchange
www.wildernessexchange.com
1407 San Pablo Avenue
Berkeley, CA 94702 (510) 525-1255

APPENDIX C: HIKING STORES

Sports Basement
www.sportsbasement.com
1301 6th Street
San Francisco, CA 94107 (415) 437-0100

Building 610 The Presidio of San Francisco
San Francisco, CA 94129 (415) 437-0100

REI
www.rei.com
1338 San Pablo Avenue (near Gilman)
Berkeley, CA 94702 (510) 527-4140

213 Corte Madera Town Center
Corte Madera, CA 94925 (415) 927-1938

1119 Industrial Rd. Suite 1-B
San Carlos, CA 94070 (650) 508-2330

The Willows Shopping Center
1975 Diamond Blvd., Suite B-100
Concord, CA 94520 (925) 825-9400

43962 Fremont Boulevard
Fremont, CA 94538 (510) 651-0305

400 El Paseo de Saratoga
San Jose, CA 95130 (408) 871-8765

2715 Santa Rosa Avenue
Santa Rosa, CA 95407 (707) 540-9025

840 Brannan
San Francisco, CA 94103 (415) 934-1938

Any Mountain
www.anymountain.net
2777 Shattuck Avenue
Berkeley, CA 94705 (510) 665-3939

20640 Homestead Road
Cupertino, CA 95014 (408) 255-6162

4906 Dublin Avenue
Dublin, CA 94568 (925) 875-1115

71 Tamal Vista Boulevard
Corte Madera, CA 94925 (415) 927-0170

The Willows 1975 Diamond Boulevard
Concord, CA 94520 (925) 674-0174

928 Whipple Avenue
Redwood City, CA 94063 (650) 361-1213

2598 Taylor Street
San Francisco, CA 94133 (415) 345-8080

1160 Blossom Hill Road
San Jose, CA 95118 (408) 264-5553

Westgate Mall 1600 Saratoga Avenue
San Jose, CA 95129 (408) 871-1001

1342 Broadway Plaza
Walnut Creek, CA 94596 (925)977-9090

Marin Outdoors
www.marinoutdoors.com
935 Andersen Drive
San Rafael, CA 94901 (415) 453-3400

2770 Santa Rosa Avenue
Santa Rosa, CA 95407 (707) 544-4400

3900A Bel Aire Plaza
Napa, CA 94558 (707) 256-1680

Lombardi Sports
www.lombardisports.com
1600 Jackson Street
San Francisco, CA 94109 (415) 771-0600

G & M Sales
www.gmoutdoors.com
1667 Market Street
San Francisco, CA 94103 (415) 863-2855

Wilderness Exchange
www.wildernessexchange.com
1407 San Pablo Avenue
Berkeley, CA 94702 (510) 525-1255

Sonoma Outfitters
www.sonomaoutfitters.com
145 Third Street
Santa Rosa, CA 95401
(707) 528-1920 or (800) 290-1920

INDEX

All Lakes, Ponds, and Reservoirs are listed by name under the heading of Lakes.

INDEX

INDEX

INDEX

INDEX

INDEX

INDEX

INDEX

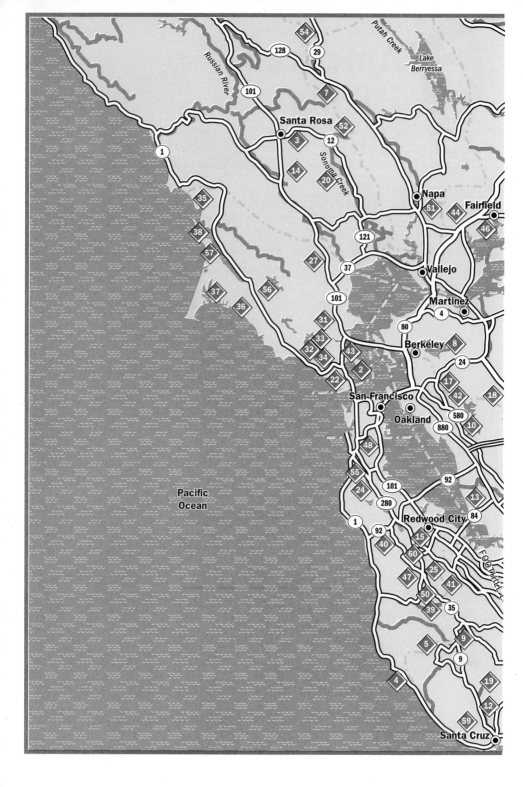